SEVENTH EDITION

INTERVIEWING

*Principles
and
Practices*

Charles J. Stewart
Purdue University

William B. Cash, Jr.
National College of Education

**WCB Brown &
Benchmark**
PUBLISHERS

Madison, Wisconsin•Dubuque, Iowa•Indianapolis, Indiana
Melbourne, Australia•Oxford, England

Book Team

Executive Editor *Stan Stoga*
Developmental Editor *Kassi Radomski*
Production Editor *Deborah J. Donner*
Photo Editor *Robin Storm*
Visuals/Design Developmental Consultant *Marilyn A. Phelps*
Visuals/Design Freelance Specialist *Mary L. Christianson*
Publishing Services Specialist *Sherry Padden*
Marketing Manager *Carla J. Aspelmeier*
Advertising Manager *Jodi Rymer*

WCB Brown & Benchmark

A Division of Wm. C. Brown Communications, Inc.

Executive Vice President/General Manager *Thomas E. Doran*
Vice President/Editor in Chief *Edgar J. Laube*
Vice President/Sales and Marketing *Eric Ziegler*
Director of Production *Vickie Putman Caughron*
Director of Custom and Electronic Publishing *Chris Rogers*

Wm. C. Brown Communications, Inc.

President and Chief Executive Officer *G. Franklin Lewis*
Corporate Vice President, President of WCB Manufacturing *Roger Meyer*
Vice President and Chief Financial Officer *Robert Chesterman*

Cover design and illustration by Tessing Design, Inc.
Chapter opener design by Tessing Design, Inc.

The credits section for this book begins on page 299 and is considered an extension of the copyright page.

*To Jane, and to Chris, Jason, Whitney, and Nathan for their
continuing patience and perseverance*

Contents

4

Questions and Their Uses   62

5

The Journalistic/Probing Interview   85

6

The Survey Interview   111

Contents

Preface

This seventh edition of our book reflects the growing sophistication with which interviewing is being approached, the ever-expanding body of research in all types of interview settings, and the effects of interpersonal communication theory and equal opportunity laws on interviewing practices. We have made a concerted effort to include the latest research findings and developments and to make the book readable through careful editing and writing.

This seventh edition discusses both the general and the specific. The first four chapters address principles applicable to all interview settings. Chapter 1 defines the interview, identifies types of interviews, and addresses the uses of interviews. Chapter 2 discusses the interview as a process, introduces two fundamental approaches to the interview—directive and nondirective, and addresses important communication components such as relationships, listening, language, and nonverbal communication. Chapter 3 discusses the structure of the interview with particular emphasis on openings, interview guides and schedules, and closings. Chapter 4 discusses and illustrates types and uses of questions, phrasing of questions, common question pitfalls, and question sequences.

The last seven chapters deal with specialized types of interviews—the journalistic/probing interview (Chapter 5), the survey interview (Chapter 6), the selection interview (Chapter 7), the performance appraisal and discipline interviews (Chapter 8), the counseling interview (Chapter 9), the persuasive interview (Chapter 10), and the health care interview (Chapter 11).

In this edition, we have provided a more thorough explanation of our definition of interviewing and both the types and uses of interviews. We have expanded our discussions of: language, nonverbal communication (with emphasis on appearance and dress), listening, the interview situation (including environment and climate), question pitfalls, and closings. In the chapters dealing with specific types of interviews, we have placed more emphasis on approaching interviews systematically, and we have provided new figures and restructured chapters to present this emphasis more effectively to students. There are also expanded guidelines for interviewees.

Some of these principles and techniques may seem simple or obvious. However, in our experiences as teachers, practitioners, and consultants of interviewing in academic, professional, and business settings, we have found that overlooking the simple and the obvious often creates problems in real-life interviews.

We have included a sample interview at the end of each chapter, *not* as a perfect example of interviewing but to illustrate various interviewing types, situations, approaches, techniques, and *mistakes*. We believe that students can learn a great deal by applying the research and principles learned in a chapter to a realistic interview that allows them to detect when interview parties are right on target as well as when they miss the target completely. The role-playing cases at the ends of Chapters 5 through 11 provide students with opportunities to design and conduct practice interviews and to observe others' efforts to employ the principles discussed. Student activities at the end of each chapter provide ideas for in- and out-of-class exercises, experiences, and information gathering. Updated readings at the end of each chapter will help students who are interested in delving more deeply into specific topics, theories, and types of interviews.

This book is designed for courses in such departments as speech, communication, journalism, business, industrial supervision, education, political science, nursing, and social work. It will also be useful in workshops in various fields. We believe this book will be of continuing value to beginning students and seasoned veterans alike. We have treated theory and research findings where applicable, but our primary concern is with principles and techniques that can be translated into immediate practice in and out of the classroom.

We wish to express our gratitude to students at Purdue University and to past and present colleagues for their inspiration, suggestions, exercises, theories, criticism, and encouragement. Special thanks are extended to Fred Jablin, Ralph Webb, and Craig Allen Smith for their assistance with our treatment of the interview as a relationship; to John and Denise Bittner for information on broadcast interviews; to Andrew Wolvin for suggestions on reorganizing and expanding the discussion of listening; to Rebecca Leonard and Robert Norton for resources on counseling and health care interviewing; to Buck Blessing and Todd White for special insights into career development and performance appraisals; to Baxter/Travenol Laboratories of Deerfield, Illinois, and Chris Janiak for helping develop and permitting us to include the performance appraisal model in Chapter 8; to Robert E. Smith, Mary Alice Baker, Patrice Buzzanell, and Tommie Ems for their interest and many suggestions; and to the reviewers who reviewed the sixth and seventh editions carefully and gave us many constructive suggestions for improvements: Joann Keyton, Baylor University; Corwin King, Central Washington University; Elizabeth Kizer, University of Missouri–St. Louis; Steven Ralston, East Tennessee State University; James Quisenberry, Morehead State University; and Dorothy Williamson-Ige, Indiana University.

We would also like to thank those who took the time to respond to a sixth edition questionnaire: Gary Aday, Virginia Highlands Community College; James Benson, University of Wisconsin–Oshkosh; Jane Cater, University of the Ozarks; Roger Conaway, University of Texas; David Doyle, Phoenix College; Ray G. Ewing, Southeast Missouri State University; Robert Greenstree, East Central University; Bill Hyman, Sam Houston State University; Frederic Jablin, University of Texas; Diane Krider, Sangamon State University; Kathleen Krone, University of Nebraska; Elaine Lyons, Luzerne County

Community College; Dennis McGough, University of New Haven; Donald MacDonald, University of Tulsa; Robert Netter, Christopher Newport College; Tyra Phipps, Frostburg State University; Harvey Pitman, Boise State University; Craig Reis, Youngstown State University; Tim Sellnow, North Dakota State University; and John Weispfenning, Indiana University.

A very special note of appreciation to W. Charles Redding—colleague, advisor, and friend—for his assistance and encouragement since the authors' first efforts to teach the principles and practices of interviewing.

An Instructor's Manual to accompany *Interviewing: Principles and Practices,* seventh edition, is available through a Brown & Benchmark sales representative or by writing to Educational Services, Brown & Benchmark, 2460 Kerper Boulevard, Dubuque, Iowa 52001.

CJS
WBC

1

An Introduction to Interviewing

By the time you are in college, you have undoubtedly taken part in thousands of interviews even though you did not call them that. For instance, you participated in an *interview* every time you obtained information from or gave information to a teacher, physician, or friend; asked for help from a counselor, employer, or parent; bought or sold an object, service, or idea; answered a survey over the phone or at a supermarket; helped to recruit members for an organization or team; gave advice to a co-worker or a younger brother or sister; or interviewed for a job. The interview is the most common form of purposeful, planned communication. It may range from formal to informal; be highly structured, moderately structured, or unstructured; deal with personal problems and needs or those problems and needs of schools, corporations, and governments; involve sophisticated theories, principles, and practices or simple facts; and last for hours or seconds. Unfortunately, in everyday life, we apply the term *interview* to a few formal settings in which we are only occasionally involved (the job interview, the survey interview, the journalistic interview) and that are conducted by highly trained professionals (recruiters, social scientists, reporters, attorneys).

The Interview Defined

We define interviewing as a *process of dyadic, relational communication, with a predetermined and serious purpose designed to interchange behavior, and involving the asking and answering of questions.*[1] The word *process* denotes a dynamic, everchanging interaction, with many variables operating with and acting upon one another, and a degree of system or structure. Although each interview is somewhat different, all involve basic communication ingredients, including the exchange of verbal and nonverbal messages, immediate and direct feedback, perceptions, listening, motivation, degrees of sensitivity, expectations, and assumptions. An interview, regardless of its intent, does not occur in isolation from other influences. Each participant brings a set of experiences, expectations, fears, pressures, and personal or organizational limitations to the interview. Events before and after as well as the physical surroundings influence the interview as it unfolds. Like all processes, once an interview commences, participants' impressions enter into their mental programming that are not reversible or stoppable and affect the perceptions of one another regardless of length or depth of the interaction.

The word *dyadic* denotes that the interview is a person-to-person interaction between two parties or units. Thus, more than two people may be involved in an interview (for example, two recruiters interviewing an applicant, a panel of five faculty

Perhaps the greatest single problem with human communication is the assumption of it.

members interviewing a student for an award, or a residence hall counselor interviewing two roommates), but never more than two parties—an *interviewer party* and an *interviewee party*. If three parties are clearly involved, (for example, a student, a faculty member, and the chair of the grade appeals committee talking about a possible grade change) a small group discussion, not an interview, is taking place.

The word *relational* suggests an interpersonal connection between the interview parties. This connection may result from the roles being played (parent, academic counselor, work supervisor, recruiter), group memberships (social, professional, political, religious), personal characteristics (gender, race, age, ethnic background, ancestry, disabilities), and status differences (student/professor, parent/child, coach/athlete, president/vice president, superior/subordinate). Relationships involve interactions and mutual interest in their outcomes. The dyadic nature of the interview, however, may lead to polarization of the parties into "me vs. you" or "we vs. they" and require application of the principles of negotiation or conflict resolution. Just as it takes "two to tangle," it takes two parties to produce an effective interview with results satisfactory to each party. Once a party enters into a relationship, the party cannot avoid the ongoing dynamic potential of the relationship.

Predetermined and serious purpose means that at least one of the two parties comes to an interview with a goal—other than mere enjoyment of the interchange—and has planned the interview to focus on specific subject matter. The predetermined and serious purpose distinguishes the interview from mere social conversation, although polite conversation, chitchat, or digressions are often important in interviews. Each party in the interview usually has a purpose and some content to communicate, either planned in advance or developed during the interview. The degree to which each party's purposes are achieved is a measure of how productive and successful the interview is. While conversations are rarely organized in advance, all interviews must have a degree of planning and structure, ranging from a purpose and topics in mind or jotted on a piece of paper to a prepared opening statement with each question carefully phrased in advance.

Interchanging behavior connotes a sharing of expectations, roles, feelings, attitudes, perceptions, and information. In successful interviews, both parties use words and nonverbal signals—touches, hugs, punches on the arm, handshakes, winks, and looks of concern or understanding—that express interest, concern, and feelings of joy, fear, loneliness, satisfaction, trust, anxiety, anger, and so on. Close interpersonal interchanges involve risk that can be minimized but never eliminated, and if one or both parties elect to "play it safe," the interview will fail. Interchanging behaviors also means that each party speaks and listens from time to time. If one party does all of the speaking and the other all of the listening, a *speech* to an audience of one, not an interview, is taking place. We believe that participation should follow a ratio of 70 percent to 30 percent, with the interviewee doing most of the talking. However, a few types of interviews such as information giving and sales may require a reversal of this ratio. Interview parties often exchange the roles of interviewer and interviewee as an interview progresses, such as when a buyer makes a counteroffer, an applicant asks questions of a potential employer, or a respondent asks a poll taker to clarify a question.

Asking and answering questions are crucial to the interviewing process. Questions are the tools interviewers and interviewees use to obtain information, check the accuracy of messages sent and received, and verify impressions and assumptions. While many interviews consist entirely of questions and answers and others involve occasional questions for strategic purposes, few interviews could take place or achieve any degree of success without purposeful questions (thought out in advance and asked at appropriate times) and appropriate responses.

Interview Scenarios

A model of the interviewing process in Chapter 2 details the components of the process and how they interact, including the two parties, perceptions, levels and types of communicative interactions, feedback, and situational variables. The scenarios below will also help you to understand the complex nature of the interview and some of its common problems.

Scenario #1: A reporter for the university daily newspaper is searching a large audience of students, staff, faculty, and administrators attending an emergency meeting to discuss severe budget cuts for the next academic year. In order to meet these cuts, the university may have to raise tuition by 10–12 percent, cut courses, eliminate some academic and athletic programs, and lay off dozens of staff, faculty, and administrators. The reporter wants to interview a cross section of reactions and has spotted three prospects. One is a man of about thirty-five wearing a denim jacket and pants and a farm implement cap, an obvious member of the maintenance staff. A second is a woman in her late forties wearing a tailored business suit, an apparent member of the faculty. And a third is a young man in his late teens or early twenties wearing a sweatshirt with the school name and logo, an obvious representative of the student point of view.

Scenario #2: An applicant for medical school is waiting in the admissions office for her appointment with a panel consisting of a student, an alumnus, a faculty member, and an assistant director of admissions. She wonders how she should address the student; whether the student will ask easy questions because of their similarity in age, status, and goals; and whether the alumnus and faculty member will ask most of the questions.

Scenario #3: A salesperson at an automobile dealership approaches a young man and woman who have been looking at foreign and domestic compact models. The following exchange takes place.

Salesperson: (addressing the man) Can I be of assistance?

Man: Yes . . .

Salesperson: (interrupts and begins to explain the features and costs of several models) As you can see, we have several models ranging in options and prices from $8,900 to nearly $20,000. What kind of car do you have now?

Man: I have a Ford Probe, but . . .

Salesperson: (interrupts) Well, the model you're looking at is a bit smaller than your Ford Probe, but it has all of the same features and about the same power for several thousand dollars less.

Man: That's interesting, but . . .

Salesperson: Say, if you're a graduating senior, we can give you a 10 percent discount on this Saturn Coupe.

Man: That sounds like a good deal, but you'd better make the deal with Jane. She's looking for a new car, not me.

Salesperson: Oh, uh (turning to the woman) well let me show you, uh, some of this model's features. I suppose you've checked some of these out already, huh?

The participants in each of these scenarios were preparing for or taking part in *interviews,* processes of dyadic, relational communication, with predetermined and serious purposes designed to interchange behaviors and involving the asking and answering of questions. Although each scenario is different, each involves the exchange of verbal and nonverbal messages, feedback, perceptions, listening, motivation, sensitivity, expectations, and assumptions. Unfortunately, the reporter assumes not only that dress reveals status, occupation, and economic level but that each stereotyped person will respond in a stereotypical manner. The medical school applicant expects a thorough and professional interview but apparently assumes that her relationship with the student will make that panelist an ally. She fears that the alumnus and faculty member will dominate the interview and dismisses the assistant admissions director as unimportant. And the salesperson assumes that only men purchase new cars, so he treats the woman as if she were a mere appendage to the interview. These scenarios illustrate that *perhaps the greatest single problem with human communication is the assumption of it.* Too often we assume that people will act in prescribed ways in specific settings because of our relationship with them or because of their dress, age, sex, race, occupation, marital status, or education.

Because we are involved in interviews every day, we assume that the process is simple and requires little, if any, formal training. But if you think interviewing skills come naturally, think of the scenarios above and your recent experiences: the inept company recruiter who kept answering her own questions; the alumni fund-raiser who was determined to get a $500 donation from you as a recent graduate of Jefferson High School even though you were overburdened with large student loans; the counselor who told you all of his problems instead of listening to yours; the political poll taker who asked leading questions; and the magazine sales representative with the canned pitch over the telephone. Most of us have learned how to interview by observing untrained "model" interviewers and then practicing what we had observed. This approach passes on the mistakes of models and is based on the assumption that we can learn interviewing merely through practice. Wines may improve with age, but interviewing rarely does. For example, a study in England revealed that physicians who did not receive formal training in interviewing patients actually became less effective interviewers as the years went on, not more effective.[2] We would be wise to amend the old saying "practice makes perfect" to "practice makes perfect if you know what you are practicing." Twenty years of experience may be one year of flawed experience repeated twenty times unless you intersperse the learning of principles and practices as you go along.

We want to show in this book that there is a vast difference between skilled and unskilled interviewers and interviewees. Our purpose is to introduce you to the basic skills applicable for all interviews and the specific skills needed in specialized settings such as those outlined in the next section of this chapter.

Types of Interviews

Now that you have a basic understanding of what an interview is and is not, let us examine a variety of interviewing dyads. Charles Redding has developed a "situational schema" into which interviews fit according to their functions.[3] Figure 1.1 is an elaboration of Redding's classification to include all types of interviews. During this discussion of interview types, it will become increasingly obvious that you are involved in interviews far more often than you ever imagined.

The first category, *information giving*, includes all interviews in which the primary function is to give information, data, directions, instructions, orientation, and clarifications. For instance, we use interviews to orient new employees, students, and members of organizations or to train, instruct, or coach people in specific behaviors necessary for performing work tasks, playing games, counseling others, or developing skills. Common examples include explaining insurance benefits to new employees or registration procedures to new students, clarifying procedures for submitting research proposals or applying for student financial aid, training people to fill out application forms or develop resumes, and coaching sales representatives on how to avoid the "door in the face" or students on how to study for multiple choice examinations. Job-related instructions are critical daily interviews in organizations: the outgoing shift of nurses, police officers, and production crews must relay information about patients, crimes and arrests, and

Figure 1.1   Types of interviews

1. Information giving
   a. Orientation
   b. Training, instruction, coaching
   c. Job-related instructions
   d. Briefings

2. Information gathering
   a. Surveys and polls
   b. Exit interviews
   c. Research interviews
   d. Investigations: insurance, police, etc.
   e. Medical, psychological, case history, diagnostic, caseworker, etc.
   f. Journalistic

3. Selection
   a. Screening
   b. Determinate
   c. Placement

4. Problems of interviewee's behavior
   a. Appraisal, evaluative, review
   b. Separation, firing
   c. Correction, discipline, reprimand
   d. Counseling

5. Problems of interviewer's behavior
   a. Receiving complaints
   b. Grievances
   c. Receiving suggestions

6. Problem solving
   a. Discussing mutually shared problems
   b. Receiving suggestions for solutions

7. Persuasion
   a. Selling products and services
   b. Recruiting members
   c. Fundraising and development
   d. Changing the way a party feels, thinks, or acts

completed products to incoming shifts. Chapter 11 on the health care interview discusses the causes for loss and distortion of information and ways to transmit information more effectively through interviews.

The second category, *information gathering*, includes all interviews in which the primary function is to obtain facts, opinions, data, feelings, attitudes, beliefs, reactions, and feedback. For instance, groups use surveys and polls to determine reasons for actions, trends in beliefs, attitudes toward political candidates, the effects of advertising campaigns, habits of television viewers, and voting intentions. Organizations use exit interviews to discover why employees are leaving positions for ones in competing organizations and what might be done to retain quality employees. College students, professors, and others use interviews as research tools. Students use interviews to obtain clarification of assignments or readings, learn how best to prepare for a final examination, and discover

More than two people may be involved in an interview, but never more than two parties—an interviewer party and an interviewee party.

why a paper received a grade of C instead of A. Journalists, police officers, and insurance claims adjusters use investigative interviews to determine causes of crimes and accidents and the parties responsible. Counselors and health care professionals use interviews to diagnose learning, psychological, and medical problems and to prescribe solutions. Chapter 5 on the journalistic/probing interview, Chapter 6 on the survey interview, and Chapter 11 on the health care interview discuss ways to gather information effectively through a variety of interview types.

The third category, *selection*, includes all interviews in which the primary function is to screen, hire, and place job applicants, employees, and members of organizations. Organizations of all types employ *screening* interviews (the typical campus interview for instance) to reduce large numbers of applicants by weeding out those who do not meet basic qualifications. They use *determinate* interviews (what most students call plant trips) to decide whether a select group of applicants or a specific applicant should be tested and interviewed further or hired. Organizations use *transfer* or *placement* interviews to promote members or move them from one position or location to another. All selection interviews are designed to assess the training, experiences, abilities, and personal characteristics of applicants or employees to determine their "fit" with an organization, position, and location. Chapter 7 on the selection interview addresses the "employment interview" from both sides of the table—the applicant and the employer.

The fourth category, *problems of interviewee's behavior,* includes all interviews in which the primary function is to perceive accurately a person's behavior, problems, or performance with the goal of helping this person to see its nature, causes, effects, and possible solutions. For instance, employers use appraisal interviews primarily to motivate employees to continue excellent performance or to improve average or poor performance, and secondarily to assess training needs, enhance communication, strengthen staff relationships, and create a positive atmosphere. Schools, corporations, churches, and professional associations use interviews to reprimand and discipline, to correct behavior, and to fire or expel individuals if performance or behavior is severe or seems incorrectable. Professionals, such as academic counselors, placement counselors, psychologists, and psychiatrists, and lay counselors, such as parents, teachers, and colleagues, all use interviews to help patients, clients, students, and friends understand and alleviate personal problems ranging from learning disabilities, substance abuse, and psychological phobias to poor grades, attendance, negative attitudes, and low self-concept. Chapter 8 on performance appraisal and discipline interviews, Chapter 9 on the counseling interview, and Chapter 11 on the health care interview discuss interviewing principles that deal with problems of the interviewee's behavior.

The fifth category, *interviews dealing with problems of the interviewers behavior,* includes all interviews in which the primary function is for the interviewer to receive complaints, grievances, or suggestions and to work out resolutions acceptable to both parties. Common interviews in this category are customer complaints, student grade appeals, employee grievances (over unfair treatment, inadequate raises, poor working conditions, or sexual harassment), and patient's challenges of medical bills or proposed treatments. Complaints may be informal customer, student, or employee "gripes," or formal union or consumer grievances. The complaint may be directly against the interviewer as owner, professor, department head, or physician, or the complaint may be against a manufacturer, retail outlet, department, university, corporation, or medical center. The interviewer acts as manufacturer representative, manager of customer relations, dean, or medical center administrator who must resolve the complaint.

The sixth category, *problem solving,* includes all interviews in which the primary function is to analyze and resolve a problem of mutual concern to both interviewer and interviewee. These are not personal problems of either party but genuinely shared concerns or problems both parties wish to explore and solve. Such mutual concerns might be loss of a client, need for better campus housing for next semester, a computer breakdown, decline in sales, a research problem, or a budget crisis.

The seventh category, *persuasion,* includes all interviews in which the primary function is to change an interviewee's ways or thinking, feeling, and/or acting. Too often students think of persuasive interviews only as *sales* interactions, and we do use interviews to purchase or sell sports tickets, automobiles, clothing, houses, computers, insurance, and services ranging from painting houses for tuition to market investment. But we also use persuasive interviews to *gain support* for a team, political candidate, proposed course of action or position on an issue. We use interviews to *recruit* persons for our teams, housing units, schools, churches, political campaigns, and social movements. We use persuasive interviews to *urge actions* such as voting, attending class, going to a convocation, spending spring break in Florida, eating at a specific restaurant, studying instead of partying, and proposing marriage. We employ interviews when seeking to *change or reinforce beliefs* whether they be political, social, religious, scientific, or economic. And we use interviews when seeking to *change or reinforce attitudes* toward people, places, things, groups, or actions. Chapter 10 discusses ways to prepare for and take part in a variety of persuasive interviews.

As you have now seen, the interview is a complex communication process, and there are many types of interviews with a wide variety of purposes and functions. Each type demands the application of specific principles and skills as well as personal traits and abilities. The combination of these characteristics may make a person highly suitable for one type of interview and poorly suited for another. For instance, an expert sales representative might be a poor counselor; an excellent investigative reporter might be a poor survey taker; an experienced recruiter might be a poor applicant.

Uses of Interviewing

One final question seems in order for this chapter. When should you use an interview instead of a questionnaire, letter, speech, or small group discussion to inform, obtain information, select persons for employment, counsel, resolve problems, or persuade? The answer often depends upon the situation, time demands, availability of respondents, purposes, subject matter, and the relationship between interviewer and potential interviewees. Here are some general guidelines. First, use interviews when you must be able to verify that an interviewer or interviewee is who he or she claims to be or when you must match interviewees with specific requirements such as age, sex, race, educational level, income range, political beliefs, and so on. Second, use interviews when it is important to control timing, the presence of other people, the questions and answers, and the situation. It may be critical, for instance, that questions be answered in a specific order or so that no other person (wife, roommate, fellow employee) is present to influence answers. Third, use an interview when it is important to motivate people to take part, listen, and respond freely, openly, and accurately. The face-to-face or ear-to-ear interview in which you can give a party your personal and undivided attention, exhibit sincere interest in *this* party, and discover the most relevant "buttons to push" is more effective in motivating people than speeches, form letters, and questionnaires. Fourth, use interviews when you want to adapt to each interviewee. For instance, you might not want to ask the same questions, provide the same answer options, or make the same arguments to every member of the football team, to all staff members at your church, or to all residents at your sorority or fraternity. Fifth, use interviews when you need detailed and lengthy answers or the ability to probe into answers. People will not write lengthy, detailed answers on questionnaires or respond at length before audiences; therefore, probing or follow-up questions are often necessary because answers may be brief, vague, inaccurate, incomplete, or suggestible. Sixth, use interviews when you need to examine in depth emotions, beliefs, feelings, and attitudes. People will not reveal these before audiences, and only the interview allows you to probe into answers for true self-disclosure and to observe how a person reacts nonverbally through eye contact, facial expressions, and vocal inflections. Seventh, use interviews when you might need to explain, clarify, or justify questions or answers. It is frustrating when filling out questionnaires to be unable to ask about the phrasing of questions or to explain why you are answering as you are, and it is equally frustrating to receive completed questionnaires only to discover that respondents have misinterpreted your questions and how you wanted them to respond. Eighth, use an interview when it is important to observe closely the interviewer's or interviewee's appearance, dress, manner, and nonverbal communication. Such observations are impossible in written communications and inadequate in small groups or audience situations. Obviously interviews are valuable supplements or follow-ups for questionnaires, application forms, written responses, small groups, and speeches. One technique, for example, is to follow a written questionnaire with random interviews or a group interview. The interviews or group interview may discover reasons why the results are as they are, serve as a validating method, discover problems with the survey questionnaire, and bind the *hard* data with oral expression.

The telephone interview, conference call, and video talk-back meeting are becoming common. Unfortunately, too many organizations abuse the telephone interview by, for example, pretending to be conducting research when they are actually selling products or services. The use of the video talk-back and conference call is increasing among organizations with multiple locations or clients scattered over a wide geographical area. The interviewer or interviewee can talk to many people at one time, answer or clarify questions directly, be seen or heard while responding, and receive immediate feedback. Time and money saved, problems resolved, and directness of communication will increase the use of talk-back and conference calls.

Critics of interviewing ask whether information gained in face-to-face encounters is valid or reliable. As you will see in later chapters, the interviewer can select interviewees carefully, train other interviewers thoroughly, develop question schedules, devise scale questions, employ question strategies, build in check questions, detect nonverbal cues, probe into answers, and apply reliability formulas to aid in the validity of results. The interviewer might also check an interviewee's responses in other interviews or questionnaires or interview the same person more than once. Research shows that respondents tend to be open and honest in trusting, supportive atmospheres. Thus, reliability is not an inherent problem. The interview is a useful tool on its own and as a supplement but, like any tool, it is best used by skillfully trained and trustworthy individuals.

Summary

We define interviewing as a process of dyadic, relational communication with a predetermined and serious purpose designed to interchange behavior and involving the asking and answering of questions. Thus, the interview is a dynamic, ongoing, ever-changing interplay of many variables. It is a person-to-person interaction with pervasive feedback between two parties that have a mutual connection and interest in the outcome. An interview has the predetermined and serious purpose of interchanging behavior, often through asking and answering questions. This definition encompasses a wide variety of interview settings. Successful interviewing requires training, preparation, interpersonal skills, flexibility, and a willingness to face the risks involved in intimate person-to-person interaction.

An Interview for Review and Analysis

John Deaver is polling his neighborhood for the local Democratic party about two months prior to state and local elections. Bill and Mary Dobbins are residents of the neighborhood but are not acquainted with John. As you read this interview, think about answers to such questions as: What makes this a "process"? Why is it a dyadic process instead of a triadic process? How can this interview be "relational" when it is between strangers? What is the "predetermined and serious purpose," and how is it shared between the two parties? In what ways does this interview involve a true "interchange of behavior"? Can you detect an exchange of interviewer and interviewee roles during the interview? What functions do questions serve for each party? What assumptions has the interviewer made prior to the interview? What type of interview is this? What makes this interview fundamentally different from a speech, small group discussion, or conversation?

1. **John:** Hi, I'm John Deaver, and I live about two blocks up the street. I'm polling for the local Democratic party and wonder if I might have three or four minutes of your time this evening.
2. **Bill:** Hi, John, I'm Bill Dobbins. You must live close to the Frankforts. We work together at the Mars Insurance Agency.
3. **John:** Yes, in fact, they live just across the street from us.
4. **Mary:** Who is it, Bill?
5. **Bill:** It's a fellow from up the street who's polling for the Democrats.
6. **John:** Hi, I'm John Deaver, and I'd like just three or four minutes to ask you some questions about this fall's election.
7. **Mary:** Okay, but we're not involved much in politics.
8. **John:** That's fine; we're just trying to determine who is registered and how they feel about the coming election. Are both of you registered in this county?
9. **Bill:** Yes, we are.
10. **John:** And would you consider yourselves Republicans or Democrats?
11. **Mary:** We don't really belong to either party; we vote for the best candidates.
12. **John:** Would you say you generally vote for Republican or Democratic candidates?
13. **Bill:** I suppose I usually vote for Republicans.
14. **Mary:** I'm really independent and split my ticket nearly all the time.
15. **John:** Okay. Do you plan to vote for Pete Dickerson or David O'Brien for mayor?
16. **Mary:** Oh, I think we'll vote for Pete.
17. **Bill:** Yes, we've known Pete for years and feel he'll make an excellent mayor.
18. **John:** And for state senator, are you likely to vote for Marcia Kransky or Mike Cody?
19. **Bill:** I'll probably vote for Marcia.
20. **Mary:** I haven't decided yet because I don't know much about either of them.
21. **John:** That's all the questions I have. May I have your telephone number?
22. **Bill:** Why do you need our phone number?
23. **Mary:** We don't want to be pressured over the telephone during the campaign.
24. **John:** We probably won't contact you, but we'd like your telephone number in case you need further information about the candidates or where you will cast your vote.

25. **Mary:** We'd rather not give out our phone number.
26. **Bill:** We know where to vote.
27. **John:** I understand, and I want to thank you for your time this evening.
28. **Bill:** Glad to help. Perhaps we'll see you sometime when we're out biking.

Student Activities

1. Keep a log of interviews you take part in during a week and think about the following ideas:
   Sharing: To what degree?
   Caring: How much?
   Risks: What kinds and how much?

2. Select another person to form a dyad; then each of you take five minutes to discover everything you can about the other. At the end of ten minutes, discuss the following questions with your partner:
   How much do you know about each other?
   What assumptions proved to be faulty?
   How much time did you spend speaking, listening, thinking?
   How could preparation have helped these interview segments?
   How were the interviews like and unlike "normal" conversation?

3. Observe several interviews or interview segments on television and decide if they are "good" or "bad." What are the characteristics of the good and bad interviews? How do these characteristics coincide with the terms used in the definition of interviewing presented in this chapter?

4. Observe several interviews (between students, customers and salespersons, students and professors, police officers and accused traffic violators, superiors and subordinates) and try to detect the assumptions parties have made prior to interviews, and the ones they make during interviews. How do these assumptions affect both interactions and interview outcomes?

5. How might you describe the interview as a relationship in miniature? Think of interviews you have taken part in recently, for example, with an employer, instructor, physician, sales representative, or counselor.

Notes

1. This definition of interviewing is based on ones in Walter Van Dyke Bingham, Bruce V. Moore, and John W. Gustad, *How to Interview* (New York: Harper and Row, 1959), 3; Robert L. Kahn and Charles F. Cannell, *The Dynamics of Interviewing* (New York: John Wiley & Sons, 1964), 16; and Robert S. Goyer, W. Charles Redding, and John T. Rickey, *Interviewing Principles and Techniques: A Project Text* (Wm. C. Brown Co. Publishers, 1968), 6.

2. R. A. Barbee and S. A. Feldman, "Three Year Longitudinal Study of the Medical Interview and Its Relationship to Student Performance in Clinical Medicine," *Journal of Medical Education* 45 (1970), 770–76.

3. Robert S. Goyer, W. Charles Redding, and John T. Rickey developed the notion of interview "parties."

Suggested Readings

Babbie, Earl. *The Practice of Social Research.* Belmont, CA: Wadsworth, 1989.

Benjamin, Alfred. *The Helping Interview.* Boston: Houghton-Mifflin, 1987.

Einhorn, Lois J.; Bradley, Patricia Hayes; and Baird, John E., Jr. *Effective Employment Interviewing: Unlocking Human Potential.* Glenview, IL: Scott, Foresman, 1981.

Gorden, Raymond L. *Interviewing: Strategy, Techniques, and Tactics.* Belmont, CA: Wadsworth, 1987.

Kreps, Gary, and Thornton, Barbara. *Health Communication: Theory and Practice.* Prospect Heights, IL: Waveland Press, 1988.

Manning, Gerald I., and Reece, Barry I. *Selling Today: A Personal Approach.* Dubuque, IA: Wm. C. Brown Publishers, 1989.

Metzler, Ken. *Creative Interviewing.* Englewood Cliffs, NJ: Prentice-Hall, 1989.

Peters, Thomas J., and Waterman, Robert H., Jr. *In Search of Excellence.* New York: HarperCollins, 1982.

Sherwood, Hugh C. *The Journalistic Interview.* New York: HarperCollins, 1972.

2

The Interviewing Process

In Chapter 1, the interview was defined as a complex process of dyadic, relational communication. This chapter explains and illustrates this process by developing step-by-step the Cash-Stewart Model of Interviewing which contains all the fundamental elements of an interview. We will explain and illustrate each part of the model and discuss the relationships between the most fundamental element—the two parties—and the other elements that make the interview a dynamic and sometimes perplexing process.

Two Parties in the Interview

The two overlapping circles in figure 2.1 represent the two parties present in an interview. Each individual within the parties is a unique product of environment, training, and experiences and has an interesting mixture of personality traits. Each adheres to specific and general stereotypes, attitudes, beliefs, and values and is guided by an ever-changing variety of expectations, desires, motives, and interests. In a very real sense, "the whole person speaks and the whole person listens" during the intimate, face-to-face interactions we call interviews.[1] No single interviewing approach is appropriate for all, or even similar, interviews because each interaction involves different human beings.

Common Ground Between the Interview Parties

The circles representing the two parties overlap to signify that the two parties are likely to *share* some environmental influences, training, experiences, personality traits, attitudes, values, and expectations. For example, both parties may come from the same geographical area, be optimistic, have similar religious beliefs, adhere to many of the same traditions, desire to be treated fairly, want accurate information, or have a sincere interest in one another. Do not be oblivious to the differences between you and the other party, but recognize important characteristics you share. Awareness of similarities allows interview parties to understand one another, establish areas of common ground, and adapt the interview to one another's needs, perceptions, desires, and customs. You will be able to communicate more effectively with the other party if you expand the area of perceived similarities and reduce the area of perceived differences.

Relationship Dimensions

The overlapping circles also signify that each interview is a relationship with three underlying dimensions: inclusion, control, and affection.[2] *Inclusion* is the degree to which each party desires to take part in the interview. For instance, an applicant may be eager to meet

Figure 2.1   The interview parties

Parties

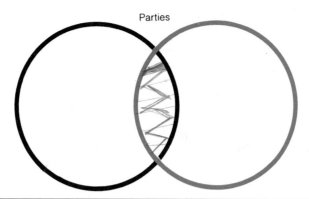

a recruiter for a major corporation, but the recruiter, having conducted seven interviews since morning, may dread the interview. Inclusion also refers to how much each party desires to include others in the interview. A teenager, for example, may not want parents involved in an academic counseling interview. Inclusion involves each party's commitment to making the interview a success. Does an appraisal interviewer, for instance, view the session as a valuable means of helping the worker or as a routine and unimportant organizational task? And finally, inclusion encompasses the willingness and ability of each party to become actively involved in the interview. Personality traits, physical condition, mental health, emotional involvements, skills, and information often affect willingness and ability. The inclusion dimension is particularly important in interviews that involve more than two people where one person may elect, or be forced, to play a passive role.

Control refers to how much power the interviewer or interviewee has to determine the nature and outcome of the interview. The power to control may be situational. For example, if you do not wish to respond to a survey, you may close the door or hang up the telephone. During a selection interview, an applicant may exert a great deal of control if there are few other qualified candidates for the job. Control may be determined by organizational hierarchy or chain of command: president over vice-president, bishop over priest, sales director over sales representative, dean over professor, professor over student, parent over child. Social customs or traditions may dictate control in some communities and groups. Thus, women, elders, old money, or descendants of founders may exert control in some interviews. Control may emanate from persons who have attained prestige through accomplishments in sports, entertainment, science, politics, military actions, or feats of bravery. Powers attained through situation, hierarchy, custom, or prestige dictate if an interview will occur; when, where, and how it will be conducted; who the other party will be; the results; and how the results may be used. Whether or not the interviewer or interviewee decides to exert these powers depends upon their relationship, their perceptions of societal, organizational, and situational constraints, and their needs, personalities, ego involvement, health, and interviewing philosophies.

Affection is the degree of warmth or friendship between the parties. Do they like one another? Do they trust one another? Is each capable of getting and giving affection during the interview? Some people fear affection or becoming too close to others, particularly in formal interviews with clients or subordinates. Others come to interviews with ambivalent or hostile attitudes because of unpleasant past experiences. Affection is often influenced by incompatible or opposing needs, desires, demands, and perceptions or by the history of the relationship. For example, an interview is more likely to be successful if the two parties have had previous positive encounters with one another. Ideal affection occurs in an interview when the two parties establish a "we" feeling instead of a "we-they" feeling. Both parties can adapt best to a relationship if they have assessed ahead of time that it is likely to be hostile, indifferent, or warm.

The interview relationship is mutual because both parties must contribute in order to gain. Even in surprise interviews at shopping centers, on the street, at the front door, or over the telephone, interviewees perceive within seconds why they are being interviewed, what will happen to the information they share, and whether they want to participate. If they decide to continue, these perceptions will determine the amount and type of information they give and how deeply they enter into the relationship. Once interviewees agree to listen further or answer questions, both parties become interdependent. Even when they have agreed in advance to participate, interviewees are initially dependent upon interviewers for context and content. Interviewers depend upon interviewees to provide adequate and accurate information, feelings, and attitudes.

Interchanging Behavior During Interviews

The small circles within the two large circles in figure 2.2 signify that behavior is constantly interchanged. Both parties are likely to ask and answer questions, to speak and listen from time to time, and to take on the roles and responsibilities of interview*er* and interview*ee*. Neither party can sit back and expect the other to make the interview a success single-handedly. For instance, if you feel that a survey taker's question is not phrased to obtain your true feelings about a political issue, point this out and explain your answer. During this brief interchange, you have taken charge and become the interviewer. A short time later, the survey taker is likely to regain control while you return to the role of interviewee. An aggressive interviewee may take command of a sales, counseling, or selection interview and become the interviewer for the remainder of the exchange. The degree to which behavior is interchanged is affected significantly by one of two fundamental approaches the interviewer may select: directive or nondirective.

Directive Approach

In a *directive interview*, the interviewer establishes the purpose of the interview and, at least at the outset, controls the pacing. An aggressive interviewee may take command as the interview progresses, but the initial intent is for the interviewer to control. Typical directive interviews include information giving, information gathering (surveys and opinion polls), employment selection, and persuasive interviews (sales). The directive interviewing approach has several advantages and disadvantages:

Figure 2.2 The switching of roles

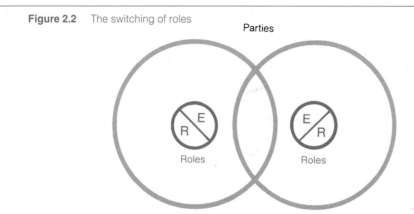

Advantages

1. It is easy to learn.
2. It takes less time.
3. It can provide quantifiable data.
4. It can supplement other methods of data collection such as questionnaires and observations.
5. It can be replicated by controlling variables such as voice, facial expressions, and appearance.

Disadvantages

1. It is inflexible
2. It is limited in variety and depth of subject matter.
3. It limits the interviewer's range of techniques.
4. It often replaces more effective and efficient means of collecting data.
5. The validity of the information may be questioned because of variables such as voice, facial expressions, and appearance.

The following is a directive interviewing exchange:

Interviewer: You are working at the present time, aren't you?
Interviewee: Yes, down at The First National Bank.
Interviewer: And how long have you been with The First National Bank?
Interviewee: About two and a half years.
Interviewer: I assume you went to work for First National as soon as you graduated from college?
Interviewee: Yes, that's correct.
Interviewer: What is your current job title?

Nondirective Approach

In a *nondirective interview,* the interviewee, by decision of the interviewer, may control the purpose, subject matter, and pacing of the interview. Typical nondirective interviews are counseling, performance appraisal, and problem solving. The nondirective approach has several advantages and disadvantages:

Advantages	Disadvantages
1. It allows the interviewer to probe deeply into subject matter.	1. It is time-consuming.
2. It gives the interviewer greater flexibility.	2. It requires acute psychological insight and sensitivity.
3. It gives the interviewee greater freedom to give lengthy answers and to volunteer information.	3. It often generates unneeded information.
4. It tends to generate more information.	4. It tends to generate excessive information.
5. It allows the interviewer to adapt to each interviewee.	5. Adaptation to each interviewee may reduce replicability.

The following is a nondirective interview exchange.

Interviewer: Tell me about your present position.

Interviewee: I'm in personnel with The First National Bank and have been with the bank since I graduated from college about two and a half years ago.

Interviewer: Um-hmm?

Interviewee: I began as a manager trainee and discovered that I really enjoyed working with people, particularly in employee selection and appraisal. When an opening in personnel occurred last October, I applied for the position and got it.

Interviewer: What are your responsibilities in personnel?

Interviewers, such as journalists, social service counselors, personnel directors, and sales representatives, often need to use an appropriate *combination* of directive and nondirective approaches. For example, a social service counselor might use a nondirective approach while assessing a family's problems and switch to a directive approach when explaining benefits and requirements. A personnel director might use a nondirective approach early in an interview to relax the applicant and establish a feeling of trust, then switch to a more directive approach while asking challenging questions, and return to the nondirective approach at the end by giving the applicant an opportunity to ask questions. Each interviewer must be able to determine when a particular approach seems most appropriate and when to switch from one approach to another. Chapter 9 on counseling and Chapter 11 on health care interviewing further discuss directive and nondirective interviewing approaches.

Perceptions of the Interviewer and Interviewee

Perceptions affect the way interviewers and interviewees respond to one another. Each party comes to an interview with perceptions of the other and of self which may change as the interview progresses. These perceptions are symbolized in the model by the double-pointed arrows between the interview parties (see figure 2.3).

Figure 2.3 Perceptions of self and others

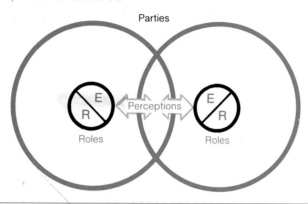

Perceptions of the Other Party

Each party may be influenced by the other's reputation—a tough boss, a reporter who asks embarrassing questions, a shady used car dealer, a counselor who cares. Previous encounters with a person may make you look forward to (or dread) an interview, posing either an advantage or a disadvantage for both parties. Endorsements by persons or groups you like or dislike may affect how you view an interviewer or interviewee.

Perceptions may change as the interview progresses and both parties react to questions and answers. Positive perceptions result from the use of clear, logical language and supporting evidence as well as from appearance factors such as hairstyle, manner, clothing, and cleanliness. Members of governmental and business groups often react positively to well-tailored suits, white shirts and blouses, gold watches, conservative shoes, and clean fingernails. Whether you want to admit it or not, your perceptions are affected by the other party's age, sex, race, size, ethnic group, and association with other groups, persons, values, beliefs, and attitudes.

Perceptions of Self

Perceptions of self, or self-concept, come from the physical, social, and psychological perceptions that you have derived from experiences and interactions with others.[3] Your experiences include all past behaviors, how you have interpreted them, and how you perceive others to have interpreted them. Others include groups to which you belong or desire to belong as well as "significant others" who influence you interpersonally. The roles you play within these groups also affect your self-concept.

Self-concept may determine whether a person is willing to take part in an interview. For instance, you may refuse to take part in a counseling session because you fear failure or think you did poorly in a previous session. Or you may take part, but fail because you were convinced that you would—a self-fulfilling prophecy: "I told you I couldn't do it"; "I just knew I wouldn't get that job"; "I couldn't help it, that's just the way I am." Perceptions of self influence the messages sent and received, how they are sent and received, risks taken, and degree of self-disclosure.

Figure 2.4 Communication interactions

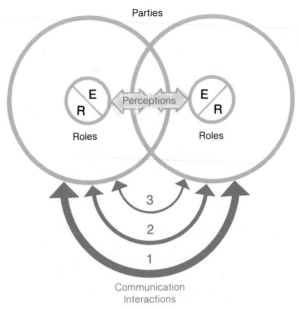

Communication Interactions

Communication interactions, symbolized by the curved arrows that link the parties in figure 2.4, are the most obvious behavioral interchanges during interviews. Each level of interaction differs in degree of self-disclosure, amount of risk, perceived meanings, and amount and type of content.

Levels of Interactions

Level 1 interactions deal with relatively safe, nonthreatening areas of inquiry and produce answers that are usually superficial, socially acceptable, comfortable, and replete with ambiguities. The following exchanges illustrate Level 1 communication interactions.

Interviewer: Good morning, Glenn. How are you this morning?
Interviewee: Fine, thanks.
Interviewer: And your family?
Interviewee: They're doing real well. Mom and Dad said to say hello.
Interviewer: Be sure to give them my best. How did you find out about our opening?
Interviewee: I was reading the *Dallas Morning News* and saw your ad.

Level 2 interactions deal with more intimate and controversial areas of inquiry— behaviors, thoughts, attitudes, beliefs, feelings. Responses tend to be half-safe, half-revealing. The interviewee strives to satisfy the interviewer while not revealing too much. The following exchanges illustrate Level 2 interactions.

Interviewer: How do you feel about interviewing with an old friend of the family?

Interviewee: Truthfully, a little bit uncomfortable. I want to get this position based on my own abilities and not on a friendship. I hope that will be the case.

Interviewer: Believe me, Glenn, my interest is in finding the best sales representative for my company.

Level 3 interactions deal with highly intimate and controversial areas of inquiry and produce answers that fully disclose a person's feelings, beliefs, attitudes, and perceptions. Level 3 interactions rarely take place without a high level of trust between interviewee and interviewer which may be unattainable until a second or third interview. The following exchange illustrates a Level 3 interaction.

Interviewer: Why are you interested in leaving your present position?

Interviewee: A major reason is the position that your company has open. It's exactly the type I have been waiting for.

Interviewer: And other reasons?

Interviewee: Well, frankly, I am not getting along with my immediate superior. We disagree on the philosophy of selling and how much freedom I should have in doing my job.

Levels of communication interactions are like doors. The door is merely ajar in Level 1 interactions, so only some general ideas, feelings, and information may pass through. An interviewee may close the door quickly and safely during Level 1 exchanges. The door is half open (the optimist's view) or half closed (the pessimist's view) in Level 2 interactions so that more specific and revealing ideas, feelings, and information may pass through. An interviewee is willing to risk both disclosure and ability to close the door quickly. The door is wide open in Level 3 interactions, allowing highly specific and revealing ideas, feelings, and information to pass through. The risk is great to an interviewee but so are the potential rewards.

The question-answer-question sequence that dominates many interviews often makes interaction levels difficult to predict, distinguish, or change. The levels reached depends upon self-perceptions, perceptions of the other party, situational variables, levels of trust, potential risks, topics being discussed, defensiveness of each party, how questions are asked and answered, and motivation to partake effectively. Unlike small groups or audiences for speeches into which we can blend (or hide), the intimate, interpersonal nature of the interview is often very threatening. The typical interview places your ego and sometimes your financial, social, professional, psychological, or physical survival on the line because it deals with *your* behavior, *your* performance, *your* reputation, *your* decisions, *your* feelings, *your* loss, *your* money, or *your* future—not those of others in a group or audience or some hypothetical being. The good interviewer and interviewee understands how interviews are threatening and what motivates people to take part at Levels 2 and 3 instead of merely Level 1.

1. People are likely to communicate beyond Level 1 if they understand what you expect of them. Avoid tricks, gimmicks, and white lies; be straightforward and honest.
2. People are likely to communicate beyond Level 1 if they are interested in you, the organization you represent, or the subject matter of the interview.

3. People are likely to communicate beyond Level 1 if you treat them with respect and give them your full attention.
4. People are likely to communicate beyond Level 1 if you offer a tangible reward (money, products, services) or an intangible reward (appreciation, feeling of accomplishment, pride in a contribution).

The thickness of the arrows in figure 2.4 symbolizes that Level 1 communication interactions are most common, particularly during the early minutes of interviews when parties are sizing up the situation and one another. The length of the arrows symbolizes the relational distance between parties and reveals that Level 3 interactions require a close relationship. If you find it difficult to advance beyond Level 1, try to determine why by observing, listening to, and questioning the other party. The reasons may be motivational, relational, perceptual, situational, or personal (such as poor communication skills or personality). Try to ease the other party into Level 2 and Level 3 exchanges. Level 2 interactions are fairly common when the interviewer is acting as an information source and asking tactful, nonthreatening questions. Be cautious when employing evaluative comments such as "*Why* do you say *that?*," especially with threatening or accusatory nonverbal emphases. Level 3 interactions require a close, positive relationship and high levels of trust, self-confidence, and motivation.

Communication interactions may be verbal or nonverbal, intentional or unintentional. Often during an interview, it is impossible to separate the verbal from the nonverbal and the intentional from the unintentional, but for discussion purposes we will do so.

Verbal Interactions

Words are merely arbitrary connections of letters that serve as symbols for people, animals, things, events, ideas, beliefs, and feelings. They are imperfect vehicles for communication learned in a particular environment under particular circumstances. Why do you call an elephant an elephant, a house a house, a democracy a democracy? Other English-speaking people do not use the same words the way you do. For instance, football identifies one form of sport in England and a very different sport in the United States. Irving Lee has written of a person who exclaimed, "Just get people to use words in their right meaning and then everyone will understand everyone else."[4] If only communication were that simple. The arbitrary nature of language has led to a host of communication problems.

Many words have multiple meanings which can cause communication breakdowns between persons of different ages, professions, geographical backgrounds, economic statuses, experiences, or educational levels. A "strike" means one thing to a factory owner and quite another to a bowler, baseball pitcher, or batter; and each feels differently about strikes. Be careful with slight changes in words that alter meanings (such as revocable and irrevocable clauses in contracts) or you will "talk past" the other party.[5] Talking past the other party often occurs because of the connotations placed on common words. You can speak of an "inexpensive" or a "cheap" suit, of your business partner having "convictions" or "prejudices," of a client being "tenacious" or "stubborn," or of a supervisor "leading" or "dictating to" subordinates. Not many people would admit to "manipulating" others during interviews, but the verb "to manipulate" has as many positive as negative meanings:

Negative meanings	Positive meanings
cunning	touch
undermine	handle
trick	join
gerrymander	meet
scheme	use
deceive	exercise
intrigue	operate
beguile	set in motion

Remember, words don't mean; people do! Choose language carefully and be aware of how your listener will interpret each word and phrase.

Keep up-to-date with changing usages of common words. For example, fast cars went from "keen" and "neat" in the 1940s and 1950s to "hot," "cool," "groovy," and "far-out" in the 1960s and 1970s to "decent," "tough," "mean," and "awesome" in the 1980s. It takes two to communicate. Know the current meanings of words and words preferred in specific situations so you can share language with others. Listen to people talk in a variety of situations; read popular and local materials; pay close attention to "in" words used in television programs and interviews. All of these sources will keep you informed about the latest meanings of words. As a general rule, avoid slang in interviews, do not limit your vocabulary to "in" words, and do not try to be what you are not.

Confusion often results during interviews when words sound alike and look alike but have different meanings. *Sail* and *sale* refer to selling and sailing; *bowl* and *bull* can refer to anything from a stadium, cereal bowl, or game to a male animal or shoving one's way through a crowd; and *game* may connote a chess match, basketball game, wild animal, or person willing to try something new. Listen carefully to what is being said by you and the other party, and do not assume that accurate communication is taking place.

Each profession has its own jargon. Teachers refer to "underachievers" when they mean students who are failing; sociologists speak of "culturally deprived environments" instead of slums; a highway engineer may recommend a "vehicular control device" instead of a stoplight; and a communications professor may speak of dyads instead of interviews. Jargon may lead interview parties to talk "at" or "past" one another.

Each of us also uses personal jargon in the form of euphemisms and differentiation or renaming. Euphemisms are substitutions of better sounding words for common words, often to mask or hide reality. Thus, we speak of our "life-like" rather than artificial Christmas tree, of going to the "powder room" instead of restroom or bathroom, of our "sales associates" rather than clerks, and of "women's sizes" in place of sizes for large women. Differentiations or renamings are attempts to redefine something to alter how we and others view reality. Recession or "down turn" in place of "depression" helps us to see an economic crisis as less serious than the "Great Depression"; "friendly fire" alters how we view the accidental killing of our own soldiers in combat; and calling something a "political" rather than a "scientific" document or report changes the fundamental way we see the document. Euphemisms and renaming can not only lead us to *talk past* one another but to *fool* one another intentionally or unintentionally.

Everyone is guilty of using ambiguous words. What is a "nice" vacation, an "affordable" college education, a "simple" insurance policy, a "moderate" increase in salary, or a "typical" work day? Who is not "middle-class" in America? When is a person "young," "middle-aged," or "old"? When is something "one of the best," or, perhaps more accurately, when is it not "one of the best"? Strive for specificity in language to minimize problems and maximize communication. Each time you use an ambiguous word or phrase, you invite misunderstandings, misperceptions, and false expectations. Never assume that accurate communication has taken place. Explain or illustrate what you mean by a nice vacation; give a figure for moderate cost; explain what a simple insurance plan includes; give age ranges for middle age. If the other party uses an ambiguous word or phrase, ask for an explanation, example, or figure.

Nonverbal Interactions

Some writers claim that 65 percent to 93 percent of communication is carried through nonverbal behavioral acts, appearances, and manners of dress that reveal emotions, personality traits, attitudes, reactions, certainty, interest, happiness, status, role-playing, and time availability.[6] Not only do we communicate largely through nonverbal means, but many writers claim that nonverbal acts and appearance are more effective than verbal symbols. Research suggests that nonverbal actions: exchange feelings and emotions more accurately; convey meanings and intentions relatively free of deception, distortion, and confusion; are more efficient; are most suitable for suggestion or imparting ideas and emotions indirectly; and are critical for high quality communication.[7]

When you take part in an interview, observe the other party for nonverbal clues that reveal how well the interview is proceeding. The other party is likely to be detecting everything you do and do not do, assigning meanings to the simplest behavioral acts: head nods, vocal expressions, touches, pauses, and glances at your watch. The intimate nature of the interview (with parties often a mere arm's length apart) magnifies nonverbal communication. Sometimes a single behavioral act conveys a message. For example, poor eye contact may "tell" a party (rightly or wrongly) that you have something to hide, a limp handshake that you are timid, a serious facial expression that you are sincere, touching a hand or arm that you are sympathetic or understanding, or a puzzled expression that you are confused. The rate of speaking and conducting an interview may communicate urgency (fast speed), the gravity of the situation (slow speed), lack of interest (fast speed), lack of preparation (slow speed), nervousness (fast speed and breathless voice), or indecision (halting voice). Silence may encourage the other party to talk, signal that you are not in a hurry, show agreement with what is being said, and keep a party talking.

More often, however, you send and receive messages from a combination of behavioral acts. For instance, leaning forward, good eye contact, nodding the head, and serious facial expression may show you are interested in what a person is saying. Fidgeting, crossing and uncrossing your arms and legs, sitting rigid, looking down, furrowing your brow, and a high pitched voice may reveal a high level of fear, anxiety, or agitation. A drooping body, frowning, and slow rate of speaking may reveal sadness or resignation to anticipated failure or discipline. Leaning backward, staring at the other party, raising an eyebrow, crossing your arms, and shaking your head may signal disagreement, anger, or disgust. The way you shake hands and look another in the eyes may signal a degree of trust and trustworthiness. Body movements, gestures, and posture may show dynamism or lack of it.

Physical appearance and dress are particularly important during the first few minutes of interviews, the critical first impression before the interview parties get to know and respect one another. Whether we like to admit it or not, we respond more favorably to generally attractive persons who are neither too fat nor too thin, tall rather than short, shapely rather than unshapely, pretty and handsome rather than plain or ugly. You may not be able to do much about your height, weight, shape, or handsomeness, but you can be neat and clean with well-groomed hair. Wear neat, clean, pressed clothing that is appropriate for the occasion and fits well. Keep accessories such as earrings, bracelets, necklaces, rings, and watches to a bare minimum. Makeup and cologne should enhance appearance rather than call attention to themselves or stun the other party. As a rule of thumb, be conservative in dress, appearance, and makeup, particularly for business or professional meetings. Remember, how you dress and prepare yourself physically for an interview reveals a great deal about how you feel about yourself, the other party, and both the nature and importance of the interview. Also, how you dress and prepare yourself physically will affect your self-concept, determine credibility with the other party, reveal status within an organization or group, and gain appropriate or inappropriate attention.

All interviewers and interviewees interpret and assign meanings to what they observe, and these meanings are affected by relationships, experiences, and personalities. For example, you may see a yawn and interpret it as a sign of boredom or merely as a lack of sleep. Or you may note poor posture and interpret it as a sloppy habit or as being at ease, or you may hear a soft voice and interpret it as a sign of weakness or as a measure of self control. Or you may note rumpled or out-of-style clothing and see a party as unprofessional or perhaps as a creative person who is not concerned about unimportant things. Therefore, it's important to be aware of how you and others interpret what you observe.

Verbal and nonverbal messages are usually intertwined, and the nonverbal may *complement* the verbal.[8] Vocal stress may call attention to an important word: "I am *not* going to Chicago" or "The *net* income last year was $325,000." Inflection may give a specific meaning to a word. If, for instance, you must release an employee, you may complement the verbal message with a sincere tone of voice, deliberate speaking rate, serious facial expression, and direct eye contact. The nonverbal accentuates and verifies your words. People often assess the verbal and the nonverbal before interpreting messages. For example, if a client remarks, "That's a nice looking outfit; you ought to have it cleaned and burned," you are likely to listen to the voice, observe the facial expression, and look for a twinkle in the eye to determine if the client is joking or serious. Since words are imperfect collections of symbols, they often cannot express inner feelings, exact meanings, or attitudes. Nonverbal actions join with words to express subtle meanings and feelings.

Nonverbal communication plays many roles in the interview setting.

Nonverbal actions may *reinforce* verbal messages: a head nod while saying yes, a head shake while saying no, an extended arm with the hand up while saying stop, a wave while saying hello or goodbye. You may point to a chair and say, "Sit here, please." "We're number one!" would not be the same without a raised arm and an extended finger. "Give us two beers" may be repeated with two raised fingers. "I love you" may be said and accentuated with a touch, a wink, or a squeeze of the hand.

A nonverbal action may stand alone as a *substitute* for words. For instance, you may point to a chair without saying, "Sit here, please," and the interviewee will get the message. People express "We're number one!" by raising and shaking an index finger. They say "I don't know" by shrugging shoulders or express "I don't care" with a shrug and a sour look. You may say "I approve," "please continue," or "I'm interested in what you're saying" by nodding your head. Nonverbal substitutes—a kind of everyday sign language—may be as effective as and less disruptive than words. A pause or moment of silence may communicate a variety of messages: Go on; I agree (disagree); I do (don't) believe you; I am interested (disinterested); I have confidence (no confidence) in you; or I don't understand. Silence is not a void; communication is taking place.

Nonverbal symbols may be *inconsistent* with words. For example, if a supervisor says, "Go ahead and take tomorrow off . . . if you want to," you are likely to observe his nonverbal signals as well—not merely *what* is said but *how* it is said. You may interpret the real message as "I don't approve!" or "It'll create problems." People often mean the opposite of what they say. For instance, the tone expressed in "What a choice!" may mean there is no choice, and verbal emphasis in "That was a great raise!" may mean the raise was ridiculously low. A misplaced pause may communicate different messages: "What's up the road ahead?" or "What's up the road (pause) ahead?" Messages sent and messages received are inseparable combinations of the verbal and the nonverbal. Research suggests that when one party's voice, face, gestures, eye contact, or posture communicates an attitude or feeling inconsistent with the words used, the other party typically responds to the nonverbal rather than the verbal—the *how* dominates the *what.*

Remember, any behavioral act, verbal or nonverbal, may be interpreted in a meaningful way by the person receiving it. The message may be *intentional* or *unintentional,* and the fact that you did not intend to communicate boredom with a yawn is irrelevant if the other person interprets it that way. A counselor, for instance, may agree with a solution but communicate disagreement nonverbally. As noted in Chapter 1, perhaps the greatest single problem with communication is the assumption of it. Faulty assumptions and transmissions are revealed when a person replies, "But I didn't mean it *that* way."

Feedback

Feedback, represented by the large arrow at the top of the interviewing model (see figure 2.5), verifies what is communicated to the other party and how that party is reacting. Feedback between interviewer and interviewee is continuous and more immediate and pervasive than in any other form of communication. No interview can be successful without meaningful feedback.

Feedback Options

Feedback is more than a means of checking word translation. It is a knowledge of results that may be inferred or observed. A response to a question may signal whether or not the correct message got through. Based on your own perceptions and your relationship with the other party, you compare the response to your intended message and then decide how to react. The three feedback alternatives are to (1) *confirm* that the message got through, (2) *readjust* the message, or (3) *deny* reception and try again. Imagine that a supervisor states, "I need you to work the second shift on Saturday." You may frown, an apparent rejection of the request. The supervisor may then deny the feedback message and reply, "I was hoping you would not react that way," or adjust to your feedback by saying, "I know you had planned to go to the football game, but this is the first time I have asked you to work on Saturday in more than a year." You may confirm the feedback, "Yes, I've had these tickets for more than a month"; or deny the feedback, "No, it's not that big a deal"; or adjust to the feedback, "I'm sorry; you have given me a break on weekend shifts. I'll see if someone else can use the tickets."

Feedback is continuous, but correct detection and interpretation depend upon the sensitivity, receptivity, and perceptiveness of each party. For example, an interviewee may display uneasiness through lowered eyes, fidgeting, or trembling voice every time an interviewer gets close to a particular sensitive area. The skilled interviewer will detect these signals and decide whether to probe into the area or avoid it.

Figure 2.5 Feedback

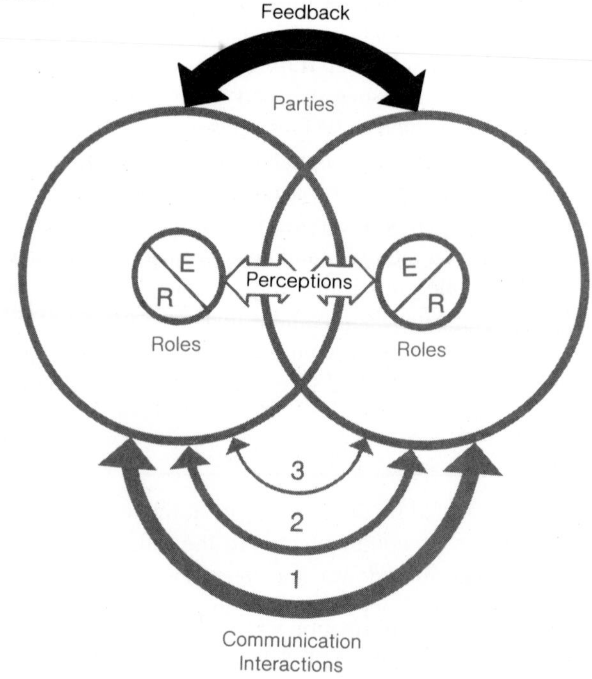

Listening

Poor listening habits guarantee loss of information; failure to detect feedback clues; and failure to motivate the other party to respond, express feelings, listen, and interact. You cannot hear and assess the steady stream of feedback in interviews when you have your mouth open and your ears closed. Even when spending half or more of an interview listening, few people listen well. In a series of studies during the 1950s, Ralph Nichols discovered that the average white collar worker demonstrated only about 25 percent listening efficiency. Recent surveys have found poor listening to be rated as the number one communication barrier for accountants and first-line supervisors.[9]

Many times, when we play the role of interviewer, we do not listen carefully either to the question we ask or to the answer we receive; and when we play the role of interviewee, we do not listen carefully either to the question we are asked or to the answer we give. Only occasionally will a friendly critic remark following an interview, "You should have heard what you asked (said.)" Many times we do not listen effectively because we are not really interested in what the other party is asking or answering. Also, we may be too easily distracted or are unaware of listening approaches and principles.

The three approaches to listening are (1) listening for comprehension, (2) listening for empathy, and (3) listening for evaluation. Each approach has a particular emphasis that may help you receive and process information during interviews, and any one approach may dominate all or part of an interview. Physicians, sales representatives, journalists, and counselors may use all three approaches in a single interview.[10]

Listening for comprehension is primarily a method of receiving content and requires little or no feedback from the listener. The purpose is to understand and remain objective, not to inspect critically each question, answer, or reaction. This listening approach is common during the first minutes of interviews when both parties are trying to determine how to react. Here are some guidelines for listening for comprehension:

1. Clarify questions and answers through repetitions and reflective questions.
   Why should you act now?
   You say now is not a good time for you to act?
   Which policy is selected most often by people in your field?
   Are you concerned about what might happen in the future if . . . ?
2. Obtain additional information through probing questions.
   Tell me more about . . . .
   Why do you think this program is not for your firm?
   And then?
   What do you know about . . . ?
3. Ask for specific information when a question or response is vague.
   What do you mean by APR financing?
   When do you think an employee's performance should be appraised?
   Which issue was that report in?
   Where have you worked before?
4. Identify types and nature of beliefs, attitudes, and feelings.
   Why do you feel that way?
   How would you describe your feelings at this time?
   Why do you think diversification is the way to go today?
   How do you feel about beginning a new career at age fifty?
5. Listen for critical content and main ideas, no matter how difficult they are to understand.
6. Be patient, particularly when information seems irrelevant or uninteresting.
7. Listen to the answer before planning your next question.
8. Take notes both to retain information accurately and to show that you are listening.

Listening with empathy is a method of responding beyond merely receiving and comprehending messages. It communicates to the other party an attitude of genuine concern, understanding, and involvement.[11] Listen with sensitivity and provide extensive feedback. Strive to put yourself in the other's place to understand and appreciate what the other person is feeling. Empathic listening is total response, not a series of principles. It reassures, comforts, expresses warmth, and reveals unconditional positive regard for the other party. Highly personal and emotional issues, such as poor performance in a course, dropping out of school, an illness, family problems, divorce, bankruptcy, and changes in college majors or careers, require empathic listening. The genuineness of empathic listening is a measure of its success. Empathic listening and responses point the way to possible actions. Listening for empathy is not synonymous with showing sympathy. Sympathy implies feeling sorrow, while empathy is the ability to put oneself in the situation of the other party. The empathic listener says verbally and nonverbally, "As much as I can, I will try to put myself in your place in order to understand your thoughts, feelings, beliefs, and limitations." Here are some guidelines for listening with empathy:

1. Respond to questions and answers with candor.
   Yes, there are some unprofessional organizations involved in direct mail advertising today. However . . .
   I can understand your concern about investing several thousand dollars at this time, but . . .
   No, I don't like to talk about cancer either; on the other hand, . . .
2. Try to remain nonevaluative unless you have no choice.
   (evaluative) That's not a good choice because . . .
   (nonevaluative) That's one option, of course. Another is . . .
   (evaluative) Well, if you want my opinion, I must say that I think you're making a big mistake in choosing . . .
   (nonevaluative) You must realize that my situation is not exactly like yours, but if I were choosing, I would probably select . . .
   because . . .
3. Listen carefully with an eye toward giving options and directions.
   If you are trying to keep the total cost below $3,500, here are some selections available at this time.
   I can understand your financial problems since many of our clients have been affected by the layoffs. Perhaps you could consider . . .
4. Strive to be comfortable with strong displays of emotion.
   Let a person talk out hostilities toward you or others. Do not interrupt or become defensive without hearing everything the person wants to say.
   If a person begins to cry, be silent and give the person adequate time to become composed. Little that you can say will help the situation; phrases such as "I know" do not help much.
   If a person launches into a morbid account of a problem, hear it out without showing discomfort or impatience.
5. Let the other party know you are listening and interested.
6. Do not react too quickly to comments and questions that contain controversial or emotional ideas.
7. Do not interrupt the other party.

Listening for evaluation should follow comprehension and empathy in most interviews because you are not ready to judge information until you have comprehended it. Evaluative listening is crucial, but you must guard against expressing evaluations verbally and nonverbally during interviews if you desire continued cooperation and disclosure. Above all, do not become defensive. Here are some guidelines for evaluative listening:

1. Keep your cool, particularly if you are "baited" by an interviewer or interviewee with leading questions or emotion-laden words.
2. Listen carefully to the entire question or response before making any judgment or drawing any conclusions.
3. Listen carefully to the words used and how they are used.
4. Observe all nonverbal clues and behavior for nuances that will give you a clear idea of how to proceed.
5. Listen to the content of questions and responses, including rank order of points, logic, and evidence.
6. If you have any doubts about a question or answer, ask for clarification before evaluating and responding.
7. Withhold final evaluations until an entire point of the interview is concluded. Only then can you understand adequately and judge appropriately.

Although insightful listening is critical to both interviewer and interviewee, most people find it difficult to listen, let alone to choose the appropriate listening approach. Listening is an invisible skill. Many people learn to be passive listeners as children, students, employees, and subordinates. They do not react verbally or nonverbally, but merely sit and accept (or appear to accept) what they hear. You have had experiences with people who would not listen to you. Friends of one of the authors recently wanted to purchase an insurance policy from an agent who was determined to discover the specifics of their business income, mortgage, debts, and so on. Even when they dodged such questions and asked the agent to show possible plans by using national averages, he continued to ask personal questions. This agent made the couple angry and did not make the sale.

You can be an effective listener if you work at it.[12] First, you must want to be a listener as much as you want to be a talker. Strive to be as satisfied when listening to others talk as when listening to yourself talk. Second, you must overcome the "entertainment syndrome," the expectation that you must be entertained in all settings and pay attention only to what you determine is not "boring." Little in the world, in or out of the classroom, is continually exciting and entertaining, but most of it is important to listen to and to consider seriously. Third, you must be an active listener who listens carefully and critically to words, arguments, and evidence, and observes all nonverbal clues from voice, face, gestures, eye contact, and movements. And fourth, you must concentrate on listening despite distractions, including your biases and prejudices, the physical surroundings, and the other party's mannerisms, appearance, and dress.

All interviews come about because of an *exigency*—a need or problem marked by a degree of urgency. For example, a married couple feels their marriage could be improved with counseling, a student needs a part-time job for spending money, a lawyer must get information from a reluctant witness to prove a client is innocent, a sales representative must reach a quarterly goal to retain a position, and a physician must obtain accurate information from a patient who may have a terminal illness.

Need or problem and degree of urgency determine the type and affect the atmosphere of each interview. The atmosphere of a screening or placement interview is very different from that of a separation or reprimand interview. A survey creates an atmosphere different from a grievance, sales, or interrogation interview. Each type of interview places special restraints on the initiation of the process, the parties, and the levels of interactions. Need, urgency, and type of interview determine the roles played by interviewer and interviewee and how these roles may switch. For instance, an applicant who desperately needs work may play a more active interviewer role during an interview than an applicant who has a good position and is merely shopping around to see what is available.

The situation (need, problem, and urgency) may determine whether the interviewing approach is directive or nondirective. For example, although most persuasive interviews tend to be directive, counseling interviews tend to be nondirective, and employment interviews tend to be a little of each, although urgent problems may dictate an unusual approach or combination of approaches. An organization controlling the interview may determine the approach. Survey groups, for instance, prescribe in detail how, when, and where each interview is to be conducted. Some companies are now prescribing the questions their recruiters are to ask of all applicants.

No interview takes place in a vacuum tube in which parties interchange behavior oblivious to the world beyond the rarefied atmosphere of the tube. Each interview occurs not only because of a predetermined and serious purpose but also at a given time and place, and is subjected to a variety of situational variables. Location, architecture, temperature, seating arrangement, furniture, distance between parties, territoriality, noise, interruptions, privacy, time of day and week, and events that precede and follow the interview all affect the interview either negatively or positively. The interviewing situation is symbolized in figure 2.6 by the circle that encloses all other variables. The arrows pointing inward symbolize the "implosive" effect of situational variables on the interviewing process.

Time of Day, Week, and Year

Individuals communicate best at different times of the day, week, and year. For instance, you might be a morning, afternoon, or night person, meaning this is the optimum time for your performance, production, communication, handling of conflicts, and dealing with highly important, intricate, or delicate matters. Late in the work day or shift or just before lunch or dinner might allow too little time to handle significant issues or give information adequately. Monday mornings and Friday afternoons are times when moods tend to be dark and motivation low. Holidays such as Christmas, Memorial Day, Thanksgiving, and

Figure 2.6 Situational variables

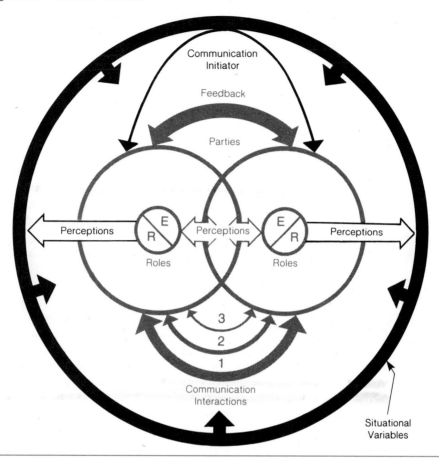

Yom Kippur are good times for some types of interviews (sales, employment selection, journalistic) but bad times for others (dismissals, reprimands, investigations). Counselors note marked increases in crisis interviews with lonely people during family-oriented and happy seasons such as Christmas, Thanksgiving, and Passover.

Be aware of events that may precede or follow an interview. Tuesday afternoons might ordinarily be good times for a manager or professor, but not *this* Tuesday afternoon because of a poor production report delivered before your interview or a budget cut meeting that will follow. An applicant facing another job interview immediately afterward may be thinking of the next interview instead of listening carefully during this one. Events related or unrelated to your interview topic and purpose, such as a traffic accident, plant closing, personal problem, or troublesome interview prior to your meeting may affect concentration, mood, and ability to communicate.

Initiating the Interview

The arrows that emerge from the top of the situational circle in the interviewing model and touch each party (see figure 2.6) signify that either party may initiate the interview. For example, a student may walk into a professor's office and ask for help with an assignment, or a professor may call a student in to talk about an assignment. An insurance representative might call a friend about the possibility of selling a term policy, or a friend might call an insurance representative about purchasing a term policy.

The situation often determines who initiates an interview. For instance, a police officer must interview those involved in a traffic accident; a reporter must interview a member of the school board about a controversial drug testing policy; and a college senior must interview for positions relevant to his or her major. Conversely, the person who initiates an interview affects the situation more because the initiator often determines when and where the interview will take place and the emotional climate. For example, an appraisal interview may be very different when a supervisor stops an employee and says, "See me in my office at three o'clock!" from when an employee stops a supervisor and asks, "Could I meet with you at three o'clock to discuss my progress?" The first is far more threatening than the second. Initiating the interview is dealt with at length in Chapter 3.

Perceptions of the Situation

Perceptions of the situation are symbolized in the interviewing model (see figure 2.6) by the arrows that run from the parties to the situational circle. It is critical to remember that each person comes to an interview with unique perceptions of the situation (need, problem, urgency, timing, setting, and initiation). An interviewer may see the interview as a *routine* and not very exciting daily activity, while the interviewee may see it as a *major event* likely to affect future career, marriage, and financial plans, health, or social status. Thus, a recruiter may interview a dozen college seniors a day; it is merely business as usual. But for a particular college senior, this interview may be the chance of a lifetime, an event anticipated since high school.

The setting may be perceived quite differently by interview parties. For example, a supervisor may view the conference room as a neutral setting, while an employee may see it as a hostile environment, particularly if workers tend to get fired there. A dean of students sitting behind a desk may feel very relaxed, but a student sitting in front of the desk may feel very threatened. Both parties have vested interests in the outcome of an interview, but often their goals are quite different. The sales representative wants to sell a set of encyclopedias and the customer wants to spend available money on a stereo; a journalist wants to produce an exciting news story and a campaign worker does not want to embarrass a candidate; a recruiter wants to hire a hard worker and an applicant wants an easy job with good salary with fringe benefits.

Interview parties are most likely to communicate beyond Level 1 interchanges if they perceive the situation to be informal rather than formal, warm rather than cold, private rather than open to others not involved in the interview, and close physically, socially and psychologically rather than distant. We also tend to communicate more openly in familiar and open settings.[13] Most organizations attempt to enhance the other party's concentration and motivation with well-lighted, pleasantly painted, moderate-sized rooms with comfortable furniture, temperature, and ventilation. While other organizations strive to create business and professional settings that resemble living rooms, dining rooms, family rooms, and studies to make clients feel more "at home" during interviews.

Territoriality

All of us are territorial. We tend to stake out our physical and psychological space and to resent those who violate it with their eyes, voice, or body. Think of your negative reactions when you were talking to a professor and another student was obviously listening to the interaction, or when you were having a luncheon meeting and a person at the next table stared at you. Or when you were talking with your supervisor at your work station and fellow workers were talking loudly at the next station, or when you were tutoring a student and another student took a seat at the same small table. We do tend to react less negatively to territorial invasions by friends, peers, high status persons, or people who explain why they are encroaching on our territory.

Seating arrangement may help or hinder an interview. You are likely to feel uncomfortable with a person who insists on talking nose-to-nose, and you may react by backing up, placing furniture between you and the other person, or terminating the interview. Two or three feet—approximately an arm's length—seems to be an optimum distance. Status, sex, furnishings, cultural norms, relationship between the parties, and personal preferences may influence the seating arrangement in an interview. For example, a superior and a subordinate may sit across a desk from one another (arrangement A in figure 2.7),

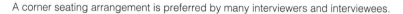

A corner seating arrangement is preferred by many interviewers and interviewees.

Figure 2.7   Seating arrangements

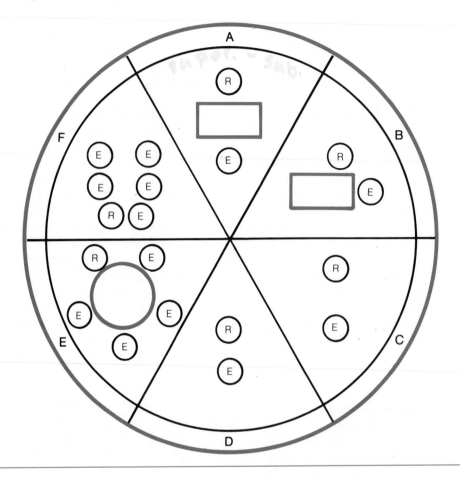

providing appropriate distance in a formal setting where one party desires to maintain a superior position. Two chairs at right angles near the corner of a desk or table (arrangement B) create a less formal atmosphere and a feeling of equality. Many students have remarked that they prefer this arrangement with college professors. You may remove physical obstacles and reduce the superior-subordinate atmosphere further by placing chairs on opposite sides of a small table or by omitting the table altogether (arrangements C and D). A circular table (arrangement E) is growing in popularity, especially in counseling interviews or interviews involving more than two people, because it avoids a head-of-the-table position, allows participants to pass around materials, and provides a surface on which to write, review materials, or place refreshments. The circular table or chairs around a small coffee table works well for panel or group interviews. Arrangement F is suitable when one or both parties consist of several persons.

It is also important to take into consideration whose turf you will be on during an interview. You are likely to feel more comfortable, relaxed, and less threatened in your own home, room, office, or place of business than on another's turf, particularly that of a stranger, supervisor, or high status person, such as dean of the college, editor of the newspaper, or president of the company. We all tend to be protective of our turf. Think of how you felt when you last walked into your room or office and found another student, employee, or stranger in your chair or at your desk. When you have a choice, select the location most conducive to effective communication. The location might be a neutral setting, such as a restaurant, to avoid turf problems. Or it could be another's residence because you want to talk about home insurance or improvement, another's place of business because you want to discuss business investments, or your office because you have designed it carefully to show you have a highly professional and well-established public relations agency.

Noise

Noise in an interview refers to anything that interferes with the communication process.[14] It may, for instance, be background noise such as machinery, ringing telephones, doors opening and closing, squeaking chairs, music, others talking, objects being dropped or unloaded from trucks, footsteps outside the room, and traffic or aircraft noise. Other frequent distractions include people coming in and out of the room, walking by an open door, or asking the other party or you for answers or assistance. You may generate your own "noise" by coming to an interview fatigued, angry about an incident unrelated to the interview, overwhelmed with personal problems, or thinking about the next interview. Also, you may be easily distracted by a headache, stomachache, or hangover. Additionally, you may succumb to looking out a window at traffic, building construction, or interesting scenery. Or you may be concentrating on pictures, objects, and furniture in the room or the other party's notetaking, dress, appearance, or mannerisms. You can limit the negative influences of noise by selecting locations relatively free of background noise. Sometimes, "noise" can be alleviated by merely closing the door; taking the phone off the hook; turning off your printer, television set, radio, or stereo; closing a window or blinds; and telling others you do not wish to be disturbed. You can limit self-generated noise by coming to interviews physically and psychologically ready to concentrate on the matters at hand. Chapter 5 offers suggestions for notetaking that avoids unwarranted distractions.

Summary

This chapter presents a model of the interviewing process and explains the many variables that interact. Interviewing is a dynamic, complicated process between two complex parties operating with imperfect verbal and nonverbal symbols guided and controlled by the situation. A thorough understanding of the interviewing process and the relationship that exists between the parties is a prerequisite for successful interviewing. Both parties must be aware that perceptions of self, the other party, and the situation determine how interviews progress and outcomes are achieved. The abilities to listen (for comprehension, empathy, and evaluation) and to employ silence strategically are often more important than the ability to talk.

An Interview for Review and Analysis

Joe is a production foreman with twenty-five years of experience and a very good record. The boss is considering him for a promotion, but company policy stipulates that a foreman is *not* to be informed when being actively considered for a promotion. Hence, Joe does not know he is promotion material. Furthermore, because of company policy, the boss is compelled to avoid tipping his hand. Company policy does allow mentioning, in general terms, overall considerations related to the current work force situation and to established company criteria for promotions. This interview is exploratory rather than decision-making. Two hours prior to the interview, Joe receives a call from the boss's secretary asking him to report to the boss. No reason is given.[15]

Use the dimensions of inclusion, control, and affection to assess the relationship that exists between Joe and the boss. How did this relationship affect the interview? How did situational variables, particularly the initiation, affect the interview? What perceptions do Joe and the boss have of themselves, of one another, and of the situation? When, if ever, do the roles of interviewer and interviewee switch? At which levels are most of the interactions, and why? Which listening approaches do Joe and the boss use most often, and how do these approaches affect the interview? Which feedback options are used? How does the nonverbal affect the verbal? Does the boss use a directive or nondirective approach? How appropriate was this selection? What suggestions would you give to Joe and the boss to improve their interviewing skills?

1. **Boss:** Well, Joe, come on in. (smiling) Sit down. It's been quite a while since we've had time for a real chat.
2. **Joe:** (sitting in chair opposite desk, facing the boss) Thank you, Sir. (low, soft voice)
3. **Boss:** (very serious facial expression and tone of voice) How are things moving along these days, Joe? Everything under control in your section?
4. **Joe:** Oh, yeah, fine. No complaints. (fast speaking rate)
5. **Boss:** I'm *glad* to hear that there are no complaints. (pause) You think, then, that you're doing a pretty good job?
6. **Joe:** As good a job as I know how, Sir. (shifts weight in chair)
7. **Boss:** Good. (pause; looks Joe directly in the eye) By the way, have you ever thought of . . . uh, doing *something else?*
8. **Joe:** (pause; speaks slowly) Well . . . uh, yes and no, I guess. However, I do like this job very much. (rapidly) It's a job I really know very thoroughly.
9. **Boss:** Hmmm, I see. You mean you would not like to change your job, then?
10. **Joe:** Uh . . . no . . . no . . . I really don't think I would.
11. **Boss:** (looking closely at Joe; measuring his words) I see. Just why do you want to stay on your present job?

12. **Joe:** Well, I get along fine. I know the work real well, and everybody seems to like me.

13. **Boss:** *Seems* to like you? (looks Joe directly in the eye)

14. **Joe:** Oh . . . now and then there may be one or two fellows who don't like one of my decisions. But we always manage to get along.

15. **Boss:** Some fellows perhaps don't like you, then? (sounds accusatory)

16. **Joe:** Well, I wouldn't exactly say *that.* I've had a couple of guys who have been sore because I didn't give them some overtime when they thought they were entitled to it.

17. **Boss:** You mean that's the *only* reason some of the men haven't been too fond of you?

18. **Joe:** Really, Sir, that's the only thing of any importance I can think of. And even those two guys were not really hotshots. They're not the kind who deserve overtime. They goof off too much. (firm voice, direct eye contact)

19. **Boss:** You don't like men who loaf on the job?

20. **Joe:** No, absolutely not! Everyone should pitch in and do his share.

21. **Boss:** I assume, of course, that you do yours!

22. **Joe:** Oh, yes indeed!

23. **Boss:** (after a pause) Uh . . . Joe, answer me this: did you ever think of . . . uh, *bettering* yourself?

24. **Joe:** Think of bettering myself? Well, yes, lots of times. I guess anyone who has any brains or any ambition wants to try to do better.

25. **Boss:** Just what do you mean by *that?*

26. **Joe:** Well, I only mean that anyone—or at least almost anyone—could find ways to improve. (looks down)

27. **Boss:** You think, then, that there's room for improvement in the way you're handling your job right now?

28. **Joe:** Oh, I'm sure there's always room for improvement. Did you have anything *special* in mind, Sir?

29. **Boss:** Let me put it this way, Joe; have you ever thought of bettering yourself on . . . *another* job?

30. **Joe:** Oh, I really do like my job very much, Sir! This is a job I feel I know very well. I feel I'm on top of it, if you know what I mean.

31. **Boss:** I'm not sure you were listening *carefully* to my question, Joe. Let me ask it again: have you thought of bettering yourself on *another* job?

32. **Joe:** Well, that's hard to answer, Sir, because I'm really very enthusiastic about my present job.

33. **Boss:** You haven't considered the *possibility* of another job?

34. **Joe:** Well, I suppose there are times when anybody daydreams a little about how things would be on another job. But I really haven't given it much serious thought.

35. **Boss:** I take it, then, that you prefer very definitely to *stay* on your present job; is that right?

36. **Joe:** Oh, yes, definitely. As I have said, I feel very happy in my job. Did you have anything in mind about me being on another job, Sir? (rapid speaking rate)

37. **Boss:** Oh, don't worry about that, Joe. I see I have another appointment coming up in a couple of minutes. It's been good to have a little chat with you. We'll have to get together again before too long. Lots of luck. See you later. (shakes Joe's hand firmly without meeting his eyes)

Student Activities

1. An important quality of a good listener is the ability to shift from one listening approach to another when necessary. Listen to a local news interview or a classroom interview and see if you can identify the kinds of listening being employed and when the approaches seem to change.

2. Go on a shopping trip to a clothing store, car dealership, hardware store, or other retail outlet and observe how verbal and nonverbal symbols and actions are both intertwined and separate in communication interchanges. How do parties react when they detect that the verbal and nonverbal seem to convey different messages?

3. Read an interview in *Time, Newsweek, U.S. News,* or a similar source and see how many levels of interactions are used. Try to determine why Levels 1, 2, and 3 occur when they do and why one level dominates or appears infrequently or not at all.

4. Go to a variety of professional offices and observe the physical surroundings. How are they designed for the types of interviews that take place there? Which do you find most comfortable, and why? Which do you find least comfortable, and why?

5. Observe an interview in class or on television for several minutes, keeping the three relational dimensions in mind: inclusion, control, and affection. How did these dimensions affect the interview? How did they change as the interview progressed? Which dimension seemed most critical to the success or failure of the interview?

6. What types of interviews are most likely to require a directive approach, a nondirective approach, or a combination of approaches? How do you determine which to use and when? Which approach seems to be most common in your day-to-day interactions?

Notes

1. Robert S. Goyer, W. Charles Redding, and John T. Rickey, *Interviewing Principles and Techniques: A Project Text* (Dubuque, IA: Wm. C. Brown Publishers, 1968), 23.

2. Our treatment of the interview as a relationship is influenced by several sources: W. C. Schutz, *FIRO: A Three-Dimensional Theory of Interpersonal Behavior* (New York: Holt, Rinehart & Winston, 1958); Paul Watzlawick, Janet H. Beavin, and Don D. Jackson, *Pragmatics of Human Communication* (New York: Norton, 1967); Gerald M. Phillips and Julia T. Wood, *Communication and Human Relationships: The Study of Interpersonal Communication* (New York: Macmillan, 1983); and Judee K. Burgoon and Jerold L. Hale, "The Fundamental Topic of Relational Communication," *Communication Monographs* 51 (1984), 193–214.

3. William D. Brooks and Robert W. Heath, *Speech Communication* (Dubuque, IA: Wm. C. Brown Publishers, 1985).

4. Irving J. Lee, *How to Talk with People* (New York: Harper & Row, 1952), 23.

5. Lee, 11–26.

6. Ray L. Birdwhistell, *Kinesics and Context* (Philadelphia: University of Pennsylvania Press, 1970), 158; Albert Mehrabian, "Communication without Words," *Psychology Today* 2 (1968), 51–52.

7. Dale G. Leathers, *Nonverbal Communication Systems* (Boston: Allyn and Bacon, 1976), 4–7.

8. Mark L. Knapp, *Essentials of Nonverbal Communication* (New York: Holt, Rinehart and Winston, 1980), 11–14.

9. Ralph C. Nichols, "Listening Is a Ten-Part Skill," *Nation's Business* 45 (1957), 56; Lyman K. Steil, Larry L. Barker, and Kittie W. Watson, *Effective Listening: Key to Your Success* (Reading, MA: Addison-Wesley, 1983), 9–10.

10. Andrew W. Wolvin and Carolyn G. Coakley, *Listening* (Dubuque, IA: Wm. C. Brown Publishers, 1988); and Lyman K. Steil, Larry L. Barker, and Kittie W. Watson, *Effective Listening* (Reading, MA: Addison-Wesley, 1983).

11. Richard E. Crable, *One to Another* (New York: HarperCollins, 1981), 169; James J. Floyd, *Listening: A Practical Approach* (Glenview, IL: Scott, Foresman, 1985), 119–125.

12. Floyd, *Listening*, 20–28.

13. Knapp, *Essentials of Nonverbal Communication,* 54–55.

14. Stephen W. Littlejohn, *Theories of Human Communication* (Belmont, CA: Wadsworth, 1992), 52; Floyd, *Listening,* 50–54; Florence I. Wolff, Nadine C. Marsnik, William S. Tracey, and Ralph G. Nichols, *Perspective Listening* (New York: Holt, Rinehart and Winston, 1983), 187–192.

15. This interview has been revised and adapted by W. Charles Redding from an original appearing in Benjamin Balinsky and Ruth Burger. Adapted from pp. 24–25 in *The Executive Interview* by Benjamin Balinsky and Ruth Burger. Copyright 1959 by Benjamin Balinsky and Ruth Burger. It is reprinted by permission of Harper & Row and W. Charles Redding.

Suggested Readings

Adler, Ronald B.; Rosenfeld, Lawrence B.; and Towne, Neil. *Interplay: The Process of Interpersonal Communication.* New York: Holt, Rinehart & Winston, 1989.

DeVito, Joseph A. *The Interpersonal Communication Book.* New York: Harper & Row, 1988.

Floyd, James J. *Listening: A Practical Approach.* Glenview, IL: Scott, Foresman, 1985.

Knapp, Mark L. *Essentials of Nonverbal Communication.* New York: Holt, Rinehart & Winston, 1980.

Lair, Jess. *I Ain't Much Baby—But I'm All I've Got.* New York: Doubleday, 1978.

Leathers, Dale G. *Successful Nonverbal Communication.* New York: Macmillan, 1986.

Littlejohn, Stephen W. *Theories of Human Communication.* Belmont, CA: Wadsworth, 1992.

Mehrabian, Albert. *Silent Messages: Implicit Communication of Emotions and Attitudes.* Belmont, CA.: Wadsworth, 1981.

Steil, Lyman K.; Barker, Larry L.; and Watson, Kittie W. *Effective Listening.* Reading, MA: Addison-Wesley, 1983.

Stewart, John. *Bridges Not Walls.* New York: Random House/Alfred A. Knopf, 1989.

Wilmot, William W. *Dyadic Communication.* New York: Random House/Alfred A. Knopf, 1987.

Wolvin, Andrew W., and Coakley, Carolyn Gwynn. *Listening.* Dubuque, IA: Wm. C. Brown Publishers, 1988.

3

Structuring the Interview

While each type of interview (survey, probing, journalistic, employment, appraisal, persuasive, counseling, and health care) requires a somewhat different structure, certain principles and techniques are applicable to all. This chapter focuses on these principles and techniques and divides the interview into three major parts: (1) the opening, (2) the body, and (3) the closing.

The Opening

The few seconds or minutes spent in the opening is often the most important period of the interview because what you do and say, or fail to do and say, sets the tone for the interview and often determines whether you will be able to get beyond Level 1 interactions. The tone may be serious or lighthearted, formal or informal, professional or nonprofessional, threatening or nonthreatening, relaxed or tense. However, be sure the tone is the one *intended* and most *appropriate* for each encounter. The opening's primary function is to motivate both parties to participate freely and communicate accurately. A poor opening may lead to a superficial interview, inaccurate information, or no interview at all. If dissatisfied with your initial approach, a person may say no, walk away, close the door, or hang up the phone.

The Two-Step Process

A two-step process of establishing rapport and orienting the other party encourages participation. Situation, interviewer preference, and the relationship between interviewer and interviewee determine which step comes first, what is included in each step, and how content is communicated. Establishing rapport is a process of creating goodwill and trust between interviewer and interviewee, and it often begins with a self-introduction ("Good morning, I'm Melissa Johnson") or a greeting ("Good morning, Bob") accompanied by nonverbal actions such as a firm handshake, eye contact, a smile, a nod, and a pleasant, friendly voice.[1] The rapport stage may then proceed to personal inquiries ("What's new?" "How are things going?" "How have you been?") and on to small talk about the weather, sports, families, current events, and so on. You may flavor the personal inquiry and small talk with tasteful humor. Customs of the geographical area or the organization, relationship and status differences between the parties, formality of the occasion, and interview type and setting determine the appropriate verbal and nonverbal rapport building

What you do and say in the opening seconds sets the tone for the remainder of the interview.

techniques in each interview. Be careful of overdoing this stage because you can turn off an employer, client, or respondent with too much sweet talk, particularly if you appear to be insincere.

Orientation, the second step in the opening, may explain the purpose, length and nature of the interview, the organization responsible, how the information will be used, and why this interviewee was selected. Rapport and orientation are often intermixed, but whether separate or not, they reduce "relational uncertainty" so that each party is aware of the degree of warmth or friendliness (affection) that will pervade the interview, how *control* will be shared, and how interested each is in taking part (inclusion). An inadequate opening may mislead one or both parties and create problems during or following the interview. The rapport and orientation steps are illustrated in the following opening from a persuasive interview:

Persuader: Good evening, Mr. Warwich. I'm Jessie Addison from World Auto Insurance. I talked to your wife a few days ago.

Persuadee: Oh yes, she said you were coming over this evening. Come in and sit down.

Persuader: You have a very nice home in a lovely neighborhood. How long have you lived here?

Persuadee: About seven years. We enjoy the home and the area, and it's been a great place to raise a family.

Persuader: When I called your wife, she said you have two policies coming due, one on a 1991 Honda and the other on a 1993 Oldsmobile wagon.

Persuadee: Yes, that's correct.

Persuader: My main purpose this evening is to introduce you to the policies, benefits, services, and low prices of World Auto. What do you know about our company?

Common Opening Techniques

The following are common opening techniques. Each may serve as an entire opening, aid in rapport building, or initiate the orientation.[2]

1. *Summarize the problem.* This technique is useful when an interviewer is unaware of the problem, vaguely aware of it, or unaware of details. For example:

   > Since we installed the word processors nearly five years ago, there has been a steady increase in the number of errors in our records. The attitude of the staff seems to be that since errors can be corrected easily, they are no problem. But many of these errors are going undetected until our customers ask questions or complain about accounts. I would like to discuss some ways to solve this problem.

   There are occasions when stating the purpose of the interview would make its achievement impossible. This is true, for example, in research interviews and in some survey interviews. You may need to withhold your purpose or disguise it to get honest, unguarded answers.

2. *Explain how the problem was discovered.* This technique explains how the interviewer discovered the problem and then usually summarizes it. Be honest and specific in revealing sources of information. For example:

   > Last evening I was reviewing our third-quarter audit and discovered that losses to shoplifting increased nearly 12 percent over the second quarter. I would like to get your reactions to some new security procedures I'm developing.

3. *Mention an incentive or reward for taking part.* This technique can be effective if the incentive is appealing to the respondent, a monetary reward, for example. Be careful of this technique because many salespersons use a gift to motivate people to listen to sales pitches. For instance, if you begin an informational interview with this opening, you may never convince the interviewee that you are not a salesperson pretending to be a pollster. The following is an incentive opening.

   > Good evening. I'm Terry Keck from the Washington County Planning Commission. We are conducting a study of current zoning laws and how they are affecting older housing areas such as this one. We hope this study will result in zoning changes that will protect and enhance the value of older homes and neighborhoods.

4. *Request advice or assistance.* This is a common opening technique because assistance is often what an interviewer needs. The request may begin the orientation process, so be clear, precise, and sincere. For example:

> Kathy, I'm preparing a market survey for Model X3, which was released to several stores two months ago. Would you respond to a series of questions I've worked up and tell me if any of them are unclear?

5. *Refer to the known position of the interviewee.* This opening technique refers to the respondent's position on an issue or problem. Be cautious in using it because a tactless reference to a known position may create antagonism or a defensive attitude. Here is a tactful opening:

> Hi, Louise. I understand that you have some reservations about my proposal to expand the production facilities at the Webster plant and that you would prefer another location. I'd like to discuss my proposal and your reservations.

6. *Refer to the person who sent you to the interviewee.* Be sure the person did send you, and use this method only when you are fairly certain the interviewee knows and likes the person. It could be embarrassing or disastrous to discover after using a name that the interviewee dislikes or does not recall the person. Here is an example of this technique:

> Professor Thompson? Professor Tudor in the history department said you might be able to give me some information on the archaeological diggings at Fort Ouiatenon.

7. *Refer to the organization you represent.* This opening refers to a group (Gallup, the *Times,* General Motors, University of Illinois) instead of a person. Mentioning the group represented may orient and motivate an interviewee to cooperate. For example:

> Good afternoon. I'm from the Consumer Research Center at Eastern State University. We're conducting a study of automobile purchases during the past six months.

An interviewee's reaction to the name of an organization may be negative as well as positive, so lessen the potential impact by preparing for possible negative reactions. For example:

Interviewer: Hi, I'm Margie Kelley from the law firm of Kelley and Kelley.
Interviewee: Isn't that the outfit that tried to get that drunk driver off after she killed a mother and her three kids?
Interviewer: Yes, we represented Jo Adams because we felt she had the right to legal counsel and was more in need of treatment than punishment.

8. *Request a specific amount of time.* "Got a second?" is perhaps the most *overused* and *misused* opening technique. You cannot explain who you are or what you want in a second. State a realistic time and, by the end of it, either complete or begin to close the interview. If the interviewee has more time or wants to continue, the interviewee can say so. Here is an example of this technique:

> John, do you have ten minutes to discuss a problem with me?

If you tell a person you need forty-five minutes, the person may say no, but if you do not reveal the time needed, the person may have to end the interview early because of another appointment. Either way, your purpose is not achieved. The best solution is to make an appointment for any interview that requires more than five or ten minutes.

9. *Ask a question.* Begin an interview with an open-ended question such as "What can I help you with?" "How may I be of assistance?" or "What types of computers are you most interested in?" Avoid closed questions such as "Can I help you?" or "Do you need assistance?" that a person can answer with a quick "No."[3] To enhance trust and cooperation, you should pose an open-ended question that is easy to answer. You should not put the interviewee on the spot. Avoid questions such as "Do you want your children to have a good education?" which have a single, obvious answer and may be insulting to the interviewee. An open question may serve as a transition from the rapport-building and orientation functions of the opening to the informational, counseling, or persuasive functions of the body of the interview. Make these transition questions easy to answer and clearly relevant to your stated purpose.

10. *Combination opening.* The nine standard opening techniques are not the only ones available to an imaginative interviewer. As illustrated in these samples, you may combine two or more techniques:

A: Good morning. I'm George Williams from the telephone company, and I would like about five minutes of your time to get your opinions on the new billing system we initiated recently.

B: Hello. I'm George Williams from the telephone company. Your neighbor Cynthia McAlister said you might be willing to help with a study we are conducting to determine how we can improve the new billing system. Changes as a result of this study should make billings easier to understand and may even reduce charges.

Nonverbal Communication in Openings

The opening techniques discussed above must be accompanied by appropriate nonverbal communication because an effective opening also depends upon how you act, look, and say what you say.[4] Therefore, you should always knock before entering a room or office, even if the door is open, and wait until the other party signals for you to enter, even if you are a superior or you own the house, building, or organization. Also, never take a seat until you are given a signal to do so; a verbal "come in" or merely a smile, head nod, or wave are common examples of acknowledgement. The space you are invading is the other party's territory; any apparent violation of this space is likely to begin the interview on poor footing. Maintain good eye contact with the other party (do not stare) because eye contact shows trust and trustworthiness and enables you to pick up signals such as "come in," "be seated," and "I'm interested/willing to talk to you."

As noted in Chapter 2, your appearance and dress add a great deal to the important first impression you make. Both should communicate attractiveness, neatness, maturity, professionalism, and a knowledge of what is appropriate for *this* interview and setting. Your voice and facial expression should signal the gravity or seriousness of the situation and your relationship to the other party: stranger, nodding acquaintance, colleague, business contact, friend. Do not let your countenance signal catastrophe when the interview deals with routine matters of little significance, friendliness when you are about to discipline or discharge a person, warmth when you are quite angry, happiness when a major problem needs attention, or closeness when you have never met the other party or are lower on the organizational ladder. If you shake hands, give a firm but not a crushing handshake. Be careful of overdoing handshaking with acquaintances, colleagues you work with everyday, or persons during brief encounters. Touching another on the hand, arm, or shoulder is generally appropriate only when both parties have an established and close relationship and the occasion warrants it.

Quiz #1—Interview Openings

How satisfactory are the following openings? Consider the interviewing situations and types, the techniques used, and what is omitted. How might each be improved? Do not *assume* that each opening is unsatisfactory.

1. This is a counseling interview taking place in a professor's office. The student has not made an appointment.

   > Professor Taylor, got a second? (walks into the office) Are we going to do anything important in class on Friday? (laughs)

2. This is a survey interview taking place at the front door of a home. The parties do not know one another.

   > Good evening. (smiling, shakes hands vigorously) I would like to ask you some questions concerning your feelings about the recent teacher strike in Swiss County.

3. This is a journalistic interview taking place in the hallway near the Senate chamber between a reporter and a United States senator. The senator is heading toward a committee meeting.

   > Senator Smothers! (waving, shouting) Would you comment on your committee's actions on short-term steps to relieve the balance of payments crisis?

4. This is an informational interview taking place in the office of a production line supervisor.

   > Hi! (smiling) I've been sent to see you about a problem in my division; one I can't seem to handle.

5. This is a persuasive interview taking place between two business partners in an office.

   > I got a call last night, near midnight, from a person I won't name. (serious tone of voice, frowning) She said you were thinking of altering your position against unionizing our shop. What's going on?

The Body

The Interview Guide

An interview guide is an outline of topics and subtopics to be covered. Guides help interviewers develop areas of inquiry (rather than random lists of questions), remember areas of information, record answers, recognize relevant and irrelevant answers, and determine which probing questions to ask. Since the interview guide is an outline, review the fundamentals of outlining so you can impose a clear, systematic structure on each interview.

Structural Sequences

A *topical sequence* follows natural divisions of a topic. For example, an interview on road repair might be divided into three parts: budget, major projects, and equipment. An interview on a company budget might discuss research and development, production, marketing, and sales. Journalists frequently resort to single-word topic guides: what, when, where, who, how, and why.

A *time sequence* treats topics or parts of an interview in chronological order. For instance, an interview explaining a process might move from stage one to stage two to stage three. A recruiter probing into a student's educational background might proceed from junior high school to high school to college.

A *space sequence* arranges topics according to space divisions: left to right, precinct to precinct, top to bottom, east to west. A guide explaining the physical arrangement of a firm might begin by discussing the business office, then move to the printing area, and finally to the shipping room.

A *cause-to-effect* sequence deals with the causes and effects of an event, problem, or accident. An interviewer may prefer to describe an effect first (high unemployment, rising interest rates, and low production) and then move to causes.

A *problem-solution* sequence consists of a problem phase and a solution phase. For instance, a city engineer and a builder might begin an interview by discussing a zoning problem and then turn to how the problem can be settled.

Assume that you have decided to interview an experienced counselor for information to aid you in future interviews. First decide on the major areas of information you want, such as training, methods, experiences, and suggestions for the novice. Second, place possible subtopics under each major area, as in the following topical sequence guide:

I. Training in interviewing
    A. Courses in interviewing
        1. Formal
        2. Informal
    B. Reading about interviewing
        1. Books
        2. Pamphlets
        3. Trade journals
    C. Observing interviews
        1. Practice interviews
        2. Real interviews

II. Experiences in interviewing
    A. When
    B. Where
    C. Types
    D. Frequency

III. Methods used in interviewing
    A. Preparation
    B. Organization or structure
        1. Opening
        2. Body
        3. Closing
    C. Questions
    D. Special techniques

IV. Suggestions for the beginner

Some areas (such as IV) may need no subtopics to assure free and open responses or to allow discovery of subtopics as the interview progresses. You may employ two or more sequences in an interview, such as a time sequence for major divisions and a topical or spatial sequence for subdivisions. Or the problem part of a problem-solution sequence may be developed from cause to effect.

Interview Schedules

After completing an interview guide, decide if additional preinterview structuring is needed. The guide alone may be sufficient, or you may wish to turn all or part of it into questions. The outline of areas or questions you take to an interview is an interview *schedule.*

A *nonscheduled interview* may be a detailed guide or merely a list of topics and subtopics. The nonscheduled interview is most useful when: the information area is extremely broad; interviewees and their information levels differ significantly; interviewees are reluctant or have poor memories; or the interviewer has little preparation time. The two *major advantages* of the nonscheduled interview involve the unlimited freedom to (1) probe into answers and (2) adapt to different situations and persons. The *major disadvantages* are that the nonscheduled interview requires a highly skilled interviewer, is difficult to replicate, provides no easy means of recording answers, presents problems in controlling the time factor, and allows interviewer bias to creep into unplanned questions. Interviewer bias occurs when interviewees respond in ways they think interviewers want them to respond (because of verbal or nonverbal cues) rather than give their true feelings, attitudes, or beliefs.

The *moderately scheduled interview* contains major questions with possible probing questions under each. Phrases in the interview guide become questions. The moderate schedule, like the nonscheduled interview, offers freedom to probe into answers and adapt to different interviewees and situations. In addition, it imposes a greater degree of structure on the interview, forces a higher level of preparation, aids in recording answers, and is easier to conduct and replicate. Since interviews tend to wander and become unstructured, listing questions makes it possible to keep the interview on track or return to the structure when desired. Journalists, broadcasters, medical personnel, recruiters, counselors, lawyers, and insurance investigators, to name a few, rely primarily on non-scheduled and moderately scheduled structures. A moderately scheduled interview would look like this:

1. What things, events, or happenings bother you the most these days?
   a. What about natural disasters?
   b. What about crime in the streets?
   c. What about the economy?

2. What do you think economic conditions will be like four years from now?
   a. What about economic conditions in this area?
   b. What about economic conditions in this state?
   c. What about economic conditions in the nation as a whole?

3. How do you feel about the President's handling of the drug problem?
   a. How do you feel about mandatory drug testing of employees?
   b. How do you feel about using the armed forces to fight drug smuggling?

4. How do you feel about government aid to localities stricken by natural disasters such as floods, tornados, and earthquakes?
   a. What types of aid should the government give?
   b. How should the amount of aid be determined?
   c. Who should control the distribution of this aid?

A *highly scheduled interview* contains all the questions to be asked and the exact wording to be used with each interviewee, allowing no unplanned probing or deviation from the schedule. Questions are usually closed in nature so that respondents can give brief answers. Highly scheduled interviews are easy to replicate and conduct, and they take less time than either nonscheduled or moderately scheduled interviews. However, flexibility or adaptation are not possible, and probing questions, if any, must be planned into the schedule. Researchers and survey takers use highly scheduled interviews such as the following:

1. Which issue or problem facing America today bothers you the most?
   a. What is the most important reason this issue bothers you the most?
   b. When did this problem or issue begin to bother you the most?

2. Do you think economic conditions will be better or worse for you next year?
   a. (If the answer is better): Why do you think economic conditions will be better for you next year?
   b. (If the answer is worse): Why do you think economic conditions will be worse for you next year?

3. What three words would you use to describe the President's economic policies?

4. Which group of taxpayers do you think carries the heaviest tax burden?

5. Which group of taxpayers do you think carries the lightest tax burden?

The *highly scheduled standardized interview* is the most thoroughly planned and structured. All questions and answer options are stated in identical language to each interviewee who then picks an answer from those provided. Highly scheduled standardized interviews are the easiest to conduct, record, tabulate, and replicate, so that even no interviewers can handle them. However, the breadth of information is restricted, and probing into answers, explaining questions, or adapting to different interviewees are not possible. Built-in interviewer bias may be worse than the accidental bias encountered in nonscheduled and moderately scheduled interviews. Respondents have no chance to explain, amplify, or qualify answers. Researchers and survey takers interested in precise information, replicability, and reliability use highly scheduled standardized interviews because their procedures must produce the same results in repeated interviews. The following is a highly scheduled standardized interview:

1. Which one of the following issues or problems facing America today bothers you the most?
    a. Health care
    b. Taxation
    c. Crime
    d. Unemployment
    e. Drugs
    f. Foreign competition

2. Do you think economic conditions will be:
    a. Better four years from now
    b. Worse four years from now
    c. About the same four years from now

3. Do you think the President's war on drugs will be:
    a. Highly successful
    b. Successful
    c. Unsuccessful
    d. Highly unsuccessful

4. In your estimation, which of these groups carries the most unfair tax burden?
    a. Farmers
    b. The wealthy
    c. Senior citizens
    d. The poor
    e. White collar workers
    f. Blue collar workers

5. In your estimation, which of these groups carries the smallest tax burden?
    a. Farmers
    b. The wealthy
    c. Senior citizens
    d. The poor
    e. White collar workers
    f. Blue collar workers

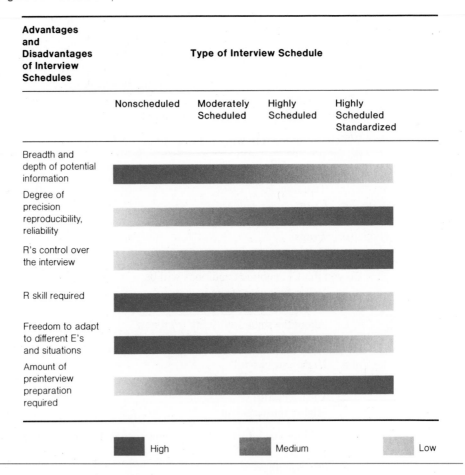

Figure 3.1 Structural options

Advantages and Disadvantages of Interview Schedules	Type of Interview Schedule			
	Nonscheduled	Moderately Scheduled	Highly Scheduled	Highly Scheduled Standardized

Breadth and depth of potential information

Degree of precision reproducibility, reliability

R's control over the interview

R skill required

Freedom to adapt to different E's and situations

Amount of preinterview preparation required

High   Medium   Low

When writing about the advantages and disadvantages of schedule types, Raymond Gorden warns: "Neither should neatness of the interview schedule, efficiency of coding, or reliability of responses be confused with the more important criterion—validity of the information."[5] Choose the schedule best suited to the interviewer, respondents, data needed, and type of interview; and do not hesitate to combine schedules: nonscheduled in the opening, moderately scheduled when probing and adaptation are needed, and highly scheduled standardized for easily quantifiable data. Although schedules are usually lists of questions, they can range from a topic outline to a manuscript. For example, you may write out major arguments for a persuasive interview or instructions for an information giving interview. Figure 3.1 summarizes the major advantages and disadvantages of each schedule.[6]

The Closing

Closings are usually brief but highly important parts of interviews. Once you have asked or answered the last question or made the last point, it is tempting to take a deep sigh of relief. However, an abrupt closing may undo the rapport and trust established during the interview and make the other party feel like a discarded container—important only as long as the interviewer needs what's inside. Each interview forms or adds to the relationship between the parties and creates expectations. Thus, future interactions are enhanced by good closings and damaged by poor ones.

Functions and Guidelines

There appears to be three primary functions for closings.[7] First, the closing may signal the termination of the interview, but not the relationship. In fact, a common element of the closing is a statement or agreement about when the next contact may take place: "See you after class in about an hour"; "Let's get together after lunch"; "See you in the morning"; "I'll be back in touch when I return from vacation at the end of August"; or "Let's meet again next year in Chicago." Simple phrases may communicate the likely interval between interviews. Phrases such as "see you" or "until next time" tend to signal short intervals; "farewell" and "goodbye" tend to signal lengthy or forever intervals; "let's stay in touch" or "don't be a stranger" tend to signal moderate intervals; and "we'll be in touch" or "we'll call you" may lead to confusion because a party may have difficulty determining if this is a moderate interval or a traditional "brush off" that means never. Second, the closing may signal supportiveness designed to bring the interview to a positive and productive close. One or both parties may express pleasure in having taken part in the interview and express hope or intention of renewing contact in the future. And third, the closing may summarize what has taken place. Even when there is no systematic summary, either or both parties may use the closing to "tidy up" the process; to bring the interview to a neat and orderly ending; and to pull together a variety of issues, concerns, agreements, and bits of information addressed.

Follow several guidelines for closing interviews. First, be sincere and honest. Make no promises you cannot keep. Second, do not rush the closing. The so-called "law of recency" suggests that people recall the last thing said or done during an interview. If it is being rushed out the door or an ill-chosen phrase, your relationship and future contacts with this party will be in jeopardy. Remember that the closing is not an entity unto itself but an integral part of the whole interview. Third, do not introduce new topics or ideas during the closing when neither party is ready to devote satisfactory attention to them. If you sense that an interview *in fact* or *psychologically* has come to a close, do not try to resurrect it. Simply bring it to an effective close. Fourth, remember that the interview is not over until it's over. The other party is likely to be noticing and interpreting everything you say and do until you are out of sight and sound of one another. A slip of the lip or an unfortunate nonverbal act might negate all that you have accomplished during the opening and body of the interview. Fifth, avoid *false closings*, language and nonverbal actions that signal the interview is coming to a close when it is not. Sixth, leave the door open for future contacts, and if additional contact is planned, explain what will happen, when, where, and why. If feasible, make the appointment before the other party leaves or escorts you out the door. And seventh, try to avoid what Irving Goffman called *failed departures*.[8] A failed departure takes place when you have brought an interview to a successful close and taken leave from the other party. Then an hour or so later you run into this party in the hall, parking lot, or a restaurant. The result is often awkward because both parties have said their "goodbyes" and now must think of something to say on the spot. Practice hypothetical situations to determine what you might say if this happens to you. For instance, what would you say to a company recruiter if you met this person later in the hallway outside your college placement service? A professor in the parking lot? A supervisor after you have said goodbye to take a position with another company?

Closing Techniques

The following are common closing techniques.[9]

1. *Offer to answer questions.* Be sincere in the desire to answer questions and give the interviewee adequate time to ask. Do not give a quick answer to one question and then end the interview.

   > Any questions?
   > Do you have any questions you would like to ask?
   > I would be happy to answer any questions you might have.

2. *Use clearinghouse questions.* The clearinghouse question allows you to determine if you have covered all topics or answered all the interviewee's questions. It can be an effective closing if your request is perceived not as a formality or an attempt to be sociable but as an honest effort to ferret out questions, information, or areas of concern not discussed adequately.

   > I think that takes care of everything I need. Can you think of anything I have missed?
   > Anything else before I leave?
   > Is there anything we have not discussed that you would like to bring up at this time?

3. *Declaring the completion of the purpose or task.* The four-letter word "well" probably brings more interviews to a close than any other word or phrase. When people hear it, they automatically assume the end is near and prepare for leave-taking.

   > Well, that's all the questions I have.
   > Okay, that should give me plenty of material for a good report.
   > Well then, with this one last signature, the contract is complete.

4. *Make personal inquiries.* Personal inquiries are pleasant ways to end interviews, but they must be sincere and show genuine interest in the interviewee. Interviewees judge sincerity by the way interviewers listen and react verbally and nonverbally.

   > When are you moving into your new home?
   > Where are you going on your vacation?
   > How's your daughter doing in law school?

5. *Make professional inquiries.* Like personal inquiries, professional inquiries are pleasant but more formal ways to end interviews if the inquiries or statements are sincere and show genuine interest in the other party's professional life. Most of us appreciate those who show interest in and concern for our careers or career preparation.

> How is your internship with WZBO working out?
> Are you going to attend the Society of Professional Journalists convention in San Francisco?
> Good luck in your new position as sales manager.

6. *Signal that time is up.* This closing is most effective when a time limit has been announced or agreed upon in the opening. Be tactful in calling time, and try not to give the impression that you are moving the interviewee along an assembly line.

> Well, that's all the time we have for today.
> Our time's up, and I have another appointment waiting.
> Wow, it's 3:30 already; our time went quickly today.

7. *Explain the reason for the close.* Tell why you must close the interview and be sure the justifications are real. If an interviewee thinks you are giving phony excuses, any future interactions will be strained.

> I have another appointment waiting; perhaps we can . . . .
> I'm sorry, but I'm going to have to end our discussion because I have a class in a few minutes.
> I must leave now to get to the airport by five o'clock.

8. *Express appreciation or satisfaction.* A note of appreciation or satisfaction is a common closing because interviewers usually have received something— information, help, a sale, a story, and so on. Be sincere and avoid any verbal or nonverbal hint of sarcasm.

> I've really enjoyed meeting you. Thanks much for your help.
> That's all the questions I have. Thank you for your time.
> I think we've accomplished a great deal today. I appreciate your willingness to come in early this morning.

9. *Exhibit concern.* Expressions of concern for the interviewee's health, welfare, or future are effective if they are sincere and not merely verbal habits. Be sure the note of concern is appropriate for your relationship with the interviewee.

> Take care, and I will see you soon.
> Be sure to get in touch with me if you run into additional problems.
> I hope all goes well for you in your new position.

10. *Plan for the next meeting*. It is often appropriate to arrange the next interview or reveal what will happen next, including date, time, place, topic, content, or purpose.

> Let's get together again on October 16 at 10:00 A.M. and see how things appear at that time.
> Okay, when we meet on the tenth, we should be prepared to review the final draft of the contract.
> We will notify you in about two weeks of the results of this interview and whether we would like you to come to Milwaukee for another one.

11. *Summarize the interview*. A summary is a common closing for informational, appraisal, counseling, and sales interviews. Summaries may repeat important information, stages, and agreements or verify accuracy and agreement.

> It's agreed, then, that I will write up a preliminary report that includes design, labor, and materials cost for phase one of the office complex while you check the figures with your home office and contact me by Friday if there are any necessary changes?

Nonverbal Closing Actions

Nonverbal actions may intentionally or unintentionally signal that the closing is commencing. Actions perceived as leave-taking signals include straightening up in the seat, leaning forward, standing up, moving away from the other party, uncrossing your legs, placing your hands on your knees as if preparing to rise, breaking eye contact, offering to shake hands, making various hand movements, smiling, and looking at the clock. Be conscious of such actions so the closing will not take you by surprise.

Remember that any behavioral act may be interpreted in a meaningful way by the party observing the act. Unconscious movements such as glancing at a watch may cause an interviewer or interviewee to feel pressure to close an interview prematurely. Be constantly aware of what your words and actions are saying to the other party.

Interviewers usually combine several techniques into a complete closing, such as the following:

> Well (glancing at a watch), I see our time is up. (leaning forward and smiling) I think it's been a good session (rising from the chair) and we are close to an agreement. (shaking hands with the interviewee) I appreciate your meeting on such short notice. Take care of yourself, and I will see you at ten next Monday (a waving hand motion).

Decide before or during each interview which combination of closing techniques is most suitable. Your role in the interview, and perhaps your relationship with the interviewee, may dictate some techniques, rule out others, and determine who will initiate the closing and when.

Quiz #2—Interview Closings

How satisfactory are the following closings? Consider the interviewing situations and types, the techniques used, nonverbal communication, and what is and is not included. How might the closing be improved verbally and nonverbally? Do not assume that each closing is completely unsatisfactory.

1. This is a counseling interview in an academic office. A student has been experiencing severe academic and relationship problems with courses, professors, and roommates. This is the third session with the counselor.

Interviewer: Well, (straightening up) our time's up. I think we accomplished a great deal today. You're making remarkable headway. (sitting back) What are your reactions to today's session?
Interviewee: I think I'm beginning to . . .

2. This is an employment screening interview in a college placement center. Pete is a senior in management with average grades and no management or supervisory experience.

Interviewer: (standing up) I've enjoyed talking with you this morning, Pete. (shakes hands) We'll be getting in touch with you soon. Good luck! (vocal stress)

3. This is a persuasive interview in a used car lot. Jan and Frank are looking for a recent model mini-van and have been talking to a sales person at B & B Quality Cars and looking at a 1993 Plymouth Voyager and a 1992 Pontiac Sportsvan.

Interviewer: Well, Jan and Frank, (smiling) it's been nice meeting you both. (waving) Come back.

4. This is a political survey being conducted by a representative of a professional polling firm. The survey takes about fifteen minutes and is occurring at the apartment door of Mary Ellen McPhee.

Interviewer: (looking at the interview form) That's all the questions I have. Really a nice evening, isn't it?

5. This is a semi-annual appraisal interview taking place in a supervisor's office. The employee is Ida Armand with a very good record with the organization. She has received three promotions since joining the organization ten years ago.

Interviewer: Well, keep up the good work, Ida. (looking at a wall clock) How's your son doing in college?
Interviewee: He's doing just fine. He made the dean's list last semester and was selected as the outstanding junior in management.
Interviewer: (moving toward the door) See you soon.

Summary

This chapter divides the interview into three parts: (1) opening, (2) body, and (3) closing. All three parts are vital to an interview's success. If the interviewer does not create the proper atmosphere during the opening, even the best lineup of questions, arguments, or information may fail. If the closing turns off the interviewee, the achievements of the opening and the body may be lost. Many structural principles and techniques are available from which the interviewer must select the ones most appropriate for each interview. The variables of the interviewing process should serve as selection guides.

Remember that the interview is not completed until the interviewer and interviewee are out of sight and sound of one another.

Later chapters on survey, probing, employment, appraisal, persuasive, health care, and counseling interviews discuss structural divisions, techniques, and strategies peculiar to each. Chapter 4 covers questions and question sequences used in the body of interviews.

An Interview for Review and Analysis

This interview is taking place between a representative of the student government and a professor of art. The student is one of several student government representatives attempting to assess reactions to a recent campus-wide evaluation of courses and instructors. The location is the professor's office.

How satisfactory is the opening? How might it be improved? What type of schedule does the student use? Which structural sequence or sequences does the student employ? How appropriate are the schedule and sequences for the student's purpose? How satisfactory is the closing? How might nonverbal communication have influenced the opening, body, and closing?

1. **Student:** Good afternoon, Professor . . . Wright (glances at the professor and then looks around the office). As I mentioned on the phone, I'm one of several students assessing recent course-instructor evaluation procedures (rapid rate of speaking).

2. **Professor:** (smiling) You must be Robert Starsky (glances at the student's tee shirt with a beer company logo). Come in and have a seat (pause). Just how can I help you?

3. **Student:** Right, I'm Bob Starsky (nervous grin). Well . . . this will only take a few seconds, and we hope to learn how we might improve next semester's evaluation (opens notebook and peruses the survey questions).

4. **Professor:** I see (looks closely at the student and his notebook).

5. **Student:** (looking at the professor) First off, do you have any reactions to the evaluation?

6. **Professor:** (shrugs shoulders) It was a typical evaluation and went okay, (pause) I guess.

7. **Student:** (smiles) Does that mean you think it was a good program?

8. **Professor:** (serious expression) No better and no worse than ones we've tried in the past.

9. **Student:** (fast rate of speaking) We're hoping to make it the best possible in a few semesters (slows rate of speaking and returns to his schedule). Now, I'd like your reaction to the procedures.

10. **Professor:** (raises hands, puzzled facial expression) What procedures?

11. **Student:** (apologetic tone) Oh, uh, how it was administered.

12. **Professor:** (sits back in chair, looks out window) I think the administration in my classes went well and was within the fifteen minutes you promised. I've heard that . . .

13. **Student:** (interrupts) Good. And how about the forms used?

14. **Professor:** (shrugs) They seemed to cover the usual questions with a five-point scale, and students didn't seem to have any problems or complaints.

15. **Student:** (nods) And how do you feel about the class time used?

16. **Professor:** (frowns, serious tone of voice) I don't like to give up class time for other things.

17. **Student:** (looking at notes) Do you see any *major* problems with the evaluation?

18. **Professor:** Well (pause), just the usual problems with student evaluations of instructors. I think it's really a popularity contest and doesn't mean much, especially in art classes.

19. **Student:** (smiles) How can we solve this problem?

20. **Professor:** People are people, and students will give good evaluations to professors they like or who give easy grades.

21. **Student:** Well, (looks over notes, closes notebook, and then looks at the professor) that's all I need. Do you have any final reactions?

22. **Professor:** No . . . (long pause) not really. Just don't place too much faith in paper and pencil evaluations of art classes and instructors.

23. **Student:** (stands up) Okay, I'll make note of that (walks out of office).

Bad Closing

Student Activities

1. Observe dyadic interactions during a twenty-four-hour period and keep a record of how they are opened. Which openings and combinations of openings are used? What techniques are employed that are not discussed in this chapter? How did nonverbal behavior affect these openings?

2. Select a topic of interest to you and conduct a ten-minute, nonscheduled interview with a friend. Note what information was gained and how the interview progressed. Then conduct a ten-minute, moderately scheduled interview with another friend on the same topic. Compare the results of the two schedules and the apparent advantages and disadvantages of each.

3. Pick an interview from *Newsweek, Time, U.S. News,* or another source and try to construct an interview guide from it. Which sequences were used? Which schedules were used? How did the interview type, situation, and parties seem to affect selection of sequences and schedules?

4. During a twenty-four-hour period, keep a record of the closing techniques used in dyads you observe. Which techniques are most commonly used? How does the relationship between the parties affect leave-taking? What causes false closings, and how can they be avoided or minimized? How did nonverbal behavior affect these closings?

5. Make an appointment with an experienced interviewer. Discuss methods used to open and close various types of interviews. How does the interview type determine which methods to employ, and when? Which schedules does this interviewer employ most, and how has this use changed over the person's career?

Notes

1. Paul D. Krivonos and Mark L. Knapp, "Initiating Communication: What Do You Say When You Say Hello?" *Central States Speech Journal* 26 (1975), 115–25.

2. For discussion of openings, see Robert S. Goyer, W. Charles Redding, and John T. Rickey, *Interviewing Principles and Techniques: A Project Text.* (Dubuque, IA: Wm. C. Brown Publishers, 1968), 10–11.

3. *The Wall Street Journal,* March 2, 1981, 19.

4. Krivonos and Knapp, "Initiating Communication," 116–120.

5. Raymond L. Gorden, *Interviewing: Strategy, Techniques, and Tactics* (Homewood, IL: Dorsey Press, 1975), 49. Reprinted by permission.

6. This figure is based on one in Bernard Berelson and Gary Steiner, *Human Behavior: An Inventory of Scientific Findings* (New York: Harcourt Brace Jovanovich, 1964), 30.

7. Mark L. Knapp, Roderick P. Hart, Gustav W. Friedrich, and Gary M. Shulman, "The Rhetoric of Goodbye: Verbal and Nonverbal Correlates of Human Leave-Taking," *Speech Monographs* 40 (1973), 182–98.

8. Erving Goffman, *Relations in Public* (New York: Basic Books, 1971), 88.

9. Knapp, et al, "The Rhetoric of Goodbye," 188–198.

Suggested Readings

Benjamin, Alfred. *The Helping Interview*. Boston: Houghton-Mifflin, 1987.

Gorden, Raymond. *Interviewing: Strategy, Techniques, and Tactics*. Belmont, CA. Wadsworth, 1987.

Goyer, Robert S.; Redding, W. Charles; and Rickey, John T. *Interviewing Principles and Techniques: A Project Text*. Dubuque, IA: Wm. C. Brown Publishers, 1968.

Knapp, Mark L.; Hart, Roderick P.; Friedrich, Gustav W.; and Shulman, Gary M. "The Rhetoric of Goodbye: Verbal and Nonverbal Correlates of Human Leave-Taking." *Speech Monographs* 40 (1973), 182–98.

Krivonos, Paul D., and Knapp, Mark L. "Initiating Communication: What Do You Say When You Say Hello?" *Central States Speech Journal* 26 (1975), 115–25.

Manning, Gerald L., and Reece, Barry L. *Selling Today: A Personal Approach*. Dubuque, IA: Wm. C. Brown Publishers, 1989.

Richardson, Stephen D.; Dohrenwend, Barbara S.; and Klein, David. *Interviewing: Its Forms and Functions*. New York: Basic Books, 1965.

Zunin, Leonard, and Zunin, Natalie. *Contact: The First Four Minutes*. Los Angeles: Nash Publishing, 1986.

4

Questions and Their Uses

Whether you are talking to a professor, interviewing for a job, conducting a poll, working with a counselor, getting information from a supervisor, appraising an employee, talking to a government official, or selling a product or service, your knowledge of the types and uses of questions is crucial. Even when giving information, you will use questions to check on facts, verify the accuracy of statements, and clarify what you have heard. Virtually no interview takes place without questions, and a great many interviews consist entirely of questions and answers. We define a question as *any statement or nonverbal act that invites an answer;* it need not be an interrogative utterance followed by a question mark.

This chapter focuses on literally the "tools of the trade" for interviewers and interview65ees: the many types of questions, the criteria for phrasing questions, and the question sequences most effective for interviewing purposes. As you are introduced to one question type after another, you are likely to wonder why you need to learn all of these types of questions and what they are called. After all, "Isn't a question merely a question?" Yes, but in the same sense that a screwdriver is a screw driver, a wrench is a wrench, and a saw is a saw. For instance, you can do a repair job more effectively and efficiently if you pick out the ideal size, length, and type—slot, Phillips head, Torx, square—of screw driver; socket, ratchet, crescent, open-end, or pipe wrench; a coping, mitre, crosscut, sabre, hack, or keyhole saw. It helps a great deal to know the types of tools available and what they are called so you can ask for or pick out the most appropriate one without wasting time, experiencing frustration, and delaying the completion of the task. This is also true with questions and interviewing. If you are aware of the many types of questions available and their unique capabilities, then you will be able to conduct or take part in interviews more effectively and efficiently and enjoy the process. For example, you will not ask a question designed to obtain a yes or no answer when you want a lengthy answer, ask a question that introduces a new topic when the previous topic remains largely unexplored, or ask a question that leads interviewees to respond the way they think you want them to respond instead of how they really feel.

Types of Questions

Although a listing of types and subtypes of questions can stretch as far as the imagination, each question has three characteristics: (1) open or closed, (2) primary or secondary, and (3) neutral or leading.[1]

An open question lets the respondent do the talking and allows the interviewer to listen and observe.

Open and Closed Questions

Open questions are broad, often specifying only a topic, and they allow the respondent considerable freedom in determining the amount and kind of information to give. Some questions are *highly open* with virtually no restrictions, such as the following:

Tell me about yourself.
What do you know about Ford Motor Company?
What are your feelings about legalized abortion?
How do you think this city can be improved?

Other questions are *moderately open* with some restrictions:

Tell me about your hobbies.
What do you know about the foreign operations of Ford Motor Company?
How do you feel about Representative Smiley's stand on legalized abortion?
How do you think the parks in this city can be improved?

Market researchers and public opinion surveyors may hand a statement, picture, or product offer to a person and ask, "How would you respond to this statement?" "What comes to mind when you look at this picture?" or "What are your feelings about this offer?"

Open questions have several *advantages*. For instance, they let interviewees do the talking and volunteer information, thus allowing them to reveal what they think is important and determine the nature and amount of information to give. Therefore, open questions communicate interest and trust in the interviewee's judgment. Answers to open questions can reveal interviewee uncertainty, intensity of feelings, frames of reference, prejudices, or stereotypes. Additionally, open questions are easy to answer and pose little threat to the interviewee.

Open questions also have *disadvantages*. Answers may consume a large amount of time because interviewees are dwelling on irrelevant information. On the other hand, interviewees may withhold information thought to be irrelevant or obvious. Interviewers must be skilled in controlling and recording lengthy answers, and replication of the interview is difficult because each interviewee determines the length and nature of answers. Finally, results from lengthy, rambling answers may be impossible to code and tabulate.

Closed questions are restrictive in nature and may supply possible answers. Some are *moderately closed*, asking for a specific piece of information, such as the following:

What salary range do you have in mind?
How old were you when you first got involved in organized sports?
When did you last have a physical examination?
Which brands of gasoline have you used during the past six months?

Other questions are *highly closed*, where the interviewee selects an appropriate answer from a list. Multiple-choice questions such as the following are common in surveys and research interviews:

Which of these brands of gasoline did you purchase last?

_____ Amoco

_____ Phillips 66

_____ Union 76

_____ Sunoco

_____ other _____

What educational level have you achieved?

_____ some high school

_____ high school graduate

_____ some college

_____ college graduate

I would like you to rate the following brands of coffee on a scale from one to five. If you strongly like the brand, give it a five. If you like the brand, give it a four. If you neither like nor dislike the brand, give it a three. If you dislike the brand, give it a two. If you strongly dislike the brand, give it a one.

Folgers	1	2	3	4	5
Maxwell House	1	2	3	4	5
Sanka	1	2	3	4	5
Nescafe	1	2	3	4	5
Stewart	1	2	3	4	5

The *bipolar* question limits the interviewee to one of two choices, for example:

Do you usually purchase colas with or without caffeine?
Do you live in a rural or urban area?
Are you a blue-collar or white-collar worker?

Other bipolar questions ask for an evaluation or attitude:

Do you agree or disagree with the new tax proposal?
Do you approve or disapprove of mandatory drug tests?
Do you like or dislike diet soft drinks?

Perhaps the most common bipolar questions ask for a yes or no response.

Did you vote in the last Presidential election?
Do you smoke?
Are you familiar with the new safety requirements?

Bipolar questions assume that there are only two possible answers and that the answers are poles apart: like/dislike, approve/disapprove, high/low, yes/no. What about interviewees who are undecided, have no opinion, do not know the answer, or are mildly or strongly for or against only a part of the question? Too many interviewers ask bipolar questions out of habit or carelessness when they actually do not want a simple yes or no. Think before asking bipolar questions.

Closed questions have several *advantages*. For example, the interviewer can control answers and ask for specific information. Closed questions require little interviewer effort and allow more questions, in more areas, in less time. And answers are easy to replicate, code, tabulate, and analyze.

Closed questions also have *disadvantages*. Answers to closed questions often contain too little information, requiring additional questions, and they do not reveal *why* an interviewee has a particular attitude. Interviewers tend to talk more than interviewees when asking closed questions, and interviewees have little opportunity to volunteer information. And finally, it is possible for interviewees to rate, rank, select an answer, or say yes or no without knowing anything about the topic.

Figure 4.1 illustrates the major advantages and disadvantages of open and closed questions.[2] As the interviewer applies more constraint to a question, the amount of data decreases. As the amount of data decreases, the interviewer's control increases, less time

Figure 4.1   Question options

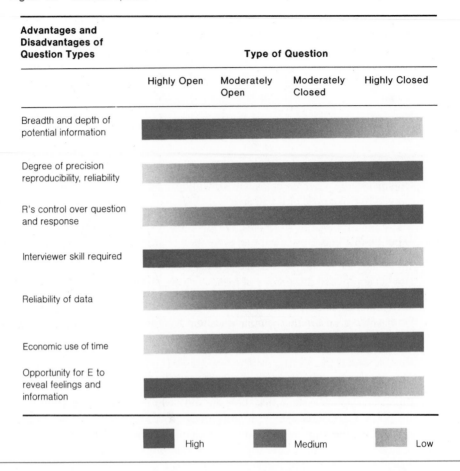

Advantages and Disadvantages of Question Types	Type of Question			
	Highly Open	Moderately Open	Moderately Closed	Highly Closed
Breadth and depth of potential information				
Degree of precision reproducibility, reliability				
R's control over question and response				
Interviewer skill required				
Reliability of data				
Economic use of time				
Opportunity for E to reveal feelings and information				

■ High   ■ Medium   ▫ Low

and skill are required, and the degree of precision, reliability, and reproducibility increases. On the other hand, as the interviewer lessens constraint, the amount of data increases, and interviewees reveal knowledge level, understanding, reasons for feeling or acting, and hidden motives. Many interviews include open and closed questions with varying degrees of constraint in order to get the information desired.

Primary and Secondary Questions

Questions may be primary or secondary.[3] *Primary* questions introduce topics or new areas within a topic and make sense out of context: Where were you when the tornado struck your house? What is your favorite hobby? Tell me about your last accounting position. All examples of open and closed questions presented earlier are primary questions.

Secondary questions attempt to elicit further information following a primary or another secondary question. They may be open or closed and are often called "probing" or "follow-up" questions. Secondary questions are useful when the interviewee does not respond or answers seem incomplete, superficial, vague, suggestible, irrelevant, or inaccurate.

If you feel an interviewee has not completed an answer or is hesitant to continue, remain silent for a few seconds (perhaps using eye contact, facial expression, or a nod) to encourage the person to continue. If this fails, use *nudging probes* such as the following:

I see.
Go on.
And then?
Yes?
What happened next?
Uh-huh?

A common mistake of both interviewers and interviewees is the feeling that all questions must be multiple-word sentences, not nonverbal or verbal nudges. Too often instead of urging the respondent to continue, the follow-up question stifles the respondent or opens up a new area or topic, the opposite of what the situation requires. As a result, valuable information is lost. Remember, too, that silence not only encourages the other party to begin and continue talking, but shows interest in what is being said, shows respect for the party, and may communicate belief or disbelief more tactfully than words.

If you are unsure that you have elicited all important or available information, use a *clearinghouse probe.* For example:

Did Terri say anything else about the conference?
What have I not asked about that might be of importance?
Have I missed anything that you can think of?

If an answer is *superficial,* use an *informational probe* that begins with phrases such as the following:

Tell me more about . . .
What happened after . . . ?
How did you react to . . . ?
Explain further the point that . . .

If an answer is *vague,* you might reply:

I'm not sure I understand your point.
What did you have in mind when you said . . . ?
Please define "tentative" for me.
What do you mean by "a great deal of money?"

If an answer seems to *suggest* a feeling or attitude, you might ask:

Why do you feel that way?
Why do you think that happened?
What do you mean by "seems?"
How do you feel about that?

If an answer seems *irrelevant,* such as in the following exchange, you might restate the question with nonverbal emphasis:

Interviewer: What are your attitudes toward the new work rules?
Interviewee: A lot of people around here don't like them. They say they're dreamed up by
    somebody who never saw an assembly line, let alone worked on one.
Interviewer: What are *your* attitudes toward the rules?

Other tactics aimed at getting relevant information include rephrasing the question, asking a probing question, or remaining silent to encourage a more relevant answer—a *silent probe.*

If an answer is *inaccurate* (wrong date or figure, inaccurate quotation, mix-up in words), you might use a *reflective probing* question. The reflective probe reflects the answer in order to clarify or verify it. For example:

You mean 1986, don't you?
Was that net or gross income?
He didn't qualify his intention to leave next month?
Then, you are going to support this proposal?

When using reflective probes, make sure interviewees understand you are merely clarifying answers, not expressing disbelief or trying to trap them. If you are unsure of what interviewees have said or implied, reflective probes can help you resolve uncertainties:

You think, then, that you can meet the new deadline?
Are you defining a "good" raise as 10 percent or above?
You say you were *tricked* into signing the petition?
Am I correct in assuming that you will take this job if offered?

If you want to be certain that you have understood a series of answers and have retained information accurately, you might ask a *mirror* or *summary* question. The mirror question is related to the reflective probe, but the mirror summarizes a series of answers or interchanges to ensure accurate understanding. For example, an employee might ask a mirror question to be certain of instructions from a supervisor:

Okay, Margaret, let me see if I've got this straight. You want me to put three people on the
Smith job, four on the Thompson job, and keep two here to repair the equipment? Have I
got it right?

A salesperson might ask the following question after determining a customer's desires:

You want a one- or two-year-old van, preferably a mini-van with bucket seats in the
middle, that is capable of pulling a large boat, right?

If asked properly, mirror and reflective questions can help you avoid errors caused by faulty assumptions.

An interviewee may *not respond* to a question. If this happens, restate or rephrase the question, ask tactfully why the person is not answering, or abandon the question and go to your next one. Do not interpret hesitation as no response and jump in with another question. You may have to explain more fully the kind of information desired, why you need it, or how you will use it.

The use of secondary questions separates skilled from unskilled interviewers. The unskilled interviewer tends to think ahead to the next question on the schedule, in a hurry to move on. The skilled interviewer listens carefully to each response to determine if the answer is adequate. If an answer is inadequate, the interviewer determines the probable cause within a few seconds and phrases an appropriate probing question to elicit more accurate and complete information. Skillful probing questions can heighten an interviewee's motivation because the interviewer is obviously interested and paying attention.

Secondary questions may cause problems when not phrased carefully. Stanley Payne illustrates how the meaning of a simple "why" question can be altered by stressing different words.[4]

Why do you say that?
Why *do* you say that?
Why do *you* say that?
Why do you *say* that?
Why do you say *that*?

"Why" questions may communicate disapproval, disbelief, and mistrust and put interviewees on the defensive by appearing to demand justifications, explanations, and rationales. A secondary question may alter the meaning of a primary question or bias the reply. Be careful not to misquote an interviewee or put words into anyone's mouth. The respondent may feel you have not listened. Avoid *curious probing* for information you do not need, especially if the information might embarrass the interviewee.

Quiz #1—Supply the Secondary Question

Supply an appropriate secondary (probing) question for each of the following exchanges. Be sure that each question probes into the answer and is not a primary question introducing a new facet of the topic. Phrase your questions tactfully.

1. **Interviewer:** How did you like your last job?
   Interviewee: At first it was quite interesting.
   Interviewer: Tell more about your job
2. **Interviewer:** What kind of person was your supervisor?
   Interviewee: So-so.
   Interviewer: What do you mean by so-so?
3. **Interviewer:** How do you feel about close detail work?
   Interviewee: That depends.
   Interviewer: on what

4. **Interviewer:** Define cooperation for me.

   Interviewee: (no response)

   Interviewer:

5. **Interviewer:** What do you envision a sales job would be like?

   Interviewee: I think the product is important. I like a product worth being sold and with a good application. I want to sell something with a real and definite purpose.

   Interviewer:

6. **Interviewer:** Which presidential candidate do you plan to vote for?

   Interviewee: Oh, I don't know.

   Interviewer:

7. **Interviewer:** How many cups of coffee do you drink each day?

   Interviewee: Several.

   Interviewer:

8. **Interviewer:** What do you think of my painting?

   Interviewee: It's really interesting.

   Interviewer:

9. **Interviewer:** How do you feel about this work schedule?

   Interviewee: It's . . . not bad.

   Interviewer:

10. **Interviewer:** How is John doing on the football team?

    Interviewee: He didn't make the starting nine.

    Interviewer:

Neutral and Leading Questions

All questions discussed so far in this chapter are neutral questions. The interviewee could decide upon an answer without direction or pressure from the interviewer. In bipolar questions, for instance, the interviewee could choose between two equal choices: yes/no, approve/disapprove, good/bad.

Questions in which the interviewer suggests implicitly or explicitly the answer expected or desired are leading questions. As Robert Kahn and Charles Cannell have stated, the leading question "makes it easier or more tempting for the respondent to give one answer than another."[5] The person merely agrees in the direction the interviewer seems to suggest. Leading questions may be intentional or unintentional, implicit or explicit, verbal or nonverbal.

The varying degrees of direction and the distinction between neutral and leading questions are illustrated in the following questions.

Leading Questions

1. You like close detail work, don't you?
2. You're going with us, aren't you?
3. Do you oppose the union like most workers I've talked to?
4. Wouldn't you rather have a Buick?

Neutral Questions

1. Do you like close detail work?
2. Are you going with us?
3. What are your attitudes toward the union?
4. How does this Buick compare to other cars in this price range?

How you ask a question may bias the answer you receive.

5.	How do you feel about these asinine government rules?	5.	How do you feel about these government rules?
6.	When was the last time you got drunk?	6.	Tell me about your drinking habits.
7.	Have you stopped cheating on your exams?	7.	Did you cheat on your last exam?
8.	Would you classify yourself as a conservative or a radical?	8.	Would you classify yourself as a reactionary, conservative, moderate, liberal, radical, or other?
9.	Don't you think tax reform is unfair to farmers?	9.	How do you feel about tax reform?

All nine leading questions make it easier for the interviewee to respond in a particular way. The potential for interviewer bias is obvious, with the setting (persuasion, reprimand, information getting, counseling, and news gathering), the tone (formal or informal, serious or relaxed), and the manner in which each question is asked (smiling, frowning, normal, or gruff voice) determining the respondent's ability to ignore the direction provided.

The first four questions are mild in direction. Each appears to be bipolar, to ask for a yes or no response. However, the phrasing of each guides the interviewee toward one pole, so they are actually unipolar questions. Unintentional leading questions can result by accidentally phrasing bipolar questions in a leading manner, so you may avoid many leading questions by limiting the use of bipolar questions. Respondents could ignore the direction of question 1 if their being hired did not seem to depend on a yes answer or if they did not need the job. Question 3 uses a bandwagon (follow-the-crowd) technique, and the respondent's answer would depend upon attitudes toward the union, feelings toward other workers, and past experiences. A respondent with no strong feelings might just go along with the answer the interviewer seems to desire.

The last five questions provide strong direction, virtual dictation of the proper answer, and are called *loaded* questions. Loaded questions are the most extreme form of leading questions. Questions 5 and 9 are loaded because of *emotionally charged words* and *name calling.* Questions 6, 7, and 8 provide degrees of *entrapment.* Question 6 assumes the respondent has been drunk at least once. Question 7 charges the person with cheating in the past; either a yes or a no will keep the respondent in hot water. Question 8 does not offer two polar opposites (reactionary is the opposite of radical), so the respondent is likely to choose the least onerous answer (conservative).

Since leading questions have potential for interviewer bias, avoid them *unless you know what you are doing.* Introductory phrases such as "According to the law," "As you know," "As studies have shown," and "According to leading authorities" lead interviewees to give "acceptable" responses rather than true feelings. Remember, you can turn a neutral question into a leading question by the *manner* in which you ask it.

Leading questions have valuable uses. Employment and appraisal interviewers may want to see how interviewees will respond under stress. Persuasive interviewers use leading questions to obtain agreement: "I'm sure you can see the benefit of a good education." Reporters ask leading questions to provoke unguarded replies or to prod reluctant interviewees. Social workers have discovered that questions such as "When was the last time you got drunk?" show that a whole range of answers is acceptable and will not shock the interviewer.

Do not confuse neutral mirror questions and reflective probing questions with leading questions. Mirrors and reflectives appear to direct respondents toward particular answers, but their purposes are clarification or verification, not leading or direction.

Figure 4.2 compares types of questions available to interviewers and interviewees.

Quiz #2—Identification of Questions

Identify each of the following questions in four ways: (1) open or closed, (2) primary or secondary, (3) neutral or leading, and (4) whether it is a special question: bipolar, nudging probe, clearinghouse probe, informational probe, reflective probe, mirror, or loaded.

1. By middle school, then, you mean grades fifth to eighth?
2. What is your favorite sport?
3. Let me get this straight. We will leave at 7:30 in the morning and arrive in Salt Lake City at 9:45. The first session will begin at 10:00 and end at 12:00 noon. Is that correct?
4. Do you think we should continue our overly generous support of the United Nations?
5. How can you explain that?
6. Tell me about your previous working experiences.
7. Is your income tax accurate and honest?

Figure 4.2 Types of questions

	Neutral		Leading	
	Open	**Closed**	**Open**	**Closed**
Primary	How do you feel about the new labor contract?	Do you approve or disapprove of the new labor contract?	Most highly skilled workers favor the new labor contract; how do you feel about it?	Do you favor the new labor contract like most skilled workers I have talked to?
Secondary	Why do you feel that way?	Is your approval moderate or strong?	If you favor the contract, why did you speak against it?	Do you favor the new contract, then, merely because other skilled workers favor it?

8. Go on.
9. Did you vote in the last primary election?
10. Is there anything else I should know before the staff meeting?

Phrasing Questions

Careful wording of questions can motivate the respondent to answer freely, accurately, and thoroughly. Phrasing questions is not a simple task, so develop each with five factors in mind: (1) language, (2) relevance, (3) information level, (4) complexity, and (5) accessibility.

Language

Kahn and Cannell suggest that interviewers use "language that communicates successfully to the least sophisticated respondents and at the same time avoids the appearance of oversimplification."[6] They do not mean to mimic respondents' jargon or slang, but to use common words: "going to college" instead of "matriculating," "drunk" instead of "inebriated," "interviewing" instead of "dyad," and "liar" instead of "prevaricator."

Many words and names have a variety of meanings. For instance, if you are "raising a tent," are you putting it up or taking it down? If you are "moved by a gesture," do you mean physically or emotionally? By "politicians," do you mean all government officials or just currently elected officials, and what about persons running for office or serving on campaign, office, or party staffs? Frames of reference often determine the meanings applied to words. For example, when twenty students wrote down the first thing that came to mind when they heard the word "game," their responses included Monopoly, football, basketball, tennis, bridge, baseball, deer, pheasant, sport, fun, cards, wild animal, and "willingness to try something."

Common words often have vague meanings: much, many, most, average, fair, hot, cold, a lot, large, small, excellent, and superior. Does the statement "Most supervisors come up the ladder from assembly line jobs" mean 51 percent, 65 percent, 75 percent, or more? A "hot" day for one person may be "just right" for a second and "a bit cool" for a third. Key words in the following questions are so vague that yes or no answers would be meaningless. In the fourth question, for instance, is the interviewer asking about the respondent's smoking habits or weight?

Do you watch television much?

Do you obey the speed limit most of the time?

Are you familiar with the new program?

Are you a heavy smoker?

People often carelessly toss words such as *could, should, ought,* and *would* into questions, assuming they are synonymous. How might you respond to each of the following?

1. What rights *could* a woman have in deciding on an abortion?
2. What rights *should* a woman have in deciding on an abortion?
3. What rights *ought* a woman to have in deciding on an abortion?
4. What rights *would* a woman have in deciding on an abortion?
5. What rights *does* a woman have in deciding on an abortion?
6. What rights *will* a woman have in deciding on an abortion?

Similar sounding words may cause confusion: *very* and *fairly, steal* and *steel, bull* and *bowl, cereal* and *serial, weather* and *whether.* Provide context, transitions, or a preview to alleviate misunderstandings. Listen to answers for hints that the interviewee has "heard" the wrong word.

Be on guard against phrasing that may alter results from one interview to the next. In a survey on television programming, an interviewer first asked parents if they "controlled" their children's television viewing. A large majority said no, but when asked later if they "allowed children to watch any program they wanted to," a large majority also said no. Which is accurate? In a recent survey, one set of respondents was asked, "Is it okay to smoke while praying?" and another set was asked, "Is it okay to pray while smoking?" An overwhelming number said no to the first question and yes to the second. Although the questions were essentially the same, respondents saw them as different because of the wording.

Relevance

Respondents must be able to see the relevance of each question in order to communicate freely and accurately. If a question or series of questions may appear irrelevant, explain the rationale for each and phrase them carefully to avoid obtrusive language. The placing of questions may also affect relevancy. For example, ask for demographic data such as age, salary, education level, and religious preference at the beginning or end of an interview, not somewhere in the middle. The end of the interview is best for such data because by then, hopefully, mutual trust has been established. If, during a political survey, your first question is "How old are you?" the interviewee may wonder what that has to do with politics.

Information Level

Respondents must have a store of knowledge that enables them to respond intelligently. Questions above the respondent's information level may cause embarrassment or resentment, either of which decreases motivation to respond. Ask for information in common categories or frames of reference, such as pounds of sugar instead of ounces, electric costs in dollars instead of kilowatts, or number of hours of television viewing per day instead of per year. Interviewees may fake answers rather than admit ignorance. A few years ago a student asked several people what they thought about a news report that Avis Candy Company was a communist front. (Both the news report and the company were fictitious.) Some respondents said they doubted the truth of the report; some said they were surprised when they heard the report; some said they had not heard the report; and one person replied, "It's funny you ask that. They contacted me just last week."

Questions beneath a respondent's information level may insult his or her intelligence. This occurs when an interviewer uses overly simple words, requests elementary information from an expert, or provides too much explanation. Determine if the respondent is a lay person, a novice, or an expert on the subject, and whether public opinion or authoritative knowledge is needed. For instance, the following question would be acceptable for the general public but not for a communications professional: "What do you think of the FCC's (Federal Communication Commission) ban on X-rated films on cable television?" What communications professional would be unfamiliar with the initials FCC?

Do not assume respondents will have the information you want. Large numbers of people cannot name their senators, congressional representatives, or governors. Many do not know the population of their cities, their annual incomes, or their wedding dates. Current trends, world events, new books, and unemployment figures are known by surprisingly few people. Abbreviations can cause problems; for example, an interviewee may be familiar with the TVA but not know that it stands for Tennessee Valley Authority.

Complexity

Questions should contain a simple, clear request for a limited amount of information. Avoid complex questions that defy a person to answer them. If you must ask a complicated question such as the following, use sample answers to explain the scale, or provide a small card containing the scale and a sample or two.

> Now, I would like your opinion on some leading brands of detergent. I would like you to rate these brands by using the numbers from plus five to minus five. If you like the brand, give it a number from plus one to plus five. The more you like it, the bigger the plus number you should give. If you dislike the brand, give it a number from minus one to minus five. The more you dislike it, the bigger the minus number you should give it. If you neither like nor dislike the brand, give it a zero.

Some questions are complex because of poor wording. This question was used in a research project on marriage relationships:

> Pick the most appropriate response. You feel that you understand each other, but you have never told them this.
> 1. You have never felt this way, or you have felt this way and told them this.
> 2. You occasionally have felt this way, but you have never told them this.
> 3. You frequently have felt this way, but you have never told them this.

Accessibility

Accessibility refers to the respondent's ability to answer questions because of social, psychological, or situational constraints.[7] As you grow up, you learn to be humble, so that if an interviewer suggests you are beautiful, intelligent, creative, or generous, you are likely to pose an "Aw shucks, it was nothing" attitude. Some topics are traditionally "off limits" in polite society. When interviewers pose questions in taboo areas—sex, personal income, religious convictions—they are asking for answers not easily accessible to respondents. If, as a health care professional, for example, you must investigate such topics, understand your relationship with the interviewee and pay attention to situational variables such as privacy, seating arrangement, and location. A person may be psychologically unable to relate true feelings toward a supervisor, teacher, friend, or parent or to recall details and feelings about an accident, illness, or traumatic happening. Design such questions to lessen social and psychological constraints and avoid offending the respondent. If possible, delay "inaccessible" questions until you have established a good relationship with the respondent.

Quiz #3—What's Wrong with These Questions?

After reviewing the five factors of question phrasing—language, relevance, information level, complexity, and accessibility—identify the problem or problems with each question below and then rewrite it to make it a good question.

1. (First question in an interview on recent efforts to unionize state employees) Were you familiar with the platform of AFSCME? — identify
2. (Asked midway through an interview on lowering the drinking age to eighteen) Are you a registered voter?
3. What effects do you believe euthanasia would have on various age groups and religious groups, and what influence do you believe these two groups would have on the legalization of euthanasia?
4. What are your reactions to the gang-rape case in Boston?
5. Would you say that the president is doing a good job or that he could do better?
6. Do you obey the speed limit personally (a) most of the time, (b) when convenient, or (c) seldom?
7. How do you feel physically and mentally after watching an X-rated movie?
8. (First two questions) Do you approve or disapprove of bioengineered food? What is bioengineered food?

9. High taxes affect whom the most: (a) upper class, (b) middle class, (c) lower class?
10. Please place yourself into one of the following classes: I drink very little, some, quite a lot, a lot.

Common Question Pitfalls

Because interviewers often have to phrase or create many questions on the spot, they are prone to fall into common pitfalls such as the bipolar trap, the open-to-closed switch, the double-barrelled inquisition, the leading push, the guessing game, and the yes (no) response.

The *bipolar trap* occurs when interviewers ask yes/no questions when they do not want yes/no answers: "Do you know what happened next?" instead of "What happened next?" "Do you know much about our company?" instead of "What do you know about our company?" "Can you tell me the names of the researchers on this project?" instead of "What are the names of the researchers on this project?" Ask a yes/no question when you want a yes or a no, not when you want specific information or a lengthy answer. You can avoid most bipolar traps by beginning questions with words and phrases such as *what, why, how, explain,* and *tell me about* instead of *do, can, would,* and *will.*

The *open-to-closed switch* occurs when an interviewer asks an open-ended question but, before the interviewee can respond, rephrases the question into a closed or bipolar question:

What were your first reactions when you were told you had won the lottery? Did you believe the call?

Tell me about your training in electronics. Did your training include work on microcomputers?

Why did you leave school? Was it because of the economy?

The open-to-closed switch seems to occur because interviewers are still developing questions in their minds and feel they ought to add something. Unfortunately, the some-thing added is usually a bipolar question that does not get the breadth of information the original question would have gotten. When given two questions, interviewees tend to answer the second. Avoid the open-to-closed switch by listening to yourself, waiting silent-ly after you have asked a good question, and giving the person ample time to respond.

The *double-barrelled inquisition* or multiple question occurs when you ask two or more questions at the same time:

Tell me about your staff, budget, and programs for this year's fund drive.

When and how did you first get interested in civil engineering?

What are your short-range and long-range plans?

Interviewees are unlikely to remember all parts of your question and will respond to what they remember, often the last thing they heard. Some interviewees may feel they are being subjected to a third-degree inquisition. If you do not listen carefully both to what you asked and what you received, you will not ask a follow-up question and will fail to get all the information originally asked for. Ask one question at a time.

The *leading push* occurs when interviewers ask unintentional leading questions that suggest how interviewees ought to respond:

Don't you think you were partly to blame?

You do feel this is the best plan under the circumstances, don't you?

I'm sure you can understand my point of view.

Keep most of your questions neutral if you want honest answers and accurate information, because many interviewees will go along with whatever answers seem to be desired or in their best interests. Use leading questions for specific purposes, and know what you are doing. If you do not hear yourself asking a leading question, you may get erroneous information and not know you have fallen into a common question pitfall.

The *guessing game* occurs when interviewers attempt to guess information instead of ask for it: "Could the accident have been caused by faulty brakes?" instead of "What do you think caused the accident?" "Do you think the low price of oil is the major reason for lower inflation?" instead of "What do you feel is the major reason for lower inflation?" Interviewers such as health care professionals, journalists, and investigators often ask strings of guessing questions to gain information that a single open-ended question might obtain. Follow a simple rule: don't guess, ask!

The *yes (no) response* occurs when interviewers mistakenly ask questions with only one obvious answer:

Do you think you can handle this job?

Do you want to win this game?

Do you want to get a speeding ticket?

Do you want to become an alcoholic like your uncle?

You can avoid asking questions with obvious answers if you think before asking. Use open questions or ones with a variety of options to eliminate the yes (no) response pitfall.

You can avoid most common question pitfalls by planning questions prior to the interview, by thinking through questions before asking them during the interview, by stopping when you have asked a good question instead of rephrasing it, and by getting in the habit of avoiding bipolar questions. Know the pitfalls well enough so that you can catch yourself when you are about to tumble into one.

Quiz #4—What Are the Pitfalls in These Questions?

Each of the following questions illustrates one or more common question pitfalls: bipolar trap, open-to-closed switch, double-barrelled, leading push, guessing game, and yes (no) response. Identify the pitfall(s) of each question and rephrase it to make it a good question. Avoid committing a new pitfall with your rephrased question.

1. Do you want to get sick?
2. Tell me about your job and your new condo.
3. Don't you think we should buy American?
4. Tell me about your new job. Do you like the hours?

5. Do you think the engine stalling could be caused by the fuel injector, the computer, or maybe the grade of gasoline I've been using?
6. (Interviewee is putting on her coat and hat) Are you leaving now?
7. How was your vacation? Did you get out of town for a few days?
8. Do you enjoy classical music?
9. Did you come to this university for your major or because it was in your state? *Why did you come to this university?*
10. How are your classes and your internship with the development office going?

Question Sequences

Questions are often interconnected (primary with primary questions and primary with secondary questions) and may form a sequence for an entire interview or within a topic. Common sequences are the funnel, inverted funnel, quintamensional design, and tunnel.

Funnel Sequence

A funnel sequence begins with a broad, open-ended question and proceeds with ever more restricted questions, such as the following:

1. What are your reactions to the employee retraining program?
2. What kinds of retraining are most workers likely to take part in?
3. Which one is likely to be most helpful?
4. What is the cost per employee?
5. Is the program worth it?

The funnel sequence is appropriate when respondents know the topic, feel free to talk about it, and want to express their feelings. Since open questions are easier to answer, pose less threat to interviewees, and get interviewees talking, the funnel sequence is a good way to begin interviews. Also, the funnel sequence avoids possible conditioning or biasing of later responses. For instance, if you begin an interview with a closed question such as "Do you think amnesty should be given to all strikers?" you may place the respondent in a positive or negative state of mind and produce a defensive attitude for the remainder of the interview. An open question such as "What are your feelings about granting amnesty to all strikers?" may avoid polarization and enable you to ask closed questions later.

Inverted Funnel Sequence

The inverted funnel sequence begins with a closed question and gradually proceeds toward open questions, such as the following:

1. Is your employee retraining program worth the cost?
2. What is the program's cost per employee?
3. Which type of retraining is likely to be most effective?
4. What kinds of retraining are included?
5. What are your reactions to the retraining program?

The inverted funnel sequence is useful when you need to motivate interviewees to respond. Respondents may not want to talk about an unpleasant event or may feel they do not know the answers. A respondent's memory may need a bit of assistance, and an initial closed question can serve as a warm-up. For example, when an interviewer asked a person to respond to an open question about mudslinging in political campaigns, the person replied: "I don't know much about politics; you ought to try someone else." The interviewer then asked a few closed questions, and within minutes the reluctant interviewee was giving sophisticated views on political campaigning and mudslinging. Closed questions worked when open ones did not. A series of closed questions can progress toward a final clearinghouse question such as, "Is there anything else you would like to add?"

Quintamensional Design Sequence

The quintamensional design sequence was developed by George Gallup to determine the intensity of opinions and attitudes.[8] This five-step approach proceeds from an interviewee's awareness of the issue to attitudes uninfluenced by the interviewer, specific attitudes, reasons for those attitudes, and intensity of attitude. For example:

1. *Awareness:* "Tell me what you know about the south bridge proposal."
2. *Uninfluenced attitudes:* "How, if at all, might this bridge help ease traffic problems in the downtown area?"
3. *Specific attitude:* "Do you approve or disapprove of the bridge proposal?"
4. *Reason why:* "Why do you feel this way?"
5. *Intensity of attitude:* "How strongly do you feel about this—strongly, very strongly, not something you will ever change your mind on?"

Tunnel Sequence

The tunnel or "string of beads" sequence is a series of similar questions, either open or closed, which may allow for little probing. This sequence is common in interviews designed to get reactions or attitudes toward a variety of people, places, things, and issues, and when the interviewer wants to quantify the data. The tunnel sequence is unlikely to get in-depth information on a single topic and may be a series of bipolar questions. The following is a tunnel sequence:

1. Do you approve or disapprove of the new bridge?
2. Do you think it will be effective in limiting traffic through the downtown area?
3. Are you personally involved in this issue?
4. Do you prefer a different location of the bridge or no bridge at all?
5. Do most of your friends approve or disapprove of the proposal?

Quiz #5—Question Sequences

Which question sequence or combination of sequences would you employ in each of the situations described below? Why would you use this sequence or combination?

1. You are conducting a market survey for your company to assess the effect of a recent advertising campaign.

2. You are a claims adjuster for an insurance company and must interview a family only hours after their home has been totally destroyed by fire.
3. You are conducting a preelection attitude and opinion survey for a newspaper chain.
4. You are interviewing a person for the company newsletter who has just been promoted to director of research and development.
5. You are interviewing applicants for entry level positions in sales.

Summary

The interviewer has a limitless variety of questions to choose from, and each type of question has unique characteristics, capabilities, and pitfalls. Each question has three characteristics: (1) open or closed, (2) primary or secondary, and (3) neutral or leading. Five factors to bear in mind when phrasing questions are: (1) language, (2) relevance, (3) information level, (4) complexity, and (5) accessibility. And there are six common question pitfalls to avoid: the bipolar trap, the open-to-closed switch, the double-barrelled >𝘈𝘷𝘰𝘪𝘥 inquisition, the leading push, the guessing game, and the yes (no) response. Interviewers must select and phrase the kinds of questions and sequences best suited for their purposes and objectives. Common sequences include the funnel, inverted funnel, quintamensional design, and tunnel. Remember that questions and question sequences are the "tools of the trade" for both interviewees and interviewers. If you know their types and unique uses, you will be able to take part in and conduct interviews more efficiently and effectively. And, the better you conduct your interviews, the more both parties will enjoy the experience.

An Interview for Review and Analysis

This is a portion of a medical school admissions interview between a faculty member and a prospective student. Identify each question as open or closed, primary or secondary, neutral or leading, and decide whether or not it is a special question such as bipolar, nudging probe, informational probe, clearinghouse probe, reflective probe, mirror, or loaded. How well does each question meet the criteria of language, relevance, information level, complexity, and accessibility? How effectively does the interviewer probe into answers? Does the interviewer tumble into any common question pitfalls? What type of schedule is employed? Which type or types of question sequences are used?

1. **Interviewer:** Tell me how you became interested in medicine. ~ open - ended
2. **Interviewee:** I guess there were a number of things that gradually turned my attention to medicine. My uncle was a physician and often took me to his office when I was growing up. He seemed to have a very fulfilling life, one he really enjoyed every day.
3. **Interviewer:** (silence)
4. **Interviewee:** And I've always had an interest in science and would like to get involved eventually in medical research.
5. **Interviewer:** I see.
6. **Interviewee:** In medicine I would be working with people and helping them physically and psychologically. I like to work with people.
7. **Interviewer:** If, as you claim, you like to work with people, why do you plan to move into medical research? Is it because of your interest in science?

Double Quest.

8. **Interviewee:** I see research as a direct way of helping, but I would never want to devote all my life to research.

9. **Interviewer:** Okay. How happy have you been with your choice of Penn State for your undergraduate studies? As a place to live and learn, your classes, your contact with faculty?

10. **Interviewee:** Well, I chose Penn State because I was interested in engineering when I graduated from high school. I have been very satisfied with Penn State.

11. **Interviewer:** Are you saying that you would have selected a school other than Penn State if you had not been interested in engineering?

12. **Interviewee:** Perhaps.

13. **Interviewer:** You were there, so you just decided to stick it out?

14. **Interviewee:** I'm not sure at this date what I would have done because engineering dominated my thoughts at the time.

15. **Interviewer:** When and why did you switch from engineering to premed?

16. **Interviewee:** At the end of my sophomore year.

17. **Interviewer:** Are you thinking of a specialty in medicine?

18. **Interviewee:** Yes. I would like to specialize in pediatrics.

19. **Interviewer:** Why pediatrics?

20. **Interviewee:** I've always enjoyed working with children in church groups and in scouts, and think I could work well with children.

21. **Interviewer:** How do you feel about abortion? Are there circumstances when you think they should be performed?

22. **Interviewee:** I am opposed to it.

23. **Interviewer:** You mean even when a mother's life is in danger or when medical personnel know that the baby will be born greatly deformed?

24. **Interviewee:** Well . . . (long pause)

25. **Interviewer:** Most physicians I know believe that grave danger to a woman's life justifies an abortion. Wouldn't you agree?

26. **Interviewee:** I know some doctors feel that way, but I have read articles by doctors who disagree with them and say that they have never encountered such a situation.

27. **Interviewer:** If I were your patient and I had terminal cancer, would you tell my family?

28. **Interviewee:** Yes, I would.

29. **Interviewer:** Would you tell me?

30. **Interviewee:** Yes, I would.

31. **Interviewer:** What if I had AIDS? Not clear

32. **Interviewee:** Would I tell you? Yes.

33. **Interviewer:** Would you tell my family if I asked you not to?

34. **Interviewee:** Yes, I would, because they would need to take a few precautions, and you would need their help and understanding.

35. **Interviewer:** I get the impression that you are not easily swayed from a position, and I seem to hear you saying that you like and trust people. Correct?

36. **Interviewee:** Yes, I think so.

37. **Interviewer:** What have I not asked you that you would like to tell me about yourself?

38. **Interviewee:** Well, as you can see from my MCAT materials, I have served a number of volunteer functions in hospitals to get a better understanding of the medical profession. Also, I have read a great deal about the Duke medical school and feel that this is the best school for me.

Student Activities

1. Observe several interviews over a few days and note the types and uses of questions. What are the most common types used? How do they satisfy the five factors of question phrasing discussed in this chapter?

2. Prepare two sets of questions—one with neutral questions and one with some leading questions. Then, interview ten people, five with each schedule. How did the answers vary, if at all? How did different people (age, sex, education, occupation) react to your two schedules?

3. Tape-record an evening news program that includes interviews with government leaders, people in crises, community leaders, and sports figures. What kinds of questions dominated these brief encounters? How did setting, event, interviewer, and interviewee seem to affect types and uses of questions?

4. Select an interview from the *New York Times, Newsweek,* or another source and see if you can pick out the question sequence or sequences employed. If different sequences were employed, what seemed to determine their selection?

5. Select a current issue and conduct two five- to ten-minute interviews. Use only primary questions in one interview. In the second interview, probe into answers when feasible. Compare the amount and nature of the information received in each interview. How did your primary questions differ when you knew you could not probe into answers?

Notes

1. See Stanley L. Payne, *The Art of Asking Questions* (Princeton, NJ: Princeton University Press, 1951), for an excellent discussion of types and uses of questions and difficulties in phrasing questions.
2. This figure is modeled after one in Bernard Berelson and Gary Steiner, *Human Behavior: An Inventory of Scientific Findings* (New York: Harcourt Brace Jovanovich, 1964), 30.
3. Robert L. Kahn and Charles F. Cannell, *The Dynamics of Interviewing* (New York: John Wiley & Sons, 1964), 205. Reprinted by permission of John Wiley & Sons.
4. Payne, *The Art of Asking Questions,* 204.
5. Kahn and Cannell, *The Dynamics of Interviewing,* 127.
6. *Ibid.,* 112.
7. *Ibid.,* 112.
8. George Gallup, "The Quintamensional Plan of Question Design," *Public Opinion Quarterly* 11 (1947), 385.

Suggested Readings

DeVito, Joseph A. "Relative Ease in Comprehending Yes/No Questions," *Rhetoric and Communication.* Edited by Jane Blankenship and Hermann Stelzner. Urbana, IL: University of Illinois Press, 1976.

Dohrenwend, Barbara S. "Some Effects of Open and Closed Questions on Respondents' Answers." *Human Organization* 24 (1965), 175–84.

Dohrenwend, Barbara S., and Richardson, Stephen A. "A Use of Leading Questions in Research Interviewing," *Human Organization* 23 (1964), 76–77.

Kahn, Robert L., and Cannell, Charles F. *The Dynamics of Interviewing.* New York: John Wiley & Sons, 1982.

Long, Lynette, Paradise, Louis V., and Long, Thomas J. *Questioning: Skills for the Helping Process.* Monterey, CA: Brooks/Cole, 1981.

Payne, Stanley L. *The Art of Asking Questions.* Princeton, NJ: Princeton University Press, 1980.

Richardson, Stephen A. "The Use of Leading Questions in Nonscheduled Interviews," *Human Organization* 19 (1960), 86–89.

5

The Journalistic/Probing Interview

The probing interview is the most common type of interview because journalists, lawyers, police officers, health care professionals, students, teachers, insurance claims investigators, supervisors, managers, counselors, children, and parents, to name a few, are involved in them every day. Probing skills, emphasized in Chapter 4, are essential in nearly every type of interview listed in figure 1.1 in Chapter 1. The probing interview may be as brief and informal as a student asking a professor about an assignment, a broadcast journalist checking with a source before airtime, or a supervisor asking an employee how a new production procedure is working. Or it may be as lengthy and formal as a television interview with a world leader, an oral history interview with a famous inventor, or a medical intake interview with a patient. Because many of you are preparing for careers in broadcast or print journalism, this chapter will pay particular attention to journalistic/probing interviews.

Regardless of length, formality, or setting, the *purpose* of the interview is to get needed information as accurately and completely as possible in the shortest amount of time. The *method* to accomplish this consists of careful questioning, insightful listening and observing, and skillful probing. Many interviewers fail to get the information desired because they *assume* the process is simple and requires little training or preparation: "It's just a matter of asking a couple of questions." But successful probing interviews are rarely easy or accidental; they are thoroughly planned and carefully conducted by skilled interviewers. Figure 5.1 illustrates the seven-step process the probing interviewer should follow to obtain the information desired.

Preparing for the Journalistic/Probing Interview

Determining the Purpose

Before you begin to research a topic, develop an interview guide, or phrase questions, you must determine *why* you are going to conduct an interview (or a series of interviews) and the *product* you want to produce. Inevitably, this twofold purpose will both affect and be affected by the situation. For example, if the product is to be a news feature story or a research report, this use of information may determine the length and number of interviews to be conducted, interviewees selected, specific purpose (to elucidate, observe, discover, examine, or expose), and the situation. If you attend a news conference or briefing, the situation may dictate the types and numbers of questions you can ask, how you can use the information you and other interviewers extract, and whether some information will be "off the record." If you want to see how the person on the street or the worker

Figure 5.1 Stages in journalistic/probing interviews

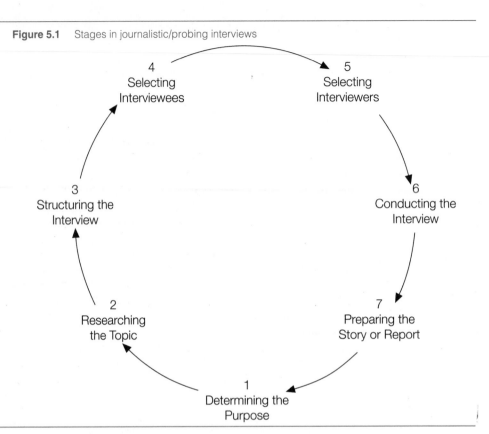

on the factory floor feels about an issue, your purpose determines the situation and product. If your purpose is to get a first-hand account of an accident, disaster, or reaction of people to a startling announcement such as a plant closing, situational factors such as broadcast or press deadlines, physical dangers of the situation, psychological state of victims or witnesses, and physical setting may determine who you interview, how you interview them, and the nature and amount of information you can obtain.

Researching the Topic

The kinds of information needed for a report, decision, diagnosis, recommendation, news story, investigation, or course of action determine the type of research you should do prior to the interview and the structure and questions you employ. Be thoroughly briefed on the interview topic so that you can go beyond basic, obvious information readily available through the media or routine reports. Search through your organization's archives and clipping files, the local library, government publications, corporate reports and publications, periodicals, and any other source that might prove helpful. A show of ignorance may anger an interviewee and embarrass you. Few events are more pathetic, for example, than an interviewer attempting to discuss a book with its author or the progress of a project with an engineer without having first read beyond the title page or checked the daily reports.

Additionally, proof that you have done your homework is likely to impress the interviewee and motivate the person to respond more readily and in more depth. Few events are more impressive than an interviewer who refers to specific pages in a book or report, is aware of published information on a project, pronounces difficult names correctly, and uses appropriate jargon and technical terms correctly.

Structuring the Interview

As you research a topic, jot down areas and subareas that you might develop into an interview guide, and look for information not included in available materials, such as interpretations of data, attitudes, and feelings. Consider who has and who has not contributed to materials or been interviewed to date. The guide you construct may be an elaborate outline or a variation of the traditional journalistic interview guide: *what* happened, *when* it happened, *where* it happened, *how* it happened, *why* it happened, and *who* was involved.

If the interview is brief or if you are highly skilled in such interviews, you may complete your preparation without an interview guide; if not, you should develop a moderate schedule that turns topic areas into primary questions, listing possible secondary or probing questions under each. The moderate schedule eliminates the necessity of creating every question at the moment of utterance and allows you to plan your wording while not in the heat of the interview. At the same time, the moderate schedule gives you flexibility to delete questions or create new ones as the need arises during the interview. Some interviewers fear digressing from a guide and thus losing their train of thought. A moderate schedule can lessen this fear because a list of questions is available to return to following a detour. Above all, a moderate schedule allows you to *adapt* to each interviewee, situation, and response.

Plan an opening that will establish an atmosphere of mutual trust and respect and begin to establish a positive relationship between you and the interviewee. In the opening minutes, you may identify yourself and the organization you represent, explain the topic you want to discuss and why, reveal how the information attained will be used and by whom, and tell how long the interview is likely to take. Review the opening techniques presented in Chapter 3 to determine which ones are best for each interview. For example, a tactful reference to the interviewee's position on an issue can get the interview underway: "I understand you disagree with the new railroad relocation plan. What are your major reasons for opposing this plan?" Do not rely on the same opening techniques from interview to interview regardless of the situation. For instance, a casual compliment, friendly remark about a topic or person of mutual interest, or a bit of small talk might create a relaxed and friendly atmosphere with one person and produce the opposite effect with a busy, hassled interviewee who does not have time for small talk.

The interview typically will end when you have the information you need or when time runs out. If an interviewee has limited you to fifteen minutes, complete your task in that time or prepare to close. The interviewee may grant you additional time; if not, close the interview and try to arrange another one. End on a positive note so the relationship established or added to during this sitting will aid future interactions with the party. Show your appreciation for the interviewee's assistance. Remember that the interview is not over until both parties are out of sight and sound of one another. Look and listen for important information or insights during the closing moments when the interviewee's guard may be down.

Selecting Interviewees and Interviewers

Selecting Interviewees

In many instances, the person or persons you must interview will be determined by your purpose or the situation: a patient in need of assistance, a home owner who has reported a robbery, a supervisor who has information about a new procedure, a client who needs legal or psychological counseling, an accident victim who needs help, a president who calls a news conference. At other times, you will have to select one or more interviewees from among several survivors, witnesses, experts, or persons with different points of view. Use the following four criteria to guide your selection of interviewees.

Does the interviewee have the information desired?

What is the person's level of expertise through experiences, education, training, and/or positions held? Was the person in a position to have observed the accident, discovery, robbery, or proceedings? How was the person involved in determining a policy or course of action? Decide if you need to interview an authority or an expert on the topic, or is your purpose to assess a person's level of expertise? For instance, an oral historian may want to interview a person who was intimately involved in a historic military action; a journalist might want to interview a political candidate to see how much the person knows about foreign policy or state tax laws; and a student might want to interview a professor about how grade appeals are conducted or the current status of research on cold fusion. Be aware, however, that interviewees will often answer questions whether or not they have accurate information. Raymond Gorden writes about "key informants"—persons who can supply information on the local situation, assist in selecting and contacting knowledgeable interviewees, and aid in obtaining their cooperation.[1]

Is the interviewee available?

A person might be too far from your home base, available for only a few minutes (when you need to conduct an in-depth interview), or unavailable until after your deadline. Many famous or high status persons—company presidents, sports or television stars, senators or congresspersons, renowned surgeons or researchers—may appear to be inaccessible. Do not assume a person is unavailable until you have tried to make an appointment. Contact a possible go-between (Gorden's key informant), talk to an aide, follow a chain of command, or work with the public relations department to reach the person with your request for an interview. You may have to be explicit about who you are, who you represent, how long the interview will take, where and when it will be held, and the topics you want to cover. Perhaps you will have to supply some sample questions or even all of your questions. But be careful of excessive demands that may make the person no longer worth interviewing.[2]

Is the interviewee willing to give the information needed?

Respondents may be reluctant for several reasons: mistrust of you, your position, or your organization; fear of revealing information potentially harmful to themselves or others; belief that the information desired is not anyone else's business; or the feeling that there is "nothing in it" for them. You may have to convince interviewees that you can be trusted for confidentiality and accuracy. People will usually cooperate if they have an interest in you, the topic, or the potential outcome of the interview. Thus, you might point out why the interests of interviewees will be better served if information or attitudes are known, perhaps employing a bit of verbal arm-twisting: "We cannot process your claim until we have your statement . . .;" "The other party has already given their side of the incident . . .;" "I can't do much for you if you're not willing to . . .;" or "If you do not talk to me, you'll have to tell your story in court." Be careful of heavy-handedness that might ruin the interview, your relationship with the interviewee, and any future contacts. Be equally wary, however, of interviewees who seem too eager to be interviewed and may desire to spread a bit of disinformation.

Is the interviewee able to transmit information freely and accurately?

Any one of several problems may make a person unacceptable as an information source: faulty memory, a state of shock, inability to express or communicate ideas, proneness to exaggeration or oversimplification, unconscious repression or distortion of information, or deliberate lying. The interviewing situation (accident, death, fire, tornado, or scandal) may contribute to interviewee transmission problems. A father or mother grieving over the death of a child (and confronted with tape recorders, investigators, lights, and cameras) cannot be treated the same as a person commenting on production quotas, Christmas decorations, or the reception of a government grant.

If time allows, get to know interviewees ahead of time by researching their work and accomplishments, personalities, reputations, and levels of information. Learn about their biases, values, idiosyncrasies, vested interests, hobbies, and interviewing traits. How skilled are they at responding to (and perhaps evading) questions? Many persons are interviewed daily (police chiefs, political leaders, candidates, corporate officers, lawyers), and a growing number have taken special courses in which they have learned to confront interviewers of all types. All of this information will reveal how interviewees are likely to act and react when you interview them. Webb and Salancik write that the interviewer "in time, should know" a "source well enough to be able to know when a distortion is occurring, from a facial expression that doesn't correspond to a certain reply."[3]

Selecting Interviewers

The ideal journalistic/probing interviewer should be a keen observer and listener who is patient, persistent, skillful at asking secondary questions, and able to write a coherent, organized, and interesting report of the interview after asking dozens of questions.[4] A particular situation or interviewee may require the interviewer to be of a specific age, sex, race, ethnic group, religion, political party, education level, or status. The similarity or difference in status between interviewer (R) and interviewee (E) may offer unique advantages for the interviewer, as shown here:[5]

R Superior to E	R Equal to E	R Subordinate to E
1. R can easily control the interview.	1. Rapport is easily established.	1. E will not feel threatened.
2. E may feel motivated to please R.	2. Fewer communication barriers.	2. E may feel freer to speak.
3. R can observe E under pressure.	3. Fewer social pressures.	3. R does not have to be an expert.
4. R can arrange the interview easily.	4. High degree of empathy possible.	4. E might feel sorry for R and want to help.
5. E might feel honored.	5. R and E will be at ease.	

6. R can reward E.

Some interviewees will not grant interviews to organizations or people they perceive to be low-status, such as a cub reporter for the *Sandcut Gazette.* As a result, many groups give important-sounding titles to their representatives: traveling sales representatives become vice-presidents, reporters become editors, assistants become associates, poll takers become research directors, and supervisors become executives.

By the time you have researched and selected interviewees and interviewers, you should have an excellent picture of the relationship that will exist during an interview. You will know the level of *affection* between the parties, how much they like, respect, and trust one another. You will know the level of *inclusion,* how eager each party is to discuss the topic with the other party at the particular time and place. And you will know the level of *control,* how much each party will share control and be able to determine interview length, topics, questions, responses, disclosure, and cooperation. A positive relationship is critical to the success of probing interviews, so try to build goodwill, motivate the party to take part, and get agreements on control prior to the interview.

In each of the following situations, who would be the ideal interviewer or interviewee? Should the interviewer be superior to, equal to, or subordinate to the interviewee? Or would there be an ideal combination of role relationships?

Situation #1. A student in mechanical engineering wants to talk to someone about the types of positions available for engineers in general and mechanical engineers in particular.

> The interviewer should be subordinate to the interviewee because the need is for an expert, someone who has far more information than the interviewer. A superior interviewee would not feel threatened by the interviewer and would likely be motivated to help the student in making career decisions.

Situation #2. The owner of a small trucking firm with thirty employees needs legal advice because of a pending lawsuit over an accident in which one of the firm's trucks was involved.

> The ideal relationship might be a middle ground between the interviewee (the owner seeking an attorney to help him with a lawsuit) and the interviewer (the lawyer). The owner is used to being "boss" and may communicate best in an equal relationship with a lawyer who is a major partner in the firm, not a young associate. Therefore, an equal relationship

would allow the parties to communicate easily, to respect and understand one another, and to be at ease. However, if the owner is also in a subordinate role, the person might be more willing to listen to and act upon the lawyer's advice, and the lawyer (the obvious expert in this situation) could control the interview more effectively.

Situation #3. A newspaper wants to interview the president of General Electric about persistent rumors that G.E. might merge with a French corporation.

The reporter would need to approach the General Electric president with impressive credentials and from a position as an editor or senior correspondent. This would make the relationship nearly equal (president to editor or well-known correspondent) to show the newspaper's acknowledgement of the president's position and stature, to establish rapport, to lessen social pressures often encountered in the superior-subordinate relationship, and to enhance communication effectiveness by avoiding communication barriers.

Situation #4. A cancer research specialist at one university wants information about research developments at another university.

These cancer specialists should be equals to enhance rapport, reduce communication barriers and social pressures, and establish a high degree of empathy. The ideal relationship would be as colleagues rather than superiors or subordinates.

Situation #5. An employer wants to know how employees feel about new grievance procedures.

The employer's role as an authority figure (and probably a major force in creating the new grievance procedures) eliminates him or her as the interviewer because employees would be reluctant to communicate beyond Level 1 with the employer. The employer should select an interviewer who is equal to or subordinate to interviewees (the employees) in order to establish rapport with them, relax them, pose little or no threat to their job security, and reduce communication barriers.

Conducting the Interview

Types and Uses of Questions

The primary questions used in probing interviews should be open-ended to motivate the interviewee to communicate freely. This is particularly true of opening questions that begin interviews, for example:

Please tell me what you saw when you arrived home.
Tell me about today's bargaining session.
Describe the incident for me.
How do you feel about the in-service seminars we've had this year?
What do you know about our organization?

Thorough answers to open-ended questions give you the opportunity to listen appropriately (for comprehension, empathy, or evaluation) and to observe the interviewee's mannerisms, appearance, and nonverbal communication. This will help you determine the accuracy and relevancy of answers and how the interviewee feels about you, the interview, and the topic. Closed questions make the interviewer talk more and listen less. If you find yourself asking question after question and doing all of the work in an interview, you are undoubtedly asking closed questions and probably trying to guess information rather than ask for it. Open up your questions and put the interviewee to work. Be patient and persistent, and do not cut into an interviewee's answer unless the person is obviously off target or promises to continue forever.

The flexible, adaptive nature of the probing interview not only permits but requires the interviewer to employ the full range of probing questions. *Informational probes* detect clues in answers and ask for additional information or explanation: What do you mean by *tentative* decision? Tell me more about the zoning variance you might ask for. Who is Bill Zalinsky? *Nudging probes* prod interviewees to continue giving information asked for in an open question. Interviewees (particularly less educated persons with small stores of information) tend to give the first opinion that comes to mind or to give a bit of information and wait to see if you want them to continue.[6] You need not phrase a sentence-length question; a word or phrase will do: I see. Go on. And then? And? *Clearinghouse probes* reveal whether you have obtained all available information on a topic before going to the next primary or secondary question: Is there anything else you can recall about this conversation? Have you told me everything about the incident on Thursday? What have I not asked about that you think might be important? Did Mary Ann have anything else to say? *Reflective probes* and *mirror questions* verify and clarify answers to check accuracy of understanding, notes, memory, and interpretation: You think, then, that the fire started near the sofa in the living room? (reflective probe) Okay. Then you first smelled smoke about 3:00 A.M., and the smoke alarm went off a few seconds later. You and your husband left your bedroom, came down the stairs, and exited through the front door. As you were leaving the house, you could see some flames and heavy smoke from the left corner of the living room near the sofa? Is this correct? (mirror question) Do not forget the *silent probe;* a bit of silence can often be more effective in eliciting information than any number of words.

Be courteous, tactful, and non-argumentative when asking both primary and secondary questions, and be understanding when delving into sensitive or personal areas. Be prepared to back off if an interviewee becomes emotionally upset or clearly feels that certain questions are irrelevant or inappropriate. Plowing ahead with probing questions could damage the relationship and the interview.

Because probing interviewers create many questions on the spot, they are prone to fall into common question pitfalls discussed in Chapter 4: the bipolar trap, the open-to-closed switch, the double-barrelled question, the leading push, the yes (no) response, and the guessing game. You can avoid most question pitfalls by thinking through questions before asking them, by stopping when you have asked a good question instead of rephrasing it, and by getting in the habit of avoiding bipolar questions. Know the pitfalls well enough so that you can catch yourself when you are about to tumble into one.

The following examples of good and bad questions should help you to sharpen your question skills and avoid the pitfalls.

1. The *bipolar trap:*
   Bad: Do you like the new one-way street proposal?
   Good: How do you feel about the new one-way street proposal?
2. The *open-to-closed switch:*
   Bad: How do you think the football team will do this fall? Do you think they'll go to a bowl game?
   Good: How do you think the football team will do this fall?
3. The *double-barrelled inquisition:*
   Bad: Tell me about the potential effects current legislative proposals might have on academic programs, building plans, and student loans.
   Good: Tell me about the potential effects current legislative proposals might have on academic programs.
4. The *leading push:*
   Bad: Don't you think we should buy now while interest rates are low?
   Good: Do you think we should buy now while interest rates are low?
5. The *guessing game:*
   Bad: Did you decide not to run for reelection because of redistricting, the recent monetary scandals in the House, or perhaps the current political climate?
   Good: Why did you decide not to run for reelection?
6. The *yes/no response:*
   Bad: Do you think you'll win the election for Mayor?
   Good: What are your chances of winning the election for Mayor?

Be sure to phrase your questions carefully not only to avoid common question pitfalls but also to obtain the information you desire. Review the information in Chapter 4 on phrasing questions. Pay particular attention to the language, the relevance of the question for your topic, the needs of the interviewee, the information level of interviewee, the accessibility of the interviewee, and the complexity of the topic. Be prepared because sometimes interviewees will play games with interviewers who phrase questions poorly. The following exchange took place during a recent presidential primary campaign in New Hampshire and was broadcast over radio network newscasts throughout the country:

Reporter: How are you going to vote on Tuesday?
Resident: How am I going to vote? Oh, the usual way. I'm going to take the form they hand me and put x's in the appropriate boxes (laughing).
Reporter: (a pause) Who are you going to vote for on Tuesday?

Take the time and effort to phrase each question effectively so it will serve your purpose best. Sometimes this means breaking the rules. For instance, it may be necessary to ask an obvious question even when you know the answer in advance: "Tell me about your major." "What is a black belt in karate?" "When did your company become one of the Fortune 500?" Such simple and obvious questions can relax the interviewee by getting the person talking about something that is well-known and easy to talk about and show that you are interested in a topic important to the interviewee. A leading push question such as "Come on now; surely you don't believe that" or "Don't you think it's time for a change in party leadership?" can provoke an interviewee into an exciting interchange (particularly for a broadcast interview) or revealing information far more interesting and valuable than a neutral question might elicit. You might have to make your only question asked at a press conference a double-barrelled one to get two or more answers for the price of one. And you might ask a yes/no response question because you need to have a yes (no) for the record. Above all, however, you must know what you are doing and why.

Note Taking and Tape Recording

Whether you should take notes, use a tape recorder, or avoid both during probing interviews is a matter of opinion. Some interviewers say you should never take notes; others warn against too few or selective notes. Some find the tape recorder the best way to record information; others never use electronic contraptions. The best advice is to select the means best suited to your objectives, the situation, the interviewee, and the interview schedule. Extensive note taking or tape recording may be necessary during lengthy nonscheduled or moderately scheduled interviews to help recall exact figures and statements and *how* answers were given. However, always ask permission before taking notes or using a tape recorder and explain why you want to do so and how the notes or recording will be used. Some interviewers such as police officers and insurance claims investigators are required to tape-record interviews.

Note Taking

A major advantage of note taking is that it increases your *attention* to what is being said and how, and this increased attention improves your ability to comprehend and to retain information.[7] If you take notes, you do not have to worry about a machine breaking down or running out of tape, and you can be selective in what you write down and later choose to report. Listening to entire interviews on tape to pick out important bits of information is time-consuming, and transcriptions are costly in time and money. However, you can rarely take notes fast enough to record exactly what was said, especially if an interviewee speaks rapidly, and it is difficult to concentrate on questions and answers while writing notes. Note taking may hamper the flow of information. In an in-depth interview with a newspaper publisher, a student discovered that whenever she began to write, the interviewee would stop answering until she stopped writing, apparently to let her catch up. Before long, he was trying to arrange his chair so he could see what she was writing. Failing to accomplish this, he occasionally asked her to read what she had written and noted what she could and could not quote directly. Halfway through the interview, the publisher became concerned about the interviewer's pencil and interrupted to sharpen it and provide additional pencils.

A few guidelines can reduce problems in note taking. First, preserve effective communication with the interviewee by being as inconspicuous as possible—maintain eye contact while taking notes, use abbreviations or a form of shorthand to speed up note taking, and write down only important information. Second, avoid communicating to the interviewee what you think is important by not taking notes frantically during one answer and waiting until the interviewee is answering another question before writing anything down. One good suggestion is to develop the habit of taking some notes throughout. Third, reduce interviewee curiosity or concern by asking permission before taking notes, by explaining why notes are necessary, or by showing the interviewee your notes

Effective note taking entails maintaining eye contact as much as possible.

occasionally to check accuracy. Fourth, avoid interviewee concern by agreeing to follow ground rules for the interview, explaining how you will use the information, or perhaps agreeing to let the interviewee see your report prior to submitting or publishing it. And fifth, ensure accurate reporting by reviewing your notes immediately after the interview.

Andrew Wolvin and Carolyn Coakley discuss four methods of taking notes.[8] You may *outline* the information you receive in answers. This method works best if you interview from a carefully developed guide or schedule that makes outlining easy. Outlining can be very difficult if your interview is unstructured or takes strange or unanticipated twists and turns. You may record in *precis* form what you have heard during several minutes of an interview. Instead of taking notes during each response, you write a summary of information from several primary and secondary questions. You may employ a *fact versus principle* method by writing main ideas on one side of a note page and important facts on the other. This method helps you retain both ideas and facts and their interrelationships. And finally, you may employ a *mapping* method in which you first write and encircle main ideas, second you write significant details or facts and connect them with lines to appropriate main ideas, and third you write minor details or facts and connect them with lines to significant details or facts. This produces a map of the information you have obtained during the interview and is particularly effective when you obtain details and facts relevant to a particular main idea during widely spaced parts of an interview.

Tape Recording

By using a tape recorder, you can relax and concentrate on questions and answers during the interview and rehear *what* was said and *how* it was said afterward. A tape recorder may record unwanted discussions in a crowd, but it can also pick up answers that might be inaudible at the time. Unfortunately, tape recorders can malfunction. A student used a tape recorder during a lengthy interview for a class project and took no notes. Returning to his room, he discovered the tape did not contain a single word, and he had to rely on his memory. Realize also that some people fear tape recorders and view them as intruders in the intimate interviewing situation. Tapes do, however, provide permanent, undeniable records of answers.

A few guidelines can reduce tape recording problems. First, avoid mechanical difficulties by knowing and testing the recorder thoroughly before the interview and by taking extra cassettes and batteries with you. Second, reduce fears and objections by asking permission to use the recorder prior to the interview, by explaining why the recorder is advantageous to both parties, by placing the recorder in an inconspicuous location, and by relying on either the built-in microphone or a small one that need not be stuck in the interviewee's face. Third, reduce problems with an interviewee who fears being recorded too accurately by offering to turn off the recorder when desired, by revealing how the recording will be used, and by volunteering to let the interviewee check and edit statements before using them. And fourth, always tell the interviewee in a telephone interview that the conversation is being recorded, and why.

Handling Difficult Situations

The Press Conference or Group Interview

The press conference or group interview poses special problems for interviewers because they usually have little or no control over the situation or the interviewee. The interviewee or a staff member may announce when and where the interview will take place and impose ground rules such as length, topics allowed, and interviewers who may attend. Protocol often enables interviewees or staff members to end the interview without warning, perhaps to avoid or escape a difficult exchange. You may or may not get to ask the questions you have prepared, and you are not likely to have an opportunity to probe into answers. Listen carefully to answers other interviewers receive, because they might provide valuable information or suggest other questions you should ask.

Your relationship with interviewees at press conferences may be critical. If interviewees like and respect you, they may pick you from among several interviewers to ask questions and even give you an opportunity to probe. On the other hand, if interviewees are hostile, perhaps because you are known for asking tough or embarrassing questions, they may refuse to recognize you or give vague, superficial answers and then quickly turn to another interviewer to evade your follow-up questions. Since you might be recognized only once at a press conference, asking double-barrelled questions may be your only opportunity to get responses on more than one topic.

The Broadcast Interview

The broadcast interview, whether over radio or television, presents unique problems.[9] Being on real or figurative stages may cause both parties to be extremely nervous or to engage in a bit of playacting because of audiences, cameras, microphones, and lights. Prepare for broadcast interviews by becoming familiar with the physical setting, including seating for you and the interviewee, audio and video equipment, technicians, and perhaps program format and purpose. Pay close attention to the briefing you will receive concerning time limits, beginning and closing signals, and microphone use, levels, and locations. Adequate preparation will reduce nervousness and enhance your efficiency and performance.

Some utterances and actions in interviews cannot be broadcast or may be embarrassing, such as profanities, obscene gestures, poor grammar, and excessive "uhs" and "ahs." Deadlines and extreme time limitations require questions that are direct, to the point, and moderately open at most. You may normally have an hour or two to discuss a problem with a client, customer, or employee, but a broadcast interaction may last no longer than a few seconds or minutes. Know your questions well enough to ask them from memory or from a few small cards because forms and lists of questions may make noise or cause you to appear awkward, amateurish, or unprepared. If you want the interview to be, and appear to be, spontaneous, do not provide questions to the interviewee prior to the broadcast. Ken Metzler notes that spontaneous questions get spontaneous answers.[10]

Handling Difficult Interviewees

Probing interviews (particularly journalistic interviews) delve into feelings, attitudes, and reasons for actions, so they often hit raw nerves and evoke reactions ranging from tears to hostility. The settings of disasters, crimes, defeats, ceremonies, deaths, and scandals are often tense, emotional, or embarrassing. Be prepared for difficult situations and know how to handle each.

Emotional Interviewees

Interviewees may burst into tears during probing interviews, and the problem is not helped when family or friends exclaim, "Oh, God!" or "Now, stop that Amy!" or when interviewers blurt out, "I know just how you feel" or "Want a kleenex?" Reactions such as the following may help if they are used *tactfully* and *sincerely*.

Don't be embarrassed; it's perfectly okay to cry.
Take your time; we're in no hurry.
Would you like to come back later?

If you have a close relationship with the interviewee, holding the person's hand or placing an arm across the shoulders might be appropriate. Remember the value of silence. Give people an opportunity to gather their thoughts and calm down, and they will usually be ready to continue within a few minutes. John and Denise Bittner suggest that you ask only direct and necessary questions at such times. "Remember, people in crisis situations are under a great deal of stress," they write. "A prolonged interview won't provide additional information; it will only upset people."[11]

Above all, do not compete for the "really dumb question of the day" award. On almost any evening, you can turn on the radio or television news and hear a journalist ask the parents of a child just killed in a car accident, in a drive-by shooting, or in a sports accident: "How did you feel when you heard the news of your child's death?" or "Was the family devastated by this tragedy?" Be considerate and use good sense when asking questions of emotional interviewees.

Hostile Interviewees

If you detect hostility in an interviewee, first try to determine if it is real or merely perceived on your part and second, what is its cause. A person may feel angry, depressed, helpless, or frightened because of circumstances, and an interviewer becomes a convenient target for releasing feelings. Hostility may be toward you, your organization, your position or profession, or the way the information will be used. Bad experiences with similar interviewers may lead an interviewee to expect the worst from you. A person may become hostile because of a question's timing, wording, or nonverbal message or because the interviewer seems to have pushed too far. Be careful of unwarranted pressure tactics. Allow a hostile interviewee to blow off steam while you remain friendly and nondefensive. A nondirective strategy such as the following might reveal the source of hostility and reduce it:

"You seem very upset; would you like to talk about it?"
"Do I detect a note of anger in your answers?"
"You appear to be very angry at the moment."

As Phillip Ault and Edwin Emery comment, "Treat the average person with respect, and he will do the same."[12]

Reticent Interviewees

If a person seems unwilling or unable to talk, try to discover why. The person may be inhibited by you, the situation, the topic, the surroundings, other people nearby, and so on. Often reticence is a personal or family trait that cannot be resolved during an interview. You might change your style (from formal to informal, cool professional to warm associate, disapproving to approving) or your question strategies (open questions to closed questions, nondirective to directive) until the interviewee is warmed up and ready to give longer answers. A careful self-introduction and orientation about the nature of the interview will open up some reticent interviewees. Use silence to encourage persons to talk, nudging probes to keep them talking, and good listening techniques (particularly empathic listening) to show you are interested. Discuss easy, nonthreatening topics during the early minutes so interviewees can reply easily and openly.

Evasive Interviewees

Interviewees often try to evade questions that force them to reveal inner feelings or prejudices, or questions that make them take stands on issues, make decisions, give specific pieces of information, or incriminate themselves. Evasive strategies include humor, "put-on"

Courtesy and respect will help to alleviate an interviewee's hostility.

hostility, counter questions, answers to a different question, requests for rephrasing or giving a rationale for a question, and long, impressive answers that say little and dodge the issue. President John Kennedy often used humor to evade questions during press conferences. This is how he answered one poorly phrased question:[13]

Reporter: Mr. President, Senator Margaret Chase Smith has proposed that a watchdog committee be created. What is your reaction?

President: To watch congressmen and senators? Well, that will be fine if they feel they should be watched.

The people at the press conference laughed, and Kennedy avoided the question. On occasion you may ask a question even when you know the interviewee will not answer it because the way the question is evaded may be revealing. You may have to resort to leading or loaded questions such as the following to evoke a meaningful response: "Isn't this a weak proposal . . .?" "But a few minutes ago you said. . . ." "Every member of the board of directors agrees with this merger proposal; how do you feel about it?" "Are you saying that you would rather have us go bankrupt than meet the government regulations?"

Embarrassing Interviewees

Interviewees may intentionally or unintentionally embarrass themselves, you, or both. "Bloopers" are difficult to handle tactfully when you are alone with an interviewee, but they are even more so when others are witnessing the interview. Art Linkletter hosted the CBS program "House Party" for several years. A regular feature was brief interactions with young children, which often proved embarrassing, such as the following:[14]

Linkletter: What animal would you like to be, and why?

Youngster: I'd like to be an octopus, so I could grab all of the bad boys and bad girls in my room and spank them with my testicles.

Linkletter: (interrupting hastily) An octopus has eight tentacles, Johnny, and he . . .

Youngster: (breaking in and clutching Linkletter's arm impatiently) Mr. Linkletter, you've got that all wrong. Not tentacles, testicles.

The best approach to many embarrassing situations is to drop the subject and if necessary, come back to it later. Never purposely try to embarrass an interviewee.

Confused Interviewees

Closely related to embarrassing situations are ones in which people are confused by the topic or question. Be prepared to handle confused persons without making them feel embarrassed or hostile so that you can get the information needed. You may rephrase a question tactfully or ask the original or rephrased question later in the interview. Watch how you react nonverbally. The following scenario demonstrates another way of handling confused interviewees.

A severe national strike by coal miners during President Jimmy Carter's administration led a reporter from station WIBC to Monument Circle in Indianapolis to get citizen views on actions the President might take. The following exchange took place between the reporter and a person in her early twenties.

Reporter: This is Channel 8 News. Do you think President Carter should order the miners back to work?

Interviewee: No! The adults!

Reporter: The adults?

Interviewee: Yes. President Carter should order the adults back to work not the minors. Many of them don't have cars and can't get to work.

The reporter, realizing that similar sounding words (miner and minor) had caused confusion and a potentially embarrassing situation for the interviewee, exhibited not a hint of a smile or shock, thanked the young woman, and went to the next passerby as if the exchange had made perfect sense.

Talkative Interviewees

Some people love to talk about anything, especially if they feel important because of the interview. You may have difficulty shutting them off and keeping them on track. You may resort to closed questions to give the talkative person less verbal maneuverability. Look for natural openings or slight pauses for a chance to insert a question or redirect the interview. Use obvious interruptions only as a last resort.

A number of nonverbal actions may signal that you wish to go on to another question or topic because you have all information needed for the previous question. You might nod your head as if to say "I've got it; that's enough"; look at your schedule of questions or lean forward to hint that you are about to ask another question; stop taking notes to suggest you have all information you need for this question; glance at your watch or a clock to suggest that you need to move on or that time is about up. Whether wedging in new questions, saying that you need to go to another question, or signalling nonverbally that you have enough information, be tactful and sensitive.

Preparing the Story or Report

You are now ready to review the information and observations obtained by one or more interviews to see if you have obtained the information necessary to satisfy your purpose. Jog your memory, read through notes, and listen or view tape recordings. You may have to sift through hundreds or thousands of words, statements, facts, opinions, and impressions to locate newsworthy items. Check answers with other sources, especially if there is reason to suspect that an interviewee lied or gave inaccurate information.

Once you know what you have obtained from the interview stage, perform several editing chores. If you are preparing a verbatim and complete interview for publication, determine whether you should include grammatical errors, mispronounced words, expletives, slang and vocalized pauses such as "uh," "and uh," "um," and "you know." What about repetitive statements, long and rambling explanations, and simple errors made by interviewees who do or do not know differently? Readers and listeners may enjoy the account with all of the warts showing, but both interview parties may be embarrassed and lose credibility. You might never get another interview with this person or organization.

Determine if it is necessary to preface specific answers and questions so readers and listeners will have a clear understanding of each. You might edit some of your questions to make answers more pointed and meaningful. When quoting from notes or memory, strive for accuracy. Do not put words in an interviewee's mouth. Be sure proper qualifiers are included. Do not understate or overstate an interviewee's opinions, attitudes, intentions, or commitments. Be sure both questions and answers are reported in context. Above all, be honest and fair.

The technical steps of report or story preparation are beyond the scope of this book (see the suggested readings at the end of the chapter), but we want to close with a few precautions. Remember the ground rules agreed to and which information is "off the record." Violations of agreements will harm you and future interviewers. Sherwood reminds us that an interviewer asserts that a statement was made, not that it is true.[15] Be patient. Be careful of assumptions. Not long after Chinese leader Mao Tse-tung died, a television network interrupted its programming to announce that Mao's wife and other radicals were dead. An overzealous journalist had assumed that a report of "liquidation from the party" meant death. It did not, much to the network's embarrassment. Strive for accuracy in every fact and interpretation.

Figure 5.2   Responding in the journalistic/probing interview

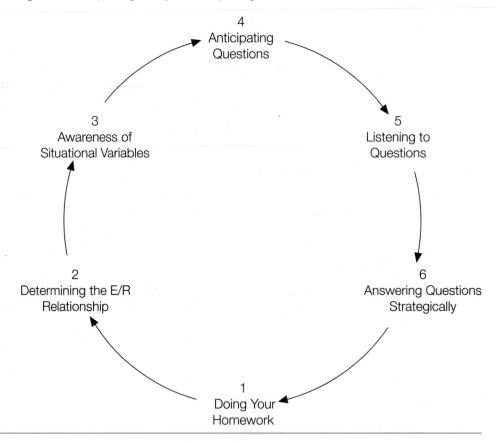

The Respondent in the Journalistic/Probing Interview _____

Attention in books on interviewing is naturally focused on the *interviewer* because most readers are concerned with learning to play that role more effectively. But all of us are *interviewees* at least as often, and probably more often, than we are interviewers. Let's turn attention, then, to how you can be a more effective respondent in interviews. Figure 5.2 illustrates the six step process the interviewee should follow in responding effectively in the journalistic/probing interview.

Doing Your Homework

Do your homework. Be thoroughly briefed on topics that might come up, including recent events, accidents, controversies, innovations, decisions, and administrative actions. Think about your role in any of these topics. Learn everything you can about who will interview you, including such characteristics as age, education and training, special interests, experiences, and attitudes toward you and the topic: friendly/hostile, trusting/suspicious, formal/informal, interested/disinterested. What is the interviewer's reputation? What questioning techniques does the interviewer usually employ?

Interviews often take place without prior warning, such as when a person calls you on the phone; stops by your office; appears at your front door; or approaches you on the street, factory floor, or at the scene of an event or accident. When this happens, be sure the opening is thorough so you understand who the person is, who the person represents, how long the interview will take, what information the person wants, and how this information will be used. A thorough opening, perhaps including a bit of small talk, not only orients you of the topic, purpose, and relationship with the interviewer but gives you time to collect your thoughts and prepare to answer questions strategically.

Determining E/R Relationship

A major problem encountered in journalistic/probing interviews is the interviewee's role relationship with the interviewer. Quite often the interviewer is in a superior position, such as supervisor, physician, lawyer, counselor, or media celebrity. The interviewee, trying to communicate "upward," may be overawed by the interviewer: "J. B. wants to see *me!*" "I'm going to be interviewed by Dan Rather." "The chairman of the board wants *my* opinion." Feelings of subordination and obligation to answer any question asked, particularly in the presence of cameras and microphones, turn normal people into "silly putty." As an interviewee, try to maintain your equilibrium, and if you have a choice, determine whether you should speak to a particular person at a particular time. Realize, of course, that refusals of interviews sometimes lead interviewers, particularly journalists, to state ominously: "Jean Prosky was unavailable for comment" or "Officials of the Catbird Corporation refused to grant us an interview." Such statements infer guilt, but are preferable to foolish comments that become headlines.

Awareness of Situational Variables

Be aware of situational variables. When will the interview take place? Defer some interviews until you are informed and mentally ready to cope with difficult questions. Why should the interviewer be totally prepared and the interviewee totally unprepared? Where will the interview take place? You may wish to establish some ground rules for an interview such as time, place, and length, which topics are off-limits or off-the-record, and who the interviewer(s) will be. Occasionally you may require that questions be submitted in advance. How much control you have depends upon your relationship with the interviewer, the situation, and how eager you are to be interviewed. What will be the physical setting? Will an audience be present? If the interview will be a broadcast, review the discussion on such interviews presented earlier in this chapter.

Anticipating Questions

Your homework should allow you to *anticipate* most questions that may be asked. Think about how you might respond to specific questions. What might be the most important thing to say or to avoid? Which words should you use or avoid? How can you support your answers? Are there organizational policies on how you can respond to specific questions? How will you respond to questions you cannot answer because of lack of information or because of organizational or legal constraints?

Listening to Questions

What should you do while an interviewer is asking a question? First, *listen* carefully and *think* before answering. Every evening persons on television newscasts make statements at the scenes of accidents, crimes, or controversies that they will regret the next day. Some will be fired for their verbal indiscretions, while others will be sued, arrested, investigated, reprimanded, or merely embarrassed. Listen to what is being asked. Listen for words you may not know or may misinterpret. Listen for verbal and nonverbal cues that reveal feelings as well as facts. Second, be patient. Do not assume you know what a question is before it is completed. React to a question only after fully hearing and understanding it. And do not interrupt the interviewer. Third, focus your attention on the question being asked at the moment, not on past or future questions. Fourth, focus on the interviewer and the question, not on other persons or the surroundings. This is particularly important during broadcast interviews that involve several persons, studios, cameras, monitors, and microphones. Fifth, do not dismiss a question too quickly as irrelevant or stupid. The interviewer may have a very good reason for asking the question. And sixth, do not become defensive even when baited by an interviewer. You cannot think clearly when angry, and you may blurt out words, claims, or accusations you will regret immediately. Remember, becoming hostile reduces you to the level of the interviewer.

Answering Questions Strategically

Design answers with several criteria in mind. A good answer is concise, precise, carefully organized, clearly worded, logical, well-supported, and to the point. Avoid either underkill or overkill in answers. Give answers, not sermons, lectures, or tirades. Do not make excuses; give reasons and explanations. Be pleasant, polite, and tactful. Do not underestimate the interviewer's knowledge or intelligence. When you give a personal opinion on a subject, be sure the interviewer understands that you are speaking for yourself and not for your organization. If you do not know an answer, say so. You may promise to get the information as soon as possible.

Insist upon adequate time to think through and present your answers. This is particularly true when answering tough, thought-provoking, or tricky questions. If an interviewer cuts you off in mid-answer or apparently wants brief answers, cooperate as long as it suits *your* purpose. If brief or interrupted answers may compromise you or your organization, refuse to continue until given adequate time to reply, and if the interviewer still tries to plow ahead, terminate the interview. Do not allow the interviewer to put words in your mouth; think and speak for yourself.

Learn the many strategies for handling questions. One strategy is to ask the interviewer to repeat, rephrase, or explain long, complicated, or unclear questions. A second strategy is to preface some answers carefully and tactfully. Note why a question is bad, tough, or tricky, do not merely say that it is so. Preface a long answer by explaining why it must be so. Provide a substantial explanation why you must refuse to answer or simply say "No comment." A third strategy is to rephrase a question for the interviewer or an audience that may be listening: "If what you're asking is . . .," or "She is asking. . . ." A fourth strategy is to challenge the content of questions. Question unsupported assertions, assumptions, inferential leaps, causal fallacies, and inaccurate "facts" or quotations. And a fifth strategy is to answer a question with a question, but use this strategy sparingly because it can create hostility between interview parties.

Respond to specific types of questions to your benefit. If a question is *double-barrelled,* reply to the part you can recall and can answer most effectively, and let the interviewer worry about the remainder. If a question is *bipolar* or *multiple choice,* be sure the choices are fair and the only ones possible; if they are not, explain or qualify your answer or insist upon additional options. For example, the question "Do you think coal or synthetic fuels are the best solution to our future energy needs?" does not allow for solar energy. If that is your preferred answer, comment, "Of the two choices you have given, I think synthetic fuels are better; however, I believe solar energy is the best solution to our future energy needs." Answer a yes/no bipolar question with a simple yes or no when it is to your advantage, and elaborate when it is not. Take full advantage of *clearinghouse* questions to present information you would like the interviewer to hear. And search *reflective* and *mirror* questions for accuracy and completeness because they may provide you with the best opportunities to detect misinterpretations, gaps, and inaccuracies in the interviewer's memory and notes.

Organize long answers like mini-speeches with an introduction, body, and conclusion and use signalling phrases such as "First . . . Second . . . Third . . ." so interviewers can understand what you are saying and remember information accurately. Be careful of abbreviations because not everyone knows what FCC (Federal Communication Commission), NOW (National Organization for Women), NRA (National Rifle Association), and org. com. (organizational communication) refer to. Use humor carefully. Good humor in answers is tasteful, tactful, spontaneous, appropriate (for you, the interviewer, and the situation), fresh, and satirical rather than sarcastic. Use examples to illustrate points: "It will look like the station on Concord Road." We all like good stories, whether fictional or nonfictional, and they maintain an interviewer's attention, illustrate points, and are easy to recall. Use analogies and metaphors to compare unknown or complicated things, procedures, and concepts to ones with which the interviewer is familiar.

Summary

The journalistic/probing interview is the most common type of interview because it is used daily by persons ranging from journalists and police officers to health care professionals and parents. Length and formality vary, but the purpose and method are the same: to get needed information as accurately and completely as possible in the shortest amount of time through careful questioning, listening, observing, and probing. Although preparation of an interview guide or schedule is important, the interviewer must be flexible and adapt to each interviewee, situation, and response.

Interviewees need not be passive participants in journalistic/probing interviews. When given advanced notice, interviewees should be thoroughly prepared. They should share control with the interviewer, not submit meekly to whatever is asked or demanded. And they should know the principles and strategies of effective answers. The result will be a better interview for both parties.

An Interview for Review and Analysis

The interviewer is a claims adjuster for North American Casualty, and the interviewee recently had his semi stolen from a motel parking lot while on his way to Omaha, Nebraska. How satisfactory is the opening of this interview? What types of probing questions are used? How well does the interviewer listen and detect clues in answers? What question pitfalls does the interviewer tumble into? How satisfactory is the closing? Also, decide how effective the interviewee is in this interview by analyzing answer strategies and the role being played.

1. **Interviewer:** Good evening. I'm Meg Turner from North American Casualty. Are you Jock McMasters?

2. **Interviewee:** Yes, I am. Won't you come in?

3. **Interviewer:** As you know, I'm here to talk to you about the incident that occurred on June 1 of this year. I'm going to be tape recording the interview, but don't let that bother you.

4. **Interviewee:** Oh . . . okay.

5. **Interviewer:** Why don't you tell me about the incident from the time you started the trip?

6. **Interviewee:** Well . . . I picked up a load at the IBM plant just outside Raleigh and headed for Omaha about 1:30 in the afternoon, along I-85 and I-40, you know.

7. **Interviewer:** Um-hmm?

8. **Interviewee:** And I got into Knoxville at about, oh, 7:00 or 7:15, and parked in the lot by the Red Roof Inn just north of town, there on I-75.

9. **Interviewer:** And you didn't make any stops between Raleigh and Knoxville?

10. **Interviewee:** Well, yeah, I stopped in Asheville for coffee, but I was there only about fifteen or twenty minutes.

11. **Interviewer:** Okay. And then what did you do?

12. **Interviewee:** I checked in and asked the person at the counter if it was okay to park my rig where I did. And she said that's where the trucks were supposed to park.

13. **Interviewer:** Were other trucks parked there?

14. **Interviewee:** Yeah, a couple of tank trucks and a car carrier—and a fancy sports car.

15. **Interviewer:** Go on.

16. **Interviewee:** Well, I got a bite to eat and went to bed. About 7:00 the next morning, I got up, got dressed, and went outside. All the trucks were gone, including mine. That whole area was empty.

17. **Interviewer:** What did you do then? Did you call the police?

18. **Interviewee:** Well . . . the motel manager did, and some sheriff showed up in about ten minutes.

19. **Interviewer:** You did lock the rig, didn't you?

20. **Interviewee:** Oh, yes! I always lock my cab doors and check the lock on the trailer before going to sleep.

21. **Interviewer:** And then what happened?

22. **Interviewee:** I told the sheriff I had been driving a 1989 Ford cab with a National trailer loaded with computers and electronic components from the IBM plant near Raleigh to Omaha. Then I showed him the bill of lading with the computers and things listed on it.

23. **Interviewer:** Okay. Who knew you were going to make this trip to Omaha? Did you talk to other drivers at the warehouse?

24. **Interviewee:** No . . . there weren't any other drivers there when I picked up the load.

25. **Interviewer:** Did anyone at the warehouse besides the dispatcher know where you were heading?

26. **Interviewee:** Not that I know of.

27. **Interviewer:** Did you talk to anyone at the rest stop near Asheville?

28. **Interviewee:** No . . . not really.

29. **Interviewer:** What about people at the motel in Knoxville?

30. **Interviewee:** Not about what I was carrying, no.

31. **Interviewer:** What about members of your family?

32. **Interviewee:** Hey, wait a minute! You don't think my wife or kids had something to do with this, do you?

33. **Interviewer:** I'm just trying to learn who might have known where you were going and what you were hauling. Did you watch the loading of your trailer and see the contents?

34. **Interviewee:** Well, I didn't inspect each piece. I just counted the boxes to make sure I had as many boxes as the bill of lading showed.

35. **Interviewer:** Then, you did count each box?

36. **Interviewee:** Yes, I did.

37. **Interviewer:** You called our office right away, didn't you?

38. **Interviewee:** Well, yeah, pretty much so.

39. **Interviewer:** So you left Raleigh about 1:30, arrived in Knoxville about 7:00 in the evening, discovered the rig was missing around 7:00 the next morning, and contacted the police immediately; correct?

40. **Interviewee:** Yep.

41. **Interviewer:** Do you own your own rig?

42. **Interviewee:** The `89 Ford, not the trailer.

43. **Interviewer:** When did you make your last payment?

44. **Interviewee:** Oh, I don't have the Ford paid for yet.

45. **Interviewer:** Do you know how much you owe on the cab?

46. **Interviewee:** Well, yeah . . . at least my wife does. She keeps track of the books for me.

47. **Interviewer:** You weren't behind in payments, were you?

48. **Interviewee:** No, ma'am. We'd be caught up after this haul.

49. **Interviewer:** I see. Tell me about your loan—the amount, monthly payments, duration, and the lender.

50. **Interviewee:** We bought the truck through the Ford finance plan, one of those sixty-month deals, and we've been paying on it each month for a little over a year now.

51. **Interviewer:** Well, that's all the questions I have for now. Is there anything else you'd like to add concerning the *facts* of the incident?

52. **Interviewee:** No, not any facts that I can think of.

53. **Interviewer:** And the statements you have made during this interview give the true version of this incident to the best of your knowledge?

54. **Interviewee:** Uh, sure, to the best of my knowledge.

55. **Interviewer:** Thank you, and I'll be in touch.

Probing Role-Playing Cases

A Case of Cheating

A student named Pat Fullmer, a junior in history with a C—average, has been accused of cheating by two instructors at Florida Central College. The instructors questioned a couple of students about the incident and then took the matter to the dean of students' office. The interviewer is an assistant dean of students in charge of student standards and ethics. She has an appointment with Roy Brown, the English Department instructor who accused Fullmer of cheating.

A Police Brutality Case

A few months ago, John T. Sawyer, fifty-six years old, was arrested in a Chicago park. There was much confusion at the time, and charges were never filed against Sawyer. Not long after the incident, Sawyer brought charges against the arresting officers. After an initial hearing, the police department took minor disciplinary action against the officers, but this did not satisfy Sawyer. He is continuing to press charges. The National Association of Law Enforcement Officers has sent an investigator to Chicago to check into the case. The investigator has an appointment with Lou Harris, a local attorney hired by the accused officers.

A Hero Citation

Several years ago, a natural disaster struck a Boy Scout camp near Elizabeth, Tennessee. A local resident has written the governor's office about the possibility of a state commendation for Rex Ingram for his actions during the disaster at the camp. The governor has sent a member of her staff to Elizabeth to interview Max Witmore who has gathered facts and community feelings about Rex, his actions, and whether he deserves a commendation.

A Missing Child

A few years ago, five-year-old Steven Dye disappeared from his home near Cottonville, Texas, and has not been found. The interviewer is an investigator for a national organization that searches for missing children. He has made an appointment with Mr. and Mrs. Dye who have become reluctant to speak with investigators of any type because their hopes have been dashed so many times.

Student Activities

1. Compare and contrast the sample attitude survey in Chapter 6 with the probing interview in this chapter. How are openings similar and different? What types of schedules seem to be employed? What are apparent question sequences? What interviewer skills are required for each interview?

2. Interview a newspaper journalist and a broadcast journalist about their interviewing experiences and techniques. How does the nature of the medium affect the interviewer and the interviewee? How does the medium affect the interview? How does the end product differ, and what constraints does this place on each interviewer?

3. Conduct two twenty-minute interviews. Take detailed notes during the first and no notes during the second. After each interview, reconstruct the information gained, and note interviewee actions, reactions, and attitudes. Which interview worked out best? How did note taking or lack of note taking affect the interviews? Try this same experiment with a tape recorder.

4. Attend a press conference or group interview in which one person is answering questions from several interviewers. How is this situation similar to and different from one-on-one interviews? What skills are required of interviewers and interviewees?

5. Interview a police or insurance investigator about the skills and techniques required in conducting investigative or interrogation interviews. How often do they use the famous "good guy/bad guy" technique, and how well does it work? How do investigators determine when they receive a truthful or untruthful answer to a leading or stress question?

Notes

1. Raymond L. Gorden, *Interviewing: Strategy, Techniques, and Tactics* (Homewood, IL: Dorsey Press, 1975), 106.

2. Hugh C. Sherwood, *The Journalistic Interview* (New York: Harper & Row, 1972). Pages 22–38 contain excellent suggestions on how to get an interview.

3. Eugene C. Webb and Jerry R. Salancik, "The Interview or the Only Wheel in Town," *Journalism Monographs* 2 (1966), 18.

4. Sherwood, 3.

5. Gorden, 137–53; Robert K. Bain, "The Researcher's Role: A Case Study," *Human Organization*, Spring (1950), 23–28; Lewis Dexter, "Role Relationships and Conception of Neutrality in Interviewing," *American Journal of Sociology* 62 (1956), 153–57.

6. George F. Bishop, Robert W. Oldendick, and Alfred J. Tuckfarber, "Effects of Presenting One Versus Two Sides in Survey Questions," *Public Opinion Quarterly* 46 (1982), 69–85.

7. Andrew D. Wolvin and Carolyn Gwynn Coakley, *Listening* (Dubuque, IA: William C. Brown Publishers, 1985), 81.

8. Wolvin and Coakley, 184–90.

9. Ken Metzler, *Creative Interviewing: The Writer's Guide to Gathering Information by Asking Questions* (Englewood Cliffs, NJ: Prentice-Hall, 1989), 142–51; John R. Bittner and Denise A. Bittner, *Radio Journalism* (Englewood Cliffs, NJ: Prentice-Hall, 1977), 51–58.

10. Metzler, 97.

11. Bittner and Bittner, 53.

12. Phillip H. Ault and Edwin Emery, *Reporting the News* (New York: Dodd, Mead, & Co., 1959), 125; George M. Killenberg and Rob Anderson, "Sources Are Persons: Teaching Interviewing as Dialogue," *Journalism Educator* 31 (1976), 16–20.

13. Bill Adler (ed.), *The Kennedy Wit* (New York: The Citadel Press, 1964), 83. This press conference occurred on March 21, 1963.

14. Art Linkletter, *Kids Say the Darndest Things* (Englewood Cliffs, NJ: Prentice-Hall, 1957), 25.

15. Sherwood, 18.

Suggested Readings

Benjaminson, Peter, and Anderson, David. *Investigative Reporting.* Bloomington, IN: Indiana University Press, 1990.

Banaka, William H. *Training in Depth Interviewing.* New York: Harper & Row, 1971.

Binder, David A., and Price, Susan C. *Legal Interviewing and Counseling: A Client-Centered Approach.* St. Paul, MN: West Publishing, 1977.

Bittner, John R., and Bittner, Denise A. *Radio Journalism.* Englewood Cliffs, NJ: Prentice-Hall, 1977.

Brand, John. *Hello, Good Evening and Welcome: A Guide to Being Interviewed on Television and Radio.* London: Shaw & Sons, 1977.

Hilton, Jack. *How to Meet the Press: A Survival Guide for Media Interviews.* New York: AMACOM, 1990.

Metzler, Ken. *Creative Interviewing: The Writer's Guide to Gathering Information by Asking Questions.* Englewood Cliffs, NJ: Prentice-Hall, 1989.

Pomerantz, Anita. "Offering a Candidate Answer: An Information Seeking Strategy," *Communication Monographs* 55 (1988), 360–73.

Royal, Robert F., and Schutt, Steven R. *The Gentle Art of Interviewing and Interrogation: A Professional Manual and Guide.* Englewood Cliffs, NJ: Prentice-Hall, 1976.

Sherwood, Hugh C. *The Journalistic Interview.* New York: Harper & Row, 1972.

Wicks, Robert J., and Josephs, Ernest H., Jr. *Techniques in Interviewing for Law Enforcement and Corrections Personnel.* Springfield, IL: Thomas, 1972.

6

The Survey Interview

The survey is the most meticulously planned and executed interview because its purpose is to establish a solid base of fact from which to draw conclusions, to make interpretations, and to determine future courses of action. Manufacturers use surveys to gauge consumer desires, intents, and trends. Advertisers use market research surveys to predict and judge the results of campaigns and methods. Politicians rely upon survey interviews to determine voter preferences, concerns, and beliefs. Journalists employ survey techniques to get solid facts on which to base news reports and interpretations, so-called "precision journalism."[1] Colleges conduct surveys to determine how students feel about proposed changes in curriculum, housing policies, and school calendars. Students conduct surveys to determine which music groups to bring to campus or how fellow students feel about proposed changes in student government. Most Americans are involved in either taking or using surveys on a regular basis.

Whereas flexibility and adaptability describe the probing interview, reliability (assurance that the same information "would have been collected each time in repeated" interviews) and replicability (the ability to duplicate interviews regardless of interviewer, interviewee, or situation) describe the survey interview.[2] Sloppy preparation and techniques will not do. A systematic approach that begins with determining purpose and conducting background research and ends with careful analysis of data is the best assurance of a successful survey. Figure 6.1 illustrates the ten step process for planning, utilizing, and analyzing the results of successful surveys.

Determining the Purpose and Researching the Topic

What do you need to discover about a topic: attitudes of college students toward star athletes, voters' images of presidential candidates, how interviewers' dress may bias survey results, or how workers feel about the new union contract? Your purpose and research will determine the structure, questions, topic areas, interviewers, and degree of precision most appropriate for your survey.

Delineating the Purpose

Long interviews cover more areas and tend to be more reliable than short interviews.[3] Consider several factors when delineating the purpose of a survey. First, how soon must you complete the survey and compile the results? A college professor might have months to devote to a project, while a market surveyor may have weeks and a journalist only days. Second, how much time will you have for each interview? However, respondents

Figure 6.1   Steps in conducting surveys

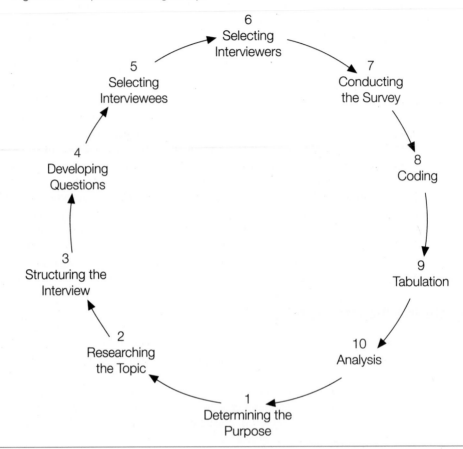

will not stand on a street corner or in a supermarket for thirty-five or forty minutes to answer questions. What can you accomplish in five or ten minutes? Third, how will you use the information—for example, to assess general feelings or attitudes or to generate precise statistics for decision-making? Uses of the results dictate how accurate and reliable a survey must be, and accuracy and reliability determine question schedule, types and uses of questions, and the number and types of people surveyed. Fourth, what are your short- and long-range goals? Do you need to assess opinions or attitudes at a specific time: the end of a sales campaign, immediately after a disaster, following a political convention? If so, a _cross-sectional_ study is sufficient. But if your purpose is to determine trends over a period of time, such as during different stages of a political campaign or how student attitudes toward college change throughout their freshman, sophomore, junior, and senior years, a *longitudinal* study is necessary. And fifth, what resources are available? A grand purpose is unrealistic if time, funds, interviewers, and means of analyzing data are limited. Surveys are expensive and may require hundreds or thousands of dollars to generate significant data.

Conducting Research

Once a purpose is delineated, investigate all aspects of the problem or issue. Do not *assume* that you already have enough information for structuring the survey. Investigate past, current, and proposed solutions to a problem. Check every potentially valuable resource: files and archives of organizations, correspondence and interviews with knowledgeable people in the field, government documents, professional journals, books, previous surveys on the topic, newsmagazines, and newspapers. Research should reveal information available in other sources that need not be obtained by your survey. Become a mini-expert on the topic so you will be familiar with unique terminology and technical concepts and can detect weaknesses in previous surveys. Research may reveal past attitudes, opinions or speculations about current attitudes and opinions. A thorough knowledge of the topic should provide insights into the nature and size of the population you will sample, the complexities of the issue, and intentional or unintentional inaccuracies in answers during your interviews.

Structuring the Interview _____

With a purpose determined and research conducted, you should develop an interview guide with major topics and subtopics. An interview guide will help you structure the interview clearly and be certain you cover all areas of information needed. The following is part of a guide developed for a county-wide survey into the needs of persons over age sixty.

I. Transportation
    A. Means of transportation
        1. Personal auto
        2. Transported in other autos
        3. Use of Council on Aging mini-bus
        4. Taxi
    B. Periodical transportation needs
        1. Doctor
        2. Groceries
        3. Banking
        4. Drugstore
        5. Other
    C. Suggestions for improving county transportation

II. Legal help
    A. Needs
        1. Wills
        2. Property
        3. Income tax
        4. Other legal needs
    B. Frequency of legal needs each year
    C. Adequacy of legal help

III. Housing
    A. Number of persons in the household
    B. Type of residence
        1. House
        2. Apartment
        3. Mobile home
        4. Other
    C. Rent or own residence
    D. Walking distance to
        1. Doctor
        2. Grocery
        3. Bank
        4. Drugstore
    E. Help needed to maintain residence
        1. Lawn
        2. Maintenance of exterior of residence
        3. Maintenance of interior of residence
        4. Snow removal

The traditional journalistic guide may be sufficient for simple surveys: who, what, when, where, how, and why.

The survey is structured so that all respondents will go through as identical an interview as possible, so the *opening* is usually written out and recited verbatim. For example:

> Hello, my name is _____, from Opinion Research Associates, a national polling firm. We are conducting a survey of people's opinions toward government and politics. We have been asking questions of some of your neighbors, and I would like to ask you a few questions. (Go to first question.)

    1. Are you registered to vote? (If yes, go to q. 3. If no, ask q. 2.)
        Yes _____ 1–1
        No _____ 1–2
    2. Do you plan to register to vote within the next month? (If yes, go to q. 3. If no, terminate the interview.)
        Yes _____ 2–1
        No _____ 2–2

3. Did you vote in the 1990 senatorial campaign when Willard Smith and Charles Gibson were running? (If yes, go to q. 5. If no, go to q. 4.)

    Yes _____ 3–1

    No _____ 3–2

4. Did you vote in the 1992 presidential election when George Bush and Bill Clinton were running? (If yes, go to q. 5. If no, terminate the interview.)

    Yes _____ 4–1

    No _____ 4–2

This opening identifies the interviewer and the survey organization and gives a general purpose. The interviewer does not identify the group that is paying for the poll (the Democratic or Republican party) or the specific purpose (to determine which strategies to employ during the remainder of the campaign) because such information is likely to influence how interviewees respond. When a newspaper such as the *New York Times* or the *St. Louis Post Dispatch,* a cable or television network such as CBS or CNN, or a well-known polling group such as Harris or Gallup conducts a poll, the oganization's name is used to enhance the prestige of the poll and the interviewer, to reduce suspicion that a candidate or party is behind the survey, and to motivate respondents to cooperate. Notice that the respondent is not asked to respond; the interviewer moves smoothly and quickly from orientation to the first question without wasting time or giving the respondent an opportunity to refuse. The first four questions determine the interviewee's qualifications. Each person must be registered or plan to register before election day and must have voted in one of the previous two elections. (Persons who did not vote in either election are unlikely to vote in the next.) The survey organization has provided instructions on the schedule for each interviewer to follow and has precoded questions for ease of tabulation.

The *closing* of surveys is usually brief and expresses appreciation, for example:

> Those are all the questions I have. Thank you very much for your help.

If the survey organization wants a respondent's telephone number to verify that a valid interview took place, the closing might be:

> That's all the questions I have. May I have your telephone number so my employer can check to see if this interview was conducted in the prescribed manner? (gets the number) Thank you for your help.

If the interviewer can provide respondents with results of the survey, a common practice in research interviews, the closing might be:

> That's all the questions I have. I want to thank you for your help, and if you'll give me your address, I'll be sure that you receive a copy of the results of my study (gets the address).

Respondents are often curious about the survey you are conducting and wish to discuss it with you. You may do so if time allows, if the respondent will have no opportunity to discuss the survey with future respondents, and if the survey organization has no objections. A friendly closing might motivate the respondent to cooperate with you or other interviewers in future surveys.

Phrasing Questions

Phrase each question with great care because survey takers cannot rephrase, explain, or expand questions or ask nonplanned secondary questions. Each question must be clearly worded, relevant to the survey, appropriate to the respondent's level of knowledge, not too complex, and socially and psychologically accessible. This is not a simple task. Respondents may be of either sex and may represent many different ages, income levels, education backgrounds, degrees of intelligence, occupations, and geographical areas.

Here is how a simple question on highway speed limits might be developed:

How do you feel about the federally imposed 55-mph speed limit?

"Federally imposed" is unnecessary and may bias results. The openness of the question may obtain a range of responses such as: "Angry," "Frustrated," "It's another step toward socialism," "I don't know," or "I think it's a (choice four-letter word) dumb law." Or some interviewees may give long speeches on the pros or cons of the speed limit. The variety and length of responses would create a recording nightmare and require secondary questions for clarification.

Close up the question:

Are you for or against or have no feelings about the 55-mph speed limit?

For	_____	1–1
Against	_____	1–2
No feelings	_____	1–3

This precoded, closed question eliminates any bias associated with "federally imposed" and solves potential problems in recording and coding answers, but it may be too closed. A respondent may not be simply for or against the speed limit, feeling, for instance, that 55 mph is unacceptable for trucks and buses on interstates but acceptable for cars on state highways. The "no feelings" option may generate a large percentage of "undecided" or "don't know" answers.

Try a third version:

Do you strongly agree, agree, disagree, or strongly disagree with this statement? The 55-mph speed limit should be maintained for all vehicles on all highways.

Strongly agree	_____	1–1
Agree	_____	1–2
Disagree	_____	1–3
Strongly disagree	_____	1–4
Undecided or have no feeling	_____	1–5

Why? (Only for respondents choosing strongly agree or strongly disagree)

_____ 1–6

This version assesses degree of feeling and specifies all vehicles and all highways, thus avoiding questions from puzzled respondents. A secondary "why" question may discover reasons for strong feelings, such as concern about one rather slow speed for all vehicles and highways. All answers have spaces and are precoded to aid in recording, coding, and tabulating results. Work with each question until it satisfies all basic requirements for phrasing and is designed to obtain the information desired.

Again, be aware that a single word may greatly alter how people respond to a question, thereby altering the results. Several years ago researchers asked the following question of several respondents: "Do you think the United States should allow public speeches against democracy?" The results were "should allow" 21 percent and "should not allow" 62 percent. Then researchers substituted a single word and asked several respondents: "Do you think the United States should forbid public speeches against democracy?" The results were "should not forbid" 39 percent and "should forbid" 46 percent. Clearly respondents viewed the word "forbid" as a much stronger and dangerous action than "not allow" even though results of the government policy would be the same. The arrangement of words may also affect interviewee responses. In a religious survey some years ago, one group of respondents was asked: "Do you think it is okay to smoke while praying?" Almost 90 percent said no. When a second group was asked, "Do you think it is okay to pray while smoking," almost 90 percent said yes. Obviously respondents saw the act as very different, the first being sacrilegious and the second being a nice thing to do while relaxing with a cigarette, even though both sets of smokers would be doing the same thing. Always think carefully of what you are asking and how an interviewee might respond. The following interaction took place recently over the telephone in one of the author's homes:

Interviewer: Good evening, I'm calling preferred customers of Antonio's Pizza [the name is changed to protect the guilty party] about our Preferred Customer Club. Have you ever tried Antonio's pizza?

Interviewee: How could I be a preferred customer if I have never eaten Antonio's pizza?

Interviewer (long pause) Gee, no one ever asked me that before. The manager just gave me a list of customers to call.

Avoid embarrassment and confusing or inaccurate results by phrasing all questions with great care. Later we will address the pretesting of surveys to detect potential problems with phrasing of questions.

Question Strategies

Survey interviewers employ several question strategies to determine interviewee knowledge level, consistency, or honesty. Stanley Payne recommends a *filter approach* to assess knowledge level.[4] For example:

Interviewer: Are you familiar with Proposition B?
Interviewee: Yes, I am.
Interviewer: What is Proposition B?

A *repeat* question consists of asking the same question several minutes apart to see if the response remains the same. A variation of this strategy is to rephrase the question slightly.

Are you in favor of Proposition B?
Do you think Proposition B should be approved?

Another example of a repeat strategy is:

What is your annual income?
I am going to read a series of annual incomes. Stop me when I read the range that includes your income.

Under $10,000	_____
$10,000–$14,999	_____
$15,000–$19,999	_____
$20,000–$24,999	_____
Over $25,000	_____

A *leaning* question is designed to reduce the number of undecided respondents. For example:

1a. If the congressional election were held today, who would you vote for? (If undecided, ask q. 1b.)

Jablonski	_____	1–1
Baker	_____	1–2
Undecided	_____	1–3
Will not vote	_____	1–4

1b. Well, do you lean more toward Jablonski or Baker at this time?

Jablonski	_____	1–5
Baker	_____	1–6
Undecided	_____	1–7

A variation of this leaning question would be, "Well, if you had to vote today, would you vote for Jablonski or Baker?" Clearly stated undecided and don't know options tend to invite large percentages of these answers, particularly when a question asks for censure of people, organizations, or products.[5]

A *shuffle* question varies the order of questions or answer options from one interview to the next to prevent order from influencing survey results. The last few choices in a question such as the following may get negative or superficial evaluations because respondents are bored or tired. Or they may be selected because they are the last heard.[6]

Now I'm going to read a list of famous vacation cities, and I want you to tell me if you have a generally favorable or unfavorable opinion of each. (Rotate the order of cities from interview to interview.)

	Favorable	Unfavorable	No Opinion
New York	1	2	3
Atlantic City	1	2	3
Washington, D.C.	1	2	3
Miami	1	2	3
New Orleans	1	2	3
Salt Lake City	1	2	3
Las Vegas	1	2	3
San Francisco	1	2	3

The shuffle strategy may eliminate order bias but can cause confusion unless interviewers are well-trained and the coding system is easy.

A *chain* or *contingency* question provides one or more secondary questions if a respondent gives a specific initial answer. The following is a typical chain strategy for a market survey, including built-in instructions and precoding.

1a.　During the past three months, have you received any free samples of toothpaste?

(20)

Yes　❒　1—Ask q. 1b.

No　❒　2—Skip to q. 2a.

1b.　What brand or brands of toothpaste did you receive? (Do not read the list.)

(21)

Clear　1

Aim　2

Ever Bright　3

Gleem　4

Crest　5

Other _____　6　(Please specify.)

1c.　(Ask only if Ever Bright is not mentioned in q. 1b., otherwise skip to q. 1d.)

Did you receive a free sample of Ever Bright toothpaste?

(22)

Yes　❒　1—Ask q. 1d.

No　❒　2—Skip to q. 2a.

1d.　Did you use the free sample of Ever Bright?

(23)

Yes　❒　1—Skip to q. 2a.

No　❒　2—Ask q. 1e.

1e.　Why didn't you use the free sample of Ever Bright toothpaste?

_____(24) _____(25)

Question Scales

A variety of *scale* or *multiple-choice* questions may avoid bipolar responses, supply a range of clear and unbiased choices, delve more deeply into topics than bipolar questions do, and reduce recording and tabulation problems. *Interval scales* provide distances between measures. For example, *evaluative interval scales* (often called Likert scales) ask interviewees to make judgments about persons, places, things, or ideas. The scale may range from five to nine answer options (five is the most common) with opposite poles such as "strongly like . . . strongly dislike," "strongly agree . . . strongly disagree," and "very important . . . not important at all." For example:

Do you strongly agree, agree, have no opinion, disagree, or strongly disagree with the recent NCAA rules changes concerning freshman eligibility to play varsity sports?

Strongly agree	5
Agree	4
No opinion	3
Disagree	2
Strongly disagree	1

Please use the phrases on this card to tell how the advertisement you just viewed for Blue Steel Cookery will affect your interest in purchasing this new line.

Increases my interest a lot	5
Increases my interest a little	4
Will not affect my interest	3
Decreases my interest a little	2
Decreases my interest a lot	1

Frequency interval scales ask interviewees to select a number that most accurately represents how often they do something or use something. For example:

How frequently do you use the Denver bus system?

5 or more times a week	5
3–4 times a week	4
1–2 times a week	3
Less than once a week	2
Never	1

Numerical interval scales ask interviewees to select a range or level that accurately reflects their age, income, educational level, rank in an organization, and so on. For example:

I am going to read several age groupings. Please stop me when I read the one in which you belong.

18–24	1
25–34	2
35–49	3
50–64	4
65 and over	5

Nominal scales provide mutually exclusive variables and ask respondents to pick the single most accurate variable. These are often "self reports" and do not ask respondents to rate or rank choices or to pick a choice along an evaluative or frequency continuum. For example, interviewers might ask:

Are you currently:

Employed outside of the home	1
A homemaker	2
Unemployed	3
Retired	4
Other _____	5

When you purchase colas by the carton or case, which of the following are you most likely to purchase?

Pepsi	7
Diet Pepsi	6
Coke	5
Diet Coke	4
Royal Crown	3
Supermarket brand	2
None of the above	1

Ordinal scales provide a list of variables and ask interviewees to rate or rank the variables in their relationship to one another, not individually as in other scales. For example:

On this card there are several reasons frequently cited for support of the proposed dam on Sugar Creek outside Bennington. Rank the top three in order of importance.

_____ Recreation
_____ Flood control
_____ Economic growth for Bennington
_____ Increased water supply
_____ Orderly development of the environment

The *Bogardus Social Distance Scale* determines how people feel about social relationships and distances. The scale usually moves progressively from remote to close relationships and distances in order to detect changes in feelings and attitudes as proximity narrows. For example, you might use the following scale to determine how male coal miners feel about female coal miners.

1. Are you in favor of allowing women to work in American coal mines?
2. Are you in favor of allowing women to work in West Virginia coal mines?
3. Are you in favor of allowing women to work in your coal mine?
4. Would you be willing to work with a woman in your coal mine?
5. Would you be willing to work for a woman boss in your coal mine?

Answer scales are designed to obtain a range of results, but studies suggest that many respondents try to "psyche out" survey takers. For instance, respondents may try to pick "normal" answers in nominal and ordinal scales and safe, moderate, or middle options in interval scales (2–4 instead of 1 or 5). Rather than admit they do not know the correct answer, respondents may pick the option that stands out, such as the second in a list that includes 10 percent, 15 percent, 20 percent, 30 percent, and 40 percent. Respondents who first agree that a certain activity would make most people uneasy are less likely to then admit ever engaging in that activity and will probably respond in an effort to change the subject.[7] Interviewers should phrase scales carefully, and observe reactions during interviews to detect patterns of responses and interviewee comprehension. For instance, long scales may confuse respondents without either interview party realizing it.[8]

Question Sequences

The question sequences discussed in Chapter 4 can be selected to suit the purpose of any survey. The tunnel or string-of-beads sequence is common in surveys when no strategic lineup of questions is needed. Gallup's Quintamensional Design Sequence described in Chapter 4 (or a variation) is appropriate if you want to explore intensity of attitudes and opinions. Because funnel and inverted funnel sequences include open-ended questions, answers are often difficult to record and may pose coding and tabulation problems. However, a study of the effects of question order suggests that general questions should come first and then more specific questions should follow—a funnel sequence.[9]

Selecting Interviewees _____

Developing a Sample

A clear definition of the *population,* what Charles Redding calls the "target group," is essential for each survey.[10] For instance, the population may be all workers for a company, all full-time workers, all full-time hourly workers, or all full-time, hourly union workers. To determine how residents of an apartment complex feel about its management, your population might include all residents, only adult (over age twenty-one) residents, or the head of the household in each apartment. The final population should include all persons who are able to respond meaningfully to your questions and about whom you want to generalize in your findings.

If the target population is small (members of a football team, the forty-five full-time workers in a factory, or the front office personnel), it is possible to interview all members. Most surveys are concerned, however, with populations that far exceed time, financial, and personal limitations (all drivers over eighteen, all 5,000 workers in Plant 3, all registered voters in Virginia). One or dozens of interviewers could not interview all of these populations, so the survey taker selects a sample of the target group. Since you cannot interview all drivers over eighteen, for example, you interview *some* of them and extend your findings to *all* of them. Effective sampling solves time, financial, and personnel problems.

Several principles govern sampling techniques. First, you must have a clear definition of the population to be sampled. Second, your sample must truly represent the total population and be a miniature version of the whole. Third, each potential respondent from the designated population must have an equal chance of being selected. Fourth, you must know the probability that each person might be selected to determine the acceptable *margin of error*. The precision of the survey is the "degree of similarity between sample results and the results from a 100 percent count obtained in an identical manner."[11] Most surveys are designed to attain a 95 percent *level of confidence*, the mathematical probability that 95 times out of 100 interviewees would give results within 5 percentage points (your margin of error) either way of the figures that would be obtained if the entire population were interviewed. The tolerable margin of error depends upon the use of the survey results. For instance, if you hope to predict the outcome of an election, you must strive for a small margin of error. If you are conducting a survey to determine how people feel about the city in which they live, you could tolerate a moderate margin of error. The size of the sample is then determined by the size of the population and the acceptable margin of error. There is no magical formula for determining number of interviewees. The Gallup organization produces accurate national surveys from a sample of 1,500. Size of sample is less important than how the sample is taken. Standard formulas reveal that as a population increases in size, the percentage of the population necessary for a sample declines rapidly. In other words, you would have to interview a larger percentage of 5,000 people than of 50,000 people to attain equally accurate results. Formulas also reveal that you must increase greatly the size of your sample to reduce the margin of error from 5 percent to 4 percent or 3 percent. The reduction of the margin of error may not be worth the added cost. Philip Meyer offers the following table that shows the sample sizes of various populations necessary for a 5 percent margin of error and a 95 percent level of confidence.[12]

Population Size	Sample Size
Infinity	384
500,000	384
100,000	383
50,000	381
10,000	370
5,000	357
3,000	341
2,000	322
1,000	278

Sampling Techniques

If you have a complete roster of all persons in a target population, place their names (or numbers assigned to each) *in a hat* and draw out the number needed. Or you might assign a number to each potential respondent and create or purchase a *table of random numbers*. With your eyes closed, place a finger on a number and decide whether to read a combination up, down, across to left or right, or diagonally. If you decide to read the last digit of the numeral touched (46) and the first digit of the numeral to the right (29), you would contact respondent number 62. Repeat the process until the sample is completed. A *skip interval* or *random digit* approach chooses, for instance, every tenth number in the telephone book, every twentieth name on the employee roster, or every other person who walks into a supermarket. If a population has clearly identifiable groups (males and females; Catholic, Protestant, and Jewish voters; education levels; or income levels), you may employ a *stratified random sample* that includes a minimum number of respondents from each group or a percentage representing the percentage of the group in the target population. Some survey organizations give a *sample point* to each interviewer (perhaps a square block that includes white, blue-collar workers) with instructions to skip the corner house (corner houses are often more expensive) and then try every other house on the outside of the four-block area until two interviews with males and two with females have been completed. The sample point or block sampling method gives the designer control over selection of interviewees without resorting to lists of names, random digits, or telephone numbers.

Several factors affect sampling methods. For instance, time of day or the location of a supermarket may determine the type of person most likely to be at home or to walk through the supermarket door. As much as 15 percent of the population may have unlisted telephone numbers, and some groups (students, the poor, migrant workers, or persons who have recently moved) may not have telephones or their names in directories. An employee roster might be divided according to areas of the plant, seniority, and job classification and thus produce a nonrepresentative sample. A simple random sampling procedure may not provide an adequate sampling of subgroups within a population, even when drawn from a hat.

Selecting Interviewers

Select interviewers carefully with three questions in mind. First, *how many are needed?* If you plan to interview a small number of persons and the interviews will be brief, one interviewer may be sufficient. However, you will need several interviewers if the interviews are lengthy, the sample is large, the time allotted for the survey is limited, or if respondents are scattered over a wide geographical area. Large and difficult interviewing assignments result in serious interviewer fatigue and decline in motivation.[13]

Second, *what special qualifications are required?* A highly scheduled or highly scheduled standardized interview does not require an interviewer who is an expert on the topic or especially skilled in phrasing questions and probing into answers. But it does require a nonthreatening person who is interested in the topic and able to listen, follow instructions, and remain neutral. College students and middle-aged homemakers tend to be excellent survey interviewers because they have these qualifications and are inexpensive to employ. If a survey requires probing and adaptation, professionally trained interviewers tend to be both more efficient and to produce more accurate results.[14]

Third, *what personal characteristics are optimal?* Interviewers who are older or who have an optimistic outlook get better response rates and cooperation, regardless of their experiences. Apparently age generates credibility and self-confidence, and optimism motivates interviewees to cooperate.[15] A recent study discovered that the personality and attitude of the interviewer is by far the most important element in shaping interviewee attitudes toward surveys.[16] An in-group relationship with an interviewee (black to black, senior citizen to senior citizen, Italian to Italian, or female to female) may avoid etiquette and communication barriers and enhance trust because the interviewer is perceived to be capable of understanding and being sympathetic.[17] An out-group relationship (white to black, young citizen to senior citizen, English to Italian, male to female) may pose no ego threat, and the interview may be perceived as a new experience and a means of recognition.

The typical survey relationship is between two strangers, lasts only from the opening through the closing, and deals with subject matter ranging from noncontroversial (market surveys on soap or soft drinks) to controversial (surveys on abortion or neighborhood rezoning). The interviewer's opening technique, qualifications, and personal characteristics, including appearance and manner, must create a favorable image (affection), persuade the interviewee to take part (inclusion), and establish the proper amount of control by not being too demanding or insistent. Recent studies report that nearly one-third of respondents believe that answering survey questions will neither benefit them nor influence decisions, that there are too many surveys, that surveys are too long, and that interviewers ask too many personal questions. Some 36 percent of respondents in one study said they had been asked to take part in "false surveys," sales interviews disguised as surveys. The percentages of persons reporting that their last survey experiences were "unpleasant" increased from 6 percent in 1982 to 12 percent in 1984.[18] Clearly, survey interviewers must be aware of the relational dimensions of affection, inclusion, and control, and must make every effort to establish a positive relationship with each respondent.

Conducting the Survey

Training Interviewers

Poor execution of interviews can undo the most thorough preparation, so you should provide both a training session and written instructions for interviewers. Training, for example, will result in greater use of appropriate probing questions, feedback, and giving instructions.[19] Discuss common interviewee criticisms, and stress the importance of following the question schedule exactly as printed. Explain complex questions and recording methods. Be sure interviewers understand the sampling techniques employed. Emphasize the need to replicate interviews to enhance reliability and attain an acceptable margin of error and level of confidence. The following is a typical list of instructions provided for interviewers:

1. Study the question schedule so you can "ask" rather than "read" questions and record answers quickly and accurately.
2. Dress appropriately; do not wear buttons or insignia that may identify you with a particular group or position on the issue being surveyed and thus bias the survey results by encouraging interviewees to respond in particular ways.
3. Be on time for all appointments.
4. Be friendly, businesslike, and sincerely interested in the interview and the interviewee.

5. Speak clearly and loudly enough to be heard easily. Maintain good eye contact, and do not rush through the interview.

6. If persons say they do not have time, use statements such as, "This will only take a few minutes" or "I can ask you questions while you're working." Do not pressure the respondent to take part.

7. If a respondent does not answer the question as asked, repeat the question but do not rephrase it because rephrasing may alter the survey results.

8. Record answers as prescribed on the schedule; write or print answers to open questions carefully and clearly.

9. Give respondents adequate time to think and respond; do not fidget or look at your watch.

10. When you have obtained the answer to the last question, thank the respondent for cooperating and excuse yourself.

Pretesting the Interview

Pretest the interview schedule and procedures to detect potential problems because the best plans on paper may not work in actual practice. Conduct complete interviews with persons from the target population, trying out the opening and closing, asking all questions, and recording answers. Do not leave anything to chance. For instance, in a political poll conducted by a college class, interviewers deleted the question "What do you like or dislike about living in Indiana?" because it took too much time and generated little useful data. When given a list of candidates and asked, "What do you like or dislike about . . .?" many respondents became embarrassed or gave vague answers because they did not know some of the candidates. This question was replaced with a Likert scale from "strongly like" to "strongly dislike" including a "don't know" option, and interviewers probed into reasons for liking or disliking only for candidates ranked in the extreme positions on the scale. Interviewers also discovered that scales tended to confuse older respondents, so they added a special explanation. Ask several questions when pretesting a survey interview, such as:

1. How well did interviewees understand what was wanted and why?
2. Which questions required explanation?
3. How effectively did questions elicit the kind and amount of information desired?
4. Which questions elicited information already obtained through prior questions in the survey?
5. To which questions did interviewees react hesitantly or negatively?
6. How adequate were answer options?
7. Was interviewer bias apparent at any time during the interviews?
8. How easily and meaningfully can answers be tabulated?

Once you have analyzed the pretest results and made necessary alterations in the procedures and questions, you are ready to conduct the survey with confidence.

A growing number of interviewers are turning to the telephone for easier and less expensive means of conducting surveys and polls.

Interviewing by Telephone

A growing number of interviewers are using the telephone for an easier, faster, and less expensive means of conducting surveys. Some studies comparing telephone and face-to-face interviews suggest that the two methods produce similar results, with respondents giving fewer "socially acceptable" answers over the telephone and preferring the anonymity it provides (particularly in certain neighborhoods).[20] However, more recent studies have urged caution in turning too readily to the telephone for surveys. One study discovered that many interviewers do not like telephone interviews, and this attitude may affect interviewee responses. Another study found that fewer interviewees (particularly older ones) prefer the telephone, that there is a lower degree of cooperation in telephone interviews, and that people feel uneasy about discussing sensitive issues with strangers over the telephone.[21]

Regardless of the potential problems with telephone surveys, they will become ever more frequent than face-to-face surveys because (1) one face-to-face or "personal" interview is estimated to cost more than $100.00, (2) locating respondents at home is more difficult because fewer and fewer homemakers exist and flexible working hours make it difficult to predict when a person might be home, (3) fewer than 50 percent of large city respondents who are contacted are willing to consent to an interview, and (4) organizations want to interview persons over a wide geographical area.[22]

The opening of the telephone interview is critical to interviewee cooperation because the great majority of refusals occur prior to the first question: one-third in the opening seconds, one-third during the orientation, and one-third at the point of listing household members. Speaking skills during the opening, including pitch, vocal variety, loudness, rate, and distinct enunciation, seem to be more important than the content. As one study concluded, "Respondents react to cues communicated by the interviewer's voice and may grant or refuse an interview on that basis."[23] Telephone interviewers apparently must establish trust through vocal and verbal analogs to the personal appearance, credentials, and survey materials that enhance trust in face-to-face interviews.

Special instructions to telephone interviewers include:

1. Develop an informal but professional manner that is both courteous and friendly, avoiding any hint of pressure or defensiveness.
2. Get the interviewee involved as quickly as possible in answering questions because active involvement will motivate the person to take part in the interview and respond effectively; try not to give the person a reason or opportunity to hang up on you.
3. Pay complete attention to what you are saying, doing, and/or hearing. Do nothing else during the interview, this includes smoking, chewing gum, eating, sorting papers on your desk, or communicating with other people in the office.
4. Say nothing you do not want the interviewee to hear, even if you try to cover the mouthpiece.
5. Talk directly into the mouthpiece of the phone, be neither too loud nor too soft.
6. Speak clearly, distinctly, and slowly. The respondent must rely solely on your voice because the person is unable to see you, your nonverbal signals, your answer cards, or your visual materials.
7. Give each answer option distinctly and pause between them to aid the respondent in recalling them.
8. Use vocal emphasis so the respondent can answer accurately: "What is the *most* important reason . . ." or "What is *your* attitude toward . . .?"
9. Listen and prove it with signals such as "Uh huh," "Yes," and "I see."
10. Explain any pauses or long silences: "Just a minute while I write down your answer," "I'm recording your answers," or "I'm writing down this information."

Coding, Tabulation, and Analysis

Begin the final phase of the survey by coding all answers that were not precoded, usually the open-ended questions. For instance, if question 10b is "Why did you not vote in the last presidential election?" a variety of answers are possible. If 10b is coded #20, each answer would be coded 20 plus 1, 2, 3, etc.

20–1 I didn't know enough about the candidates.
20–2 Both candidates were jerks.
20–3 It doesn't matter who you vote for; things always stay the same.

All "I didn't know enough about" answers would be coded 20–1.

Answers to open questions may require analysis before you can develop a coding system. For example, in a study of voter perception of mudslinging in political communication, the interviewer asked, "What three or four words would you use to describe a politician who uses mudslinging as a tactic?" Answers included more than a hundred different words, but analysis revealed that the words tended to fit into five categories: untrustworthy, incompetent, unlikable, insecure, and immature.[24] A sixth category, "other," included words that did not fit into the major categories. All words were placed into one of these six categories and coded from one to six.

Interviewers may create chaos by recording answers in a confusing manner. For example, answers to a question in a political survey, "Who is Matthew Welsh?" were recorded: "Democrat," "governor," and "political candidate." Since Welsh was the Democratic candidate for governor and a former governor, how should the answer be coded? Did "governor" mean present governor, past governor, or candidate for governor? Did "political candidate" mean for governor, senator, or representative? Did "Democrat" mean Democratic candidate for governor, Democratic candidate, or just a Democrat? Data defied coding attempts and were discarded.

Once you have coded answers and tabulated the results, the analysis phase may begin. Analysis is making sense of the data you have obtained, but this task can be overwhelming. A few years ago one of the authors surveyed 354 clergy from 32 Protestant, Catholic, and Jewish groups to assess the training clergy had received in interviewing during their college and seminary educations and since entering the profession.[25] The 48 items on the survey (times 354 respondents) provided 16,992 bits of information. Attempts to compare respondents according to religious affiliation, years in the field, and demographic data quickly produced hundreds of pages of computer printouts. How can the survey interviewer/researcher handle such massive amounts of information? Charles Redding suggests, first, that you be *selective* and ask "What findings are likely to be most useful?" Second, *capitalize* upon the potential of your data by subjecting data to comparative breakdowns to discover differences between demographic subgroups. And third, *dig* for the gold that is probably hidden within your raw data and simple tabulations.[26] For instance, in polls of registered voter attitudes, interviewers often discover that female respondents favor a candidate far less than male respondents, that African Americans have very different attitudes toward social programs than white Americans, and that the more highly educated a person is the more likely the person will support a tax increase. Remember that what you do *not* find may be as important as what you *do* find. As you analyze data, ask yourself such questions as:

What conclusions can you draw, and with what certainty? For how much of a population can you generalize? What are the constraints imposed by the sample, the interviewing process, and the interviewers? Can you determine why people responded in specific ways to specific questions? Are you in danger of making mountains out of molehills of data? What unexpected events or changes have occurred since the completion of the survey? What about undecided answers and nonresponses? For example:

Who do you plan to vote for in November, Williams or Adams?

Williams—37 percent   Sample = 1,000
Adams—36 percent
Undecided—15 percent
Nonresponse—12 percent

If you eliminate nonresponses (maybe interviewers failed to record all answers or maybe some people refused to answer the question), the sample equals 880, and the new percentages are:

Williams—42 percent
Adams—41 percent
Undecided—17 percent

What if you discard the undecided? Williams and Adams look better, but the large undecided figure may be the most important finding of the survey. Can you say with confidence that Williams is ahead, even if you ignore the undecideds? What is the margin of error? The most sophisticated survey rarely has a margin of error less than 3 percent, so Adams could be ahead by 2–3 percent or Williams could be ahead by 4–5 percent. Journalists must be cautious when writing headlines and making predictions, and organizations must be cautious in basing policy decisions on survey results. You might subject data to a statistical analysis designed to test reliability or significance of results. Several sources listed at the end of this chapter provide detailed guidelines for conducting sophisticated statistical analyses of survey data. When you have completed the analysis of your data, you must determine if the purpose and objectives of your survey were achieved and how best to report the results.

The Respondent in Survey Interviews

The proliferation of surveys assures that you are likely to take part in one several times a year. You have the right to walk away from the interviewer or hang up the telephone, but if you do, you may forfeit the opportunity to play an important role in improving commercials, selecting political candidates, influencing legislation, or bettering the environment.

Listen to the interviewer's explanation to learn who the interviewer is and who he or she represents, why the survey is being conducted, how answers will be used, and how you were chosen. Decide whether to take part after thorough orientation, not before the

Trust may be high when the survey interviewer is perceived as capable of understanding and being sympathetic with the interviewee's situation.

interviewer can explain the survey. This is a good time also to determine if this is truly a survey or a slick sales effort under the guise of a survey. Never agree to take part merely to sabotage the interview.

When taking part in surveys, listen carefully to each question, particularly to answer options in interval, nominal, and ordinal scale questions. If you have trouble remembering a question or all of the options, ask the interviewer to repeat the question slowly. Avoid replays of earlier answers, especially if you think you "goofed." Do not try to guess what a question is going to be from the interviewer's first words because you might be wrong and give a stupid answer or force the interviewer to restate the question. If a question or a series of answer options is unclear, ask the interviewer for clarification. Listen to each question, think through the answer, and respond clearly and precisely. Give the answer that best represents your views, not the one you think the interviewer wants to hear.

Respondents have rights. For example, you can refuse to answer a poorly constructed or leading question or to give data that seems irrelevant or an invasion of privacy. Expect and demand tactful, sensitive, and polite treatment from interviewers. Insist on adequate time to answer questions. Remember, you can always walk away or hang up the telephone. Survey interviews can be fun, interesting, and informative if both parties treat one another fairly.

Summary

The survey interview is systematic and meticulously planned, beginning with a clear purpose and ending with careful tabulation and analysis of results. The general purpose is to establish a solid base of fact from which to draw conclusions, make interpretations, and determine future courses of action. The survey creator must carefully choose sampling techniques, schedules, question strategies and scales, interviewers, face-to-face or telephone contacts, and coding and recording methods. Each choice has advantages and disadvantages; there is no one correct way to handle all survey situations. Survey respondents must determine the nature of the survey and its purposes to decide whether to take part. If the decision is to take part, then the respondents have a responsibility to listen carefully to each question and to answer it accurately.

A Survey Schedule for Review and Analysis

As you read through this survey schedule, notice the parts of the standard opening, and identify the question strategies (filter, repeat, leaning, shuffle, and chain), the question scales (evaluative interval, frequency interval, numerical interval, nominal, ordinal, and Bogardus Social Distance), and the question sequences (funnel, inverted funnel, tunnel, and quintamensional design). Notice the built-in probing questions, instructions for interviewers, precoding of answers, and inclusion of open questions.

(Speak to any person eighteen years or older who lives in the household.)

Hello, my name is _____, from National Opinion Research Institute, a nationwide survey research organization located in Chicago. We're conducting a study of people's opinions about a number of current issues confronting the United States today. The results of this study will be supplied to government groups and to the public through the news media. We've been interviewing people in your neighborhood and would like to ask you a few questions.

1a. When you think of a serious national problem, which problem comes to mind first?

    1.1 _____

1b. What do you think is the major cause of this problem?

    1.2 _____

1c. What are other possible causes of this problem?

    1.3 _____

    1.4 _____

    1.5 _____

2. Many people feel that inflation is a serious problem facing America today. This card *(hand card to interviewee)* gives some of the reasons people feel that we have an inflation problem. Which one of these reasons do you feel is the greatest cause of inflation? *(Record answer.)* Which is the next most important cause? *(Record answer.)* And which would be the next? *(Record answer.)*

	First	**Second**	**Third**
Taxes	1	1	1
Government spending	2	2	2
Farm prices	3	3	3
Foreign imports	4	4	4
Union demands	5	5	5
Profits for big corporations	6	6	6
Military spending	7	7	7
Interest rates	8	8	8
Don't know	9	9	9

3. I'm going to read several statements, and I would like you to tell me whether you strongly agree, agree, don't know, disagree, or strongly disagree with each. *(Record answers on the space below and rotate the order in which the statements are given from interview to interview.)*
    a. We should have a national health insurance plan that would guarantee basic medical care for all individuals and would be paid for by the government.
    b. We should place limitations on the number of cars imported into the United States.
    c. A compulsory draft should be instituted to replace the volunteer army.
    d. Standards of the Clean Air Act should be reduced to allow the burning of high sulfur coal that could reduce reliance upon foreign oil.
    e. We should work toward an international treaty that would ban all military uses of space.

	a	**b**	**c**	**d**	**e**
Strongly agree	1	1	1	1	1
Agree	2	2	2	2	2
Don't know/undecided	3	3	3	3	3
Disagree	4	4	4	4	4
Strongly disagree	5	5	5	5	5

4. Many people tell us that they are interested in the abortion issue. This card *(hand interviewee a card)* lists several positions on abortion. Please tell me which one is closest to your feelings about abortion.

There should be a constitutional amendment making abortions illegal.   1
Abortions should be legal only when the life of the mother is endangered.   2
Abortions should be legal only when the mental or physical health of   3
the mother is endangered, when the child will be deformed, or in cases
of rape.
There should be no restrictions on abortions because it is a matter of   4
free choice.
Don't know/undecided   5

5a. Are you familiar with the proposed Hyde Amendment to the Constitution?
Yes _____ 5.1 *(If yes, ask q. 5b.)*
No _____

5b. What do you know about the Hyde Amendment?

_____ 5.2

_____ 5.3

6. Thousands, and some say millions, of refugees are fleeing to the United States each year from eastern Europe, the Middle East, the Far East, and Central America.
a. Are you in favor of these refugees being allowed to come to the United States?
Yes _____ 6.1   No _____ 6.2
b. Are you in favor of their coming to live in this part of the country?
Yes _____ 6.3   No _____ 6.4
c. Are you in favor of their coming to live in this state?
Yes _____ 6.5   No _____ 6.6
d. Are you in favor of their coming to live in this city?
Yes _____ 6.7   No _____ 6.8
e. Are you in favor of their coming to live in this neighborhood?
Yes _____ 6.9   No _____ 6.10

7a. What do you know about foreign ownership of farmland in the U.S.?

_____ 7.1

_____ 7.2

7b. What, if any, contributions do you think foreign ownership of farmland makes to the U.S. economy?

_____ 7.3

_____ 7.4

7c. Do you approve or disapprove of foreign ownership of U.S. farmland?

Approve _____ 7.5   Disapprove _____ 7.6

7d. Why do you feel this way?

_____ 7.7

_____ 7.8

7e. How strongly do you feel about this?
Strongly _____ 7.9
Very strongly _____ 7.10
Something about which you will never change your mind _____ 7.11

8. How would you rate the job Bill Clinton is doing as president: excellent, good, average, not so good, poor? *(Encircle answers in the scales provided at the end of q. 10.)*

9. How would you rate the job Congress is doing: excellent, good, average, not so good, poor? *(Encircle answers in the scales provided at the end of q. 10.)*

10. How would you rate the job the Supreme Court is doing: excellent, good, average, not so good, or poor? *(Encircle answers in the scales provided below.)*

	Clinton	Congress	Supreme Court
Excellent	1	1	1
Good	2	2	2
Average	3	3	3
Not so good	4	4	4
Poor	5	5	5

11. Here is a card *(hand card to interviewee)* that lists some of the problems people say the federal government ought to take care of. As I read each one, please tell me which political party is most likely to solve the problem. The first problem is
_____. *(Rotate the order from one interview to the next.)*
Do you think the Republican or Democratic party is most likely to solve this problem?

	Dem.	Rep.	Either	Neither	Don't know
National debt	1	2	3	4	5
Unemployment	1	2	3	4	5
Taxes	1	2	3	4	5
Farm prices	1	2	3	4	5
Imports	1	2	3	4	5
Crime	1	2	3	4	5

Now I would like to ask you some personal questions so we can see how people with different backgrounds feel about the issues facing the United States today.

12. I'm going to read you several age ranges. Stop me when I read the one that includes your age.

18–24	1
25–34	2
35–49	3
50–64	4
65 and over	5

13. How often do you attend government meetings, including local, state, and national?

More than 12 times a year	1
10–12 times a year	2
7–9 times a year	3
4–6 times a year	4
1–3 times a year	5
Less than once a year	6
Never	7

14a. Do you generally consider yourself a Democrat or a Republican? *(If independent, ask q. 14b.)*

Democrat	1
Republican	2
Don't know	3
Refuse	4

14b. Well, do you generally vote for Republican or Democratic candidates for public office?

Independent/Republican	1
Independent/Democrat	2
Independent	3

15. Is your religious affiliation Catholic, Protestant, Jewish, Muslim, other, or none?

Catholic	1	
Protestant	2	
Jewish	3	
Muslim	4	
Other	5	_____ (Write in.)
None	6	

16. What was the last grade level of your formal education?

0 to 8 years	1
9 to 11 years	2
12 years	3
13 to 15 years	4
College graduate	5
Postgraduate	6

Thank you very much for your time and cooperation. The survey results should be made public within five to six weeks.

Student Activities

1. Select a current local, national, or international issue and research it. Prepare a twenty-minute, highly scheduled/highly standardized interview. Include an opening, all questions, appropriate answer spaces or options, and a closing. Use a variety of questions and interviewees. Vary the interviewing situations and your recording techniques. Write an analysis of your interviewing experiences, the strengths and weaknesses of your methods, and the data obtained.

2. Try a simple interviewer bias experiment. For example, conduct ten brief opinion interviews on a current issue (religious, political, economic, or social). All questions are to be identical. In five of the interviews, wear a conspicuous button or badge that identifies a position (a Republican elephant, a religious symbol, a slogan). In the other five interviews, do not wear the button or badge. Compare results to see if your apparent bias affected answers to identical questions.

3. Compare and contrast a market survey and a political survey. How are openings similar and different? Which types of schedules are employed? How are question types, strategies, and sequences similar and different? How is the information obtained similar and different?

4. Interview a person experienced in survey interviewing. How does this person (or the person's organization) prepare surveys? Which types of questions and schedules are used most often? Which sampling techniques are used? How are interviewers selected?

5. Volunteer to be an interviewer for a survey being conducted by a company, political party, or government organization. What instructions did you receive? If you were given one or more sample points, how was this decided? What problems did you have with the survey schedule? What problems did you have in locating suitable and cooperative interviewees? What problems did you encounter during interviews? What was the most important thing you learned from this experience?

Survey Role-Playing Cases

Desire for a Local Weekly Newspaper

The interviewer is working for a local printing firm that is seriously considering starting a free weekly newspaper. The newspaper would concentrate on local news and events and would carry inexpensive ads for baby-sitters, garage sales, local businesses, and so on. The firm has assigned the interviewer the task of creating and conducting a survey of community attitudes toward and interest in a free weekly to be called the *Good News Courier*. The interviewer has completed a draft of the public opinion interview to be used in the survey and has made an appointment to pretest the interview on a neighbor.

A New School Calendar

The interviewer is a student at a large state university and has been asked by the student government to create and conduct a survey of student attitudes toward the current school calendar and a number of proposals for revising it. The student must create a question schedule and determine both the size and nature of the survey sample. The university has graduate and undergraduate programs in several different schools and a large continuing education program.

Market Survey

The interviewer works for Market Studies, Inc., and must design a telephone survey instrument that will assess the effectiveness of a recent advertising campaign that promoted an improved version of a long-established brand of toothpaste. The advertising campaign consisted of three phases: full-page ads in major newspapers, thirty-second spots on three television networks, and free samples mailed to 200,000 randomly selected homes. The interviewer must create a set of instructions that others will use to train the dozens of interviewers necessary for conducting this survey.

A Political Preference Survey

The interviewer is on the staff of a state senator who is running for a United States congressional seat. The interviewer's task is to design a political preference survey that will determine how people in the congressional district feel about the senator and a number of local, state, national, and international issues. The survey must be done quickly and inexpensively. Thus, the time for each interview cannot exceed ten minutes. Major decisions involve which issues to cover; the proportion of each interview to devote to local, state, national, and international issues; how to assess the image of the senator; and what demographic data to obtain.

Notes

1. Philip Meyer, *Precision Journalism* (Bloomington, IN: Indiana University Press, 1979).
2. Earl Babbie, *The Practice of Social Research* (Belmont, CA: Wadsworth, 1989).

3. Stanley L. Payne, *The Art of Asking Questions* (Princeton, NJ: Princeton University Press, 1951), 129–37.

4. Payne, 21.

5. George F. Bishop, Robert W. Oldendick, and Alfred J. Tuckfarber, "Effects of Presenting One Versus Two Sides of an Issue in Survey Questions," *Public Opinion Quarterly* 46 (1982), 69–85; Payne, 23.

6. Laure M. Sharp and Joanne Frankel, "Respondent Burden: A Test of Some Common Assumptions," *Public Opinion Quarterly* 47 (1983), 36–53; Payne, 72.

7. Norman M. Bradburn, Seymour Sudman, Ed Blair, and Carol Stocking, "Question Threat and Response Bias," *Public Opinion Quarterly* 42 (1978), 221–34; Payne, 80–83 and 177–202.

8. Jean Morton-Williams and Wendy Sykes, "The Use of Interaction Coding and Follow-Up Interviews to Investigate Comprehension of Survey Questions," *Journal of the Market Research Society* 26 (1984), 109–27.

9. Sam G. McFarland, "Effects of Question Order on Survey Responses," *Public Opinion Quarterly* 45 (1981), 208–15.

10. W. Charles Redding, *How to Conduct a Readership Survey: A Guide for Organizational Editors and Communications Managers* (Chicago: Lawrence Ragan Communications, 1982), 5.

11. Morris James Slonim, *Sampling in a Nutshell* (New York: Simon and Schuster, 1960), 23.

12. Meyer, 123 For discussions of formulas and tables to determine error margin and sample size, see Slonim, 60–99, and Redding, 25–49.

13. Eleanor Singer, Martin R. Frankel, and Marc B. Glassman, "The Effect of Interviewer Characteristics and Expectations on Response," *Public Opinion Quarterly* 47 (1983), 68–83.

14. Robin T. Peterson, "How Efficient Are Salespeople in Surveys of Buyer Intentions," *Journal of Business Forecasting* 7 (1988), 11–12.

15. Singer, Frankel, and Glassman, 68–83.

16. Stephan Schleifer, "Trends in Attitudes Toward and Participation in Survey Research," *Public Opinion Quarterly* 50 (1986), 17–26.

17. Raymond L. Gorden, *Interviewing: Strategy, Techniques and Tactics* (Homewood, IL: Dorsey Press, 1969), 141–43. Reprinted by permission.

18. Schleifer, 17–26; Sharp and Frankel, 36–53; Theresa J. DeMaio, "Refusals: Who, Where, Why?" *Public Opinion Quarterly* 44 (1980), 223–32; and Burns W. Roper, "Evaluating Polls and Poll Data," *Public Opinion Quarterly* 50 (1986), 10–16.

19. Jacques Billiet and Geert Loosveldt, "Improvement of the Quality of Responses to Factual Survey Questions by Interviewer Training," *Public Opinion Quarterly* 52 (1988), 190–211.

20. Theresa F. Rogers "Interviews by Telephone and In Person: Quality of Responses and Field Performance," *Public Opinion Quarterly* 39 (1976), 51–65; S. Stephen Kegeles, Clifton F. Frank, and John P. Kirscht, "Interviewing a National Sample by Long-Distance Telephone," *Public Opinion Quarterly* 33 (1969–1970), 412–19.

21. Lawrence A. Jordan, Alfred C. Marcus, and Leo G. Reeder, "Response Style in Telephone and Household Interviewing," *Public Opinion Quarterly* 44 (1980), 210–22; Robert M. Groves, "Actors and Questions in Telephone and Personal Survey Interviews," *Public Opinion Quarterly* 43 (1979), 190–205; and Peter V. Miller and Charles F. Cannell, "A Study of Experimental Techniques for Telephone Interviewing," *Public Opinion Quarterly* 46 (1982), 250–69.

22. Robert M. Groves and Robert L. Kahn, *Surveys by Telephone: A National Comparison with Personal Interviews* (New York Academic Press, 1979), 2–5.

23. Lois Okenberg, Lerita Coleman, and Charles F. Cannell, "Interviewers' Voices and Refusal Rates in Telephone Surveys," *Public Opinion Quarterly* 50 (1986), 97–111; A. Regula Herzog, Willard L. Rodgers, and Richard A. Kulka, "Interviewing Older Adults: A Comparison of Telephone and Face-to-Face Modalities," *Public Opinion Quarterly* 47 (1983), 405–18.

24. Charles J. Stewart, "Voter Perception of Mudslinging in Political Communication," *Central States Speech Journal* 26 (1975), 279–86.

25. Charles J. Stewart, "The Interview and the Clergy: A Survey of Training, Experiences, and Needs," *Religious Communication Today* 3 (1980), 19–22.

26. W. Charles Redding, *How to Conduct a Readership Survey* (Chicago: Lawrence Ragan Communications, 1982), 119–123.

Suggested Readings

Babbie, Earl R. *The Practice of Social Research.* Belmont, CA: Wadsworth, 1989.

Fowler, Floyd J. *Survey Research Methods.* Newbury Park, CA: Sage Publications, 1988.

Fowler, Floyd J. and Mangione, Thomas W. *Standardized Survey Interviewing.* Newbury Park, CA: Sage Publications, 1989.

Frey, James H. *Survey Research by Telephone.* Newbury Park, CA: Sage Publications, 1989.

Groves, Robert M., and Kahn, Robert L. *Telephone Survey Methodology.* New York: Wiley, 1988.

Lavrakas, Paul J. *Telephone Survey Methods.* Newbury Park, CA: Sage Publications, 1987.

Marsh, Catherine. *The Survey Method.* London: George Allen & Unwin, 1982.

Meyer, Philip. *The New Precision Journalism.* Bloomington, IN: Indiana University Press, 1991.

Redding, W. Charles. *How to Conduct a Readership Survey: A Guide for Organizational Editors and Communications Managers.* Chicago: Lawrence Ragan Communications, 1982.

Rivers, William L. and Harrington, Susan L. *Finding Facts.* NJ: Prentice-Hall, 1988.

7

The Selection Interview

Researchers for decades have pointed out that the selection interview is a poor and costly means of screening, hiring, and placing applicants.[1] All too often employers are untrained, ill-prepared, biased, ask discriminatory questions, see physically attractive applicants as most qualified, and pick employees most like themselves in temperament. And all too often applicants are equally untrained and ill-prepared, naive about the process, unable to perform their best because of anxiety and tension, and lie or leave out negative information about themselves. Employers tend to push applicants for information to make a decision while applicants pull employers into an information giving, story-telling, and advising mode.[2]

In spite of the selection interview's well-documented deficiencies in predicting success and its susceptibility to bias and distortion, it remains "a central component of most organizational selection procedures."[3] Selecting employees and positions is an elaborate courtship process, and few people want to select an organizational partner sight unseen. The authors of this text have more than fifty years of combined experiences in hiring employees, and they remain amazed at how awful paper-perfect applicants are when they are met in person and asked a few thought-provoking questions. No matter how elaborate résumés, application forms, paper and pencil tests, handwriting analyses, and background searches may be, there is still no substitute for face-to-face interactions. Applicants have had much the same experience with employers after reviewing organizational propaganda and being on the receiving end of elaborate public relations campaigns. Organizations use interviews not only to select new employees and determine where they best fit into organizations but to sell themselves to applicants and to create favorable public relations with potential consumers of products and services.[4] Applicants use interviews not only to compete for specific positions and market themselves but to gain valuable experiences and determine which offers to accept and reject.

This chapter cannot give you simple formulas for success, provide shortcuts in the process, or provide surefire answers to questions, but it can prepare you for the hard work of selecting employees and obtaining positions, provide guidelines for typical interviews, and introduce you to valuable resources. We have three goals in this chapter. The *short range goal* is to help you seek and secure a good position. The *intermediate range goal* is to help you select employees because, unless you are very unusual, you will play the employer role far more often in your lifetime than the applicant role, regardless of the positions you may hold. And the *long range goal* is to improve the selection process.

Figure 7.1 Steps for the employer

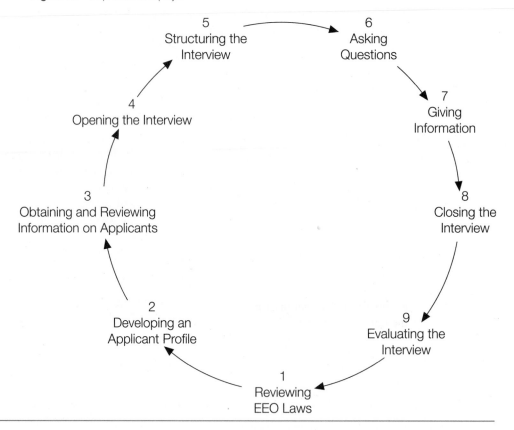

Since the selection interview is certain to remain a central component of selecting employees and attaining positions, both employers and applicants must approach the process systematically and learn how to prepare for, participate in, and evaluate interviews. Although Part 1 focuses on the employer in the selection process and Part 2 focuses on the applicant in the selection process, read and study both parts carefully because you can be an effective employer or applicant only if you understand how the other party is likely to participate.

Part 1—The Employer and the Selection Interview _____

Organizations must make interviewing a systematic and structured part of the selection process, and this involves a series of steps illustrated in figure 7.1. An essential first step is to review relevant Equal Employment Opportunity (EEO) laws.

Step 1: Reviewing EEO Laws

If you are involved in any way with hiring employees for your organization, you must be acquainted with the equal employment opportunity laws passed by Congress to eliminate discrimination in the selection of employees. In a study of 157 organizations in Wisconsin, Springston and Keyton found that an amazing 96 percent would or might ask at least one unlawful question in each interview.[5] And in a study reported recently in the *Wall Street Journal,* 70 percent of 200 interviewers and recruiters for Fortune 500 companies thought at least five of twelve unlawful questions were "safe to ask."[6] Ignorance or disregard of the law can lead to noncompliance and lawsuits against your organization. EEO laws pertain to all organizations that (1) deal with the federal government, (2) have more than fifteen employees, (3) have more than $50,000 in government contracts, and (4) engage in interstate commerce. You should be familiar with the following laws and Executive Orders:[7]

1. The Civil Rights Acts of 1866, 1870, and 1871 prohibited discrimination against minorities.
2. The Equal Pay Act of 1963 required equal pay for men and women performing work that involves similar skill, effort, responsibility, and working conditions.
3. The Civil Rights Act of 1964, particularly Title VII, prohibited the selection of employees based on race, color, sex, religion, or national origin, and required employers to discover discriminatory practices and eliminate them. Congress created the Equal Employment Opportunity Commission to ensure compliance and was concerned with the *results,* not the *intents,* of hiring practices.
4. Executive Order 11246, issued in 1965 and amended in 1967, prohibited discrimination and required government contractors to take "affirmative action" to assure that applicants were treated equally.
5. The Age Discrimination in Employment Act of 1967 prohibited employers of twenty-five or more persons from discriminating against persons because of age.
6. The Equal Employment Opportunity Act of 1972 extended the Civil Rights Act of 1964 to public and private educational institutions, labor organizations, and employment agencies.
7. The Rehabilitation Act of 1973 ordered federal contractors to hire handicapped persons, and included alcoholism, asthma, rheumatoid arthritis, and epilepsy as handicaps.
8. The Vietnam Era Veterans Readjustment Act of 1974 encouraged employers to hire qualified Vietnam veterans, including those who were disabled.
9. The Immigration Reform and Control Act of 1987 prohibited discrimination on the basis of citizenship.
10. The Americans with Disabilities Act of 1990 (effective July 25, 1992) prohibited discrimination against persons with physical or mental impairments which substantially limits or restricts the condition, manner, or duration under which they can perform one or more major life activities.

Compliance with EEO laws and guidelines is relatively easy if everything you do, say, or ask during the selection process pertains to *bona fide occupational qualifications* (BFOQs), requirements essential for performing a particular job.[8] BFOQs usually include work experiences, training, education, skills, physical attributes, and personality traits, and usually exclude sex, age, race, religion, physical appearance, handicaps, citizenship, and ethnic group. Exceptions are made if an employer can demonstrate that one or more normally unlawful traits are essential for a position.

A few simple guidelines will help you avoid most EEO violations. First, the test is called the "test of job relatedness," so be sure all questions are related to the specific position for which you are interviewing applicants. For example, if transportation is not a concern for this position, do not ask about it. Second, ask the same questions for all applicants. If you are asking certain questions only of female, handicapped, older, or minority applicants, you are almost certainly asking unlawful questions. When in doubt, use the "white male over 40 test." If you are about to ask a question about child care, age, physical ability to perform a task, or ethnic background that you would never ask a white male applicant over 40, alarm bells should go off in your head. And third, avoid general interest or curiosity questions. These will rarely deal with BFOQ's and may lead you into a thicket of EEO violations unintentionally.

Test your knowledge about what you can and cannot ask during selection interviews by rating each question below as *lawful* (can be asked), *probably lawful/unlawful* (may be asked under certain circumstances), or *unlawful* (cannot be asked).[9]

1. Who will take care of your children when they are ill?
    This may be lawful if you ask it of all applicants, but it is unlawful if asked only of women. Probably unlawful.
2. Do you have friends who work for Williams Pharmaceutical?
    This question might reveal a bias toward white, middle class males who are likely to dominate employees of most companies and thus would be unlawful. This is in a gray area, so avoid it and similar questions. Probably unlawful.
3. How have you kept such a great body if you graduated from high school in 1970?
    This is not a BFOQ and, since it would probably be asked only of females, could be used as a basis for a sex discrimination charge. Unlawful.
4. The only wheel chair access restroom is on the sixth floor. Would you mind going up there to use it?
    Organizations are required to make "reasonable accommodations" if they have more than 25 employees each workday and have had such a number for 20 or more weeks this year or the preceding year. Restrooms must be made equally available to all employees. Unlawful.
5. Would you mind if I called you by your first name?
    It is often a good idea to use an applicant's first name to avoid the cumbersome and formal Ms., Miss, Mrs., or Mr. Lawful.
6. Are you a citizen of the United States?
    You may ask this question if citizenship is a BFOQ. If the answer is no, you may ask, "When do you intend to become a citizen?" or "Do you have legal sanction to remain in the United States?" You cannot ask how or when citizenship was obtained unless the position involves national security. Lawful.

7. Are you married or living with someone?
   Marital or living status is not a BFOQ. Unlawful.
8. What professional societies do you belong to?
   This is likely to be a BFOQ. You may not ask about social, religious, or political memberships. Lawful.
9. Because of your limited vision, you will need a braille keyboard at your computer, won't you?
   You must be willing to make "reasonable accommodations," and specific needs such as a braille keyboard can be determined after a person is hired. Unlawful.
10. Would your wife be available to entertain clients?
    This question probes into marital status and a person's availability who will not be on the payroll. Unlawful.
11. Could you work or travel on the weekends?
    If this is a BFOQ, it would be lawful. However, if it is not a justifiable BFOQ, it might violate the religious beliefs and practices of some applicants and be unlawful. Probably Lawful.
12. What foreign languages can you write or speak?
    If speaking or writing a foreign language is a BFOQ and you are not asking how or where the person learned the language, it is lawful.
13. How long would you expect to work for us?
    This question is most likely to be asked of female and older applicants. Unlawful.
14. What kinds of people do you enjoy working with the most?
    This may be asked if both you and the applicant avoid such characteristics as age, sex, race, religion, and ethnic groups. However, you are opening yourself up for receiving prejudicial information and legal charges. Probably lawful.
15. Describe for me your greatest strengths as an employee.
    This question seems to probe into working strengths. Lawful.

You must keep abreast of EEO laws and interpretations, or you may be the cause of an expensive lawsuit against your organization. A study by Wilson discovered that the most common areas probed into unlawfully were arrest record, age, and handicaps followed by marital and family status and religion.[10]

Keep several rules in mind when asking questions. First, federal laws supersede state laws unless the state laws are more restrictive. Second, the Equal Employment Opportunity Commission (EEOC) is not concerned with intent but with effect. Third, advertise each position where *all qualified* applicants have a *reasonable opportunity* to learn about the opening: newspapers, placement centers, company bulletin boards and publications, and professional journals. Fourth, your organization is liable if unlawful information is maintained or used even if you did not ask for it. If an applicant volunteers unlawful information, stop the applicant and explain that your organization does not use such information for hiring purposes. Fifth, do not write or make notes on the application blank. In the past, some organizations used notes or codes to indicate race, ethnic group, and physical appearance of applicants. Even doodling on an application may appear to be a code. And sixth, never ask certain questions only of female, minority, handicapped, ethnic, or older applicants.

Step 2: Developing an Applicant Profile

With EEO laws clearly in mind, conduct a job analysis to determine the knowledge, skills, and personal traits necessary to perform a position satisfactorily, and then develop a specific *profile* of the ideal employee for the position. There are a number of ways to develop this profile. You can develop, with the help of managers and human resources personnel, a competency model of traits, skills, and motives from research on individuals who do the job well. You may develop a profile by searching literature, interviewing incumbents, supervisors, and associates, observing and analyzing actual performance on the job, and standardizing job requirements. You might do a systematic study of outstanding people in the field. Or you may analyze existing employee responses to job performance questions to distinguish good from bad performance characteristics.[11]

Competency based employee profiles typically include specific skills, abilities, experiences, education, knowledge levels, personal characteristics, and interpersonal relationships.[12] Each applicant is measured against this profile in an effort to choose the applicant that comes closest to the ideal employee. The profile approach helps organizations follow EEO guidelines, makes the selection process more objective, encourages all interviewers to cover the same topics, and reduces the "birds-of-a-feather syndrome" in which interviewers tend to favor applicants who are most similar to themselves.[13]

Some organizations such as Bristol Myers have begun to employ a "behavior-based selection technique" to assure that each interviewer matches each applicant with the ideal employee profile.[14] Four principles underlie this technique: (1) behavior that is observable can be rated; (2) behavior that is not seen must be probed for; (3) the best predictor of future behavior is past behavior; and (4) job-related behavior in the interview is a good indicator of future job performance. The behavior-based selection technique begins with a needs and job analysis to determine which *behaviors* are essential for performing a particular job. The following are observable behaviors that might be important for specific positions:

achievement	empathy	persistence
affiliation	endurance/stamina	responsibility
aggressiveness	honesty	responsiveness
ambition	impulsiveness	self-confidence
assertiveness	initiative	self-starter
competitiveness	leadership	sensitivity
consistency	listening	sincerity
courage	motivation	sympathy
decisiveness	oral communication	tenacity
dependability	organization-oriented	tough-minded
discipline	people-oriented	

Behaviors being sought must be job-related and clearly defined so that all interviewers are looking for the same ones. Once the relevant behaviors are determined, the organization creates a moderately or highly scheduled interview to elicit these behaviors. A structured interview is essential for skillful patterning and selecting of questions, recording responses, and rating applicants on behaviorally defined dimensions.[15] In the following example, the interviewer would employ a five-point scale to rate each answer according to the degree to which it exhibits or gives information about one or more behaviors: 5 = strongly present and 1 = minimally present.

Rating	Behavior	Question
_____	Initiative	What have you done to take an idea from birth to implementation?
_____	Energy	How many times have you done this?
_____	General intelligence	What was the outcome?
_____	Decisiveness	How did you feel about the results you got?
_____	Adaptability	When faced with a difficult obstacle, what did you do?

When listening to the answer to the first question, for example, the interviewer would be looking for the kinds of projects or ideas the applicant had implemented, their complexity, originality, and success, and the plan the applicant created and carried out. The answer would likely reveal a number of other behaviors such as organizational ability, meeting of deadlines, time taken to complete tasks, and ability to think. Three to five interviewers may interview the same applicant and rate each applicant on a five-point scale with the goal of reaching a .5 interrater reliability or agreement.

While the behavior based interview focuses on how an applicant did handle actual work-related situations in the past, a critical incidents approach or hypothetical approach focuses on how an applicant would handle work related situations.[16] Each is based on a carefully prepared applicant profile and relies on a carefully structured interview. In a critical incidents approach, an organization selects actual critical incidents that occurred on the job and asks applicants how they would have handled the incidents. In a hypothetical approach, an organization creates highly realistic hypothetical situations and asks applicants how they would handle each. All three approaches are based on the belief that responses to "How did you" and "How would you" questions produce more valid results than traditional interviews that rely upon "theoretical" questions for which applicants have already prepared canned answers: "What do you believe is the best way to handle conflict?" or "What qualities are essential for leadership?"[17]

Step 3: Obtaining and Reviewing Information on Applicants

Try to obtain as much information as possible on applicants prior to interviews through application forms, résumés, letters of recommendation, and objective tests. You want to begin to develop a "sense of the professional and personal qualities of each job applicant."[18] Design the application form with the ideal employee profile in mind, and avoid traditional categories that violate EEO guidelines: marital status, physical characteristics, age, arrest records, type of military discharge, and request for a picture. Provide adequate space for applicants to answer all questions thoroughly, and include a few open-ended questions similar to ones you will ask during the interview. Review each résumé to see how well the applicant's career objective meets the employee profile, and then how well the applicant's education, training, and experiences complement the stated career objective. Be sure to delete any unlawful information from the résumé (picture, age, marital status, religious organizations, etc.); you and your organization cannot be accused of using what you do not have. Review letters of recommendation with skepticism because most are written by friends or admirers and rarely contain negative information. Letters can reveal who an applicant knows, who will write letters for the applicant, and bits of information about how well the applicant fits the profile.

If you use objective tests such as honesty, personality inventory, self-assessment, and customized specialty tests (as an increasing percentage of employers are), use them as only one measure of suitability. Be sure all such tests (1) are designed to reveal relevant occupational qualifications, (2) have been validated on a cross-section of the population, and (3) meet EEO guidelines. Ensure confidentiality of results, and obtain the applicant's written consent to be tested and a waiver of liability claims for use or reliance on test results.[19]

Now that polygraph (lie detector) tests can no longer be used in the employee selection process, many organizations are resorting to *honesty tests* to determine if applicants are honest. If your organization chooses to use such a test, be sure the test will do what you want it to do, distinguish honest from dishonest applicants. The best advice, as with any test, is to use it as *part* of the total selection process. One recent study recommends that truth can best be determined through an analysis and comparison of factual information about the applicant, an honesty test, and a thorough probing interview.[20] The study concludes that an accurate reading of the applicant's verbal and nonverbal reactions to questions can help the interviewer separate truth from deception. Truthful applicants tended to identify in some detail the issue under investigation, acknowledge the probability of employee theft, respond without hesitation, suggest harsher punishment than deceptive counterparts, reject the idea of leniency, and expect favorable test results.

A task force of the American Psychological Association reviewed over 200 studies and concluded that honesty tests identify individuals who have a high propensity for stealing in the work place.[21] But what about applicants who fall into the moderate to low ranges? Robert Fitzpatrick, a Washington attorney who specializes in employment law, warns, "While they (honesty tests) might screen out some undesirable job candidates, they also screen out (like the old polygraph tests) a tremendous percentage of perfectly honest, upstanding citizens."[22] And Wayne J. Camara, Director of Scientific Affairs for the American Psychological Association, warns that "An honest applicant may not be the best qualified. Poor performance may mean greater losses than theft."[23] Whether or not you use an honesty test, protect your organization in case you discover, after making an offer or bringing a person on board, that the individual was dishonest during the hiring process. Place the following statement on all application forms: "Falsification of information in the application or interview will be viewed as grounds for refusal or termination of employment."[24]

Previewing information on the applicant should serve not only as an initial screening step but also as an important part of the total selection process. For example, the preview should give you a fairly clear notion of your relationship with the applicant by revealing how much each of you wants to take part in the interview, the degree of affection you have toward one another, and how control is likely to be shared. The preview should also reveal areas to probe and allow you to compare the applicant's oral and written answers. Jablin and Miller discovered that employers who review applicant credentials thoroughly

Review the applicant's credentials prior to the interview so you can devote full attention to questions and answers.

tended to ask more questions, a wider variety of questions, and to probe more into answers.[25] The preview should not prejudice you so that favorable impressions from paper credentials guarantee favorable impressions during the interview regardless of what the applicant does and says. On the other hand, Macan and Dipboye found that interviewers asked questions biased in a negative way of applicants with what they perceived to be poor credentials.[26] The preview or the interview should not dominate the final hiring decision. The decision should be based on all available information gathered to that time.[27]

Step 4: Opening the Interview

Approach each interview in a positive manner, realizing that it is likely to be a major event in the applicant's life and is a great public relations opportunity for your organization. Try to give the impression that this interview is the day's top priority. There is a clear correlation between how applicants are treated and the way they talk about organizations later.[28] You are your organization as far as the applicant is concerned, and the applicant is more likely to accept an offer if you are perceived to be a good representative of your organization. Applicants describe ideal representatives as warm, thoughtful, sensitive, and nondirective interviewers who listen well, exhibit empathy, and show interest in them.[29] Many organizations are experimenting with group or "board" interviews in which two or more interviewers interview an applicant at the same time, but research indicates that this approach has no advantage over the single-interviewer interview and that both applicants and interviewers prefer the "sequential" interview in which the applicant meets a series of interviewers one at a time.[30] Other organizations are experimenting with group interviews in which one recruiter interviews several applicants at the same time. This approach is subject to the pitfalls of individual interviews, but it takes less time and provides greater scope and insight as interviewees build on each others' comments.[31] And other organizations are resorting to group or panel interviews in which members divide up the client's résumé and application form with one member asking about previous work experiences, a second asking about education and training, and a third asking about specific job-related skills. The increasing use of assessment center methodologies and behavior selection strategies is making the group or panel interview more popular.

Begin the selection interview by greeting the applicant by name in a warm, friendly voice and with a firm but not crunching handshake. Introduce yourself and your position with the organization. If appropriate, you might engage in a bit of small talk about a non-controversial topic, but do not prolong casual conversation or fall into overworn questions such as "What do you think of this weather?" and "How was your trip down?" Prolonged idle chatting heightens tension by creating anxiety and suspense.[32]

Proceed to the orientation phase of the opening in which you tell the applicant how the interview will proceed: first, questions from you; second, information about the position and the organization; and third, questions from the applicant. You might tell the applicant how long the interview will take and approximately how much time you will devote to each part. If the interview is taking place during a "plant trip," you might provide the applicant with an agenda for the visit and the names and positions of people who will be involved in the selection process. Then ask an open-ended, easy-to-answer first question that gets the applicant talking about a familiar subject: education, experiences, background, and so on. The common "Tell me about yourself" is too open, often leaving the applicant in a quandary about where to begin and how much information to give. Do not put the applicant on the spot too early because studies reveal that interviewers tend to put more weight on negative information, and the earlier it comes in the interview, the more devastating it tends to be.

Step 5: Structuring the Interview

Interviewers have traditionally approached the interview in an unstructured manner, often having no more than a few favorite questions in mind. Research during the last several years has revealed the hazards of the *unstructured* selection interview:[33]

1. Interviewers tend to talk more than applicants rather than the preferred rate of 80 percent for applicants and 20 percent for employers.
2. Interviewers tend to make their decisions within the first four minutes, long before all data has been obtained from the interview.
3. Only factual biographical information (easily obtainable through written application forms) is covered consistently.
4. Ratings of applicants differ significantly among an organization's interviewers.
5. Interviewers are more susceptible to stereotyped biases and more likely to ask unlawful questions.

Use at least a moderately scheduled interview to avoid the hazards of the unstructured interview. Many organizations that employ a behavior-based selection technique are beginning to use highly scheduled interviews to improve the reliability of the selection process. Specific questions are designed to elicit specific observable behaviors. Structured interviews may be more reliable than unstructured interviews because all interviewers are forced to ask the same or very similar questions and to pay more attention to the applicant throughout the interview instead of just during the first few minutes. Therefore, there is an increased use of highly structured, tailored interviews rather than the traditional chit-chat unstructured interview because some studies show that the structured interview is twice as valid as the unstructured interview.[34] The tailored interview may be structured around specific traits in the applicant profile or around an interview guide such as: (1) whether the person can do the job, (2) whether the person will do the job, and (3) whether the person will fit into the organization.[35]

Selecting a sequence of questions is an important structural decision. A study by Tengler and Jablin discovered that interviewers tend to use the inverted funnel sequence by asking closed primary questions during the early minutes of the interview and open-ended secondary questions in the later minutes.[36] Some interviewers apparently use the inverted sequence to "test" applicants and then switch to a funnel sequence with applicants they perceive to be most qualified.[37] Since applicants tend to give short answers to primary questions while they "feel out" the interviewer's purpose and longer answers and more information to secondary questions, interviewers who are prone to making snap judgments within the first few minutes or who test applicants within this time base their decisions on minimal information.[38] Also, the best way to relax an applicant is to get the person talking, but the inverted funnel sequence begins with closed questions and permits the interviewer to dominate the conversation. The solution is to begin with a funnel sequence to get the interviewee talking and begin obtaining maximum information immediately.

Step 6: Asking Questions

Questions are the primary tools interviewers use to obtain information and determine how well applicants match the ideal employee profile. Questions should be open-ended, neutral, and job-specific.[39] Open-ended questions are critical to successful interviews. They encourage applicants to do the talking while you can listen, observe behavior, and formulate effective secondary questions. Not only do applicants give longer answers to open-ended questions, but they feel greater satisfaction with interviews that are dominated by open primary and secondary questions.[40] Like all probing interviewers, however, employers often create many questions on-the-spot to detect relevant behaviors and probe for specifics, clarity, and implied meanings. This spontaneity makes employers susceptible to several question pitfalls.

1. The *bipolar trap* in which the interviewer asks yes/no questions instead of open-ended questions.

    > **Bad:** Do you have experiences with computer record systems?
    > **Good:** What experiences do you have with computer record systems?

2. The *open-to-closed switch* in which the interviewer asks an open-ended question but rephrases it as a closed question before the applicant can respond.

> **Bad:** Tell me about your duties at Jones Memorial Hospital. Did you work with terminally ill patients?
>
> **Good:** Tell me about your duties at Jones Memorial Hospital.

3. The *double-barrelled* question in which the interviewer asks two or more questions and is likely to get an answer to only one of the two and is unlikely to get a revealing answer to either question.

> **Bad:** Tell me about your training and experiences in sales.
>
> **Good:** Tell me about your training in sales.

4. The *leading push* in which the interviewer suggests how the applicant ought to respond and thus may not get a truthful answer.

> **Bad:** I assume you would be willing to work a night shift?
>
> **Good:** How would you feel about being assigned to a night shift?

5. The *guessing game* in which the interviewer tries to guess information instead of asking for it.

> **Bad:** Did you leave your last position because you went back to school?
>
> **Good:** Why did you leave your last position?

6. The *evaluative response* in which the interviewer expresses judgmental feelings about an answer and may affect the applicant's willingness to be frank in later responses.

> **Bad:** That wasn't a good reason to quit a job, was it?
>
> **Good:** How do you feel now about that reason for leaving a job?

7. *EEO violation* questions in which the interviewer asks an unlawful question.

> **Bad:** What organizations do you belong to?
>
> **Good:** What professional organizations do you belong to?

8. *Yes (or No) response* questions in which the interviewer mistakenly gives the applicant only one possible choice.

> **Bad:** Do you feel you can handle this position?
>
> **Good:** What in your background do you feel will enable you to handle this position?

9. The *résumé-application* question in which the interviewer asks for information already available on the résumé or application form.

> **Bad:** Where did you get your training in accounting?
>
> **Good:** Tell me about your training in accounting.

The following are typical selection questions that avoid pitfalls and gather important job-related information.

Interest in the Organization
1. Why would you like to work for us?
2. How did you hear about this opening?
3. What material have you read about our organization?
4. What do you know about our products and services?
5. What do you know about the history of our organization?

Work Related (General)
1. Tell me about the position that has given you the most satisfaction?
2. How have your previous work experiences prepared you for this position?
3. Why did you choose this career?
4. What did you do that was innovative in your last position?
5. What do you think your previous supervisors would cite as your strengths?

Work Related (Specific)
1. What tactics do you use to get your point across?
2. Describe a typical strategy you would use in a sales call.
3. What criteria do you use when assigning work to others?
4. Tell me about a situation in which you made a wrong decision and how you corrected it.
5. How do you follow up on work assigned to subordinates?

Education and Training
1. What special skills do you have?
2. Which aspects of your education have prepared you best for this position?
3. Which courses did you like most in college?
4. If you had your education to do over, what would you do differently?
5. Why did you choose _____ as your major?

Career Plans and Goals
1. What are your long-range career plans?
2. If you join our organization, what would you like to be doing five years from now?
3. How do you feel about the way your career has gone so far?
4. What are you doing to prepare yourself for advancement?
5. Who influenced you most in your career choice?

Job Performance
1. What do you believe are the most important performance criteria in your area of expertise?
2. How do you ensure that you are receiving feedback pertaining to your performance?
3. All of us have pluses and minuses in our performance; what are some of your pluses?
4. What criteria do you use when making decisions?
5. How were you evaluated during your last two evaluations?

Salary and Benefits

1. What kind of salary would you need to join us?
2. What would you consider to be a good annual increase?
3. Which fringe benefits are most important to you?
4. How does our salary range compare to your last position?
5. If you had to do without a fringe benefit, which would it be?

Career Field

1. What do you think is the greatest challenge facing your field today?
2. What do you think will be the next major breakthrough in your field?
3. Which area of your field do you think will expand the most during the next five years?
4. How do you feel about government controls in your field?
5. What do you see as the major trends in your field?

Many interviewers are employing information getting tactics beyond the typical interview question.[41] For instance, some organizations create idealistic employee policy statements and observe the reactions of applicants as the statements are read. Only about 20 percent of applicant reactions are considered positive. Other organizations are using job simulations that involve the applicant in actual job tasks related to the position. A variation of this is the elaborate hypothetical situation question or an actual role-play, with the interviewer acting as a reluctant prospect, a hostile employee, or a client. Some applicants are asked to make technical presentations to members of an organization who then evaluate the presentations.

Regardless of the methods used, design the questioning phase of the interview to explore how well the applicant meets the ideal employee profile. Get specifics, explore suggestions or implications in responses, clarify meanings, and force the applicant to get beyond Level 1 responses to reveal feelings, preferences, knowledge, and expertise. Remember that there are always two applicants in an interview, the *real* and the *make-believe,* and your task is to determine how much of what you see and hear is a facade for the interview and how much is genuine. Research suggests that interviewers have difficulty making this distinction.[42] Listen carefully to all that is and is not said, and be responsive. Use silent, reflective, and content probes. Applicants feel less threatened and more respected when interviewers respond with simple verbal and nonverbal signals and do not interrupt them.[43] However, do not fall into the trap of saying "Good!" after each response, acting as a kind of selection cheerleader.

Step 7: Giving Information

Before you begin to give information, ask two important transition questions: What do you know about this position? and What do you know about our organization? These questions reveal what the applicant knows about the position and organization and can provide valuable information. First, they show how much homework the applicant has done, thus revealing the applicant's level of interest and willingness to work. And, second, they tell you how much the applicant already knows so that you can begin where the knowledge leaves off.

Give adequate information to facilitate the matching process between your organization and the applicant. Information about an organization's reputation, the position, and advancement opportunities have been found to be the most important factors in acceptance of job offers.[44] Compare yourself to your competitors, but do not be negative. Sell the advantages of your position and organization. Do not lie to applicants, intentionally hide negative aspects of the position or organization, or inflate applicant expectations. Such practices are likely to result in a high rate of employee turnover. Tell applicants what a typical day at work will be like. Avoid gossip and do not talk too much about yourself. While you want to inform applicants thoroughly, do not allow your information giving to dominate interviews. Some studies suggest that applicants speak for only ten minutes in the typical thirty-minute interview.[45] Reverse this figure, because you can learn more about the applicant by listening than by talking.

Step 8: Closing the Interview

If you have the authority to hire on the spot (rare in campus interviews but frequent when interviewing for hourly workers), either offer the position or terminate further consideration. If you do not have hiring authority or this is merely a screening interview, explain specifically what the applicant can expect after the completion of the interview. For example:

> Well, Elizabeth, as you know, we are interviewing a number of people for this position and will invite four or five to go through an additional interview at our home office in Cleveland. You will be notified from my office by mail within the next week to ten days as to whether or not you will be asked to come for the next round of interviews. Do you have any final questions?

Thank applicants for their time, give them your address and telephone number (perhaps a business card), and encourage them to write or call you personally if they have any questions.

Do not encourage or discourage applicants needlessly. If you have many excellent applicants for a position, do not give each the impression that he or she is at the top of the list. If you know an applicant will not be considered further, do not "string the person along" with false hope. Let the individual down gently. An applicant you cannot use at this time may prove ideal for a future opening.

Be sure that your office follows up on all prospects. If possible, have all letters typed and signed by you or your representative. A personal touch, even when rejecting an applicant, can maintain a feeling of goodwill toward you and your organization.

Step 9: Evaluating the Interview

Record your impressions of each applicant as soon as possible after each interview. Many organizations provide interviewers with standardized evaluation forms to match applicants with the ideal employee profile for each position.[46] If the interview was a screening interview, you must decide whether to invite the applicant for a plant trip. If the interview was a determinate interview during a plant trip, you must decide whether to offer a position or send a rejection notice (the infamous "ding letter").

Figure 7.2 Interviewer's evaluation report

INTERVIEWER'S EVALUATION REPORT

Applicant _____ Position _____

Interviewer _____ Date _____ Location _____

	Poor	Fair	Good	Very Good	Ex.
Interest in This Position	——	——	——	——	——
Knowledge of the Company	——	——	——	——	——
Education/Training	——	——	——	——	——
Experiences	——	——	——	——	——
Maturity	——	——	——	——	——
Adaptability	——	——	——	——	——
Assertiveness	——	——	——	——	——
Ability to Communicate	——	——	——	——	——
Appearance	——	——	——	——	——

1. What are the applicant's major strengths?

2. What are the applicant's major weaknesses?

3. How does this applicant compare to other applicants for this position?

Overall Rating: Unfavorable   1   2   3   4   5   Favorable

The interview evaluation often consists of two parts: a set of standardized questions and a set of open questions (see figure 7.2). The standardized part should consist of bona fide occupational qualifications for each position and be extensive enough to allow you to determine how well the applicant matches these qualifications. The following are typical open-ended questions:

1. What are the applicant's strengths?
2. What are the applicant's weaknesses?
3. How does this applicant compare to other applicants for the position?

4. How well would this applicant fit into our organization?
5. How accurate is the applicant's conception of what this position entails?

You should also evaluate your own interviewing skills and performance. The following can serve as self-evaluation questions:

1. How successfully did I create an informal, relaxed atmosphere?
2. How effectively did I encourage the applicant to speak freely and openly?
3. How thoroughly did I explore the applicant's qualifications for this position?
4. How thoroughly did I provide information the applicant needed?
5. Did I reserve adequate time for the applicant to ask questions?
6. Did I reserve judgment until the interview was completed?

Part 2: The Applicant and the Selection Process _____

Applicants, like organizations, must make interviewing a systematic and structured part of the job search and selection. This involves a series of steps illustrated in figure 7.3. You must prepare thoroughly for each selection interview because no two interviews or positions will be exactly the same. If you decide to "wing it," (to learn as you go), you will face many disappointments. Preparation includes the first four steps in the process.

Step 1: Analyzing Yourself

Begin by conducting a thorough and insightful inventory of yourself, including your needs, desires, strengths/weaknesses, likes/dislikes, and experiences. Self-analysis may be painful, but you must know yourself before you can determine the "ideal position" and the "ideal organization." As John Crystal and Richard Bolles write, "You have got to know what it is you want, or someone else is going to sell you a bill of goods somewhere along the line that can do irreparable damage to your self-esteem, your sense of worth, and your stewardship of the talents that God gave you."[47] The following questions can serve as guides for your personal inventory:[48]

1. What are your personality strengths? Weaknesses?·
2. What are your intellectual strengths? Weaknesses?·
3. What are your communicative strengths? Weaknesses?
4. What have been your accomplishments? Failures?
5. What things and activities give you the greatest satisfaction? The least satisfaction?
6. What do you need to be a happy human being? What do you not need?
7. What skills do you have? Need to acquire?
8. What are your abilities? Inabilities?
9. What are your educational strengths? Weaknesses?
10. Why did you select _____ as your major? How happy/unhappy have you been with this selection?
11. Why did you select _____ for your degree/training? How happy/unhappy have you been with this selection?
12. What professional experiences do you have? What do you lack?

Figure 7.3 Steps for the applicant

13. What is important to you in a position? Unimportant?
14. What is important to you in an organization? Unimportant?
15. What are your short-range career goals? Long-range career goals?

By the time you answer these questions, you should have a detailed self-inventory, a list of short-term objectives, and perhaps a career goal or life mission statement. If you know who you are, what you want, where you are, and where you want to go, your chances of determining how to get there are good. Do not settle too quickly on a position title or a narrow description. Focus rather on the kinds of activities and achievements that give you satisfaction, because you are unlikely to be aware of all the opportunities open to you now and in the future.

Step 2: Preparing Your Résumé

Once you have analyzed yourself thoroughly, prepare one or more résumés, depending upon the types of positions you have decided to apply for. Your résumé is your silent sales representative, so make it professional and persuasive.[49] Many employers spend only a few seconds with each résumé, so you must gain and maintain attention if you hope to get beyond the application stage. The following are suggestions for a typical résumé that is appropriate for most professions and positions.

Have the résumé professionally printed on white, off-white, or light beige bond paper. Although attention-getting colors such as yellow and orange may be suitable for creative positions in advertising or graphics, they are likely to be considered inappropriate by many employers. Pay particular attention to how the résumé is blocked so that it looks attractive, organized, carefully planned, and not crowded; employers like some white space on résumés. Use good grammar, check all spellings, and employ action verbs. Most employers prefer a single page but will accept a two-page résumé if the second page is necessary to give a complete picture of the applicant. If you must develop a two-page résumé, consider having it printed front to back on one sheet of paper because a stapled second page may get ripped off when the résumé is taken out of files or briefcases.

Develop carefully each part of your résumé. Be sure your name, perhaps in bold print, is set apart at the top of the page. Then include one or two complete addresses and telephone numbers where you can be reached during normal business hours and after hours. Be sure to include area codes with telephone numbers and zip codes with addresses. If an organization has trouble contacting you, it will turn to another applicant.

Prepare your career objective carefully; the employer is unlikely to read further if it is unimpressive or does not fit the ideal applicant profile. If you have more than one objective (middle management, sales, labor relations), make separate résumés for each objective. Many employers react negatively to jacks-of-all-trades. Target the résumé for particular organizations and positions. Give a detailed and precise career objective that reveals interest in the organization as well as information about yourself. The "me . . . me . . . me" syndrome in which you stress only what you hope to get out of a career may be a stopper. Avoid the word *job* which sounds like you are not interested in a career but in an 8-to-5 job you can escape as soon as the whistle blows.

Next, if you are a recent college graduate with few relevant experiences, give a persuasive account of your education and training to show that you are prepared for the position for which you are applying. In other words, lead with your strengths. If you are going to list schools, certificates, and degrees, place them in chronological order with the latest coming first. If you list key courses essential for a position or career, do not give abbreviations and numbers. The interviewer is unlikely to know whether Eng. 337 refers to an English or an engineering course. Explain courses and place them into meaningful groupings. Give your grade point average only if it is fairly high. Interviewers can always ask for GPAs during interviews if they consider them important.

After education and training, if you have chosen that order, present your work experiences, including paid and unpaid internships. Employers like to see practical experience. Place your experiences under meaningful categories and in reverse chronological order with the most recent first. Recent studies show that the primary concern of personnel administrators is applicant achievement or accomplishment.[50] Therefore, stress experiences most relevant to the position for which you are applying, and be sure your information and language show that you are a "doer" and a "winner." This will set you apart from a great many applicants. If you list activities in which you have taken part in college, community, or profession, emphasize your responsibilities and leadership positions. Prove that you get things done.

If you have professional certificates or licenses, awards such as "outstanding senior in civil engineering," or memberships in honorary societies such as Phi Beta Kappa and Golden Key, make note of them, with perhaps a brief description of ones with which the interviewer may be unfamiliar.

You may list some of your hobbies and extracurricular activities to reveal what you like to do apart from your professional life. Do not supply a list of references, merely note "References upon request."

Do not include a picture or give personal data such as marital status, age, physical appearance, race, religion, political affiliation, or ethnic group. You do not break any law if you do so, but you are providing information apart from bona fide occupational qualifications and assuming that an employer may hire you from unlawful criteria. Realize that you may *not* get a job because of this information. Many employers, keenly aware that they are liable for unlawful material you send them, employ "gatekeepers," secretaries or staff members who review all credentials, with instructions to discard pictures and place heavy black lines through such information as age, marital status, religion, and so on. As a result, your interviewer may see a mutilated version of your résumé instead of the carefully prepared professional one you sent (assuming of course that the employer will bother to interview a person with a mutilated résumé).

These résumé guidelines are applicable for most professions and positions, but you should know your field and position to determine if an unusual format, color, or presentation might be more suitable or attention-getting. Consider your strengths and weaknesses and how best to present yourself to a prospective employer. Figure 7.4 is a résumé created by a student in his thirties who has a large amount of practical work experiences but little that prepared him for a position in employee training. He opted to present his education ahead of experience. In figure 7.5, a twenty-two-year-old student included some work-related experiences but also chose to highlight a superior academic record. Her résumé lists awards and activities that reveal accomplishments and achievements. Note that specific duties are listed under each work-related experience.

Step 3: Doing Your Homework

Once you have analyzed yourself and prepared your résumé, you should study the job market, your chosen field, organizations to which you are applying, positions you are seeking, current events, and the interview process.[51]

The Changing Work Place

The world of work has changed dramatically since the late 1980s. Mergers and acquisitions have increased the number of organizations whose ownership is outside the United States, and the enormous economic growth of Japan, Korea, and Germany has made organizations focus on a global approach to doing business. Downsizing, rightsizing, and bankruptcies have eliminated some positions from the market place. "Secure" jobs in heavy industry have disappeared. Privatization of government agencies and severe state and federal budget cuts have reduced the security of government employment.

```
                    Dominic J. Leto, Jr.
                         Box 195
                 Mulberry, Indiana 46058
                     (317) 296-2350
```

Career Objective:
    An entry level position in employee training leading toward a career i
    plant operations management.

Education:
    Purdue University
        Bachelor of Science Degree in Industrial Education, May 1989
        GPA--Cumulative 5.14/6.00--Major 5.51/6.00

    Significant Courses
        Materials and Processes
          Polymer Materials and Processes, Machining of Metals and Plastic
          Forming and Fabricating Metal and Plastic, Industrial Product
          Simulation
        Power Mechanics
          Energy and Power Application and Service, Engine Problems and
          Repair
        Electricity
          Fundamentals of Electricity, Energy Conversion and Power
          Utilization, Energy Transmission and Power Control
        Education
          Educational Psychology, Industrial Education Teaching Methods,
          Organization and Management of Industrial Education Facilities,
          Student Teaching

Work Experience:
    Small Business Owner-Operator
        Diagnose and repair small engines from minor repairs to complete
        overhauls; maintain inventory and keep financial records
          Mulberry Lawn Mower Service, Mulberry, Indiana, January 1984 to
          present

    Lathe Operator
        Operated lathe while keeping parts within tolerances, changed tool
        and made machine adjustments

    Mold Operator
        Poured molten aluminum into molds to produce pistons

    Machine Set Up
        Diagnosed machine problems and set up machines for production
          Zollner Corp., Fort Wayne, Indiana, May 1980-January 1985

    Technician
        Maintained shop and Equipment, produced teaching aids for staff,
        operated a variety of wood, metal, and plastic processing machines
          Department of Industrial Education, Purdue University, March 198
          October 1989

References and additional information furnished upon request

Figure 7.5   Traditional résumé

JENNIFER MOLIERE

<table>
<tr><td><u>PRESENT ADDRESS</u></td><td><u>PERMANENT ADDRESS</u></td></tr>
<tr><td>143 Andrew Place #1
West Lafayette IN 47906
(319) 743-2208
Until May 1992</td><td>8421 Quincy Court
Fort Wayne IN 46835
(219) 485-9862
After May 1992</td></tr>
</table>

OBJECTIVE:

A position in Personnel and Human Resource Management. I particularly wish to utilize my organizational and administrative skills in support of corporate training and development programs.

EDUCATION:

Purdue University, West Lafayette, In 47907
Candidate for Bachelor of Arts Degree, May 1992
      Major: Organizational Communication
      Minor: Psychology
GPA: Major: 6.0   Cumulative: 5.88   (6.0 scale)
Selected courses: •Organizational Communication (Honors)
          •Personnel and Human Resource Management
          •Business Writing Utilizing Macintosh 4.0

AWARDS AND ACTIVITIES:

Phi Beta Kappa Honor Society
      •Selected junior year by School of Liberal Arts Faculty
Golden Key National Honors Society
      •Executive Board Member-Secretary
Phi Kappa Phi Honors Society
      •Top 5% of Junior Class at Purdue University
Fort Wayne Advertising Association Scholarship Recipient
      •Based on academic excellence in the field of communication
Women in Communication, Inc.
      •Member for 5 semesters

WORK EXPERIENCE:

Waterfield Mortgage Company   Fort Wayne, IN
  Administrative Assistant   Summer 1990 & 1991
      •Organizing complete mortgage files
      •Paying taxes for mortgagors
      •Working in Records, Taxes, and Insurance Servicing Departments

Purdue University Library System   West Lafayette, IN
  Reserve-Circulation Clerk   September 1990-Present
      •Working directly with faculty and students
      •Retrieving Reserve materials
      •Handling student inquires

Law firm of G. James Boeglin   Fort Wayne, IN
  Assistant to Legal Secretary   Summer 1989
      •Developing new legal document file organization system
      •Registering documents at city and county courthouses
        -Decrees   -Subpoenas   -Property Titles

VOLUNTEER ACTIVITIES:

Phone-a-thon for School of Liberal Arts
Conducted Residence Hall Tours

Figure 7.6   Organizational flattening of the 1990s

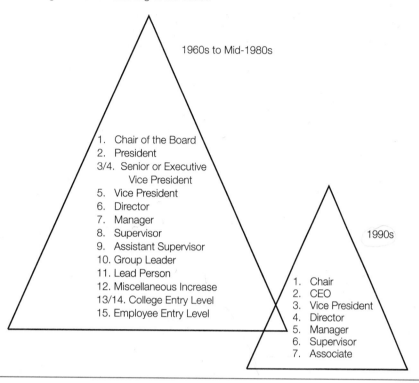

1960s to Mid-1980s

1. Chair of the Board
2. President
3/4. Senior or Executive
        Vice President
5. Vice President
6. Director
7. Manager
8. Supervisor
9. Assistant Supervisor
10. Group Leader
11. Lead Person
12. Miscellaneous Increase
13/14. College Entry Level
15. Employee Entry Level

1990s

1. Chair
2. CEO
3. Vice President
4. Director
5. Manager
6. Supervisor
7. Associate

Demographics of the work place have changed dramatically. A senior executive of a large outplacement firm stated at a recent seminar, "Any male under the age of thirty stands an 80 percent chance before his career is over of working for a woman or a minority." Women now comprise more than 50 percent of the workforce, and the growing Hispanic and Asian populations are changing profoundly the cultural mix of organizations. Workers over the age of sixty-five now account for the fastest growing part of the population; people are living longer and working longer.

What do these observations mean to you as an applicant? You will face increasing competition with larger numbers of applicants for a shrinking range of positions. The volume and range of positions available in the 1960s, 1970s, and 1980s are no longer there. "Organizational flattening" has greatly reduced the levels or steps historically available within organizations. Figure 7.6 illustrates how the 10–15 steps of a few years ago now number seven or fewer. The college graduate of the past might begin at level 14 or 15 and move up the ladder. Typical employees remained with an organization for 20, 30, or 40 years, even if they became frozen at a specific level. Career changes were two or three in the recent past; today you are likely to make five to seven career changes. The flat organization of the 1990s and into the next century with five to seven levels has fewer positions and little place for an average or below average person to hide or be pigeonholed. Employers are increasingly concerned with how applicants will fit into their organizational cultures; they are hiring more for the organization than for a particular position.[52] Therefore, you will need different characteristics and skills than your predecessors. The following are essential for the year 2000:

1. You must not only have specific job skills but be able to handle rapid change and periods of job ambiguity.
2. You must have computer literacy that enables you to enter, extract, and input data in common computer systems.
3. You must have a global perspective and understand other cultures.
4. You must have interpersonal skills both to secure a position and to move up within an organization.

Learning about Your Field, Organizations, and Positions

Learn everything you can about your field, including its history, developments, trends, areas of specialization, leaders, challenges, current and future problems, and employment opportunities. Develop a mature, realistic perception of what your field is like and what people do during a typical work day. Employers expect you to be acquainted with organizational life and to have positive attitudes toward your career, whether it be in business, academia, medicine, law, or another profession.

Learn everything you can about each organization to which you apply, including its leaders and staff, products and services (old, new, and future), geographical locations (plants, divisions, offices), expansion plans, potential mergers and growth. Also, learn about the organization's major competitors, financial status, nature of ownership, and its reputation in the field, particularly with its own clients, customers, students, or patients. You can discover information about these topics by writing to organizations or by talking to past employees, professors, and friends. Or you may consult recruiting literature, annual reports, and a variety of library sources such as the following:

Dictionary of Occupational Titles	*Occupational Outlook Handbook*
Dictionary of Professional Trade Organizations	*Open the Books: How to Research a Corporation*
Dun and Bradstreet's Middle Market Directory	*Standard and Poor's Corporation Records*
Dun and Bradstreet's Million Dollar Directory	*Standard and Poor's Industry Surveys*
Encyclopedia of Business Information Sources	*Standard and Poor's Register of Corporations, Directors and Executives*
Encyclopedia of Careers and Vocational Guidance	*The One Hundred Best Companies to Work for in America (by Levering, Moskowitz, and Katz)*
Guide for Occupational Exploration	*The Wall Street Journal*
Moody's Industrial Manual	*Thomas' Register of American Manufacturers*

Figure 7.7   The Cash position search model

All positions are comprised of these elements:

Your Talents/Skills and Abilities		The Position— What Must Be Done Daily/Weekly/Monthly

The Organization's Needs/Wants/Desires

What You Like About:	What You Dislike About:
the Organization the Position the People the Work Itself	the Organization the Position the Supervisor the Pay

You get paid for <u>EFFORT</u>, <u>ATTITUDE</u>, AND <u>RESULTS</u>.

EFFORT - Showing Up Ahead of Time and Prepared to Work

ATTITUDE - Being a Positive Influence on Others

RESULTS - Doing What Needs to be Done

Learn everything you can about the position for which you are applying, including responsibilities and duties, required experiences and training, type of supervision, advancement potential, amount of travel involved, location, starting date, job security, fringe benefits, training programs, salary and commissions, relocation possibilities and policies, and rate of turnover. A thorough knowledge of the position will allow you to (1) answer the interviewer's questions with specifics and without hesitation and (2) phrase meaningful questions of your own. The Cash Job Search Model illustrated in figure 7.7 may help you analyze each position in which you are interested.

Learning about Current Events

Learn everything you can about current events because employers expect mature applicants to be aware of what is going on in the world (locally, nationally, and internationally) and to have developed intelligent positions on important issues. Read a good daily newspaper and such periodicals as *Newsweek, Business Week,* and *Fortune.*

Learning about the Interview Process

Learn everything you can about what happens during interviews. What do employers look for? What turns them off? What kinds of questions do they ask? What kinds of interviewers will you face? How long do interviews last? What occurs during plant trips? You may find some surprising answers. For example, recent studies have revealed that 50 percent of "speech acts" in a sample of interviews were declarative statements rather than questions and answers, that most interviewers have no training in interviewing, that in a study of 49 interviews ten interviewers did not give applicants opportunities to ask questions, that interviewers may view the interview as a "work sample" and look for relevant job behaviors from applicants, and that interviewers often have three major questions in mind: can the person do the job, will the person do the job, and will the person fit into the organization.[53] When supervisors at Hughes Aircraft were asked to list the behaviors and information they looked for when evaluating applicants, they produced a pyramid (see figure 7.8). The most important behaviors and information to their organization are at the bottom and the least important are at the top.[54]

Many observers were surprised that integrity was cited as most important while specific skills were least important. The supervisors indicated that a highly skilled employee who was dishonest, narrow in knowledge, unable to communicate, immature, and unambitious would make a poor employee. Their pyramid merely visualized what a great many employers have espoused for years: honest, intelligent, well-educated persons who have the ability to communicate will go a long way with organizations. Narrowly trained specialists without other important traits will not.

Step 4: Conducting the Job Search

With résumé and homework completed, you should be ready to begin the job search in earnest. Be selective in the positions for which you apply, but choose a range of positions you would be happy with. For instance, instead of being set on a position as a cost accountant, try for a position in a good firm, with the hope of moving into cost accounting.

Networking

With the job search becoming ever more difficult, *networking* is essential for finding a good position. Take a sheet of paper and begin a "network tree" with names on one side and addresses and telephone numbers on the other. Start your tree with the most readily available sources: friends, acquaintances, relatives, former employers, internship directors, teachers, professors, insurance agents, real estate brokers, and family connections. Your primary contacts may be as many as fifty, but you can never have too many in a tight labor market. Call the person in slot number one and say you are looking for a *career opportunity,* never a *job.* The word job may give the negative impression that you are looking for anything that pays money. If this contact gives you a lead, write it down under this individual's name so you can recall who made the suggestion, and be sure to get the lead's full name and telephone number. If this contact has no opportunities, ask for three or four names of persons who might know of career possibilities. Everyone knows at least three possible leads if they think a bit or check their computer or Rolodex. Your original list of fifty may soon become one hundred or more. Be sure to thank each

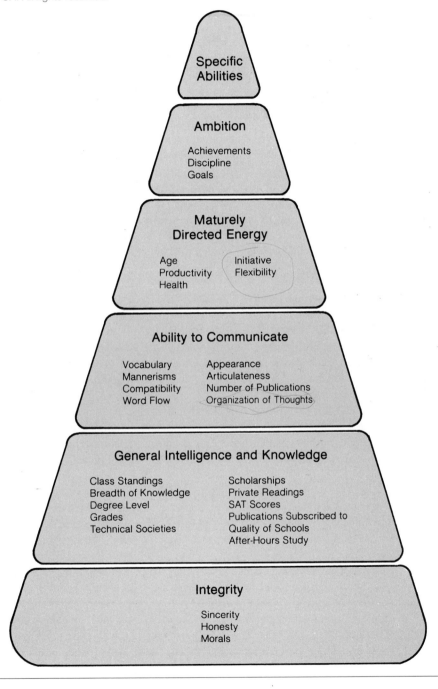

primary contact and ask, "You don't mind if I use your name when I call Fred Dugger, do you?" This yes response question is most likely going to obtain a positive response. When a networking contact leads to an interview, be sure to send a thank you note to show your gratitude.

The Placement Service or Agency

A second source is the placement agency or service. Almost every college and university has a free agency for its graduates, and others are associated with professional organizations for teachers, management majors, speech communication majors, and so on. Many "percentage" agencies will place you for a fee, usually a percentage of your first year's salary, payable upon your assuming a position they helped you obtain. Most of these agencies have "fee-paid" positions, which means that an organization has retained them on a fee basis to locate potential applicants. If you use a percentage agency, be aware that they may charge a registration fee to process your credentials. Check the contract carefully, and do not allow them to send you to interview for positions in which you are not interested or qualified. A third source is newspaper advertisements. Many organizations advertise positions in newspapers so they cannot be accused by the EEOC of reserving openings for males, whites, Anglo-Saxons, and so on. Use all of these strategies. You cannot predict which one will lead to an interview or position.

The Cover Letter

Send an original, creative cover letter and a résumé to each lead that might prove fruitful. Form letters designed for any position impress no one. Whenever possible, address your letter to the specific person who will be actively involved in filling a position. The letter should be brief (rarely more than one page), neat, typed on good bond paper with a dark ribbon, and contain no typos, grammar errors or misspellings. Begin by explaining why you are writing. Specify the position you are interested in and perhaps tell how you discovered the opening. Refer to the enclosed résumé, but do not make the letter a mere restatement of it. Stress specific education and experiences that make you well suited for *this position* with *this organization* at *this time.* Be persuasive; show interest and enthusiasm. Close the letter by asking for an interview and stating when you would be available both to be interviewed and to assume the position. Figure 7.9 is a typical cover letter.

Step 5: Creating a Favorable Impression

As you approach the interview, realize that your attitudes are critical. Be positive about yourself, past employers, and the future employer. If you go into an interview thinking, "Well, I'm gonna do it, but I know I won't do well," you probably will not. If you have the attitude, "All I want is a job," you will get a "job," if you are lucky. And if you badmouth former employers, associates, professors, or clients, the interview is likely to end quickly.

Relationship of Interview Parties

Assess the relationship that is likely to exist. How much control will you have? Degree of control is usually determined by the job market, how eager the organization is to fill the position, the strengths and weaknesses of your background, and how much you want and need the position. To what extent do you and the interviewer desire to take part in this

Figure 7.9 Sample cover letter

3379 North Cumberland Avenue
Athens, Georgia 30601
January 14, 1990

Ms. Elizabeth George
The Westin Peachtree Plaza
Atlanta, Georgia 30343

Dear Ms. George:

Mr. John Williams, my employment counselor at the University of Georgia, has informed me that the Westin Peachtree Plaza will soon be hiring managers for its expanded convention and resort programs. I believe my academic background and hotel/convention experiences have prepared me admirably for a position in hotel management.

My program in Hotel, Institutional Management at the University of Georgia has given me practical knowledge in labor-management relations, marketing, property management, and communication. This background will enable me to work effectively with employees, guests, the general public, and organizations who are interested in holding conventions at the Westin Peachtree Plaza. I chose electives in accounting and computer science so I could both understand and work effectively with the business office and the modern planning and reservation systems.

In addition to my academic training, I have had summer internships at the Hyatt-Regency Hotel in Louisville and the Opryland Hotel in Nashville. These internships provided me with experiences in managing conventions, customer relations, the operations of large hotels, and the problems and techniques of working with the many types of people that keep a modern hotel operating effectively.

During the academic year, I have worked in the cafeteria in my dormitory at the University of Georgia. I have advanced from a waiter, to a waiter captain, to the head waiter in the three and a half years I have been on campus. My experiences in the cafeteria have taught me how to work with and supervise a variety of people. As head waiter, I must schedule and supervise a staff of seventy-five waiters and waiter captains.

I would thoroughly enjoy an opportunity to talk with you about how my training and experiences have prepared me for a management position with the Westin Peachtree Plaza. Would you please call me at 404-746-2991 or write to let me know a convenient time for you to talk to me?

Sincerely,

Diana Johnson

Diana Johnson

Enclosure: Resume

interview? You may find it difficult to "get up" for an interview if you have been turned down several times during previous weeks, and the interviewer may find it equally difficult if the interview is number ten of the day. What is likely to be the level of affection (mutual trust, respect, friendship) between you and the interviewer? Both parties must be ready and able to cooperate, disclose strengths and weaknesses (of self or organization), and provide meaningful feedback.[55]

Some studies reveal that successful applicants dominate interviews but also know when to let the interviewer control the conversaion while unsuccessful applicants are submissive or try to dominate when the employer clearly wants to do so.[56] You must understand the relationship between you and the employer and adapt accordingly.

Dress and Appearance

We all think we know how to dress and prepare ourselves for interviews but the following are the five biggest mistakes men and women make:[57]

Men
1. Dirty and wrinkled clothes that do not fit properly.
2. Shirt that is too tight at the collar or around the waist.
3. Dirty hands, nails, or hair.
4. Shoes wrong color for clothes or dirty.
5. Wrong style or silhouette for body shape.

Women
1. Too much or inappropriate jewelry.
2. Too much or too little makeup, particularly overpowering perfume.
3. Scuffed or inappropriate shoes.
4. Clothing inappropriate for the work place.
5. Ill-fitting clothing.

Your budget may limit the clothing you have to wear, but there is no excuse for dirty hands, nails, and hair or rumpled, dirty, or inappropriate attire.

Advice for Men Standard interviewing apparel is a dark suit (blue, gray, or black) with a white or pastel solid shirt and a dark or contrasting tie. Try the sit-down test to check for fit. Almost anyone can wear clothes that are a bit tight when standing, but sitting down reveals quickly if the waist band or collar is too tight or the shirt gaps at the waist. Insert one finger into the collar of your shirt. If the collar is too tight, you need a larger shirt; if it is too loose, you need a smaller shirt to avoid a sloppy look. Wear brown shoes only with a brown suit; wear black or cordovan (deep wine color) with blue, gray, or black suits. Shoes must be clean and polished. Wear dark socks that complement your suit and cover at least half the leg so when you sit down and cross your legs, no skin is visible. Tie size and age depends upon what is in style, but it is always safe to wear a wide stripe tie or one that is blue and red, gray and burgundy, or black and white. Do not get caught up in the latest trendy colors and sizes. When in doubt, ask a friendly person at a men's clothing store.

Men also need to choose clothing that is appropriate for their body shapes: endomorph (regular), ectomorph (thin), mesomorph (heavy). A heavy male should not wear large plaids, thick stripes, or bright colors. Better choices are dark shades with pinstripes

Be neat, well-groomed, and dressed to look professional.

such as a dark blue suit with a blue or burgundy pinstripe or, for less formal settings, a blue blazer with light gray or beige pants. A thin male (sometimes referred to as the athletic build) may wear a greater variety of clothing, and some plaids might add size and depth to the physical appearance.

Colors may have both psychological and physiological effects on interview parties. It is claimed, for example, that black projects power and sophistication; gray projects security; blue projects harmony; red projects energy and arouses emotions, brown projects friendliness and approachability; and yellow projects intelligence and optimism.

Advice for Women Makeup, hair style, and clothing are personal decisions that reveal a great deal about your personality—who you are, your self concept, and what you think of others. Take it seriously. No makeup is probably too little, but if it calls attention to itself, it is probably too much. Recruiters suggest small earrings with one per ear, one ring per hand, and no bracelets. Coloring is essential, and a cosmetic counselor can help you determine what is appropriate for you and your clothing.

Tight clothes do not look attractive on either men or women. Try the sit-down and one-finger-in-the-collar tests we recommended for men. Wear appropriate under garments to avoid a "see-through" appearance that is both distracting and unprofessional. Low comfortable pumps are appropriate shoes, and they should be clean, polished, and appropriate for the clothing worn. Select a conservative jacket and skirt that give a professional rather than a casual appearance. Length of skirt should be appropriate to the body silhouette and not call attention to itself. And avoid "baggy panty hose" or ones with runs or snags. In all matters of clothing, be neat, comfortable, and professional.

Nonverbal Communication

Nonverbal communication, such as voice and eye-contact, is an important ingredient in the selection interview.[58] Interviewers rate applicants higher if they smile, have expressive facial expressions, and maintain steady eye contact without staring. Dynamism or energy level is communicated through the way you shake hands, sit, walk, stand, gesture, and move your body. Try to appear calm, relaxed, and in control by avoiding nervous gestures and movements. Speak in a normal conversational tone with vocal variety that exhibits confidence and interpersonal skills. Interviewers prefer *standard* or *prestigious* accents. Studies reveal that applicants with regional, ethnic, or racial accents receive lower evaluations, get shorter interviews, and receive fewer offers.[59] Do not hesitate to pause a few seconds before answering particularly difficult questions, but be aware that frequent pauses may make you appear hesitant or unprepared. Interviewers interpret pauses of one second or less as signs of ambition, self-confidence, organization, and intelligence. Remember that nonverbal communication or body language can validate or negate what you are saying.[60]

Step 6: Answering Questions

Although dress, appearance, and nonverbal communication are important ingredients in the selection process, do not overestimate their effect. A number of studies suggest that the final decision is most often based on a combination of verbal and nonverbal impressions, with the verbal (answers, questions, education, and experiences) having a clear edge over the nonverbal.[61] In short, be ready to answer and ask questions effectively. Nervousness is natural, but if you concentrate on giving the interviewer the information asked for, you will find your nervousness disappearing. If you are asked a question you do not understand, paraphrase it in your own words or ask for clarification. Interviewers assume applicants understand questions unless applicants state otherwise.

Successful applicants tend to give answers that are succinct, specific, and to the point.[62] They listen carefully to questions, do not interrupt or try to second-guess the employer, and then present organized responses with clear arguments, relevant content, good grammar, and action words that show they are "doers." Successful applicants do not prepare canned answers that employers can destroy with a single, well-placed probing question. They show enthusiasm, speak positively about experiences, have clear goals and career plans, and exhibit direct interest in both the position for which they are

ing and the interviewer's organization. They do nothing merely to make a good
ssion because experienced interviewers can detect phony applicants rather easily
ay. Successful applicants accept responsibilities for past actions and give rea-
not excuses, for those actions. They try to demonstrate the characteristics of the
iewer's ideal employee through answers and references to their education and
iences.

Unsuccessful applicants tend to give brief answers that indicate they are non-
assertive, passive, and cautious. Their answers contain qualifiers and "you knows" which
display tentativeness and powerlessness. They seem evasive and use less active, concrete,
positive language and less technical jargon. Unsuccessful applicants appear uncertain
about the kinds of positions they want and where they hope to be in the next five or ten
years. They are unable to identify their interests with the interests and needs of the interviewer and the organization. They play passive roles in both openings and closings. The
reverse of passive, and perhaps even less apt to be hired, are applicants who attempt to
manipulate interviewers by name-dropping or insincere flattery. In short, unsuccessful
applicants exhibit few of the qualities most interviewers are seeking.

Identifying Unlawful Questions

Although federal and state EEO laws have existed for more than twenty years and many
organizations train their selection interviewers to follow EEO guidelines, many applicants, particularly women, are still asked unlawful questions. These violations range from
mild infractions such as "What does your husband do?" to gross offenses such as "Will
you go to bed with me?" Apparently some violations occur because of curiosity, tradition, and ignorance of the law, while others occur because employers have exaggerated
feelings of power or desire to violate laws seen as infringements on their rights. Many
employers continue to ask unlawful questions because they are aware that the EEOC cannot sue them. Only applicants can sue for apparent violations of EEO laws, and only if
the court decision is in the applicant's favor, can the EEOC apply a fine. Obviously few
applicants will go to the trouble and expense of suing a potential employer.

Regardless of why interviewers violate EEO laws and guidelines, such questions
pose serious dilemmas for applicants. If they answer unlawful questions honestly, they
may lose positions for irrelevant and unlawful reasons. If they refuse to answer such
questions, they may lose positions because they appear uncooperative, evasive, hostile, or
"one of those." There is no gracious way to refuse to answer a question.

You must be able to recognize an unlawful question when its occurs. Recent studies
reveal that most applicants are unaware of what constitutes an unlawful question and,
regardless of knowledge level, feel they must answer whatever questions employers
ask.[63] Review the EEO laws and unlawful questions identified earlier in this chapter. You
must also be aware of tricks employers use to get unlawful information.[64] For example, a
low level clerk may ask you which health insurance plan you would choose, and your
answer reveals if you are married and have children. During lunch when you are least
expecting serious questions, an employer may address an unlawful area directly. Or perhaps during lunch or taking a tour of the plant, employers may probe into such areas as
child care in the guise of their own problems: "What a day! My daughter Emily woke up

this morning with a fever and my husband is out of town. Do you ever have days like this?" If you are not careful, your response will reveal a great deal of irrelevant, unlawful, and perhaps damaging information without knowing it.

However, many employers have learned how to get unlawful information through lawful questions. For instance, instead of asking, "Do you have children?" an employer asks, "Is there any limit on your ability to work overtime?" Others use coded questions and comments. For example, "Our employees put a lot into their work" means "Older workers like you don't have much energy;" "We have a very young staff" means "You won't fit in;" and "I'm sure your former company had its own corporate culture, just as we do here" means "You can't teach an old dog new tricks."[65]

Responding to Unlawful Questions

What, then, should you do when asked an unlawful question? First, determine the importance of the position.[66] Your primary task is to get a good position, and if you are hired, you may be able to change the hiring practices of the organization's recruiters. And second, you must gauge the severity of the EEO violation. If it is a gross violation, consider not only refusing to answer the question but reporting the interviewer to his or her superiors or to placement center authorities if you are at a school or professional facility. If a question is a moderate violation and you are interested in the position, consider a number of tactics. You may choose to *answer directly but briefly.*[67]

1. **Interviewer:** What does your wife do?
   Interviewee: She's a pharmacist.
2. **Interviewer:** Do you attend church regularly?
   Interviewee: Yes, I do.

You may pose a *tactful inquiry* such as the following:

1. **Interviewer:** What does your husband do?
   Interviewee: Why do you ask?
2. **Interviewer:** Apparently you are confined to a wheelchair; how might this affect your work performance?
   Interviewee: How is my handicap relevant for a position as a computer programmer?

You might try a *tactful refusal* such as:

1. **Interviewer:** How old are you?
   Interviewee: I don't think age is important if you are well qualified for a position.
2. **Interviewer:** Do you plan to have children?
   Interviewee: My plans to have a family will not interfere with my ability to perform the requirements of this position.
3. **Interviewer:** What do you do on Sunday mornings?
   Interviewee: If working on Sundays or weekends is a part of this position's requirements, I would prefer to discuss that after we know whether or not I am the person you wish to hire for this position.

You might answer by *neutralizing* the interviewer's apparent concern.

1. **Interviewer:** Do you plan on having a family?
   Interviewee: Yes, I do. I'm looking forward to the challenges of both family and career. I've observed many of my women professors and fellow workers handling both quite successfully.

2. **Interviewer:** Who will take care of your children while you are at work?
   Interviewee: *Our* children will attend a good day-care center until they are in the primary grades.

3. **Interviewer:** What happens if your husband gets transferred or needs to relocate?
   Interviewee: My husband and I would discuss locational moves that *either* of us might have to consider in the future.

You might answer and *take advantage* of the question to support your candidacy.

1. **Interviewer:** Where were you born?
   Interviewee: I am quite proud that my background is _____ because it has helped me to deal effectively with people of various ethnic backgrounds.

2. **Interviewer:** How would you feel working for a person younger than you?
   Interviewee: I have worked for and with many people younger and older than myself. This has never posed a problem because I admire and appreciate competence regardless of age.

3. **Interviewer:** How old are you?
   Interviewee: I have always felt that age is unimportant. Some people are too old at 25, others at 30, and others at 40. My attitude, enthusiasm, and abilities to learn and to adapt are far more important than my age. I'm 54.

4. **Interviewer:** Are you married?
   Interviewee: Yes I am, and I think that's a plus. As you know, many studies show that married employees are more stable and dependable than unmarried employees.

Or you might try what Bernice Sandler, a nationally recognized authority on discrimination in hiring, calls a *tongue in cheek test response* that sends an unmistakable signal to the interviewer that he or she has asked an unlawful question. This strategy must be accompanied by appropriate nonverbal signals to avoid offending the interviewer.

1. **Interviewer:** Who will take care of your children?
   Interviewee: (smiling, pleasant tone of voice) Is this a test to see if I can recognize an unlawful question in the selection process?

2. **Interviewer:** How long do you expect to work for us?
   Interviewee: (smiling, pleasant tone of voice) Is this a test to see how I would handle an unlawful question?

These are a few examples of how you might handle questions that violate EEO laws. Such questions are never easy to answer, but you may handle them more effectively if you are prepared. Remember, you need not answer every question an interviewer asks.

Step 7: Asking Questions

Most interviewers will give you an opportunity to ask questions.[68] If they do not, request time to ask questions you consider important in determining if this is the best position and organization for you. Some applicants feel obligated to ask superficial questions if they have no real ones in mind. Suppress this urge. Your questions reveal a great deal about your values, interests, intelligence, maturity, homework, and so on, so ask them carefully and thoughtfully. Successful applicants, for example, tend to ask more questions that are open-ended and that probe into the position, the organization, and the interviewer's opinions. Unsuccessful applicants ask closed questions and more miscellaneous information questions. Avoid too many "me" questions that show little interest in the organization. Ask position-related questions rather than ones about salary and benefits.

An applicant acts as a probing interviewer and is prone to tumble into the common question pitfalls—double-barrelled, leading, yes/no response, bipolar, guessing game, and open-to-closed switch. But applicants also have a few question pitfalls all their own:

1. The *have to question* in which you make it sound like you would be an uncooperative employee if hired.

   Bad: Would I have to travel much?
   Good: How much travel would this position entail?

2. The *typology question* in which you ask for *type* when you want an open-ended answer.

   Bad: What type of training program do you have?
   Good: Tell me about your training program for this position.

3. The *pleading question* in which you seem to beg for the answer.

   Bad: Could you please tell me about the expansion of your plant in Jacksonville?
   Good: Tell me about the expansion of your plant in Jacksonville.

4. The *little bitty question* in which you may indicate lack of interest by appearing to want very little information.

   Bad: Tell me a little bit about the position you mentioned earlier.
   Good: Tell me about the position you mentioned earlier.

5. The *immature question* that shows you lack professional maturity and have not done your homework.

   Bad: Do you have any benefits?
   Good: Tell me about the stock sharing plan you have for employees.

The following sample applicant questions show interest in the position and the organization, are not overly self-centered, and meet question guidelines.

1. Describe your ideal employee for me.
2. How does your organization encourage employees to come up with new ideas?
3. How much choice would I have in selecting geographical location?
4. What would a typical day be like?
5. How does your organization evaluate its employees?
6. How might your organization support me if I wanted to pursue an MBA?
7. How much supervision would I get as a new employee?
8. What, in your estimation, is the most unique characteristic of your organization?
9. How might an advanced degree in engineering affect my position with your company?
10. How does the cost of living in Boulder compare to Denver?
11. Tell me about where other entry level management personnel have moved within your organization.
12. What have you liked most about working for this organization?
13. What can you tell me about the possible merger with GM?
14. I noticed in the *Wall Street Journal* last week that your organization was listed among the 200 fastest growing mid-size corporations. How can you account for such phenomenal growth?
15. How much contact would I have with management?

Step 8: Evaluation and Follow-up

Do a thorough review of each interview, with the goal of repeating strengths and eliminating weaknesses in future interviews. Be careful, however, not to overreact to your impressions and the interviewer's feedback. Your perceptions of what happened during the interview, how the interviewer reacted, or what specific nonverbal actions meant may be greatly exaggerated or plain wrong. Ask questions such as the following during your postinterview evaluation:

1. How adequate was your preparation: background study, résumé, answers, questions?
2. How effective was your role during the opening?
3. How comfortable were you during the interview?
4. How appropriate was your dress?
5. Which questions did you handle well? Poorly?
6. Which opportunities to sell yourself did you miss?
7. How thorough were your answers?
8. How well did you adapt your questions to this organization and position?
9. How effectively did you show your interest in this organization and position?
10. Did you obtain enough information on the position and the organization to determine if you wanted to remain interested?

Be sure to follow up the interview with a brief note thanking the interviewer for the time given you, and stress your interest in the position. The thank-you note provides you with an excuse to contact the interviewer, keep your name alive, and provide additional information that might help the organization decide in your favor.

Summary

The selection interview can be a productive two-way communication event that allows an employer and an applicant to determine whether the position/organization and prospective employee are well matched. Both parties must be familiar with EEO laws and guidelines and with recent research into the selection process. Both must approach the process in a systematic manner and do adequate homework. Both must listen, ask insightful questions that avoid common pitfalls, and answer questions thoroughly and succinctly. And both must evaluate interviews carefully to determine the next course of action and to improve selection interview techniques.

A Selection Interview for Review and Analysis

This simulated selection interview was conducted by two management majors at Purdue University. Steven Mitchener is applying for a position as a consumer lending officer with the national department of Mellon Bank. Mary Ann Ellabarger is a personnel director and college recruiter for Mellon Bank.

How satisfactory are the rapport and orientation stages of the opening? How well do the questions of employer and applicant meet EEO guidelines and avoid common question pitfalls? How effectively does the employer probe into answers? Does the employer appear to have an ideal employee profile in mind? How appropriate, thorough, to the point, and persuasive are the applicant's answers? What image does the applicant present during the interview? How adequate is the employer's information giving? How adequate is the closing? Does the employer control the interview too much, too little, or about right?

1. **Employer:** Good morning; Steve Mitchener?
2. **Applicant:** Yes.
3. **Employer:** I'm Mary Ellabarger, personnel director of Mellon Bank of Pittsburgh. Won't you have a seat? And how are you today?
4. **Applicant:** Just fine, thanks. I had a good trip out.
5. **Employer:** What I would like to do today is, first of all, ask you some questions concerning yourself and your interests, then I would like to tell you a bit about what Mellon Bank has to offer you, and finally, I will be more than happy to answer any questions you have for me.
6. **Applicant:** Fine. I have been looking forward to the interview.
7. **Employer:** First of all, what made you decide to come to Purdue?
8. **Applicant:** Well, I'll go back to my senior year in high school. I took a computer science course in high school, and I really enjoyed it. I thought I would enjoy programming and data processing. In my decision to attend Purdue University, I sought out some colleges that I thought had good computer science programs. Purdue has an excellent program. It offers bachelor's, master's, and doctoral degrees in computer science, so I thought I would try it out. I planned to minor in business. Once I got here, I realized that computer science was not what I wanted to do. I would be cooped up in a corner, and I would not be working with people, which is what I enjoy doing more than anything else. So I switched my minor to my major and shifted to an accounting and finance major. So that is how I ended up at Purdue with the major that I have.

9. **Employer:** You say that you like to work with people. Why do you like to work with people?

10. **Applicant:** Well, it seems like my whole life has been centered around people. Through the activities and the things that I have done, I see that I am a very people-oriented person. That's something that I enjoy; I can't explain why. I just enjoy working with people.

11. **Employer:** What kind of qualities do you think you possess that would enable you to work well with people on a job and in different situations?

12. **Applicant:** I think that in several activities that I've been involved with at school, I have learned to understand different types of people. You come to college and you get away from a very condensed version of people in high school. When you come to college, it's diversified. Suddenly you meet people from all different cultures and from different locations across the nation and across the world. This is something that I've learned to live with, to work with many different types of people.

13. **Employer:** Um-hmm. Are you speaking of your activities? I noticed when reviewing your application that you've been very active in the Purdue Glee Club and Purdue Service. What is Purdue Service?

14. **Applicant:** The Purdue Service is the glee club honorary. Within the glee club there are twelve servers, and each one heads up a committee within the glee club. We have public relations and campus relations, just to name a few. We are elected by our peers to head up particular committees.

15. **Employer:** And I see that you're the manager of the glee club.

16. **Applicant:** Right.

17. **Employer:** And what does this position as manager entail? In other words, what are your duties, responsibilities, problems?

18. **Applicant:** Basically, I act as a liaison between the director and the guys in the glee club. I'm responsible for lining the guys up, making sure they know where they're supposed to be, what they're supposed to wear at what particular time. If there are any problems that arise within the glee club, I take it upon myself, as my responsibility, to take care of these problems, to put the guys at ease, or to communicate these problems to the director. If the director has something that needs to be said to the glee club, he works through me, and I talk to the guys in the glee club and, if there's a problem, I try to straighten it out or get the information that's needed to them.

19. **Employer:** You have been manager now for a year?

20. **Applicant:** Right.

21. **Employer:** What has been the most difficult situation that you have had to deal with?

22. **Applicant:** Well, like I was saying earlier, I think each guy in the glee club is a different person; no two guys in the glee club are alike. And you are going to confront different types of personalities and no one is going to agree on everything. So you have to learn to deal with different types of personalities. Someone is going to like something and another person is not going to like it, and you have to work with each one of these differences and you have to compromise and work with the guys in each case.

23. **Employer:** If I were to walk into a glee club practice and choose maybe ten members at random and ask them to tell me a little bit about you, what would they tell me about Steve Mitchener?

24. **Applicant:** This is a kind of conceited question, I realize . . .

25. **Employer:** I know; that's why I would like for you to tell me.

26. **Applicant:** I'm sure they would say that I am a very caring individual, that I'm open, willing to listen to problems that they might have, that I do care about each individual in the glee club, that I don't show partiality to guys in the club, and if there's a problem, they feel that I'm open and that they can come to me with the problem.

27. **Employer:** How do you feel that these qualities or characteristics you possess, that you can work well with people, will help you in a job with Mellon Bank as a consumer lending officer, which is the position you are applying for?

28. **Applicant:** I feel that not only the experience that I have had within the glee club but the people I have met when we do our shows has helped me get a better understanding of individuals, the way they function and the way they think. And I feel this equips me to work in many jobs. Specifically relating to Mellon Bank, I feel that it is going to help me in working with people, and helping me with the job so that when I come across problems, we will be able to talk about them openly and get the solutions that are needed.

29. **Employer:** Very good. Why are you interested in a position with Mellon Bank?

30. **Applicant:** My major is accounting and finance, and I realize that banking is included in finance. I'm definitely interested in the banking field, and I feel that my accounting can give me a good background for a job with Mellon Bank working as a lending officer. And again, with my interest in people, I feel that I will be able to go out and work with people and apply my finance and accounting training to the job and to the people that I will be working with at Mellon.

31. **Employer:** Okay. Please tell me what you think a position as a consumer lending officer would entail.

32. **Applicant:** The way I look at it, it would be a job where I would be responsible for going out to different companies within the Pittsburgh area and getting them to take out loans from Mellon Bank. For each loan that I would get, I would get credit and I would be paid on a commission basis. I would enjoy a position where I would go out to get people to take loans.

33. **Employer:** So why should we choose you over other applicants for this position?

34. **Applicant:** That's a pretty tough question. I feel that the work experience I have had, that I mentioned on the application, as a student service captain in one of the residence halls has helped me on a work basis, as opposed to being manager with the glee club, and has helped me to cope with problems in the actual work process. I've learned to deal with people and their problems and to come up with solutions. This experience, as well as being manager of the glee club and a finance major with an accounting background, make me a very strong candidate for the job as a lending officer.

35. **Employer:** You mentioned something about being a student service captain. Was this during college?

36. **Applicant:** Yes. This was during the last two years.

37. **Employer:** What were some of your specific duties and responsibilities in this position?

38. **Applicant:** I was responsible for about thirty-five waiters. I use the term waiters but they're not really that because it's a cafeteria. Anyway, I was responsible for making sure that the meal ran smoothly, that the waiters knew where they were supposed to be, and I made myself available for any problems. Also, I made sure there was enough food on the lines and made sure that each captain was familiar with his or her job. I had to be available for whatever came up.

39. **Employer:** Going back to your education at Purdue, you mentioned on your application that you chose your major because you had a strong interest in accounting and finance. You've already said that once you got to Purdue University you changed over into this major. Would you please elaborate a little bit more on why the interest in accounting and finance?

40. **Applicant:** After I got here I realized that being in computer science was not what I really wanted to do. I'm people-oriented; I talked to quite a few people who were in computer science and they felt that it was leading up to a programming job where I would be pretty much in a secluded area and I would not have much access to or spend any time with people. Well, after talking to these individuals, I was convinced that was not what I wanted to do. So I shifted my minor to my major. I chose the accounting and finance major in the School of Management where I knew I would definitely be working with people and where I could apply my strong interests in finance and accounting.

41. **Employer:** How do you feel about the education that you have received at Purdue?

42. **Applicant:** Purdue definitely has an excellent management school. I have been very pleased with what I have learned at Purdue. I feel that my grades definitely show how much I have learned. But aside from the academic part, I have learned a lot about myself in terms of the way I think, the way I can function with people, and the way I can solve problems. I have learned to understand other people so much better and to accept their points of view because I have become so much more open-minded from my schooling and the people I've met.

43. **Employer:** And that's very important in the type of position that you are applying for. Out of those things you just mentioned, which is the most important thing that you have gotten out of your career as a student at Purdue University?

44. **Applicant:** I think I'll go back to what I just said. The one thing that really stands out I think, aside from the academic, is that I have become a much more open person. I feel I can handle any situation, any problem that comes up, because I have become so much more open-minded. I'm open to different points of view and what different people have to say. I'm open to constructive criticism whenever I'm doing something wrong. I feel that I can accept criticism. If it's something that will improve my well-being, then I'm ready for it. So I would have to say that open-mindedness has been the most important thing for me.

45. **Employer:** Let me tell you a little bit about Mellon Bank and what we have to offer you in the position of consumer lending officer. You would be working in the national department at Mellon Bank, which is one of the largest wholesale banking operations in the country. Our lending officers are responsible for all aspects of our corporate banking relationships. The scope of this department's operations is nationwide. We do business with more than ninety of the one hundred largest United States corporations and almost three-fifths of the Fortune 500. The department is organized geographically, which provides a broad exposure for you to the United States corporate market as well as financial intermediaries. Lending officers interface with top level officers and specialists in multinational and domestic corporations as well as medium-sized and regional companies. The training program that we have available for you when you first start out with Mellon Bank is a short orientation program lasting three to four weeks, depending upon how well you adjust and perform. You'd begin your development in the national department as a credit analyst. This initial assignment will provide you with a working knowledge of the basic methods and tools to use in evaluating corporate credit situations. You would be working closely with our experienced corporate lending officers who have been with the company for a while. They would help you to apply your skills and financial analysis early in

your work with Mellon Bank. After you have completed this three- to four-week training program and gone into the credit analyst assignment, you would move into our national department in one of the geographical lending divisions. You would be responsible for commercial loan and division activities not only for existing customers but also for prospective customers, and you would then move according to your performance and your experience. Since all of our lending and operating activities do require extensive nationwide marketing, the position as a consumer lending officer entails traveling nearly one-third of the time. Do you have any questions for me?

46. **Applicant:** I have several questions that I'd like to relate specifically to Mellon Bank as a whole. You know as well as I do that over the last year the prime rate has fluctuated tremendously, and more last year than in the previous thirty years. Now, how is this going to affect Mellon Bank in the long run?

47. **Employer:** Well, of course, any change in the prime rate is going to affect any company. As far as Mellon Bank goes, we will not be affected as heavily as many companies because we are in the lending business and companies, as our customers, are going to have to borrow if they need money to meet deadlines. They are going to have to borrow no matter what the prime rate is. So in the long run it will have no effect on Mellon Bank's lending position or Mellon Bank as a whole.

48. **Applicant:** So you're saying that the prime rate is not really going to affect Mellon Bank?

49. **Employer:** Not in the long run.

50. **Applicant:** I know many states across the nation are now allowing banks to expand into surrounding counties, and banks do not have to limit business just to a particular county. Now, I know that in Pennsylvania banks can expand into counties surrounding their main area, the branches can expand, but they cannot go into the rest of the state. Should Pennsylvania pass laws that would allow banks to expand into other counties within the state, how would this affect Mellon Bank? What are your plans?

51. **Employer:** This would be very good for Mellon Bank at this time. We have made provisions to expand into other counties. Right now, as you said, we are waiting for the laws to pass. We have already planned out where to place new plants of Mellon Bank and, as soon as the law is passed, which is looking good for within the next six months, we will be expanding into surrounding counties in Pennsylvania.

52. **Applicant:** How is this going to affect your employment?

53. **Employer:** This will be excellent. We are recruiting heavily right now because, within the next four to five years, we are going to be moving people around within Mellon Bank nationwide. We do need young people to get in there right now, to start at the bottom level as you would as a consumer lending officer and to begin working. We will be opening new accounts; therefore, we will be acquiring new employees because we don't have enough employees right now to expand efficiently and effectively. So we'll be employing many new people, especially in the area you're interested in.

54. **Applicant:** I would like to turn now to your training program. You mentioned that it is a three- to four-week training program. Is this a program that is designed primarily to train individuals or one in which they try to weed out the zeros?

55. **Employer:** Well, neither. It's basically an orientation program. You'll be meeting people, getting familiar with Mellon Bank's policies and benefits, working with different individuals within different departments, and you will get familiar with the surroundings. So you're not just thrown out as a consumer lending officer and told to go for it. This program will give you some background. We do have a seminar to orient new employees. You will be training at approximately the same time as other new employees. So you will be meeting the new people that you will be working with; you will all be in the same boat; and you will be getting familiar with some of the people you will be working with and under.

56. **Applicant:** So what's the basis for the performance appraisal in this training program?

57. **Employer:** Anyone that we decide to hire as an employee of Mellon Bank, as you asked in the first question, if they are a zero, they wouldn't be hired in the first place. I think that would be quite evident while just talking to them. As far as performance appraisal, when you are hired for the position you are applying for as a consumer lending officer, we already know in which department you will be placed. There is no performance appraisal in the training program. Like I said, it is designed to get you familiar with Mellon Bank as a corporation. You're coming into this completely cold. You know a little bit about the company on the whole but not much about the different divisions that you will be working in or the different departments. So that's all it is. It's just basically getting you familiar with us. You are not judged on your performance in the orientation program. We'll be showing you around the plant and around the grounds and explaining a bit more about our policies.

58. **Applicant:** So, as long as I were to contribute to the betterment of Mellon Bank, I would be assured of being placed in a management position as a lending officer?

59. **Employer:** Oh yes, because we're looking right now for people who are interested in this job, and that's what you would be hired as. But there's a process that you go through to get there. The credit analyst position is basically an extension of the orientation, familiarizing you with our processes, how we go about working with our customers, and how you would contact potential customers. So, like you said, it is just to get you familiar with the company. You would definitely be placed in a management position in, say, the next year or two.

60. **Applicant:** That's all the questions I have. I would like to add that I'm very interested in a position with Mellon Bank.

61. **Employer:** I'm glad to hear that. If you don't have any further questions, I would like to tell you that I've enjoyed talking with you. It's been quite interesting. I feel that your qualifications fit nicely with what we are looking for as consumer lending officers. You seem to enjoy working with people, and this job requires a lot of contacts with people. I should be getting in touch with you by mail no later than the fifteenth of this month. I'm going to take your application back and review how your interests fit with what we have to offer. I would be able to tell you more then where you might be located. I notice that you have no specific geographic location on your application.

62. **Applicant:** That's correct. I will be looking forward to hearing from you.

63. **Employer:** You should be hearing from me within a couple of weeks.

64. **Applicant:** Thanks a lot.

65. **Employer:** Do have a good day.

Selection Role-Playing Cases

An Accountant for a Metal Company

The applicant, John Roberts, is an accountant in his thirties who has spent twelve years working for Hardshelled Metalworking Associates. Twice during the past five years a departmental headship has been vacant and both times an outsider was brought in to fill the position. When the same thing happened a third time, John went to his supervisor to protest what seemed to be an injustice. A bitter argument followed, and John was fired. He is now about to talk to Howard Jones, personnel manager for the All-Metal Stamping Company, about a position similar to the one he held so long. John has a degree in accounting and a record of successful work in two positions prior to going to Hardshelled where several of his suggestions for improved accounting procedures reduced office costs. He is not quite sure what to say if Jones asks why he left his last job. He wants the job at All-Metal because the pay is slightly better than it was at Hardshelled and he has a family to support and house and car payments due.

The employer, Howard Jones, has a vacancy in the accounting department. The job requires a full knowledge of accounting procedures, initiative, and loyalty to the company. With not much immediate opportunity for promotion from the position, the person who is hired will be in a dead-end spot for some years. The accounting department has good morale, and the workers get along well with each other and with the department head. Howard knows little about John except that he is a little over thirty years old, has a family, and has a good reputation in accounting. He would probably be a good person for the job, except that at his age he might be eager for a promotion. Why he left his former employer is uncertain, but he answered a classified ad for another position. It would be a relief to fill the vacancy with a steady, capable, loyal person.

A Real Estate Salesperson

The applicant, Louise Wood, is in her mid-twenties. She worked for four years as a salesperson of women's clothing in a Chicago department store. She was dissatisfied with the low salary, and six months ago she decided to take a training course in real estate. She took the state test recently and passed with a very high grade. Now she is going to talk to Wanda Connor, owner of Connor and Associates, a well-known realty company in Chicago. When Louise worked as a salesperson at the department store, she had a very good record, and many of her customers requested her help with purchases. The store did not want Louise to leave but understood her position since it could not offer her an opportunity for advancement. She has a good personality and can talk easily with people. However, she stutters sometimes when she gets nervous. When she speaks with Mrs. Connor, should she tell her about this difficulty? Louise does not want to ruin her chances for the position because she has a family to support.

The employer, Wanda Connor, has an opening for a real estate salesperson. The job requires a person with experience in selling and someone who can talk easily and persuasively with people. Connor and Associates is run on a commission basis and offers opportunity for advancement. Wanda knows little about Louise except that she is in her twenties and has a family. She knows little about her past work experience. Louise evidently wants the position since she called promptly as soon as it was advertised.

A Corporate Loan Manager

The applicant, Marilyn Haney, is a twenty-nine-year-old college graduate with a B.S. and an M.A. in accounting and economics. She has held three jobs with banks but has been asked to leave each position because of various involvements with married male employees. Her marriage is nothing more than a neutral pact between herself and her husband. Because of family problems, she is not always the easiest person to work with, and she knows it. She has been out of work about a month and needs a job badly. Should she tell the interviewer about her difficulties or let him find out on his own?

The interviewer, Arnold Jacoby, is in charge of a large bank in California. His bank is branching out into the corporate loan area, and he needs a young, aggressive person to head this area. He wants an experienced person with some education beyond the bachelor's degree. The person must have the ability to understand corporate finance and be able to deal with corporate executives. The new manager will be able to select a staff, and salary is negotiable. This bank is the old, conservative banking establishment of the community, and its leaders do not wish to hire anyone who might damage the image that has been maintained for nearly seventy-five years.

Student Activities

1. Contact your state employment office and ask about the trends in lawsuits over EEO violations during the past five years. What does this information reveal about the progress or lack of progress being made in eliminating discriminatory selection practices?

2. Interview a person in your profession who conducts selection interviews. Ask what the person looks for in applicants and how the information is obtained. Compare what you find out with the information in this chapter. How can you account for the similarities and differences?

3. Conduct a thorough self-analysis using the questions provided in this chapter. When you have completed this analysis, determine which types of positions you should and should not apply for and which types of organizations you should and should not contact.

4. Pair up with another person and conduct two simulated interviews. In one, play the role of employer, and in the other, the role of applicant. Each applicant should provide the employer with a résumé, a completed application form, and a thorough description for a position with a specific organization. Be sure to go through all stages in each interview: opening, questions from the employer, information from the employer, questions from the applicant, and closing. Ask some tough questions along with common questions. When the interviews are completed, discuss in detail with one another the strengths and weaknesses exhibited. Try to identify how you can improve your interviewing skills and the information you give and get.

Notes

1. Michael T. Motley and Nancy L. Smith, "Effects of Temperament upon Hiring Decisions: A Preliminary Examination of Global Personality Traits and Communicator Compatibility," *Communication Reports* 2 (1989), 22–29; Paula C. Morrow, "Physical Attractiveness and Selection Decision Making," *Journal of Management* 16 (1990), 45–60; Murray Porath, "Legal Questions about Legal Questions," *Early Childhood News* 3 (January/February 1991), 1 and 8.

2. Patricia G. Engler-Parish and Frank E. Millar, "An Exploratory Relational Control Analysis of the Employment Screening Interview," *Western Journal of Speech Communication* 53 (1989), 30–51.

3. Craig D. Tengler and Fredric M. Jablin, "Effects of Question Type, Orientation, and Sequencing in the Employment Screening Interview," *Communication Monographs* 50 (1983), 245; Richard D. Arvey and James E. Campion, "The Employment Interview: A Summary and Review of Recent Research," *Personnel Psychology* 35 (1982), 281–321.

4. Lowell Axtmann and Fredric M. Jablin, "Distributional and Sequential Interaction Structure in the Employment Selection Interview," Unpublished Paper, Annual Convention of the International Communication Association, Chicago 1986.

5. Jeffery Springston and Joann Keyton, "Defining and Quantifying Potentially Discriminating Questions in Employment Interviewing," Unpublished Paper, Annual Convention of the Speech Communication Association, San Francisco 1989.

6. Junda Woo, "Job Interviews Pose Risk to Employers," *The Wall Street Journal,* March 11, 1992, B1 and B5.

7. See for example, Patricia T. Bergeson, "The Americans with Disabilities Act (ADA): Practical Considerations for Employers," Chicago: Pope, Ballard, Shepard & Fowle, Ltd., 1991; Ruth G. Shaeffer, *Nondiscrimination in Employment, 1973–1975: A Broadening and Deepening National Effort* (New York: The Conference Board, 1975); Jerome Siegel, *Personnel Testing under EEO* (New York: AMACOM, 1980); Sandra Sawyer and Arthur Whatley, *Sexual Harassment: A Form of Sex Discrimination* (New York: The Personnel Administrator, January 1980).

8. Porath, 8; Ron Zemke, "Legally Speaking, Don't Take Interviews for Granted," *Training* 17 (1980), 52, 54, 56; Robert Bloom and Erich P. Prien, "A Guide for Job-Related Employment Interviewing," *Personnel Administrator* 28 (1983), 81–86; Barry Newman, "Expanded Employee Rights Increase Liability Exposure," *Journal of Compensation and Benefits* 4 (1989), 204–8; "Employment at Will: New Restrictions on the Right to Fire," *Small Business Report* 13 (1988), 60–63.

9. Porath, 8; Woo, B5; According to Rochelle Kaplan, legal counsel for the College Placement Council, no question is technically unlawful. The use of a question may be unlawful because courts assume that if you ask such a question, you will use it for unlawful purposes.

10. Gerald A. Wilson, "Instructional Implications for Responding to Discriminatory Interview Questions," Unpublished Paper, Annual Convention of the Speech Communication Association, San Francisco 1989.

11. Motley and Smith, 22–29; Buckingham, 99; Adrian Savage, "Selection Tests: Using Past Behaviour to Predict Performance," *Personnel Management* 17 (1985), 51; John Hendrickson, "Hiring the `Right Stuff'," *Personnel Administrator* 32 (1987), 70–74; Ken Miller, "Job Analysis Can Help You Find Good Employees," *Security Management* 30 (1986), 113–14.

12. See for example, Ellen Kolton, "The Educated Hunch," *Inc.* 7 (1985), 93–96; Carol Schneider-Jenkins and Norma Carr-Ruffino, "Smart Selection: Three Steps to Choosing New Employees," *Management World* 14 (1985), 38–39; Jeffrey W. Daum, "Interviewer Training: The Key to an Innovative Selection Process That Works" *Training* 20 (1983), 57–63.

13. Michael M. Harris, "Reconsidering the Employment Interview: A Review of Recent Literature and Suggestions for Future Research," *Personnel Psychology* 42 (1989), 691–726; Johanna R. Van Wert, "Absence of Bias—How to Interview Impartially for the `Best Fit'," *Management World* 12 (1983), 34–46; Anthony Dalessio and Andrew S. Imada, "Relationships Between Selection Decisions and Perceptions of Applicant Similarity to an Ideal Employee and Self: A Field Study," *Human Relations* 37 (1984), 67–80; John A. Daly, Virginia Peck Richmond, and Steven Leth, "Social Communicative Anxiety and the Personnel Selection Process: Testing the Similarity Effect in Selection Decisions," *Human Communication Research* 6 (1979), 18–32.

14. George F. Dreher, Ronald A. Ash, and Priscilla Hancock, "The Role of the Traditional Research Design in Underestimating the Validity of the Employment Interview," *Personnel Psychology* 41 (1988), 315–27.

15. Christopher Orpen, "Patterned Behavior Description Interviews Versus Unstructured Interviews: A Comparative Validity Study," *Journal of Applied Psychology* 70 (1985), 774–76.

16. Harris, 691–726; *Academic Leader* (December 1990), 4–5; Jolie Solomon, "The New Job Interview: Show Thyself," *Wall Street Journal*, BI; Donald D. DeCamp, "Are You Hiring the Right People?" *Management Review* 81 (1992), 44–47; Dennis L. Warmke and David J. Weston, "Success Dispels Myths about Panel Interviewing," *Personnel Journal* 71 (1992), 120–126.

17. Harris, 691–726.

18. "Hiring: An Expert Explains How to Choose the Best Applicant," *Effective Manager* 6 (1982), 4–5.

19. Linda D. McGill, "Psychological Tests in the Workplace: Should Your Company Use Them?" *Employment Relations Today* 17 (1990), 227–232.

20. Joseph P. Buckley, "Read Between the Lines." *Security Management* 31 (1987), 80–86.

21. Wayne J. Camara, "Employee Honesty Testing: Traps and Opportunities," *Boardroom Reports*, December 15, 1991.

22. Carol Kleiman, "From Genetics to Honesty, Firms Expand Employee Tests, Screening," *Chicago Tribune,* February 9, 1992, 8-1.

23. Camara.

24. Porath, 8.

25. Fredric M. Jablin and Vernon D. Miller, "Interviewer and Applicant Questioning Behavior in Employment Interviews," *Management Communication Quarterly* 4 (1990), 51–86.

26. Therese H. Macan and Robert L. Dipboye, "The Effects of Interviewers' Initial Impressions on Information Gathering," *Organizational Behavior and Human Decision Processes* 42 (1988), 364–87; John F. Binning, Mel A. Goldstein, Mario F. Garcia, and Julie H. Scattaregia, "Effects of Preinterview Impressions on Questioning Strategies in Same- and Opposite-Sex Employment Interviews," *Journal of Applied Psychology* 73 (1988), 30–37.

27. Robert L. Dipboye, Gail A. Fontenelle, and Kathleen Graner, "Effects of Previewing the Application on Interview Process and Outcomes," *Journal of Applied Psychology* 69 (1984), 118–28; Robert L. Dipboye, Carlla S. Stramler, and Gail A. Fontenelle, "The Effects of the Application on Recall of Information from the Interview," *Academy of Management Journal* 27 (1984), 561–75; Richard P. Herden, Frank E. Kuzmits, and Lyle Sussman, "Recruitment: Avoid the Traps of Relying on Interviews," *Personnel Journal* 63 (1984), 26–28.

28. Robin Palmer, "A Sharper Focus for the Panel Interview," *Personnel Management* 15 (1983), 34–37; "The Interview Process: A Systematic Approach to Better Hiring," *Small Business Report* 9 (1984), 57–62.

29. Mark R. Shaw, "Taken for Granted Assumptions in Simulated Selection Interviews," *Western Journal of Speech Communication* 47 (1983), 138–56; Thomas Harn and George C. Thornton, "Recruiter Counseling Behaviors and Applicant Impressions," *Journal of Occupational Psychology* 58 (1985), 57–65.

30. Rowanletcher Bayne and John Cliveolwell, "Board and Sequential Interviews in Selection: An Experimental Study of Their Comparative Effectiveness," *Personnel Review* 12 (1983), 14–19.

31. Tom Owens, "New Approach to Hiring," *Small Business Report* 15 (October 1990), 39–47; Warmke and Weston, 120–126; Jonathan Horwitz and Howard Kimpel, "Taking Control: Techniques for the Group Interview," *Training and Development Journal* 42 (1988), 52–54.

32. John W. Cogger, "Are You a Skilled Interviewer?" *Personnel Journal* 61 (1982), 842–43.

33. Arvey and Campion, 284–88; Alan Gratch, "The Interview: Who Should Be Talking to Whom," *The Wall Street Journal* 29, February 1988; Robert Zawacki, "MIS Struggles to Hire Wisely/Prepping the Perfect Interview," *Computerworld* 32 (1987), 73–74; Richard T. Case, "How to Conduct an Effective Interview," *Practical Accountant* 19 (1986), 65–70. Graeme Buckingham, "Using Structured Interviews to Measure Job Success," *Personnel Management* 17 (1985), 99.

34. DeCamp, 44–47; Mary A. Bouce, "Selecting Quality Field Managers: The Wrong Choice Can Hurt," *Market Facts* 10 (January/February 1991), 11–13; "Corporate Hiring and Executive Search Will Dramatically Change in the 1990s," *Canadian Manager* 14 (September 1989), 21 and 27; Harris 691–726.

35. Carol J. Reitz, "Be Steps Ahead of Other Candidates," *Legal Assistant Today* 5 (March/April 1988), 24–26 and 84–86.

36. Tengler and Jablin, 245–263.

37. Jablin and Miller, 51–86.

38. M. Ronald Buckley and Robert W. Eder, "B.M. Springbett and the Notion of `Snap Decision' in the Interview," *Journal of Management* 14 (1988), 59–67.

39. William Friend, "Finding People: Eight Steps to Better Employment Interviews," *Association Management* 34 (1982), 37–40; Susan M. Taylor and Janet A. Sniezek, "The College Recruitment Interview: Topical Content and Applicant Reactions," *Journal of Occupational Psychology* 57 (1984), 157–68; Jeanne Greenberg and Herbert Greenberg, "Sales Managers . . . Bad Interviews Lose Good Salesmen!" *Industrial Distribution* 73 (1984), 45–46.

40. Jablin and Miller; Fredric M. Jablin and Karen B. McComb, "The Employment Screening Interview: An Organizational Assimilation and Perspective," in *Communication Yearbook 8*, R. Bostrom (Beverly Hills, CA: Sage, 1984), 142; Thomas Sheppard, "Seeking Substance: Wipe Away the Gloss when Selecting Employees," *Management World* 14 (1985), 316–37.

41. Thomas M. Rohan, "Loaded Questions . . . Help to Hire the Right People," *Industry Week* 224 (1985), 43–44; Stephen L. Cohen and H. Frank Gump; "Using Simulations to Improve Selection Decisions," *Training & Development Journal* 38 (1984), 85–88; Robert J. Morris, "Objective Interviewing—Discerning the Best in Sales Candidates," *Business Marketing* 69 (1984), 58–62; Michael F. Wolff, "Hiring People Who Do Good Research," *Research Management* 27 (1984), 8–9.

42. David C. Gilmore and Gerald R. Ferris, "The Effects of Applicant Impression Management Tactics on Interviewer Judgments," *Journal of Management* 15 (1989), 557–564.

43. Mark R. Shaw, 138–56; Karen B. McComb and Fredric M. Jablin, "Verbal Correlates of Interviewer Empathic Listening and Employment Interview Outcomes," *Communication Monographs* 51 (1984), 353–71; Stanley M. Slowik, "Ask the Right Questions, Get the Right Answers," *Security Management* 31 (1987), 75–77; Stanley M. Slowik, "Why Applicants Lie and What to Do About It," *Security Management* 29 (1985), 41–43.

44. Daniel C. Feldman and Hugh J. Arnold, "Individual Reactions to Interviewer Behavior," *Journal of Employment Counseling* 24 (1987), 17–30; Jablin and McComb, 142.

45. Peter Herriot, "Give and Take in Graduate Selection," *Personnel Management* 17 (1985), 33–35; Thomas Gergmann and M. Susan Taylor, "College Recruitment: What Attracts Students to Organizations?" *Personnel* 61 (1984), 34–36; Bruce Horovitz, "Cut the Baloney Out of Job Interviews," *Industry Week* 219 (1983), 66; Fredric M. Jablin, "Organizational Entry, Assimilation, and Exit," in *Handbook of Organizational Communication,* Jablin, et al. (Beverly Hills, CA: Sage, 1987).

46. Cogger, 840–41; Schneider-Jenkins and Carr-Ruffino, 38–39; Loretta Schorr, "Blueprint for Effective Hiring Practices," *Supervision* 45 (1983), 14, 20, 23.

47. John C. Crystal and Richard N. Bolles. *Where Do I Go from Here with My Life?* (New York: Seabury Press, 1974).

48. Lois Einhorn, *Interviewing . . . A Job In Itself* (Bloomington, IN: The Career Center, 1977), 3–5; Marilyn A. Hutchinson and Sue E. Spooner, *Job Search Preparedness Barometer* (Bethlehem, PA: The College Placement Council 1975); *Merchandising Your Job Talents* (Washington, D.C.: U.S. Department of Labor, 1975).

49. "Most Serious Résumé Gaffes," *Communication Briefings* (March 1991); These suggestions are based on the authors' experiences as hiring agents, consultations with a variety of organizations and executive placement agencies, and interviews with hiring agents from public schools, universities, and companies in electronics, manufacturing, computer software, retail sales, and real estate. See also Melvin W. Donaho and John L. Meyer, *How to Get the Job You Want* (Englewood Cliffs, NJ: Prentice-Hall, 1976), 44–66; Lois J. Einhorn, Patricia Hayes Bradley, and John E. Baird, *Effective Employment Interviewing: Unlocking Human Potential* (Glenview, IL: Scott, Foresman, 1981).

50. "Résumé Controversy," *Into Print* (Fall 1990), 3.

51. Donna Bogar Goodall and H. Lloyd Goodall, Jr., "The Employment Interview: A Selective Review of the Literature with Implications for Communications Research," *Communication Quarterly* 30 (1982), 116–23; John M. Darley and Mark P. Zanna, "An Introduction to the Hiring Process in Academic Psychology," *Canadian Psychology* 22 (1981), 228–37; Marianne Ilaw, et al., "Reading Between the Lines/Does Your Job Work For You?/The Fine Art of Finding the Right Job/Getting a Jump on the Job Market/Your College Calendar for Career Success," *Black Enterprise* 15 (1985), 95–103, 109–11.

52. Paula Eubanks, "Hospitals Probe Job Candidates' Values for Organizational 'Fit'," *Hospitals* 65 (October 20, 1991), 36 and 38; David E. Bowen, Gerald E. Ledford, and Barry R. Nathan, "Hiring for the Organization, Not the Job," *Academy of Management Executive* 5 (November 1991), 35–51.

53. Axtmann and Jablin; Jablin and Miller; Laurie Babbitt and Fredric M. Jablin, "Characteristics of Applicants' Questions and Employment Screening Interviews," *Human Communication Research* 11 (1985), 507–35; Steven M. Ralston, "The Influence of Interviewee Communication Effectiveness on Simulated Recruitment Interview Decisions," Unpublished Paper, Annual Convention of the Speech Communication Association, New Orleans 1988; Carol J. Reitz, "Be Steps Ahead of Other Applicants," *Legal Assistant Today* 5 (1988), 24–28, 84–86.

54. Robert A. Martin, "Toward More Productive Interviewing," *Personnel Journal* 50 (1971), 359–63.

55. John Warnous, *Organizational Entry: Recruitment, Selection, and Socialization of Newcomers* (Reading, MA: Addison-Wesley, 1980).

56. William L. Tullar, "Relational Control in the Employment Interview," *Journal of Applied Psychology* 74 (1989), 971–977.

57. Harris; Cindy Rager, *The Visual Image* (Cape Coral, FL: Whitney Leadership Foundation, 1990); Arvey and Campion, 290, 303; Goodall and Goodall, 119; Sandra Forsythe, Mary Frances Drake, and Charles Cox, "Influence of Applicant's Dress on Interviewer's Selection Decisions," *Journal of Applied Psychology* 70 (1985), 374–78; Helen Carl, "Nonverbal Communication During the Employment Interview," *ABCA Bulletin,* December 1980, 14–18.

58. Neil R. Anderson, "Decision Making in the Graduate Selection Interview: An Experimental Investigation," *Human Relations* 44 (1991), 403–417; Richard L. Street, "Interaction Processes and Outcomes in Interviews," *Communication Yearbook* 9, M. L. McLaughlin, ed., (Beverly Hills, CA: Sage, 1985), 215–50; Goodall and Goodall, 119–21; Daly, Richmond, Leth, 29–31; Ronald E. Riggio and Barbara Throckmorton, "The Relative Effects of Verbal and Nonverbal Behavior, Appearance, and Social Skills on Evaluations Made in Hiring Interviews," *Journal of Applied Social Psychology* 18 (1988), 331–48.

59. R. Gifford, C. F. Ng, and M. Wilkinson, "Nonverbal Cues in the Employment Interview: Links Between Applicant Qualities and Interviewer Judgments," *Journal of Applied Psychology* 70 (1985), 729–36; Robert Hopper and F. Williams, "Speech Characteristics and Employability," *Speech Monographs* 40 (1973), 296–302.

60. Scott T. Fleischmann, "The Messages of Body Language in Job Interviews," *Employment Relations Today* 18 (1991), 161–166; Anderson.

61. Street, 217–18; Arvey and Campion, 303; Goodall and Goodall, 119; Carl, 14; Keith G. Rasmussen, "Nonverbal Behavior, Verbal Behavior, Résumé Credentials, and Selection Interview Outcomes," *Journal of Applied Psychology* 69 (1984), 551–56.

62. Lois J. Einhorn, "An Inner View of the Job Interview: An Investigation of Successful Communicative Behaviors," *Communication Education* 30 (1981), 217–28; Street, 216–18; Axtmann and Jablin; Patricia Stubbs, "Some Hints to Those Who Are Interviewed," *Management World* 13 (1984), 17–18; A. Keenan, "Candidate Personality and Performance in Selection Interviews," *Personnel Review* 11 (1982), 20–22.

63. Wilson; Jablin and Miller; Shaw, 144; Axtmann and Jablin.

64. Arthur Eliot Berkeley, "Job Interviewers' Dirty Little Secret," *The Wall Street Journal* 10, March, 1989.

65. "Job Interviews Pose Rising Risk to Employers;" Harold P. Brull, "Why Should We Hire Someone Your Age? How to Answer Questions Your Interviewer Won't Ask," *New Choices* 31 (May 1991), 68–69.

66. Fredric M. Jablin and Craig D. Tengler, "Facing Discrimination in On-Campus Interviews," *Journal of College Placement* 42 (1982), 57–61; William D. Siegfried and Karen Wood, "Reducing College Students' Compliance with Inappropriate Interviewer Requests: An Educational Approach," *Journal of College Student Personnel* 24 (1983), 66–71; Shaw, 144–45; Geraldine Tucker, "Questions That Should Not Be Asked During a Job Interview," *The Black Collegian,* February/March 1980, 112–13.

67. Gerald L. Wilson and H. Lloyd Goodall, Jr., *Interviewing in Context* (New York: McGraw-Hill, 1991), 159–162; Joann Keyton and Jeffery Springston, "I Don't Want to Answer That! A Response Strategy Model for Potentially Discriminatory Questions," Unpublished Paper, Annual Convention of the Speech Communication Association, San Francisco 1989.

68. Babbitt and Jablin, 507–35; Darley and Zanna, 232–34; Jablin and Miller.

Suggested Readings

Bolles, Richard N. *What Color Is Your Parachute?* Berkeley, CA: Ten Speed Press, 1990.

Cho, Emily. *Looking, Working, Living Terrific 24 Hours a Day.* New York: Ballantine Books, 1983.

Cho, Emily, and Grover, Linda. *Looking Terrific.* New York: Ballantine Books, 1988.

Cogger, John W. *Seven Imperatives: Fair and Effective Interviewing.* New York: Drake Beam Morin, 1980.

Crystal, John C., and Bolles, Richard N. *Where Do I Go from Here with My Life?* New York: Seabury Press, 1980.

Donaho, Melvin W., and Meyer, John L. *How to Get the Job You Want.* Englewood Cliffs, NJ: Prentice-Hall, 1976.

Eder, Robert W. and Ferris, Gerald R., eds. *The Employment Interview: Theory, Research, and Practice.* Newbury Park, CA: Sage, 1989.

Einhorn, Lois J.; Bradley, Patricia Hayes; and Baird, John E. *Effective Employment Interviewing: Unlocking Human Potential.* Glenview, IL: Scott, Foresman, 1981.

Half, Robert. *How to Hire Smart.* New York: Robert Half International, 1982.

Meyer, John L., and Donaho, Melvin W. *Get the Right Person for the Job.* Englewood Cliffs, NJ: Prentice-Hall, 1979.

Molloy, John T. *John T. Molloy's New Dress for Success.* New York: Warner Books, 1988.

8

The Performance Appraisal and Discipline Interview

Although the majority of American organizations have some form of performance appraisal, progress review, or merit rating, most supervisors and subordinates are unhappy with the methods of evaluation and motivation employed. The typical appraisal system that is designed to improve productivity often aggravates the situation and results in lower productivity and increased apathy among employees.[1] Kenneth Wexley and Richard Klimoski write, "It is becoming increasingly obvious that the way performance appraisal programs are designed and carried out has a profound impact on the reactions employees have to an organization and its human resources management efforts."[2]

The performance appraisal interview can serve many important functions for both organizations and their employees if both interviewer and interviewee learn the purposes of the interview, the keys to its success, how to prepare for it, and how to take part in it. Figure 8.1 illustrates the nine-step process for planning and taking part in appraisal interviews.

Understanding the Purposes of the Appraisal Interview

The performance appraisal interview is essentially a feedback mechanism that may serve a variety of purposes for employer and employee.[3] The most important purpose for the employer is not to review and judge performance but to bring about better future performance.[4] This is best accomplished by using a total performance and development plan to make equitable and objective decisions about pay raises, job assignments, promotions, demotions, and discharges. This plan should emphasize prospects for advancement, meaningful feedback, and the employee's strengths and accomplishments.[5] Thus, an effective performance appraisal system enables organizations to assess training and development needs, enhance superior-subordinate communication, build stronger staff relationships, and create a positive results-oriented atmosphere by recognizing good work and achievement of goals.

The most important purpose for employees is to determine their performances of predetermined and verifiable goals. Self-evaluations combined with employer evaluations will tell employees exactly how they are doing on specific jobs, where they stand within organizations, and where they might be going "up the ladder."[6] Employees should seek on-going feedback and clarifications of the extent of their authority and control of personal and organizational resources.[7]

Figure 8.1 Planning and taking part in appraisal interviews

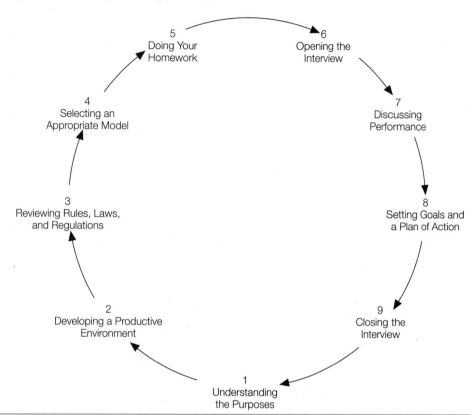

Developing a Productive Organizational Environment _____

Of the many keys to successful appraisal interviews, the most critical is the organizational environment that reflects an organization's basic "assumptions about human nature and human behavior." These *assumptions,* Douglas McGregor says, "are frequently implicit, sometimes quite unconscious, often conflicting; nevertheless, they determine our predictions that if we do A, B will occur."[8] McGregor uses these assumptions as the bases for what he calls Theory X and Theory Y. For instance, a Theory X manager assumes:

1. Human beings have an inherent dislike of work and will avoid it when they can.
2. Because human beings dislike work, they must be coerced, controlled, directed, or threatened with punishment to get them to put forth adequate effort toward the achievement of organizational objectives.
3. Human beings prefer to be directed, wish to avoid responsibility, have relatively little ambition, and want security above all.

A Theory Y manager assumes that:

1. The expenditure of physical and mental effort in work is as natural as play and rest.
2. Human beings, without external control or threat of punishment, will exercise self-direction and self-control in the service of objectives to which they are committed.
3. Commitment to objectives is a function of the rewards associated with their achievement.
4. Human beings, under proper conditions, not only accept but seek responsibility.
5. The capacity to exercise a relatively high degree of imagination, ingenuity, and creativity in the solution of organizational problems is widely, not narrowly, distributed in the population.
6. Under the conditions of modern industrial life, the intellectual potentialities of the average human being are only partially utilized.

Appraisal interviewers behaving on Theory X assumptions are likely to provide a *defensive* climate while interviewers behaving from Theory Y assumptions are likely to provide a *supportive* climate. Jack Gibb suggests that defensive and supportive climates have these characteristics:[9]

Defensive Climates	Supportive Climates
1. Evaluation	1. Description
2. Control	2. Problem orientation
3. Strategy	3. Spontaneity
4. Neutrality	4. Empathy
5. Superiority	5. Equality
6. Certainty	6. Provisionalism

Herbert Meyer recently wrote "Most modern organizations are moving away from authoritarian management toward an involvement-oriented working environment. A performance review discussion based on the subordinate's self review is more appropriate for the new climate. Research indicates that performance review discussions based on self-review are more productive and satisfying than traditional manager-initiated appraisal discussions."[10] The modern organization that Meyer refers to attempts to create a partnership with employee participation and involvement in supervisory management and to send a strong message that individual performance is highly important to the success of the organization.[11]

Employees clearly prefer a supportive climate that includes mutual trust, well-defined job descriptions, subordinate input, and a planning and review process. They want to be treated with sensitivity by a supportive, nonjudgmental interviewer. Employees want to contribute to each aspect of the review, get credit for their ideas, and know what to expect during and after the appraisal process. The appraisal is likely to be successful if an employee knows what to expect during the interview, has the ability to do what is expected on the job, receives feedback regularly, and is rewarded for a job well done.[12]

As an employer, you can create a relaxed, positive, and supportive climate by continually monitoring the employee's progress, offering psychological support in the form of praise and encouragement, helping to correct mistakes, and offering substantial

Supervisors at all levels have found it useful to talk periodically with each of their subordinates about personal or work-related issues.

feedback.[13] Above all, do not dwell primarily on negative aspects of performance, and do not let the employee do so. Base your appraisal on performance, not on the individual—attack the problem, not the person. Provide performance-related information, and measure performance against specific standards agreed upon during the previous appraisal.[14] For example, how many sales has the person made or how many claims has the person settled, and how do these compare with the standards set during the most recent appraisal session? Several studies have revealed that subordinates see supervisors as helpful, constructive, and willing to help them solve performance-related problems when those supervisors have encouraged them to express their ideas and feelings and participate equally in appraisal interviews.[15]

Frequency of appraisal interviews is a major key to success. Providing feedback on a regular basis, literally as a day-to-day responsibility, can avoid formal, once-a-year "tooth pulling" appraisals dreaded by both parties. Once a year is too infrequent, and twice seems to be a minimum. Evaluate poor performance immediately, before damage to the organization and the employee is irreparable. Avoid surprises during the interview caused by withholding criticisms until the formal appraisal session. And be sure to conduct as many sessions as necessary to do the job right; do not try to handle everything in one marathon session.[16]

Training of interviewers is another key to successful appraisal interviews. Interviewers must know how to create a genuine dialogue between themselves and the interviewee. They must realize that playing the role of evaluator will reduce the two-way communication process and negatively affect a relationship which itself is critical to the appraisal process. Interviewers who have learned how to handle performance-related information, assign goals, and give feedback are perceived by subordinates to be equitable, accurate, and clear during appraisal interviews.[17]

A primary employee complaint is the sloppy, casual attitude of too many employers toward documentation that affects their work lives, career progress, and financial gain.[18] They want interviewers and others who are involved in the appraisal to take them, their work, and their role within the organization seriously. Interviewers must be trained and have commitment to the appraisal process so that it is successful in enhancing future performance.[19]

Reviewing Rules, Laws, and Regulations

There are no shortcuts to successful performance appraisal interviews. Each must be thoroughly researched and prepared. Begin by reviewing your organization's regulations for evaluating employees, and then turn to laws, specifically Title VII of the 1964 Civil Rights Act (as amended) and Equal Employment Opportunity Commission (EEOC) guidelines and interpretations.[20] Be careful of assessing traits such as honesty, integrity, appearance, initiative, leadership, attitude, and loyalty that are difficult to judge objectively and fairly. Remember that all aspects of the employment process, including hiring, promoting, transferring, training, and discharging, are covered by civil rights legislation and EEO guidelines. Laws do not require performance appraisal by organizations; however, guidelines state that those that are conducted must be standardized in form and administration, measure actual work performance, and be applied equally to all classes of employees. Employees with equal experience or seniority in jobs requiring the same skills, effort, responsibility, and working conditions should receive equal compensation. Compensation based on sex, race, age, or ethnic group is unlawful.

The rapidly changing demographics of the workforce requires a keen familiarity with EEO laws, the nature of the appraisal interaction, and questionable assumptions have governed organizational interactions for too long. Increasing numbers of handicapped, females, and minorities are entering the workforce each year. Review carefully the EEO laws outlined in Chapter 7. Goodall, Wilson, and Waagen warn that communication between "superiors" and "inferiors" in the appraisal process leads to ritual forms of address "that are guided by commonly understood cultural and social stereotypes, traditional etiquette, and gender-specific rules."[21] If this is so, then we should not be surprised that appraisal interviewers often violate EEO laws and guidelines. The American workforce is increasingly older, and some authorities predict that age discrimination will be the most prominent area of litigation in the 1990s and beyond.[22] Incidentally, older workers perform better rather than inferior to younger workers.

Selecting an Appropriate Appraisal Model

To meet EEO guidelines and conduct fair and objective performance-centered appraisal interviews, theorists and organizations have developed several appraisal models during the past twenty years. According to the *person-product-process* model, managerial competencies lead to effective behaviors which then lead to effective performance.[23] A competency may be a motive, trait, skill, aspect of self-image, social role, or body of knowledge that leads to effective performance. Supporters of this model argue that evaluating persons in terms of competencies has two major advantages: (1) a single competency is manifest in several different actions, and (2) a manager's particular behavior is typically affected by several competencies.

In the *behaviorally anchored rating scales* (BARS) model, skills used on a specific job are identified through a job analysis, and standards are set, often with the aid of industrial engineers.[24] Typical jobs for which behaviors have been identified and standards set include telephone survey takers (at so many calls per hour), meter readers for utility companies (at so many meters per hour), and data entry staff or programmers (at so many lines of code per hour). Usually job analysts identify specific skills and weigh their relative worth and usage. With this approach, each job can have specific measurable skills that eliminate game-playing or subjective interpretation by supervisors. Employees whose supervisors use BARS report high levels of appraisal satisfaction, feel they have greater impact upon the process, and perceive their supervisors as supportive.[25] They know what skills they are expected to have, their relative worth to the organization, and how their performance will be measured. However, not every job has measurable or easily identifiable skills, and arguments often arise over when, how, and by whom specific standards are set. A recent study suggests that using the behaviorally anchored rating scale format results in more accurate performance ratings than does using the mixed standard scale format.[26]

The *management by objectives* (MBO) model, involves the manager and subordinate in a mutual (50–50) setting of results-oriented goals rather than activities to be performed. Advocates of the MBO model contend that behaviorally-based measures can (1) account for far more job complexity; (2) be related more directly to what the employee actually does; (3) minimize irrelevant factors not under the employee's control; (4) encompass cost-related measures; (5) be less ambiguous and subjective than person-based measures; (6) reduce employee role ambiguity by making clear what behaviors are required in a given job; and (7) facilitate explicit performance feedback and goal setting by encouraging meaningful employer-employee discussions regarding the employee's strengths and weaknesses.[27]

The MBO model classifies all work in terms of four major elements: (1) inputs, (2) activities, (3) outputs, and (4) feedback.[28] *Inputs* include equipment, tools, materials, money, and staff needed to do the work. *Activities* refer to the actual work performed. *Outputs* are results, end products, dollars, reports prepared, or services rendered. *Feedback* refers to the subsequent supervisor reaction (or lack of it) to the output. Figure 8.2 shows how the four major work elements interact.

If you serve as an appraisal interviewer using an MBO model, keep several principles in mind. First, *always consider quality, quantity, time, and cost.* Almost any job can be measured by these four criteria. The more of these criteria you use, the greater the chances that the measurement will be accurate. If you want to measure the effectiveness of a recruiter, for instance, you might count the number of interviews conducted by that recruiter per hire. By comparing the number of interviews per hire, you might obtain the

Figure 8.2   MBO performance appraisal model

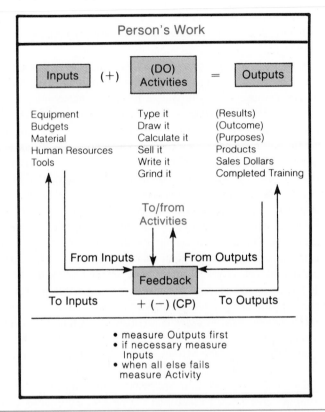

quantity and quality measure needed. You could calculate the cost in terms of time taken to fill a position, and measure quality by noting the number of people hired who received outstanding performance ratings.

Second, *state results in terms of ranges rather than absolutes.* Whether you use minimum, maximum, or achievable, or five- or seven-point scales, allow for freedom of movement and adjustment. Do not try to fine-tune the performance measure at the start, but begin with a broad range that you can adjust as the performance period continues.

Third, *keep the number of objectives small and set in a mutual environment.* If you are measuring a year's performance with quarterly or semiannual reviews, measure no more than six to eight major or critical aspects of performance. Positions such as research or development may have only one objective. The agreed-upon objectives should comprise about 70 percent of the work, with 30 percent kept in reserve to measure performance of assignments that come up unexpectedly.

Fourth, *try for trade-offs between mutually exclusive aims or measures.* An objective that is too complex may be self-defeating. For example, if you attempt to reduce labor and decrease cost at the same time, you may create more problems than you solve. Job performance is like performance in sports—when you concentrate on one aspect of the game, other parts may deteriorate. The best action might be to work on a goal step-by-step until you have achieved it.

Fifth, *when the value of the performance is abstract, initiate practices that make it measurable.* Measuring is often difficult, but anyone or anything that works can be measured. In a legal department, you might measure performance in terms of the number of cases won or lost or in terms of dollars lost to the organization. In graphic arts, you might measure response time, cost, and consumer satisfaction.

And sixth, *if you cannot predict conditions on which performance success depends, use a floating or gliding goal.* As one part of the target grows or moves, the other part does the same. This comparative measure works, for example, with production changes when people say, "You can't measure us because the production schedules change so often." You simply measure the amount produced versus the amount scheduled.

Regardless of the model you or your organization selects, *all parties* (management, interviewer, and employees) must understand the scheme and be as committed as possible to it.[29] Internal training of all parties is essential, but realize there are limits both to training and the model you select.[30] The model or appraisal scheme should be employee driven as much as possible to give employees a central role in the process and a feeling of control.[31] Many organizations are discovering that a partnership approach is most effective when it includes employee self-appraisals, peer reviews, input from each member of the employee's team, and a committee review process rather than a single appraisal interviewer. Employees perceive peer reviews to be more fair than management reviews.[32]

Doing Your Homework

Regardless of the appraisal model you employ, you must do *thorough homework.*[33] Study the employee's past record and most recent performance evaluation. Review the employee's self-evaluation. Understand the nature of the employee's position and work. Pay particular attention to the *fit* between the employee, the position, and the organization. Identify well in advance the primary purpose of the interview, especially if it is one of several with a particular employee. Prepare possible questions and any forms that you will use pertaining to the measurable goals. Know yourself and the employee as persons. For example, will you approach the interview from an *appraisal* or a *developmental* perspective? From an appraisal point of view the interview is seen as required and scheduled by the organization, superior-conducted and directed, top-down controlled, results-based, past-oriented, concerned with "what" rather than "how," adversarial, and organizationally satisfying. By contrast, from a developmental perspective, the interview is initiated by individuals whenever needed, subordinate-conducted and directed, bottom-up controlled, skillbased, now- and future-oriented, concerned with "how," cooperative, and self-satisfying.[34]

Understand the relationship that is likely to exist between you and the employee. How will control be shared during the interview? How willing are both parties to take part in the interview? Are you the best person to play the role of interviewer? Would the employee prefer someone else? How much do you like one another, and what is the history of your relationship? Realize that your relationship with the employee will affect the interview. Two or more employers often evaluate the same employee differently because their relationships differ.[35] Prepare a possible action plan to be implemented following the interview. Finally, schedule the interview several days in advance so that both parties can prepare and the employee realizes it is not a spur-of-the-moment crisis or discipline interview.

Opening the Interview

Try to put the employee at ease with a pleasant, friendly greeting. Get the person seated in an arrangement that is nonthreatening and not superior-subordinate. Researchers agree that fear of what appraisal interviews might yield "interferes with communication between interviewer and interviewee and keeps the review process from achieving its full potential."[36] Consider offering a soft drink or a cup of coffee. Establish rapport by showing support for the employee and perhaps engaging in a few minutes of small talk, but do not prolong this stage. You might orient the employee by giving a brief outline of how you want to conduct the interview. If there is something the employee would rather talk about first, do so. A slight alteration of your interview plan is worth the improved communication climate it is likely to create. Encourage the employee not to wait for a turn or the correct moment, but to participate actively throughout the interview.

Discussing Performance

Communication skills are critical to successful appraisal interviews.[37] Be aware of your own nonverbal cues and observe those emanating from the interviewee. As noted in Chapter 2, it is often not so much *what* is said but *how* it is said. Listen carefully to the interviewee, and adapt your listening approach to the changing needs of the interview, listening for comprehension when you need to understand, for evaluation when you must appraise, and with empathy when you must show sensitivity and understanding.

"Be an active listener" is good advice and common sense, but Goodall, Wilson, and Waagen warn that interviewers must know *why* they are listening actively: "Motives may include a desire to exhibit efficient appraisal behavior, to show a concern for the interviewee's well-being, and to collect evidence of talk that may be used for or against the subordinate at a later date."[38] The first two are positive, but the third may be detrimental both to the interview and future interactions with the interviewee.

Maintain an atmosphere that will assure two-way communication beyond Level 1 by being sensitive, providing feedback and positive reinforcement, reflecting feelings, and exchanging information. Feedback may be your most important skill. Consider using a panel of interviewers rather than a single interviewer. Research suggests that the panel approach produces higher validation in judgment, better developmental action planning, greater compliance with antidiscrimination laws, more realistic promotion expectations, and reduced perception of favoritism.[39] Employees tend to give favorable ratings to good interviewers and unfavorable ratings to poor interviewers.[40]

Make discussing performance an opportunity for full and open discussion between both parties aimed at improving both individual and organizational performance. Critical keys to the success of the appraisal interview are your abilities to communicate information effectively and encourage open dialogue.[41] Strive to be a counselor, coach or partner in career management rather than an authoritarian judge.

Discuss the interviewee's total performance, not just one event or a specific part of the period. Begin with areas of excellence so you can focus on the person's strengths. Strive for an objective, positive integration of work and results. Cover standards that are met, and encourage the employee to identify strengths. Communicate factual, performance-related information, and give specific examples.[42] If an employee takes special pride in a certain accomplishment and then you criticize that area, you will compound the problem. When employees believe you are attacking their personality, character, or integrity, you are left with no basis upon which to help them improve performance. The tendency of supervisors to inflate negative information when giving feedback may create conflict and reduce trust, disclosure, and cooperation. When one of the authors asked managers from a large federal agency to list the characteristics of the best manager they had ever had, the list included the following: fair, open-minded, caring, sincere, good listener, encouraging, trusting, informative, precise, knowledgeable, and a "straight shooter."

Excessive and prolonged praise can create anxiety and distrust because employees not only expect but desire to discuss their performance weaknesses. An employee who receives no negative feedback or suggestions of ways to improve will not know which behavior to change. Discuss needed improvements in terms of specific expected behaviors in a constructive, nondirective, problem-solving manner. Employees are likely to know what they are not doing satisfactorily, but unlikely to know what they should do differently. Let the employee provide much of the input. Probe tactfully and sensitively for causes of problems. Do not heap criticism upon the employee. The more you point out shortcomings, the more threatened, anxious, and defensive the employee will become. As the perceived threat grows, so will the person's negative attitude toward you and the appraisal process. Unfortunately, perceptions by employee or supervisor are not the best yardsticks for measuring performance. Where comments, suggestions, and criticisms are concerned, it is often not what is intended that counts but what the other party believes is intended. If a fault cannot be corrected by positive suggestions, do not mention it during the interview.[43]

Whether giving positive or negative feedback, you must be constantly aware of the potential effects of your biases.[44] For example, if interviewers like certain individuals or perceive them to be similar to themselves, they tend to treat them more positively and to rate their performances higher. Males continue to discriminate against women where promotions, development, or supervision are concerned. Women tend to rate achievements by other women less favorably than similar ones by men unless outside recognition influences them otherwise. You can control your biases most effectively by using objective criteria for all persons who do the same work and by being aware of common appraisal pitfalls. Terry Lowe identifies eight ways to ruin a performance review.[45] The *halo effect* comes about when an interviewer gives favorable ratings to all job duties when the interviewee excels in only one. The *pitchfork effect* leads to negative ratings for all facets of performance because of a particular trait the interviewer dislikes in others. The *central tendency* causes interviewers to refrain from assigning extreme ratings to facets of performance. An interviewer commits a *recency error* when relying too heavily on the most recent events or performance levels. The *length of service* of an interviewee may lead the interviewer to assume that present performance is high because performance was high in the past. The *loose rater* is reluctant to point out weak areas and dwells on the average or better areas of performance. The *tight rater* believes that no one can perform at the necessary standards. And the *competitive rater* believes that no one can perform higher than his or her levels of performance.

Do not start establishing goals without first summarizing the performance discussion and making sure that the employee has had ample opportunity to ask questions and make comments. Use reflective probes and mirror questions to verify information received and feedback given; use clearinghouse questions to be sure the employee has no further concerns.

Setting New Goals and a Plan of Action

Contemporary authorities agree that goal setting is the key to successful performance appraisals and should constitute 75 percent of the interview.[46] Focus, they argue, should be on future performance and career development rather than a dwelling on the past, and the interviewer should be an advisor, supporter, and facilitator rather than a judge.[47] O.L. Hill writes that "Although it is important to evaluate on the basis of past performance, it is just as important to anticipate future growth, set goals, and establish career paths."[48]

Review the last period's goals before going on to new ones. Performance is best when employees set their own goals.[49] Never intentionally or unintentionally impose goals. Avoid either/or statements, demands, and ultimatums. The goals should be few, specific, well-defined, practical, and measurable. Avoid ambiguous language such as *teamwork, cooperation, unity,* and *group effectiveness.* Both employer and employee must be able to determine when goals have been accomplished and why. Do not make the goals too easy or too difficult, but allow the employee to stretch a bit. Do not directly relate improved performance to salary increases, even though the overall evaluation may lead to a promotion and/or raise. Get the employee to suggest and agree on programs for improvement, because without cooperation the appraisal has failed. Decide upon follow-up procedures and how they will be implemented. Feedback combined with clear goal-setting produces the highest employee satisfaction.

Closing the Interview

Do not rush the closing.[50] Be sure the employee understands all that has transpired. Conclude on a note of trust and open communication. End with the feeling that this has been an important session for interviewee, interviewer, and the organization. Do not leave the impression that you are "Glad this is over until next year" or "Well, now I can get to some really important work." If you have filled out a form such as the one in figure 8.3, sign off the agreements and if organizational policy allows, permit the employee to put notes by items he or she feels strongly about. Give the employee a copy of the signed form as a record of the plan for the coming appraisal period.

Figure 8.3 Performance appraisal review form

Name:_____ Date of Appraisal:_____	
Performance Expectations	Performance Accomplishments
Employee Signature _____	Employee Signature _____
Supervisor Signature _____	Supervisor Signature _____
Manager Review _____	Manager Review _____

The Employee in the Appraisal Interview

As an employee, prepare for your appraisal interview by reviewing the objectives you were to reach during the period and the standards by which your performance will be measured.[51] Study production, attendance, and other records. Make a list of your accomplishments and problem areas. Analyze the causes of your strengths and weaknesses, and be prepared to respond to possible corrective actions with ideas for ways to improve on your own. Self-criticism often softens criticism from others, particularly superiors. Understand your relationship with the interviewer and his or her appraisal style. Check into the interviewer's mood prior to the interview. Be aware that a significant degree of sexual harassment does occur in organizations and that employees who have submitted to it tend to be judged more harshly than those who have resisted when such cases come to trial.[52]

Realize that while the interviewer runs the interview, at least half of the responsibility for making the interview a success rests with you.[53] Approach the appraisal interview as a valuable source of information on prospects for advancement, a chance to get meaningful feedback about how the organization views your performance and future, and an opportunity to display your strengths and accomplishments.[54] Be prepared to give concrete examples of your performance and how you have met or exceeded expectations. Prepare intelligent, well-thought-out questions, and be ready to discuss your career goals.

When taking part in the interview, try to maintain a productive relationship with the interviewer. Do not be eager to defend yourself unless there is something to be defensive about. If you are put on the defensive, maintain direct eye contact and clarify the facts before answering charges. You might ask, "How did this information come to your attention?" or "Who compiled these sales statistics?" This tactic will give you time to formulate a thorough and reasonable response based on complete understanding of the situation. Answer all questions thoroughly, and ask for clarification of those you do not understand. Offer explanations, but do not make excessive excuses or try to fix blame. Assess your performance and abilities reasonably, and be honest with yourself and your supervisor. Realize that what you are, what you think you are, what others think you are, and what you would like to be may describe several different people.

The appraisal interview is not a time to be shy or self-effacing.[55] Be sure to mention achievements such as special or extra projects, help you have given other employees, and community involvement on behalf of the organization. Be honest about challenges or problems you expect to encounter in the future. On the other hand, do not be afraid to ask for help. Correct any of the interviewer's false impressions or mistaken assumptions. If you are confronted with a serious problem, discover how much time is available to solve it. Suggest or request ways to resolve your difficulties as soon as possible. The interviewer is not out to humiliate you, but to help you grow for your own sake as well as for the organization. Keep your temper cool. Telling the supervisor off may give you a brief sense of satisfaction, but after the blast, the person will still be your supervisor and the problem may have worsened. Do not try to improve everything at once; set priorities with both short- and long-range goals. As the closing approaches, do not be in a hurry to get the interview over with. Summarize or state problems, solutions, and new goals in your own words. Be sure you understand all that has taken place and the agreements you are signing off for the next review period. Close on a positive note, with a determination to meet the new goals.

The Disciplinary Interview

An employer conducting a disciplinary interview must both appraise performance and advise improving behavior. As a supervisor, it may be your most distasteful task. Studies reveal that management feels discipline and punishment should be last resort efforts to change behavior. Many supervisors feel that punishment is ineffective, unethical, or somehow inhuman.[56] The working world is often difficult to separate from what goes on before and after work, but when performance standards are not met or lives are endangered by employees' conduct, you must act. Figure 8.4 illustrates the steps you should follow to handle the disciplinary interview systematically and effectively.

Preparing for Disciplinary Interviews

A helpful way to prepare for disciplinary interviews is to rehearse them by taking part in realistic role playing cases. These rehearsals can alleviate some of your anxiety and help you anticipate employee reactions, questions, and rebuttals. The variety of situations and interviewees encountered, without the pressures of a real organizational and employee crisis, can help you to refine your case-making, questioning, and responding while sticking

Figure 8.4 Handling disciplinary interviews

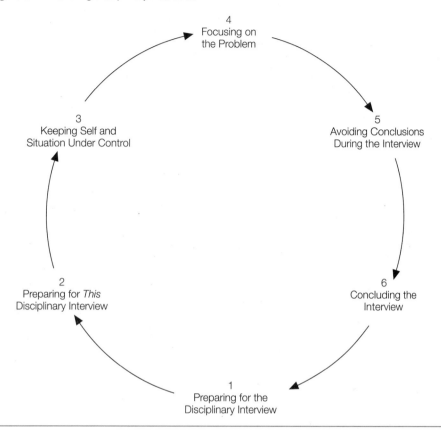

to the facts and documenting all claims with proof.[57] Role playing cases, literature reviews on disciplinary situations, and discussions with experienced interviewers will help you learn what to expect. For example, a recent study by Monroe, Borzi, and DiSalvo discovered four common responses from subjects in behavior conflict situations:[58]

1. *Apparent compliance*: over politeness and deference, apologies, promises, or statements of good intentions followed by the same old difficult or problem behaviors
2. *Relational leverage*: statements that they have been with the organization longer than the interviewer and therefore know best, that they are the best and you can't fire or discipline them, or references to friends or relatives within the organization
3. *Alibis*: claims of tiredness, sickness, being overworked, budget cuts, it's someone else's fault, or poor instructions or information
4. *Avoidance*: disappearing on sick leave or vacation, failure to respond to memos or phone calls, or failure to make an appointment

These four responses accounted for 93 percent of total incidents derived in their study.

Preparing for This Disciplinary Interview

Begin to prepare yourself by reviewing *how* you know the employee has committed an infraction that warrants a disciplinary interview. Did you see the infraction directly, as in the case of absenteeism, theft, poor workmanship, intoxication, fighting or insubordination? Or did you find out indirectly through a third party or by observing the results (such as lateness of a report, poor quality products, or goals unmet)? Are you anticipating an infraction because of stereotypes or previous incidents? For example, blacks and other minorities are often watched more closely than other employees because supervisors believe they are more likely to violate rules. On the other hand, supervisors tend to be lenient with persons they perceive as likable, similar to themselves, or possessing high status or exceptional talent.[59]

Next, decide whether the perceived infraction warrants punitive action. Absenteeism and low performance are generally considered more serious than tardiness and horseplay. Try to determine the *cause* of the infraction, because that will affect how you conduct the interview and what action you take. For example, interviewers are more likely to fire, suspend, or demote employees (1) when they feel the poor work is due to lack of motivation, interest, or drive rather than to lack of ability or technical competence and (2) when they think the employee should have been able to control the problem. Review the employee's past performance and disciplinary history. The two basic reasons for disciplinary action are poor performance or a troubled employee. When a person's performance gradually or suddenly declines, the cause may be motivational, personal, work-related, or supervisory. Drops in performance are indicated by swings in the employee's behavior; a friendly employee may suddenly become nasty, aggressive, or uncooperative. Keep an eye on other performance indicators such as attendance, quality and quantity of work, willingness to take instructions, and cooperation with other employees. A troubled employee may have an alcohol or drug dependency, a marital disturbance, or an emotional problem such as depression or anxiety. An employee may be stealing from the organization to support a gambling habit, drug, or alcohol addiction, or a boyfriend or girlfriend. Such employees need counseling, not discipline, but few organizations have effective counseling programs, and many employees refuse to take part even when they do.

For principles applicable to the disciplinary interview, review the appraisal interviewing portion of this chapter and read Chapter 9 on the counseling interview. Consider the three relational dimensions that affect interviews. Often neither party wants to take part and, as supervisor, you may have delayed the interview until there was no other recourse. As the problem came to a head, you and the employee may have come to dislike one another, even to the point of verbal and nonverbal abuse. You may decide to punish, demote, or dismiss the employee or the employee may become belligerent or resign. The employer's options are generally the most potent, unless the employee is very valuable to the organization at the particular time. Trust, cooperation, and disclosure are difficult to attain in a threatening environment.

Keeping Yourself and the Situation Under Control

You are the supervisor, and while you want to head off a problem before it becomes critical, you must not lose your temper or let the situation get out of hand. Never conduct a disciplinary interview when you are angry. *Hold the interview in a private location.* Discipline interviews are often ego-shattering, so do not worsen the situation by reprimanding an employee in the presence of peers. Meet in a place where you and the employee can discuss the problem freely and neither must play to an audience. *When severe discipline problems arise, consider delaying a confrontation and obtaining assistance.* For example, if two employees are caught fighting on a dock, have them report to your office or send them home and talk with each the next day. Depending on the situation, you may want to consult a counselor or call security before acting. *Consider having a witness or a union representative present.* The witness should be another supervisor because using one subordinate to testify against another is dangerous. If the union contract spells out the employee's right to representation, be sure to follow this procedure carefully. You may ask the witness to write down names, dates, locations, and other details relevant to the incident.

Focusing on the Problem

Deal in specific *facts,* such as absences, witnesses to the event, departmental records, and previous disciplinary actions. Do not allow the situation to become a trading contest: "Well, look at all the times I have been on time" or "How come the other guys get away with it?" Talk about this situation and this employee. *Record all available facts.* Unions, EEOC, and lawyers often require complete and accurate records. Take detailed notes, record the time and date on all material that might be used later, and obtain the interviewee's signature or initials for legal protection. *Do not be accusatory.* Avoid words and statements such as "drunk," "thief," "You're lying, aren't you?" and "Admit you stole those tools." You as a supervisor cannot make medical diagnoses of drunkenness or drug addiction, so do not even use those terms. Point to facts and leave medical judgments to professionals. *Preface remarks with phrases such as:* "From what I know . . . ," "According to your attendance report . . . ," "As I understand it . . . ," and "I have observed. . . . " Such phrases force you to be factual and keep you from accusing the employee of being guilty until proven innocent. *Ask questions that allow the person to express feelings and explain behavior:* "Tell me what happened . . . ," "Why do you feel that way . . . ," "When he said that, what did you . . . ?" Open questions allow you to get facts as well as feelings and explanations from the employee. Strive to establish the facts of the case and reach a common agreement with the employee regarding the alleged problem.[60]

Avoiding Conclusions During the Interview

Avoid verbalizing conclusions during the interview. A hastily drawn conclusion may create problems. Some organizations train supervisors to use standard statements under particular circumstances. If you are sending an employee off the job, you may say, "I do not believe you are in condition to work, so I am sending you home; report to me tomorrow at . . . " or "I want you to go to medical services and have a test made; bring a slip from the doctor when you return to my office" or "I am sending you off the job. Call me

Never conduct a discipline interview when you are angry, and when possible, hold the interview in a private location.

tomorrow at nine, and I will tell you what action I will take." This last statement gives you time to talk with others about possible actions and provides a cooling-off period for all concerned.

Closing the Interview

Conclude the interview in neutral. If discipline is appropriate, give it; but realize that delaying action may enable you to think more clearly about the incident. *Be consistent with the union contract, this employee, and all other employees.* Refer to your organization's prescribed disciplinary actions for specific offenses. Theft, except under unusual circumstances, is usually grounds for dismissal, while employees with alcohol and drug problems may be counseled the first time and fired the second time. Apply all rules equally to all employees.

Summary

Judge an employee's performance on the basis of standards mutually agreed upon ahead of time. Apply the same objectives equally to all employees performing a specific job. Research and good sense dictate that appraisal, promotion, salary, and discipline issues be discussed in separate interview sessions. Appraisal interviews should occur at least semi-annually, while promotion, salary, and discipline interviews usually take place when needed. Deal with discipline problems before they disrupt the employee's work or association with your organization.

For both employer and employee, flexibility and open-mindedness are important keys in successful appraisal interviews. Flexibility should be tempered with understanding and tolerance of individual differences. The appraisal process must be ongoing, with no particular beginning or end. Supervisors and subordinates are constantly judged by the people around them. By gaining insights into their own behavior and how it affects others, both parties can become better persons and organization members.

An Appraisal Interview for Review and Analysis

AGF Learning Systems develops custom training programs—video, audio, programmed instruction, and computer simulations—for both domestic and international clients. Nancy Jamieson is manager of Account Services (customer relations), and Jack Doyle has worked for Nancy for more than three years. He is about to receive his last quarterly performance review. AGF uses an MBO system mutually agreed to by supervisor and employee. The following key objectives are measured 70 percent by the employee's work and 30 percent by the supervisor: day-to-day duties, response to change, working with others, and so on. Each objective is measured on a five-point scale, with 5 being high and 1 being low; the higher the score, the greater the percentage of salary increase.

How effective is the opening in establishing rapport and orienting the employee? Which type of climate prevails, supportive or defensive? How effectively do supervisor and subordinate deal with positive aspects of performance first before getting into negative aspects? Does either party get into nonperformance aspects of the employee's behavior? How effectively do the parties set goals for the next appraisal period? Does either party dominate a specific phase of the interview? How effectively is the interview closed? How skilled are both the supervisor as an interviewer and the subordinate as an interviewee? How prepared are both parties?

1. **Nancy:** Good morning, Jack; please have a seat.
2. **Jack:** Thanks.
3. **Nancy:** Let me just refresh my memory and summarize where we left off last time. At the end of the third quarter when we discussed your five key objectives, you were not only on target but ahead of schedule on number one. Objectives two and three were close to being completed for the year. The real problems came in numbers four and five. Is this about what you recall?
4. **Jack:** Yes, that's pretty much where we were.
5. **Nancy:** Number four was to notify your customer base at least ninety days prior to the time their materials needed updating in order to give production and printing a maximum of 180 days lead time, with 150 days being ideal but 120 being acceptable. This one seems to be really off target.
6. **Jack:** Yeah, it is, and even some of the ideas we discussed last quarter don't seem to be working. When I call clients before sending out the Suggested Revision Lists and then make follow-up calls to make sure they have received the lists, it only seems to irritate them.

7. **Nancy:** Do you have a copy of the notes we made on this last quarter? Good. We agreed to the call-write-call strategy because too many customers were calling in complaining about our lack of response time once they had asked for revisions . . . .Why do you think this is irritating your clients?

8. **Jack:** This is just a guess, but I've had a couple of customers tell me that their account representatives had told them to ignore account services and call them when they were ready for revisions or updates.

9. **Nancy:** How did you respond?

10. **Jack:** I told them it didn't *really matter* but because our account reps were so busy, we wanted to make sure that revisions didn't get lost in the busy day-to-day business.

11. **Nancy:** Nice way of handling a rather clumsy situation, Jack! I have a feeling that sales is trying to sell up to customers, and we are trying to revise current materials. Let me take this up with Matt in Sales. Between now and year-end, let's adjust that objective to read, "When customers respond positively or give us permission to revise materials, we will . . . (Jack interrupts)

12. **Jack:** No problem. . . . We are averaging 128 days, and I think we can beat that figure.

13. **Nancy:** If you can't control it, then it's hard to hold you responsible for it; so this adjustment should help.

14. **Jack:** Yeah, that's okay, but I see no real help on number five. I've been off target for three quarters and don't see any way to get back within budget in the next three months.

15. **Nancy:** Why not?

16. **Jack:** (laughing) Why not . . . ? Well, I'm 118K over my budget on customer complaint corrections and if I can't charge back some of the Special Request Customers, there is no hope for me ever being close. . . . I may be 175K in the hole by year-end.

17. **Nancy:** Jack . . . you do good work! There seem to be only two areas of slippage. The SRC budget items and your relationship with accounting. . . . Now . . . (Jack interrupts)

18. **Jack:** Okay! Okay! So you and Accounting aren't happy. . . . Well, here's my predicament. When a customer calls me or my six operators and wants an extra tape, one more manual, a few copies of Tab II materials, I can't say no, I can't bill them, and I can't charge Sales. So I eat the cost. . . . Now what am I supposed to do?

19. **Nancy:** Jack! Come on . . . you're too nice to the customers. Why not say, "Okay, but we will need to bill you X?"

20. **Jack:** I've tried that, and they slam down the phone. . . . After I stop swearing, I usually pick up the phone myself and put NC on the bill. When Accounting sees No Charge, they bill me. I go to accounting and raise hell—why isn't this billed to Public Relations, Sales, Advertising and Promotions—hell, anybody but me. Their answer is always the same, "You sent it; you pay for it."

21. **Nancy:** (silence)

22. **Jack:** Look, what do you want me to do?

23. **Nancy:** I was going to save this for the end, but maybe now is a good time. Jack, overall your performance has been outstanding. Here is a survey we took of customers. You and your group came out on top, but the survey indicates some interesting findings. Read some of these comments.

24. **Jack:** (after a few minutes) The ratings are great, but I'm not sure I like the handle "Generous Jack!" Maybe I do too much for customers, but. . . .

25. **Nancy:** Jack, Customer Service is art and science! You have a reasonable budget, but you are way over. This is a tough area that requires a delicate sense of judgment. You need to ask yourself, "Am I doing too much for the customer?" It may sound harsh, and I don't mean it to be, but we're in the business of selling services. We must charge the customers for all of those services. Now let's see if we can't keep this item under 120K.

26. **Jack:** That's only $2,000 for three months. . . . I can't do it!

27. **Nancy:** Sure you can. Now you're meeting all the other objectives quite well, so just focus your attention on this one for the final quarter. Come see me more often if things aren't shaping up during the next few weeks. I've got another appointment now, but let's talk again soon.

28. **Jack:** Okay, I'll do my best, but it's going to be tough and I'm going to make a lot of customers unhappy.

Appraisal and Disciplinary Role-Playing Cases

A Recreation Department Assistant

The interviewer, Mac Roberts, is the director of a city recreation department. His assistant director is a young college graduate with a major in recreation. There are eight full-time members on the recreation staff and a large group of part-time or volunteer workers. Mac is in his early forties and has been involved in physical education, recreation, and industrial education most of his life. He has built a good working relationship with the local high schools and industries. Jim Morrison, his assistant, has been with the department for one year and has been eased into dealing with local industry. Much to Mac's amazement, he has received several phone calls complaining that Jim has put pressure on local industries and retailers to donate equipment. During the performance review, Mac intends to resolve this problem.

The interviewee would like the recreation department to have better and more up-to-date equipment. He thinks local merchants and industries who make money off kids should donate some new equipment each year. He has been calling on them to see if they will loosen their purse strings. He has hinted that kids ought to support only those merchants and industries that support them. Jim is up for his first performance review and, while not unhappy with the job, feels he could use more help and support.

An Instructor in a Small College

Donna Hoosier is chairperson of the history department at a small college that prides itself on its outstanding teachers. With the help and approval of her staff, Donna has initiated an annual review of each history staff member. She conducts the appraisals herself. The results of each review are noted and placed in the professor's open personnel file. Donna is interviewing Harry Lackington, an untenured professor, who seems to be an extremely weak teacher and has problems relating to students. Harry has ranked lowest on students' evaluations for the entire campus and has failed more students than the other six members of the history department combined.

Harry Lackington is in his mid-thirties and thinks he has found a place where he can teach and enjoy life. He previously taught high school and is fed up with spoon-feeding students. He does his job, and he wants plenty of time to play tennis and take some courses toward his doctorate. He is strongly opposed to the evaluation system but has to remain silent until he obtains tenure. He does not like the idea of a performance review and plans to say so during the appraisal interview.

A Secretary in Industry

Max Johnson is the manager of an office that employs eight secretaries. The company produces products for office and commercial use and has a dozen salespersons on the road. Each secretary in the office is assigned one or two salespersons and several distributors. The secretaries must be able to handle the telephone and deal with people. When an account calls directly to the factory, the salesperson assigned to that territory is given the commission. It is important that the secretary be accurate in recording the order and crediting the commission to the right person. Max is about to interview Sarah Randolph who has been with the company for nearly two years and has been above average in performance. Recently, however, she has cost the company money by inaccurately recording phone orders. She is terrible with details, causing wrong quantities and items to be shipped.

Sarah Randolph is a college graduate in her early twenties. She turns out twice the volume of most employees, but some of it must be done over. She is pleasant, enjoys her work, and loves to talk to salespersons on the telephone, especially concerning big accounts. Lately, however, one of the married salespersons has been driving her up the wall. He calls her at least twice a day, mails her funny cards, and gives her silly presents. Quite recently he has been stopping by her apartment unannounced. She has reached the frustration level but does not want to tell him off, inform her supervisor, or get the salesperson in trouble with his wife. She knows her work has been affected, but does not know what to say about it during the interview, if anything.

An Hourly Worker

Marie Pauling is a salesperson recently promoted to assistant personnel manager. Because of a recent turnover in plant personnel, she has been assigned to conduct performance reviews of several hourly workers. She is interviewing Maud Raston, who has just completed her six-month probation period. Maud's production record is above average, her waste is within the prescribed limits, and her attendance is normal. But Maud is a chronic "bitcher," a persistent cloud of gloom and doom. She complains about the insurance plan, the vending machines, the material handlers, the water fountains, and the supervision. She is constantly placing suggestions in the suggestion box.

Maud had to go to work because of her husband's back trouble. While she does not mind working, she hates being forced into it. Doctors tell her it will be two or three years before her husband can go back to construction work. Until then she will be the sole supporter of her family. She dislikes people who do not speak their minds. She feels that while this is not a bad place to work, it is not a good one either. She is surprised that some of her coworkers have been at the job ten, fifteen, or twenty years. She complains a lot but does not really mean to. Lately, some women on her shift have been giving her the cold shoulder.

A Fashion Manager

Mary Alice Tame is the manager of a large women's department in a major department store. She is ambitious, competitive, and hopes to become the head buyer for the entire department store chain. She has forty-three people working for her in three areas. The big turnover is in the college shop where the new "group leader" (Mary Alice's name for manager) is a young college graduate named Linda Wakefield. Linda is beautiful, efficient, and extremely bossy. She had two years of experience with a competitor before joining Tame's store where she improved her area's business by 13 percent in just one year. Linda is an excellent merchandiser, but complaints have reached Tame that she spends considerable company time with the male trainees and is occasionally more than friendly with some members of management. How can Tame correct her without losing her?

Linda Wakefield is twenty-five but looks nineteen, is very proud of her figure, and dresses to show it off. After all, she feels, people in the fashion business should be a picture of fashion. She wants to be a big success in fashion retailing and spends long hours at night keeping up on the latest fabrics, trends, and designs. During college, sororities, classes, part-time jobs, and beauty contests kept her too busy for much socializing. Now that she is earning a good living, she intends to make up for lost time. Her feeling toward her supervisor is not warm. She feels that if Tame would order some of the things she suggests, she could improve business by 25 percent. Linda plans to mention this at an appropriate time during their next interview.

Student Activities

1. Check with a company, a government agency, the Civil Service, or a military unit to see what kind of performance appraisal process is used. What performance indicators, standards, or objectives does the organization use? How often does the organization measure each person's performance? How is the appraisal interview structured? How does it deal with personnel who are not performing satisfactorily?

2. Obtain a union contract from a local company and examine the section on discipline. What are the steps that must be taken by management? What are the offenses for which an employee may be fired? What kinds of programs does the company have for troubled employees? What happens if an employee refuses counseling?

3. Find an organization that uses a merit rating system, one that employs a standard appraisal interview approach, and one that uses an assessment center approach. Interview a member of the personnel staff of each organization to discover the advantages and disadvantages of each system. Discuss where and how appraisal interviewing can be used best.

4. It is frequently said that there is no effective way to evaluate good teaching. With this comment as a framework, develop a means of measuring or evaluating your instructor. Use student reaction forms and faculty critiques to develop a statistical means of arriving at a rating and ranking. How could an appraisal interview be used to convey this information to your teacher? How would teachers benefit from appraisal interviews? Who should conduct the interviews?

5. Find an organization that uses an MBO approach and one that uses a BARS approach. Interview members of each organization concerning their feelings about these methods of evaluating performance. What are the major pluses and minuses of each method? What role does interviewing play in each system?

Notes

1. Mary Zippo and Marc Miller, "Performance Appraisal: Current Practices and Techniques," *Personnel* 61 (1984), 57–59; "Self-Appraisals: A Participative Technique for Evaluating and Improving Employee Performance," *Small Business Report* 9 (1984), 37–40; Edward E. Lawler III, Allan M. Mohrman, and Susan L. Resnick, "Performance Appraisal Revisited," *Organizational Dynamics* 13 (1984), 20–35; Kaye Loraine, "How Effective Are Work Evaluations?" *Supervision* 45 (1983), 7–8, 13.

2. Kenneth N. Wexley and Richard Klimoski, "Performance Appraisal: An Update," *Research in Personnel and Human Resources Management* 2 (1984), 35–79.

3. Bruce R. McAfee and Mark L. Chadwin, "How Can Performance Evaluations Be Used to Motivate Employees?" *Management Quarterly* 24 (1983), 30–35.

4. William Umiker, "Performance Review Interviews: Planning for the Future," *Health Care Supervisor* 10 (March 1992), 28–35.

5. Alice LaPlante, "Making Performance Reviews Work for You," *Computerworld* 26 (April 6, 1992), 119.

6. David Cameron, "Performance Appraisal and Review," *Management Decision* 19 (1981), 3–54; H. Kent Baker and Stevan R. Holmberg, "Stepping Up to Supervision: Conducting Performance Reviews," *Supervisory Management* 27 (1982), 20–27; "The Performance Appraisal Interview," *Managers Magazine* 57 (1982), 36–40; Don Caruth, Bill Middlebrook, and Frank Rachel, "Performance Appraisals: Much More Than a Once-A-Year Task," *Supervisory Management* 27 (1982), 28–36.

7. Clinton O. Longnecker, "The Delegation Dilemma," *Supervision* 52 (February 1991), 3–5.

8. Douglas McGregor, *The Human Side of Enterprise* (New York: McGraw-Hill, 1960), 6, 33–34, 47–48.

9. Jack R. Gibb, "Defensive Communication," *Journal of Communication* 11 (1961), 141.

10. Herbert H. Meyer, "A Solution to the Performance Appraisal Feedback Enigma," *Academy of Management Executive* 5 (February 1991), 68–76.

11. Ross E. Robson and Dalmas H. Nelson, "Supervisor and Nonsupervisor Agreement and Dissonance Regarding Performance Appraisal," *Review of Public Personnel Administration* 11 (Fall 1990/Spring 1991), 121–130; Stuart Feldman, "AMOCO Keeps Its Employees in the 'Big Picture'," *Personnel* 68 (June 1991), 24.

12. Lawler, Mohrman, and Resnick, 20–35; Loraine, 7–8, 13; Arthur Pell, "Benefiting from the Performance Appraisal," *Bottomline* 3 (1986), 51–52; Baker and Holmberg, 20–27; H. Kent Baker and Philip I. Morgan, "Two Goals in Every Performance Appraisal," *Personnel Journal* 63 (1984), 74–78; Randall S. Schuler, "Taking the Pain Out of Performance Appraisal Interviews," *Supervisory Management* 26 (1981), 8–12.

13. O.L. Hill, "Time to Evaluate Evaluations," *Supervisory Management* 37 (March 1992), 7; Umiker.

14. "The Performance Appraisal Interview," 36–40; David T. Wight, "The Split Role in Performance Appraisal," *Personnel Administrator* 30 (1985), 83–87; Caruth, Middlebrook, and Rachel, 28–36; McAfee and Chadwin, 30–35.

15. Ronald J. Burke, William F. Weitzel, and Tamara Weir, "Characteristics of Effective Employee Performance Review and Development Interviews: Replication and Extension," *Personnel Psychology* 31 (1978), 903–19; Ronald J. Burke, William F. Weitzel, and Tamara Weir, "Characteristics of Effective Employee Performance Review and Development Interviews: One More Time," *Psychological Reports* 47 (1980), 683–95; Baker and Morgan, 74–78.

16. Steven D. Norton, "Performance Appraisal Advice for the New Supervisor," *Supervisory Management* 27 (1982), 30–34; Ronald W. Clement and George E. Stevens, "The Performance Appraisal Interview: What, When, and How?" *Review of Public Personnel Administration* 6 (1986), 43–58; Schuler, 8–12.

17. John M. Ivancevich, "Subordinates' Reactions to Performance Appraisal Interviews: A Test of Feedback and Goal-Setting Techniques," *Journal of Applied Psychology* 67 (1982), 561–67; Stephen M. Duley, et al., "Training and Generalization of Motivational Analysis Interview Assessment Skills," *Behavioral Assessment* 5 (1983), 281–93; Douglas Cederblom, "The Performance Appraisal Interview: A Review, Implications, and Suggestions," *Academy of Management Review* 7 (1982), 219–27.

18. Hill.

19. Bob Losyk, "Face to Face: How to Conduct an Employee Appraisal Interview," *Credit Union Executive* 30 (Winter 1990–1991), 24–26.

20. Steven D. Norton, 30–34; Robert Layer, "The Discrimination Danger in Performance Appraisal," *Conference Board Record* (March 1976), 60–64; Robert I. Lazer and Walter S. Wirkstrom, *Appraising Managerial Performance: Current Practices and Future Directions* (New York: The Conference Board, 1977), 2.

21. H. Lloyd Goodall, Jr., Gerald L. Wilson, and Christopher L. Waagen, "The Performance Appraisal Interview: An Interpretive Reassessment," *Quarterly Journal of Speech* 72 (1986), 74–75.

22. Gerald R. Ferris and Thomas R. King, "The Politics of Age Discrimination in Organizations," *Journal of Business Ethics* 11 (May 1992), 341–350.

23. Wexley and Klimoski, 38–40.

24. Wexley and Klimoski, 40–41.

25. Stanley Silverman and Kenneth N. Wexley, "Reaction of Employees to Performance Appraisal Interviews as a Function of Their Participation in Rating Scale Development," *Personnel Psychology* 37 (1984), 703–10.

26. Philip G. Benson, M. Ronald Buckley, and Sid Hall, "The Impact of Rating Scale Format on Rater Accuracy: An Evaluation of the Mixed Standard Scale," *Journal of Management* 14 (1988), 415–23.

27. Wexley and Klimoski, 40; G. P. Latham and Kenneth N. Wexley, *Increasing Productivity through Performance Appraisal* (Reading, MA: Addison-Wesley, 1981); Daniel Ilgen, Richard Peterson, Beth Ann Martin, and Daniel Boeschen, "Supervisor and Subordinate Reactions to Performance Appraisal Sessions," *Organizational Behavior & Human Development* 28 (1981), 311–30.

28. This model and explanation come from a booklet prepared by Baxter/Travenol Laboratories titled *Performance Measurement Guide*. The model and system were developed by William B. Cash, Jr., Chris Janiak, and Sandy Mauch. The model is reprinted with permission of Baxter/Travenol, Deerfield, Illinois.

29. John Knibbs and Stephen Swailes, "Implementing Performance Review and Career Planning: Part One," *Management Decision* 30 (1992), 49–53; Elaine M. Evans, "Designing an Effective Performance Management System," *Journal of Compensation & Benefits* 6 (March/April 1991), 25–29.

30. Knibbs and Swailes; Danny L. Balfour, "Impact of Agency Investment in the Implementation of Performance Appraisal," *Public Personnel Management* 21 (Spring 1992), 1–15.

31. Umiker.

32. Carol A. Norman and Robert A. Zawacki, "Team Appraisals—Team Approach," *Personnel Journal* 70 (September 1991), 101–104; Brad Lee Thompson, "An Early Review of Peer Review," *Training* 28 (July 1991), 42–46.

33. Jaci Jarrett Masztal and Todd A. Silverhart, "Beyond the Numbers: Performance Appraisals Show the True Picture," *Managers Magazine* 67 (April 1992), 22–24; Jeanne Mancision, "The Appraisal Interview: Constructive Dialogue in Action," *Health Care Supervisor* 10 (September 1991), 41–50; Arthur Pell, 51–52; Clement and Stevens, 43–58; Douglas B. Simpson, "The Performance Appraisal Interview: Putting It All Together," *Health Care Supervisor* 3 (1985), 63–76; James F. Bolt, "Panel Interviewing at Xerox," *Human Resource Planning* 6 (1983), 55–58; Norton, 30–34; Cederblom, 219–27.

34. From a speech to a client briefing on September 30, 1983, in San Francisco by Buck Blessing of Blessing and White, Inc., a leading international career development company.

35. Wexley and Klimoski, 50–55.

36. Goodall, Wilson, and Waagen, 74–87; Pell, 51–52; Baker and Morgan, 74–78; Cederblom, 219–27, "The Performance Appraisal Interview," 36–40.

37. Simpson, 63–76; Loraine, 7–8, 13; John F. Kikoski and Joseph A. Litterer, "Effective Communication in the Performance Appraisal Interview," *Public Personnel Management* 12 (1983), 33–42.

38. Goodall, Wilson, and Waagen, 76.

39. Bolt, 55–58.

40. James P. Larson, "Role of Memory in the Performance-Evaluation Process: With Special Reference to Diary Keeping," *Psychological Reports* 57 (1985), 775–82.

41. Mancision; Knibbs and Swailes.

42. Pell, 51–52; McAfee and Chadwin, 30–35; Schuler, 8–12; Norton, 30–34.

43. Street, 224; Wexley and Klimoski, 43; Loraine, 7–8, 13.

44. Wexley and Klimoski, 52–53; B. Rosen and T. H. Jerdee, "The Influence of Sex Role Stereotypes on Evaluations of Male and Female Supervisory Behavior," *Journal of Applied Psychology* 57 (1973), 44–54; William J. Giboness, "Effect of Applicant's Sex, Race, and Performance on Employer's Ratings: Some Additional Findings," *Journal of Applied Psychology* 61 (1976), 80–84; Manuel London and John Poplawski, "Effects of Information on Stereotype Development in Performance Appraisal and Interview Content," *Journal of Applied Psychology* 61 (1976), 199–205.

45. Terry R. Lowe, "Eight Ways to Ruin a Performance Review," *Personnel Journal* 65 (1986), 60–62.

46. Willard M. Oliver, "I/O Psych and You," *Security Management* 35 (March 1991), 41–44; Umiker.

47. Umiker; Gerald A. Bricker, "Performance Agreements: The Key to Increasing Motivation," *Sales & Marketing Management* 144 (February 1992), 69–70.

48. Hill.

49. Ivancevich, 581–87; Pell, 51–52; Wight, 83–87; Baker and Morgan, 74–78.

50. Baker and Holmberg, 20–27; Baker and Morgan, 74–78.

51. Margaret A. Bogerty, "How to Prepare for Your Performance Review," *Advanced Management Journal* 47 (1982), 12–19.

52. Martin S. Remland and Tricia S. Jones, "Sex Differences, Communication Consistency, and Judgments of Sexual Harassment in a Performance Appraisal Interview," *The Southern Speech Communication Journal* 50 (1985), 156–76.

53. LaPlante.

54. LaPlante.

55. LaPlante.

56. This discussion of the discipline interview is based on a variety of sources and experiences but relies primarily upon the following for a review of recent research: Richard D. Arvey and Allen P. Jones, "The Use of Discipline in Organizational Settings: A Framework for Future Research," *Research in Organizational Behavior* 7 (1985), 367–408.

57. Joseph T. Straub, "Disciplinary Interviews: The Buck Stops with You," *Supervisory Management* 36 (April 1991), 1–2.

58. Craig Monroe, Mark G. Barzi, and Vincent S. DiSalvo, "Conflict Behaviors of Difficult Subordinates," *Southern Communication Journal* 54 (1989), 311–329.

59. Arvey and Jones, 373–75.

60. George Socrates, "The Disciplinary Interview," *Management Services* 29 (1985), 20.

Suggested Readings

Boyatzis, R. E. *The Competent Manager: A Model for Effective Performance.* New York: John Wiley & Sons, 1982.

Carroll, S. J., and Schneier, C. E. *Performance Appraisal and Review Systems.* Glenview, IL: Scott, Foresman, 1982.

Fournies, Ferdinand F. *Coaching for Improved Work Performance.* New York: Van Nostrand Reinhold and Company, 1978.

Fournies, Ferdinand F. *Why Employees Don't Do What They're Supposed to Do.* Blue Summit Ridge, PA: TAB Book, 1988.

John, R. G. *The Appraisal Interview Guide.* New York: AMACOM, 1979.

Latham, G. P., and Wexley, K. N. *Increasing Productivity Through Performance Appraisal.* Reading, MA: Addison-Wesley, 1981.

Naisbitt, John. *Megatrends.* New York: Warner Books, 1988.

Neal, John E., Jr. Effective Phrases for Performance Appraisals. Perrysburg, OH: Neal Publications, 1991.

Patton, T. H., Jr. *A Manager's Guide to Performance Appraisal.* New York: Free Press, 1982.

Peters, Thomas J., and Waterman, Robert H., Jr. *In Search of Excellence.* New York: Harper and Row, 1982.

Schneider, Katie R., and Hawk, Donald L. *The Performance Appraisal Process: A Selected Bibliography.* Greensboro, NC: The Center for Creative Leadership, 1980.

Souerwine, Andrew H. *Career Strategies.* New York: AMACOM, 1980.

9

The Counseling Interview

When you think of a counselor, you probably think of a highly trained psychiatrist, psychologist, or educational counselor listening thoughtfully to a patient, client, or student who may be lying on a couch or sitting in front of a large desk with a pensive, middle-aged figure seated on the opposite side. The movies and television have imprinted this stereotype on your mind. A remarkable fact is that most counseling interviews, including highly sensitive and critical ones, are conducted by para-professionals, professionals in other fields (physicians, clergy, lawyers, teachers, and supervisors), associates (fellow workers, students, and club members), friends, and family members. Training may range from extensive coursework to a few hours of intensive training to none at all beyond having counseled in the past. Fortunately, the "lay counselor" has proven remarkably successful, even in urban and campus crisis centers. Persons in need of help often seem to trust someone more like themselves, someone who is not part of the medical establishment, and someone who is neutral, objective and, above all, willing to listen.[1]

Whenever you are called on to help a person gain insights and cope with a physical, mental, emotional, financial, academic, or personal problem, you are a counselor. The counseling interview is perhaps the most sensitive of all interviews because it usually occurs only when a person feels incapable of handling a problem alone or when a counselor decides that help is needed. Either situation may be a blow to the person's self-concept. In addition, the problem is likely to be highly personal, involving finances, intimacy, emotional stability, physical health, drug or alcohol abuse, marriage, morals, grief, or work/academic performance. The counseling interview requires a high degree of trust and openness if the interviewee is to understand the problem and to decide how to solve it.

The purpose of this chapter is to introduce the principles of counseling interviewing so that you can work more effectively with "normal" people having "normal" problems. It is not intended to make you an instant psychotherapist ready to treat persons with psychological disorders. However, you should still approach the counseling interview systematically with considerable attention to pre-interview analysis and planning. Figure 9.1 illustrates the nine-step process the counselor should follow in helping interviewees understand and resolve problems.

Reviewing Approaches to the Counseling Interview

In Chapter 2 we introduced the two fundamental approaches to interviews, directive and nondirective, and discussed their advantages and disadvantages. The sensitive and

Figure 9.1 The counseling interview process

potentially explosive nature of the counseling interview necessitates a careful selection of interview approach, so begin interview preparation by reviewing the principles and assumptions that underlie each.

In the *directive approach,* the interviewer controls the structure of the interview, subject matter attended to and avoided and the pace and length of the interview. The counselor collects and supplies information, defines and analyzes problems, suggests and evaluates solutions, and provides guidelines for actions. In short, the directive interviewer serves as an "expert" who consults with interviewees. The directive approach is based on the assumption that the interviewer knows more about the problem than the interviewee and is better suited to analyze it and assess solutions. The accuracy of this assumption, of course, depends on the interviewer, the interviewee, and the situation. The interviewee, for instance, may not be disabled by illness, injury, or emotions, and may know exactly what solution is needed.

In the *nondirective approach,* the interviewee controls the structure of the interview, determining the topics, when and how they will be discussed, and the pace and length of the interview. The interviewer acts as a passive aide and helper, not as an expert or advisor. The interviewer *helps* the interviewee obtain information, gain insights, define and analyze problems, and discover and evaluate solutions. The interviewer listens, observes, and encourages but does not impose ideas. The nondirective approach is based on the assumption that the interviewee is more capable than the interviewer of analyzing problems, assessing solutions, and making correct decisions. In the extreme, this assumption questions the right of another person to "meddle" in another's problems or to serve as more than an indirect helper. The accuracy of this assumption, like the directive assumption, depends on the interviewer, interviewee, and situation. The interviewee may know nothing about the problem or potential solutions, or worse, may be misinformed about both. The interviewee may not be able to express or visualize a problem, make sound decisions, or consider the ramifications of decisions. A person may refuse to admit there is a problem. If the interviewee party consists of two or more people, they may be hopelessly divided over what to do and how to do it. At such times, the interviewer may serve as an objective, neutral referee, presenting pros and cons of specific courses of action. Interviewers must be able to distinguish between when they are serving as expert advisors and when, quite subtly perhaps, they are imposing personal preferences on an interviewee.

In many counseling interviews, you will find it necessary to employ a *combination* of directive and nondirective approaches. You may, for instance, begin with a nondirective approach to encourage the interviewee to talk and thereby reveal the causes of the problem. Then you may switch to a more directive approach when discussing possible solutions or courses of action. A directive approach is best for obtaining facts or making diagnoses, while a nondirective approach tends to open up large areas and bring out a great deal of spontaneous information.[2] The difficult task is to determine which approach is most appropriate at the moment and when a change in approach is needed.

Reviewing Interaction Phases and Responses

Although there is no standard structural format for counseling interviews, Hartsough, Echterling, and Zarle's sequential phase model, originally designed for handling calls to a campus or community crisis center, is applicable to most counseling situations, and it can help you determine when to use a directive and nondirective approach.[3] Figure 9.2 illustrates these phases. The *affective* or emotional phases, boxes 1 and 3, involve the interviewee's feelings of trust in the counselor and feelings about self and the problem. A nondirective approach is usually best for affective phases. The *cognitive* or thinking phases, boxes 2 and 4, involve thinking about the problem and taking action. A directive approach is usually best for cognitive phases.

The typical counseling interview begins with establishing rapport and a feeling of trust (phase 1), proceeds to discovering the basic nature of the interviewee's problem (phase 2), probes more deeply into the interviewee's feelings (phase 3), and finally comes to some decision about a course of action (phase 4). Except in emergencies, do not move from phase 1 to phase 4, or omit phase 3 without careful thought. If you do not discover the depth of an interviewee's feelings, you may not truly understand the

Figure 9.2 Phases of counseling interviews

Affective	Cognitive
1. Establishment of a Helpful Climate (a) making contact (b) defining roles (c) developing a relationship	2. Assessment of Crisis (a) accepting information (b) encouraging information (c) restating information (d) questioning for information
3. Affect Integration (a) accepting feelings (b) encouraging feelings (c) reflecting feelings (d) questioning for feelings (e) relating feelings to consequences or precedents	4. Problem Solving (a) offering information or explanations (b) generating alternatives (c) decision making (d) mobilizing resources

problem or possible solutions. Do not expect to move through all four phases in every interview or to proceed uninterrupted in numerical order. You may go back and forth between phases 2 and 3, or between 3 and 4. Unless the interviewee wants specific information (where to get medical help, how to drop a course and add another, how to get an emergency monetary loan), you may not get to phase 4 until a second, third, or fourth interview. Be patient!

Turner and Lombard summarize a client-centered approach in figure 9.3, showing the information potentially available to the interviewer and the general ways the interviewer may respond.[4] These types of information and responses may occur in any of Hartsough, Echterling, and Zarle's four interaction phases. Turner and Lombard say the interviewee is likely to talk about (1) objects, events, ideas, concepts, and so on, (2) other people, or (3) self. As an interviewer presented with these kinds of information, you should respond to what the interviewee is saying about self. You may respond by (1) giving opinions, advice, or suggestions, (2) interpreting what the interviewee is saying, or (3) accepting or clarifying "what the client has been saying from the client's own frame of reference."

With these choices, you should accept or clarify what the interviewee has been saying about self. You may respond to the interviewee's talk about self at the level of (1) content, (2) expressed feelings, or (3) unexpressed feelings, but as a client-centered interviewer, you should respond to expressed feelings.

Expressed feelings provide a fourth decision—whether to respond to feelings that are (1) positive, (2) ambivalent, or (3) negative. Turner and Lombard say the interviewer should respond to ambivalent and negative feelings rather than to positive ones in order to gain insights into the interviewee's problem.

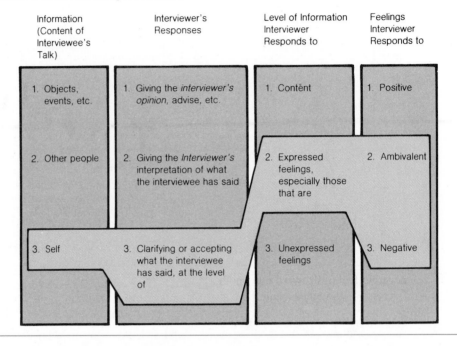

Figure 9.3 Information and responses in counseling interviews. Reprinted with permission of The Free Press, a Division of Macmillan, Inc. from *Interpersonal Behavior and Administration* by Arthur N. Turner and George F. Lombard.

Turner and Lombard's suggestions should not be interpreted as fixed rules. The situation, the interviewee, and the phase of the interview will determine what kinds of materials become available and which ones have priority. Phase 4, for example, may require advice rather than clarification of what the interviewee has said. Be flexible, but use Turner and Lombard's suggestions as guidelines.

Analyzing Self and Other

Begin with a detailed and insightful self-analysis. Although self-analysis is not easy, you will have difficulty trying to understand and help others if you do not know yourself. What are your personality characteristics? Research reveals that qualities intrinsic to the personalities, attitudes, and nonverbal behavior of counselors—rather than gender or ethnic group membership, largely account for their counseling effectiveness.[5] For example, you should be open-minded, optimistic, serious, self-assured, relaxed, and patient. You should not be argumentative or defensive when there is no need to be. You must be able to disclose your motives, feelings, beliefs, attitudes, and values if you expect others to be open with you. Do not dominate interpersonal interactions, but have a sincere desire to help others. You must be *people* rather than *problem* oriented. Educational and professional training are geared toward solving problems, but in nearly all counseling interviews, the problems are attached to people. You must be "people-centered" to be sensitive to the interviewee's needs and communicate understanding, comfort, reassurance, and warmth. In short, you must strive to be empathic.

What are your intellectual, communicative, and professional strengths? You must be imaginative, analytical, and organized. You must be able to learn quickly and recall information accurately and completely. You must be able to communicate in a variety of settings by being a good listener and skilled in verbal and nonverbal communication. Be experienced and highly trained in your profession, and keep up-to-date with research, changes, and trends. Know how other people, the present interviewee in particular, view you, and your position, organization, and profession. And be sure you have a realistic view of your counseling skills and what can be accomplished in typical sessions.

Review everything you know about the interviewee: education, work history, academic record, family background, medical/psychological test results, previous counseling sessions, statements (from physicians, acquaintances, family, supervisors, other counselors), and information about past problems and solutions. What situational variables are likely to affect this person? What relationships (social, family, professional, religious, political) do you have in common with the interviewee? Have you counseled this person before and if so, have you and the interviewee both done everything that was agreed to? What about the relational dimensions of inclusion, affection, and control? To what extent do both of you want to take part in this counseling interview? What are your positive and negative feelings toward one another? Who is most likely to control all or parts of the interview? How much control must you impose if the session is to be productive?

If you know an interviewee thoroughly prior to the interview, you will be able to anticipate and respond more effectively to common questions and comments such as the following:

I don't want (need) your help or anyone else's.

I can take care of this myself.

Get off my back.

How can we get this over with quickly and painlessly?

Why should I discuss my personal problems with you?

You wouldn't understand.

Don't tell my mom and dad.

Just tell me what you want me to do.

I can't afford to take time off.

You've never been married, so how can you help me?

No one knows how I feel.

No offense, but how can a fifty-year-old understand what a teenager faces today?

You don't know what it's like living with Jim; nobody does.

You can respond to such questions and statements in a variety of ways. For instance, you might use silence, nudging probes, or repeat questions to urge the interviewee to continue and perhaps to explain feelings, attitudes, and reasons or to give information. You might probe into the causes of feelings, attitudes, or reasons. You might provide more information to allay fears or remove misconceptions. Or you might allude tactfully to the specific training or experience that enables you to help or to understand. If you formulate possible answers, questions, and comments *beforehand,* you are less likely to be caught off guard during the interview. Be ready to respond to unusual questions and requests. Above all, do not become defensive or jump to premature conclusions. Review the question tools discussed in Chapter 4 and the probing skills in Chapter 5. A variety of interviewer responses and reactions are discussed later in this chapter.

The success of counseling interviews often depends on how much an interviewee is willing and able to disclose information, beliefs, attitudes, and concerns. Some factors may be beyond your control. For instance, females seem to disclose significantly more information about themselves than do males, especially on intimate topics such as sex, and a person's disclosure history often affects disclosure in other interviews.[6] But interviewers can encourage interviewee disclosure, for example, by disclosing their own feelings and attitudes, by assuring confidentiality, and by reducing the interviewee's perception of risk in providing information.[7]

Frequently an interviewee will ask for help without notice or explanation, and you must rely on your training and experience to get a session underway successfully. Begin with a nondirective approach as you try to discover what is bothering the person and how you may help. Do not assume that you know why the person is calling or showing up at your door. Encourage interviewees to make appointments so you have time to prepare. An appointment also lessens the risk of having to rush through an interview or close one prematurely. Either may be disastrous to the interview and your relationship with the person.

Preparing an Appropriate Climate

Provide a climate conducive to good counseling—a quiet, comfortable, private location, free of interruptions. You cannot expect an interviewee to be open and honest (Level 2 and Level 3 interactions) if other employees, students, clients, or patients can overhear the conversation. Consider using a neutral location such as a restaurant, lounge, park, or company cafeteria where the interviewee might feel less threatened. Some interviewees feel comfortable or safe only on their own turf, so consider meeting in the person's office, home, or place of business.

When possible, arrange the seating so that both interviewer and interviewee are at ease and able to communicate freely. Studies suggest that the situation is the most important variable in determining level of self-disclosure and that an optimal interpersonal distance between parties is 3.5 feet.[8] Review the discussion of seating arrangements in Chapter 2. Many people comment that an interviewer behind a desk makes them ill at ease, as though the "mighty one" is sitting in judgment. They prefer to sit in a chair at the end of the desk—at right angles to the interviewer—or in chairs facing one another with no desk in between. Arrangements of furniture can contribute to or detract from the informal, conversational atmosphere so important in most counseling sessions. Many counseling interviewers are discovering that a round table, similar to a dining room table, is preferred by interviewees. Such a setup also allows the interviewer to take notes and pass materials to more than one interviewee more easily than when seated

Provide a climate conducive to good counseling, which is a quiet, comfortable, private location, free of interruptions.

around a desk or coffee table. Interviewees also seem to like this arrangement because they often handle family matters around the dining room table and feel that a round table has no "authority" position.

Opening the Interview

The first few minutes of a counseling session set the verbal and psychological tone for the remainder. Greet the interviewee by name in a warm, friendly manner, being natural and sincere. Do not be condescending or patronizing. Accept the interviewee as he or she is. Do not try to second-guess the person with statements such as:

I'll bet I know why you're here.

I assume you want to talk about the test results.

No doubt you want to know about the committee's decision.

Grades are posted in the hall.

The interviewee may not have initiated the interview for any of these reasons but may feel pressured into agreeing to some extent with your guess. In addition, your interruption may ruin an opening the interviewee had prepared that would have revealed the *primary* concern. Avoid tactless, but all too common reactions such as:

You look terrible.

You've put on some weight, haven't you?

What's on your mind?

Have you been doing what we agreed to last week?

You should have studied more and partied less.

These comments are not conducive to the relationship and atmosphere needed for a successful counseling interview.

When you initiate a counseling session, state clearly, precisely, and honestly what you want to talk about. If there is a specific amount of time allotted for the interview, make this known so you and the interviewee can work within it. The interviewee will be more at ease knowing how much time is available. Your attire and role behavior will significantly affect the interviewee's perceptions of your "attractiveness" and "level of expertise" and thus also help determine how closely the person is drawn to you.[9]

The counseling interviewer often consumes considerable time getting acquainted and establishing a working relationship with the interviewee. This time may be necessary even when your relationship with the interviewee has a long history. The counseling interview is somehow different and more threatening than other interactions. An interviewee may begin by talking about the number of floors up to your office, the size of your office, books on the shelves, pictures on the walls, the view out the window, or recent incidents unrelated to the interview topic. Do not rush this seemingly frivolous process. The interviewee is sizing up you, the situation, and the setting, and is (perhaps) building up the nerve to face the issue of the interview.

The rapport stage, in which you attempt to establish a feeling of goodwill with the interviewee, is your chance to establish a reputation for being interested, fair, and able to maintain confidences. You can discover the interviewee's expectations about the interview and attitudes toward you, your position or organization, and counseling sessions in general. You must be comfortable with the situation (which may include an embarrassing topic such as sex, a taboo topic such as death, a crying interviewee, or one who talks about everything but the real problem) if the interviewee is to be comfortable with the situation.

When rapport is established, you may let the interviewee begin with the topic that seems of most interest, particularly if he or she initiated the contact. This is the first step toward discovering the precise nature of the problem and why the interviewee has been unable to face it or solve it. Do not rush the interviewee. Persons or parties will usually tell what they want you to know when they are ready. Above all, do not rush in with solutions as soon as you think you have discovered the problem. Observe the interviewee's nonverbal cues carefully because apparently insignificant cues may reveal inner feelings and their intensity. If you initiated the contact or the interviewee seems incapable of getting to the point, you must take charge and guide the interviewee toward discovering the nature of the problem.

Listening, Observing, Questioning, and Responding

Although you will play many roles in each counseling interview, four will dominate: listening, observing, questioning, and responding. In each of these roles, strive to help, empathize, and inform.[10]

Listening

Listening (for comprehension, evaluation, and empathy) and *observing* are perhaps your most important roles. To get to the heart of the problem, you must give undivided attention to the interviewee's words and their implications, as well as to what is intentionally or unintentionally left unmentioned. Be genuinely interested in what the person is saying. Do not interrupt or take over the conversation. Beware of interjecting personal opinions, experiences, or problems; maintain the focus on the interviewee. If the person pauses or stops talking for a few moments, do not chatter to fill in the silence. Use silence for a variety of purposes, an important one being to encourage the interviewee to continue talking. Review Chapter 2 for uses of silence and listening principles. Rebecca Leonard suggests several behaviors that communicate a willingness to listen: facing the other person squarely, adopting an open posture, leaning toward the other person, being relatively relaxed, maintaining good eye contact, reflecting attention through facial expressions, and attending with vocal cues such as "um-hmmm" and "yes."[11] Interviewees tend to interpret smiles, attentive body postures, and gestures as evidence of warmth and enthusiasm.[12]

Observing

Observe how the interviewee sits, gestures, fidgets, and maintains eye contact; listen to the voice for loudness, timidity, and evidence of tenseness. These observations may give clues about the seriousness of the problem and the interviewee's state of mind. How disturbed or relaxed is the person? How comfortable is the person with you? One study indicates that deceptive answers are lengthier, more hesitant, and characterized by longer pauses, while another suggests that people maintain eye contact longer when they lie.[13] If you are going to take notes or record the interview, explain why, and stop if you detect that either activity is affecting the interview adversely.

Questioning

Questions play important roles in counseling interviews, but asking too many questions may interrupt interviewees and break the flow of self-disclosure. Numerous questions, often asked in a rapid-fire manner, reduce the interviewee to a mere respondent and may stifle the interviewee's own questions. Open questions, both primary and secondary, encourage talkativeness and emotional expression.[14] Ask one question at a time because multiple questions tend to result in ambiguous answers with neither part answered clearly.[15] Use encouragement probes such as:

What else would you like to say?

Uh-huh?

What happened next?

I see.

Go ahead with your story.

Avoid curious probes into feelings and embarrassing incidents, especially if the interviewee seems hesitant to elaborate. Beware of questions that may communicate disapproval, displeasure, or mistrust. Avoid leading questions except under unusual circumstances, and be careful of the "why" question that may appear to demand explanations and justifications. Imagine how an interviewee might react internally or externally to questions such as:

Why didn't you come to me sooner?
Why didn't you stick with the exercise program we set up?
Why don't you do as your supervisor tells you?
Why did you sell 3 percent less last month than the month before?

Review question types and criteria for phrasing questions in Chapter 4.

Responding

The interviewer may respond or react to the interviewee's comments, revelations, questions, and answers in an infinite variety of ways.[16] These responses may be placed along a continuum from highly nondirective to nondirective, directive, and highly directive.[17]

Highly nondirective reactions and responses encourage the interviewee to continue commenting, to analyze ideas and solutions, and to be self-reliant. As the interviewer, you offer no information, assistance, or evaluation of the interviewee, the interviewee's ideas, or possible courses of action. Highly nondirective reactions and responses are used in phases 1, 2, and 3. You may even remain silent, thus encouraging interviewees to continue or to answer their own questions, as in the following example:

Interviewee: What do you think I should do?
Interviewer: (silence)
Interviewee: Well, I've thought about going home for a few days before final examinations start.

You may encourage the interviewee to continue speaking by employing semiverbal phrases, such as the following:

Interviewee: It seems so hopeless.
Interviewer: Um-hmm.
Interviewee: First there was my husband's operation, then the radiation treatments, and now the chemotherapy . . .

When reacting and responding in a highly nondirective manner, be aware of your nonverbal behaviors. Face, tone of voice, speaking rate, and gestures must express sincere interest and reveal a high level of empathy. Interviewees often look for signs of approval or disapproval, interest or disinterest. Ruth Purtilo discusses five kinds of smiles: "I-know-something-you-don't-know," "poor-poor-you," "don't-tell-me," "I'm-smarter-than-you," and "I-don't-like-you-either." For example, if a person asks, "Is this going to take long?" the interviewer merely smiles.[18] Holding the hand or a simple touch may reassure a person and show that you care and understand. An "um-mmmm!" may signal a positive or negative reaction. Either reaction may adversely affect the interview, by making the interviewee wary of expressing true feelings or desires, or by encouraging the person to express feelings and desires perceived to be more acceptable to you. Do not permit a silence to become prolonged or awkward. If a party seems unable to continue or to "go it alone," switch to more appropriate responses.

A variety of question techniques may serve as highly nondirective responses. For example, you may *restate* or *repeat* an interviewee's question or statement, instead of providing answers or volunteering information, ideas, evaluations, or solutions. The attempt is to urge the person to elaborate or come up with answers alone.

Interviewee: I don't know what to do.
Interviewer: You don't know what options are available to you?

Restatements and repetitions must be tactful and purposeful. An interviewee may become upset by a constant "echo" during the counseling interview. You may choose to *return* a question rather than answer it. Once again the attempt is to encourage the interviewee to analyze problems and select possible solutions.

Interviewee: Should I try to go back to school next week?
Interviewer: How do *you* feel about that?

Do not continue to push a decision back if you detect that the individual has insufficient information or is confused, misinformed, genuinely undecided, or unable to make a choice. To continue with a highly nondirective approach would be nonproductive and potentially harmful to the interviewer-interviewee relationship. You might *invite* the interviewee to discuss a problem or idea.

Interviewee: I have some serious reservations about taking this new assignment.
Interviewer: Care to tell me about them?

In highly nondirective invitations, the interviewee may refrain from elaborating or keep feelings concealed. The interviewer does not say "Tell me about it" or "Such as?" but asks if the person is willing or interested in discussing, explaining, or revealing. The *reflective question* is a valuable way to make sure, in a nondirective manner, that you understand what the interviewee has just said. As discussed in Chapter 4, reflective questions are designed to clarify or verify statements, not to lead a person toward your point of view.

Interviewee: We first noticed that Phil was having learning problems in early grade school.
Interviewer: That was around first or second grade?

Reflective questions require careful listening and a concerted verbal and nonverbal effort not to lead the interviewee. Interviewees are often highly vulnerable and easily swayed, even when you do not intend to influence them.

Nondirective reactions and responses tend to inform and encourage. No imposition of either information or encouragement is intended. These reactions occur primarily in phase 4 but may appear in phase 2. The following is an example of information giving:

Interviewee: What choices do I have?
Interviewer: Well, you could drop the course and pick it up next semester, or you could see if your instructor will give you an incomplete.

Be specific in answers whenever possible, and if you do not have the information, say so and promise to get it or refer the interviewee to a better qualified source. You need not have all the answers. As interviewer, you may encourage or reassure the interviewee by noting that certain feelings, reactions, or symptoms are normal and to be expected.

Interviewee: I seem to burst into tears over nothing.
Interviewer: Unexplained tears are quite common near the end of difficult semesters. The break between semesters will ease the pressures and end the tearful events.

A quick way to lose the trust of an interviewee is to give unrealistic assurances such as "There's nothing to worry about." Avoid cliches and mini-sermons such as:

Every cloud has a silver lining.

You'll laugh at this some day.

We all have to go sometime.

It's always darkest before the dawn.

You're a lucky person; why I know a person who . . .

It could have been worse.

Be careful of falling into the "we trap": "How are *we* feeling today?" "I think *we'll* make it." "*We* must take it one step at a time." The interviewee is justified in exclaiming, "What do you mean *we? You're* not in this mess, and I don't care how *you* feel!"[19]

Directive reactions and responses go beyond encouragement and information to offer mild advice or evaluations. Directive reactions are used in phases 2 and 4 and sometimes in phase 3. In the following interchange, the interviewer supports the interviewee's ideas and urges action.

Interviewee: I don't know if Frank will go along with keeping Billy in pre-school for another year.
Interviewer: Why don't you talk to him and find out?

A second type of directive response questions the interviewee's comments or ideas. Be tactful and cautious when employing this technique.

Interviewee: I'm not going to tell Mom that Dad has cancer.
Interviewer: Don't you think she has a right to know?

In a third type of directive response, the interviewer provides information and personal preference when asked.

Interviewee: Would you quit this job if you were me?
Interviewer: No, I would not, because I really like the kinds of work you're doing and enjoy the pressures. Not many people do. Why don't you contact a good career counselor to discover positions more suited to your interests and abilities?

Directive responses and reactions may challenge an interviewee's actions, ideas, or judgments, or urge the person to pursue a specific course or to accept information or ideas. It is usually wise to employ directive responses only if nondirective responses do not appear to work.

Highly directive reactions and responses should be reserved for special circumstances—when you have exhausted all less directive means. Suggestions and mild advice are replaced by ultimatums and strong advice which should be reserved for phase 4. The following are examples of highly directive responses and reactions:

1. **Interviewee:** I just can't stay on this diet.
   Interviewer: Then there's not much reason for you to keep coming back to the diet center.
2. **Interviewee:** What do you suggest?
   Interviewer: Here's exactly what you must do. Attend every class session, make up the work you have missed, and retake the first examination.

Highly directive responses are most appropriate for simple behavioral problems and least appropriate for complex ones that are based on habits or firmly held attitudes and beliefs. Try to be a helper, not a dictator, because the change or solution must come from the interviewee. A hostile person may turn you into a highly directive counselor and thus receive less understanding and more reassurances and evaluations.[20] You can rarely force people to comply with instructions and regimens, even if you have the authority to punish or fire them. Compliance is best achieved by giving adequate information about what a person should and should not do, and why.[21]

The interviewer's reactions and responses may enhance self-disclosure. Select an appropriate directive or nondirective response. For example, use highly directive responses only after you have established a close relationship with the interviewee.[22] Do not be shocked by what you hear, or at least do not reveal your shock. Preparation can reduce the number of surprises, making extreme or unusual reactions or comments less likely to shock you. Do not try to dodge unpleasant facts. Be honest and tactful, and let your voice, facial expressions, and gestures communicate a relaxed, unhurried, confident, warm, and caring image. Talk as little as possible, do not interrupt the interviewee, and listen empathically.[23] Above all, actively seek agreement with the interviewee on the problem.[24]

Closing the Interview

The closing of the counseling interview, as with all sensitive interviews, is vital to the success of the entire session. If interviewees feel they have imposed on you or been pushed out the door as though on an assembly line, much of the progress made during the interview may be erased, including the positive relationship established so carefully.

The verbal and nonverbal leave-taking actions discussed in Chapter 3 explain how interviews are closed both consciously and unconsciously. Decide which means or combination of means best suits you and the other party. There are a number of guidelines for closing counseling interviews. For instance, both parties should be able to tell when the real closing is taking place. Do not begin new topics when the interview has already come to a close, either in fact or psychologically. Do not expect to finish with a solution all worked out like a neatly wrapped package. Be content that thought has been stirred or that the interviewee was able and willing to discuss the problem. Do not be overly concerned about not meeting all expectations; remember that you and the interviewee are human beings with failings. Leave the door open for further conversation. And be sincere and honest in the ways you close interviews.

Evaluating the Interview

Think carefully and critically about the counseling interviews you take part in. Only through perceptive analysis will you begin to improve your "helping" interactions with others. Be realistic, however, because you cannot expect complete success in all counseling interviews; they are interactions between complex human beings, at least one of whom has a serious problem. Remember that your perceptions of how the interview went and how the interviewee reacted may be exaggerated or incorrect.

The following questions may serve as guides for your postinterview evaluations.

Preinterview Preparation
1. How thoroughly did I review available materials concerning the interviewee before the interview?
2. How well did I know myself and my level of counseling expertise?
3. How effectively did I assess how I communicate and come across with others, particularly *this* party?
4. How thoroughly did I review questions I might ask to get necessary information and make informed decisions?

5. How thoroughly did I review questions the interviewee might ask, and did I think about how I might respond?
6. How successfully did I prepare a climate and setting in which openness and disclosure would be fostered?

Interviewing Skills
1. How effective was the opening?
2. How skillful were my question techniques?
3. How well did I blend directive and nondirective approaches?
4. Was the pace of the interview neither too fast nor too slow?
5. If the party consisted of more than one person, how effectively did I communicate with all members?
6. How effectively did I motivate the interviewee to communicate at Levels 2 and 3?
7. Did I take adequate notes without disturbing the interview process?
8. How tolerant was I of silent moments?
9. How effective was the closing?

Counseling Skills
1. How well did I adapt to this party and situation?
2. How completely did I explain all options?
3. How effectively did I help the interviewee gain insights and make decisions without dominating the interview?
4. How accurately did I discover the real problem bothering the interviewee?
5. How effectively did I listen for comprehension, evaluation, and empathy?
6. Was I too eager to be liked by the interviewee?
7. Did I make promises I will not be able to keep?
8. Did I agree with the interviewee when I should have disagreed?
9. Did I try to handle a problem too difficult for my frame of mind or my level of counseling experience and expertise?

Your experiences and specific situations may add to or subtract from these lists of postinterview questions. The important point is to evaluate what you do in order to improve your counseling skills.

Summary

You take part in a counseling interview whenever you try to help a person gain insights into a physical, mental, emotional, or social problem and discover ways to cope. The counseling interview is perhaps the most sensitive of interview settings because it usually does not occur unless a person feels incapable of handling a problem or a counselor decides that a helping session is needed. Preparation, often the keystone to the counseling process, helps you determine how to listen, question, inform, explain, respond, and relate to each interviewee. No two interviews are identical because no two counselees and situations are identical. Thus, many suggestions but few rules are available for selecting interview approaches, types of responses, questions, and structures.

A Counseling Interview for Review and Analysis

This interview is between a college student and his academic counselor. The student has had grade problems for a number of semesters, with a history of dropping courses after the first examination. He currently wants to drop two courses six weeks into the semester.

How effectively does the counselor handle the opening? Which approach or approaches (directive, nondirective, or a combination) does the counselor use? How appropriate is this choice? How effectively does the counselor follow the four phases of a counseling interview developed by Hartsough, Echterling and Zarle? How appropriate are the counselor's reactions (highly nondirective, nondirective, directive, highly directive) during the interview? How would you evaluate the counselor's use of questions? At which levels of disclosure (Level 1, 2, or 3) are most of the counselee's revelations? How effective is the counselor as a listener? How adequate is the closing?

1. **Counselee:** Professor Smith?
2. **Counselor:** Yes, Bill, come on in. I've been waiting for you since two o'clock.
3. **Counselee:** Oh, I'm sorry. I got tied up at the house and forgot what time it was.
4. **Counselor:** I haven't seen you for several weeks. I suppose you want to talk about pre-registration for next semester?
5. **Counselee:** Well, uh, yeah, that too; but I've got another matter to talk to you about.
6. **Counselor:** What's that?
7. **Counselee:** Well, you remember last semester when I told you I wanted to take several of my electives and a heavier load than usual?
8. **Counselor:** Uh-huh.
9. **Counselee:** You tried to talk me out of it, right?
10. **Counselor:** Yes, that's correct.
11. **Counselee:** Well, you were right. I shouldn't have signed up for so many courses, particularly the ones I signed up for.
12. **Counselor:** And now you're back to drop one of the classes, just like you've done several times before! I knew this would happen.
13. **Counselee:** This is not like those other times when I was pledging the fraternity, playing sports, and over my head with activities.
14. **Counselor:** Seems like I've heard this story before.
15. **Counselee:** This time I've really tried, but the accounting and statistics classes are way above my level. Most other students are majors and have had several accounting or statistics classes.
16. **Counselor:** (silence)
17. **Counselee:** I don't even understand what they are talking about half the time. I studied over eight hours for the first accounting test and got a low D.
18. **Counselor:** Some of those courses are tough. I told you that last semester during preregistration.
19. **Counselee:** I know you told me that, but I really thought I could handle them.
20. **Counselor:** So, what do you want to do now?
21. **Counselee:** I want to drop the accounting and statistics classes and pick up a course, or maybe two, in graphics.
22. **Counselor:** Why *graphics*?

23. **Counselee:** I've been thinking about a minor in advertising, and the graphics courses would be good background.

24. **Counselor:** How do you know these would be good background courses?

25. **Counselee:** One of my fraternity brothers is in graphics, and his courses seem really interesting.

26. **Counselor:** Interesting or . . . ?

27. **Counselee:** I know what you're thinking. I'm not taking these because they're easy. I'm taking them because they should help me with an advertising minor.

28. **Counselor:** Have you talked to anyone in the advertising program?

29. **Counselee:** No, I thought I would take a couple of courses first to see if I like it.

30. **Counselor:** But these are not advertising classes; they are graphics courses!

31. **Counselee:** Well, yeah, but all advertising students take some graphics classes.

32. **Counselor:** I will approve the dropping of the two electives, one in accounting and one in statistics, but I think you need to think about the graphics classes and talk to a professor in advertising before signing up for more classes.

33. **Counselee:** Okay, but the day after tomorrow is the last day for adding classes. Couldn't you just sign the form for the graphics classes and then I'll talk to someone in advertising? That way I won't have to make another appointment with you or take up more of your time.

34. **Counselor:** No, Bill, I don't think that's a good idea. We've tried that before. You talk to someone in advertising about these courses, and I'll make time available to sign the add form.

35. **Counselee:** Okay, I'll talk to someone in advertising and get back to you as soon as I can.

36. **Counselor:** Here's the drop form, and I can see you anytime tomorrow afternoon.

37. **Counselee:** Thanks. See you tomorrow.

Counseling Role-Playing Cases

Cheating on a Test

The interviewee is a sophomore in college who has never cheated before. He recently has been having trouble with grades and needs an A in a history class to keep from going on probation. One day when the interviewee was talking to the history professor, the professor left the room for a few minutes. While he was gone, the interviewee took a copy of the final examination from his desk, knowing that the professor would never miss it because he is notorious for not keeping track of his papers. But before the day of the test, the interviewee's conscience begins to bother him, and he decides to see a counselor in the dean of students' office whom he knows quite well. The student must decide whether he should return the test and apologize to the history professor or not return it because the professor will never miss it.

The interviewer has the reputation of being a good counselor. He knows the interviewee very well and finds it hard to believe that he actually took a test from a professor's office. The interviewer has never had anyone come to him with a problem quite like this one.

An Employee-Employer Relationship

The interviewee is a legal secretary in her early twenties who has been working for a well-known lawyer. The lawyer is married and has two children, but he has repeatedly asked the interviewee to go out with him. She has told him no, but he keeps asking. The interviewee has decided to quit working for him because she does not want to get involved in his personal life. The lawyer is a nice person, an excellent employer, and pays the interviewee well. When she tells him she is quitting, should she tell him the truth or make up a story? The interviewee decides to talk the matter over with a longtime friend who is in personnel relations with a department store.

The interviewer is a thirty-year-old personnel manager at Hicks Department Store. The interviewee has asked to discuss the problem over lunch. The interviewer has a vague idea that the problem relates to the interviewee's work and knows that the interviewee enjoys the position.

A Theft and Personal Involvements

The interviewer is a counselor at a high school. Several days ago, someone broke into six vending machines in the basement of the school. The merchandise and over $70 in coins were taken. The principal has made several announcements over the public address system that if the money is returned, no charges will be pressed, but the guilty party must apologize to the entire school and pay for the merchandise and the damage to the machines. One of the better-known seniors has confessed to the interviewer that he stole the money to buy his girlfriend a watch, and he wants to know what to do.

The interviewee is the son of a widow and has never been in any kind of trouble. He met his girlfriend several weeks ago and has been seeing her every day, even though his mother disapproves. The interviewer knows that the girlfriend is from a poor family, is extremely good-looking, and all the boys think she is the greatest. She was waiting for the interviewee after school one day after basketball practice, and before they started home, she asked him to buy her a candy bar. They went to the vending machines in the basement, and she kept talking about how much money was in the machines and how nice a watch would look on her wrist. Before the interviewee realized what he was doing, he had broken open several machines and taken the money and merchandise to his car. He does not want his mother to find out but, more important, he does not want to lose his girlfriend.

Dating and Religion

The counselee is twenty-two years old and has been dating a twenty-four-year-old for over a month. She cares very much for him, and feels there could be a future to this relationship. The interviewee is a strong Catholic and her boyfriend is an equally strong Lutheran. He is coming to the interviewee's home for dinner on Friday evening, and he does not know she is Catholic. Should she tell him before he meets her family? What should she do about the entire situation? She has decided to talk to her pastor whom she has known all her life.

The interviewer has been pastor of St. Mary's Church for nearly 25 years and has known the interviewee since she was a baby. She sounded upset when she called for an appointment. He is not sure why she wants to see him but suspects it might be about a boyfriend.

Class Attendance

The interviewer is a counselor in a college dormitory where he has worked for nearly a year. The interviewee is one of 75 freshmen on the interviewer's floor. He is girl-crazy, does not like to study, loves beer, and is thoroughly enjoying the freedom of not living at home. The dorm where the interviewee lives is a coed unit that suits the interviewee just fine since his latest girl friend lives in the same building. About the middle of the first semester, the interviewer received a note from the dean of students' office stating that the interviewee had not attended one of his classes for three weeks.

The interviewee is eighteen and has been let out of the clutches of very strict parents for the first time in his life. The thrill of finally being able to do what he wishes and go whenever he chooses is almost too much for him. His mother was reluctant to let him go away to college, but his father convinced her it was the best thing to do. Since his arrival at college, the interviewee has found many new friends and activities. For some reason, he could not get through his math class, so he stopped going to it. The interview will take place in the interviewer's room.

Student Activities

1. Visit a crisis center in your community or on your campus. Observe how volunteer counselors handle telephone counseling. Talk with several counselors about their training and techniques. How does telephone counseling differ from face-to-face counseling?

2. Interview three kinds of counselors: a marriage counselor, a student counselor, and a financial counselor. How are their approaches and techniques similar and different? What kinds of training do they have and what kinds would they recommend for counselors in their occupations? In their estimation, what is a "successful" counselor?

3. Pick one of the counseling role-playing cases and develop a complete approach to the case, beginning with setting and furniture arrangement. How would you begin the interview? What questions would you ask? How much would you disclose about yourself—training, background, experiences, and so on? What kinds of reactions and responses would you use: highly nondirective, nondirective, directive, highly directive? What kind of solution would you suggest, if any? How would you hope to close the interview?

4. Make arrangements to observe a counseling interview between a teacher and student, an employer and employee, a parent and child, or a professional counselor and client. Try not to be an obvious third party. Observe the opening, questions and responses, nonverbal behavior of both parties, self-disclosures, effect of interruptions, suggestions, directive and nondirective techniques, and the closing. Write a detailed criticism of this interview, with suggestions for improvement.

Notes

1. John A. Hattie, Christopher R. Sharpley, and H. Jane Rogers, "Comparative Effectiveness of Professional and Paraprofessional Helpers," *Psychological Bulletin* 95 (1984), 534–41; John Ramirez and Jane L. Winer, "Counselor Assertiveness and Therapeutic Effectiveness in Treating Depression," *Personnel and Guidance Journal* 62 (1983), 167–70; Donald R. Atkinson, Francisco Q. Ponce, and Francine M. Martinez, "Effects of Ethnic, Sex, and Attitude Similarity on Counselor Credibility," *Journal of Counseling Psychology* 31 (1984), 589–91.

2. John Q. Quay, "The Art and Science of Effective Interviewing," *Journal of Management Consulting* 2 (1985), 14–17.

3. Lennis G. Echterling, Don M. Hartsough, and H. Zarle, "Testing a Model for the Process of Telephone Crisis Intervention," *American Journal of Community Psychiatrists* 8 (1980), 715–25.

4. Arthur N. Turner and George F. F. Lombard, *Interpersonal Behavior and Administration* (New York: Macmillan, 1969), 305–6.

5. Alfred F. Carlozzi, N. Jo Campbell, and G. Robert Ward, "Dogmatism and Externality in Locus of Control as Related to Counselor Trainee Skill in Facilitating Responding," *Counselor Education and Supervision* 21 (1982), 227–36; Barbara Goldberg and Romeria Tidwell, "Ethnicity and Gender Similarity: The Effectiveness of Counseling for Adolescents," *Journal of Youth and Adolescents* 19 (1990), 589–603.

6. John P. Lombardo and Michael D. Berzonsky, "Sex Differences in Self-Disclosure During an Interview," *The Journal of Social Psychology* 103 (1979), 281–82; Joseph Doster and Bonnie R. Strickland, "Disclosure of Verbal Material as a Function of Information Requested, Information about the Interviewer, and Interviewee Differences," *Journal of Consulting and Clinical Psychology* 37 (1971), 187; Timothy P. Johnson, James G. Hougland, and Robert W. Moore, "Sex Differences in Reporting Sensitive Behavior: A Comparison of Interview Methods," *Sex-Roles* 24 (1991), 669–680.

7. Kenneth L. Robey, "Perceived Counseling Effectiveness as a Function of Counselor's Self-Disclosure and Client's Prompting," *Psychological Reports* 47 (1980), 300; John D. Davis and Adrian E. G. Skinner, "Reciprocity of Self-Disclosure in Interviews: Modeling or Social Exchange?" *Journal of Personality and Social Psychology* 29 (1974), 779–84; Kathryn M. Woods and J. Regis McNamara, "Confidentiality: Its Effect on Interviewee Behavior," *Professional Psychology* 11 (1980), 714–21; Michael A. Westerman, A. Steven Frankel, Jeffrey S. Tanaka, and Jana Kahn, "Client Cooperative Interview Behavior and Outcome in Paradoxical and Behavioral Brief Treatment Approaches," *Journal of Counseling Psychology* 34 (1987), 99–102.

8. Robert Michael Fraum, "The Effect of Interpersonal Distance on Self-Disclosure in a Dyadic Interview Situation," *Dissertation Abstracts International* 35 (1975), 4170.

9. Patricia H. Powell and James M. Dobb, "Physical Attractiveness and Personal Space," *Journal of Social Psychology* 100 (1976), 59–64; Barbara Kerr and Donald M. Dell, "Perceived Interviewer Expertness and Attractiveness: Effects of Interviewer Behavior and Attire and Interviewing Setting," *Journal of Counseling Psychology* 23 (1976), 553–56; Mark A. Hubble and Charles J. Gelso, "Effect of Counselor Attire in an Initial Interview," *Journal of Counseling Psychology* 25 (1978), 581–82; Alice M. Vargas and John G. Borkowski, "Physical

Attractiveness and Counseling Skills," *Journal of Counseling Psychology* 29 (1982), 246–55; Alice M. Vargas and John G. Borkowski, "Physical Attractiveness: Interactive Effects of Counselor and Client on Counseling Processes," *Journal of Counseling Psychology* 30 (1983), 146–57.

10. Robert E. Doyle, "The Counselor's Role, Communication Skills, or the Roles Counselors Play: A Conceptual Model," *Counselor Education and Supervision* 22 (1982), 123–31.

11. Rebecca Leonard, "Attending: Letting the Patient Know You Are Listening," *Journal of Practical Nursing* 33 (1983), 28–29. See also, Ginger Schafer Wlody, "Effective Communication Techniques," *Nursing Management* (October 1981), 19–23.

12. Andrew S. Imada and Milton D. Hakel, "Influence of Nonverbal Communication and Rate Proximity on Impressions and Decisions in Simulated Employment Interviews," *Journal of Applied Psychology* 64 (1977), 295–300.

13. Albert A. Harrison, Melanie Hwalk, and David R. Raney, "Cue to Deception in an Interview Situation," *Social Psychology* 41 (1978), 156–61; Jo A. Burns and B. L. Klintz, "Eye Contact While Lying During an Interview," *Bulletin of the Psychonomic Society* 7 (1976), 87–89.

14. Hopkinson, Cox, and Rutter, "Eliciting Feelings."

15. A. Cox, K. Hopkinson, and M. Rutter, "Psychiatric Interviewing Techniques. II. Naturalistic Study: Eliciting Factual Information," *British Journal of Psychiatry* 138 (1981), 283–91.

16. C. Edward Watkins, Mark L. Savickas, Joan Brizzi, and Michaelene Manus, "Effects of Counselor Response Behavior on Clients' Impressions during Vocational Counseling," *Journal of Counseling Psychology* 37 (1990), 138–142; Larry Scherwitz and Richard Brand, "Interviewer Behaviors During Structured Interviews to Assess Type A/B Behavior in the Western Collaborative Group Study and the Multiple Risk Factor Intervention Trial," *Journal of Psychopathology and Behavior Assessment* 12 (1990), 27–47.

17. Robert Elliott, "Helpful and Nonhelpful Events in Brief Counseling Interviews: An Empirical Taxonomy," *Journal of Counseling Psychology* 32 (1985), 307–22.

18. Ruth Purtilo, *The Allied Health Professional and the Patient: Techniques of Effective Interaction* (Philadelphia: Saunders, 1973), 96–97.

19. Rebecca Leonard, "Communicating Responsibly," *Nursing 85* 15 (1985), 30–31; "Talking Points No. 6," *Nursing Times* (5 March, 1981), 397.

20. Lewis Bernstein and Rosalyn S. Bernstein, *Interviewing: A Guide for Health Professionals* (Norwalk, Conn.: Appleton-Century-Crofts, 1985), 49–51.

21. Shelley D. Lane, "Communication and Patient Compliance," in *Explorations in Provider and Patient Interaction,* Loyd S. Pettegrew, ed. (Louisville: Humana, 1982), 64–65.

22. Alfred F. Carlozzi, "Dogmatism and the Person of the Counselor," *The High School Journal* 68 (1985), 147–53.

23. K. Hopkinson, A. Cox, and M. Rutter, "Psychiatric Interviewing Techniques. III. Naturalistic Study: Eliciting Feelings," *British Journal of Psychiatry* 138 (1981), 406–15.

24. Elizabeth A. Siries, "Client-Counselor Agreement on Problem and Change," *Social Casework* 63 (1982), 348–53.

Suggested Readings

Benjamin, Alfred. *The Helping Interview.* Boston: Houghton-Mifflin, 1987.

Carkhuff, Robert R.; Pierce, Richard M.; and Cannon, John R. *The Art of Helping.* Amherst, MA: Human Resource Development Press, 1989.

Combs, Arthur W. *Helping Relationships: Basic Concepts for the Helping Professions.* Boston: Allyn and Bacon, 1985.

Engelkes, James R., and Vandergoot, David. *Introduction to Counseling.* Boston: Houghton-Mifflin, 1982.

Long, Lynette; Paradise, Louis V.; and Long, Thomas J. *Questioning: Skills for the Helping Process.* Monterey, CA: Brooks/Cole, 1981.

Martin, David G. *Counseling and Therapy Skills.* Monterey, CA: Brooks/Cole, 1989.

Nicholson, James A., and Golsan, Gordon. *The Creative Counselor.* New York: McGraw-Hill, 1983.

Okun, Barbara F. *Effective Helping: Interviewing and Counseling Techniques.* Monterey, CA: Brooks/Cole, 1986.

Shertzer, Bruce, and Stone, Shelley C. *Fundamentals of Counseling.* Boston: Houghton-Mifflin, 1980.

The Persuasive Interview

You take part in a persuasive interview every time you and another person attempt to affect one another's perceptions in order to bring about changes in ways of thinking, feeling, or acting. Sales interviews come to mind most often when you think of persuasive interviews, but they represent only one of many persuasive situations you encounter every day. Persuaders use interviews to recruit people for organizations, campaigns, and social movements; to urge actions or to prevent actions; to change or reinforce beliefs; and to change or reinforce attitudes. Persuasive interviews take place not only in business settings, but also in social clubs, churches, union halls, classrooms, gymnasiums, dorm rooms, and homes. They may be face-to-face or over the telephone, particularly when you are trying to eat dinner or take a nap. The fact that you take part in formal and informal persuasive efforts on a daily basis leads Roderick Hart to write that "one must only breathe to need to know something about persuasion."[1]

In previous chapters, we have urged you to remain neutral, to use leading questions only in special situations, and to avoid interviewer bias because interviewees might respond in ways they think you want them to respond instead of how they really feel. In this chapter, we focus attention on persuasive situations in which interviewers *want* and *need* to motivate interviewees to respond in specific ways to specific organizations, products, ideas, and people. For example, college recruiters want students to enroll in *their colleges;* sales representatives want customers to purchase *their computers;* lawyers want people in need of legal assistance to become *their clients;* and the political candidates want voters to vote for *them.*

The Ethics of Persuasion

As a persuasive interviewer, you have a unique advantage over the public speaker or mass persuader by being able to tailor your persuasive effort to fit a particular party, in a particular situation, in a particular setting, at a particular time. This advantage also carries with it heavy ethical responsibilities, because it is not enough to know how to persuade effectively and affect another's thoughts, feelings, and actions.

The formal concern for ethics and persuasion can be traced back to ancient Greece some 2,500 years ago, but our concern today is as strong as ever. A recent survey by *U.S. News & World Report* and CNN found that half of those surveyed believed people were less honest than ten years earlier.[2] Other news sources have included feature stories titled "What Ever Happened to Ethics?" and "A Nation of Liars?" The *Wall Street Journal* revealed that 25 percent of 671 managers surveyed said high ethics could hinder a successful career. The *Wall Street Journal* also reported a conversation with the president of a major public relations firm in which he said he would hire Lt. Col. Oliver North, a central figure in the illegal arms sale to Iran and diversion of government funds to the Nicaraguan Contras, because "If he's lying, he's lying very well, which would make him a highly excellent PR guy."[3]

Virtually every profession from professers to political consultants have created elaborate codes of ethics to guide their actions, but wholesale violations seem to occur before the printer's ink can dry on the announcements. It is not merely that humans cannot be ethical, but that we as humans have great difficulty in determining what is unethical.[4] There appears to be no absolutely and universally unethical acts, and judgments tend to focus on degrees of rightness and wrongness. Many codes seemed aimed toward the world as we would like it to be, not as it is. Each situation seems so unique that ethical principles seem inappropriate or useless. Some writers have argued persuaders must judge the ethics of their efforts according to the end being sought.[5] Others believe we must judge the means being used. But who will make the value judgments concerning degrees of right and wrong, of goodness and badness, of means and ends?

Every rule seems to have exceptions and to pose more questions than answers. For example, withholding evidence may be bad if a person is determining a school to attend or a house to purchase but good if health or security is at stake. Virtually every strategy and tactic discussed in this chapter, even careful analysis and adaptation to the interviewee, may be identified as ethical or unethical, depending on the interviewer, the interviewee, and the situation.

For instance, if you know an interviewee dislikes Jews, blacks, Catholics, Republicans, or "foreigners," is it ethical to appeal to this prejudice or even pretend to share it just to achieve your end? If an interviewee does not challenge your facts, is it ethical to keep questionable sources secret? Is it ethical to use the words of others without giving credit or to "quote" a person in *your* words, keeping the paraphrasing secret? Is it ethical to present a proposal you know is inferior to others available to the interviewee? Is it ethical to sell a product or service to a person you know does not need or cannot afford it? Does the end (an election, a successful fund drive, a sale, avoidance of a problem) justify the means? Does situation determine a code you should use?

Although there may be no single code of ethics applicable to all persuasive interviews, there are guidelines to help you as interviewer or interviewee to distinguish good from bad persuasive efforts. The Golden Rule begins the list:[6]

1. Do unto others as you would have them do unto you.
2. Perform the duty of search and inquiry by seeking accurate, complete, and relevant evidence.
3. Swear allegiance to accuracy, fairness, and justice in selection of ideas, arguments, language, and tactics employed.
4. Carefully analyze all claims and probable consequences of proposed actions.
5. Be willing to submit your private motivations to public scrutiny.
6. Achieve an ethical balance between your original ideas and proposals and how you modify them for maximum impact with a particular interviewee.

7. Tolerate dissent and divergence of viewpoints.
8. Accept responsibility for the effects of your persuasive efforts.

Kenneth Andersen has written, "Although we do not wish to force a given system of values or ethical code upon the reader, we do argue that he[she] has a responsibility to form one. We believe that it is desirable both for the immediate practical reasons of self-interest and for more altruistic reasons that a person accept responsibility for what he[she] does in persuasion both as receiver and as source."[7]

Stages in the Persuasive Interviewing Process

Success is not assured in any persuasive interview, but the possibility of success is greatly enhanced if you can convince an interviewee that your proposal meets five interrelated conditions.[8]

1. The proposal appears to satisfy an urgent need or one or more desires or motives, *and*
2. the proposal and the persuader appear to be consistent with the persuadee's beliefs, attitudes, and values, *and*
3. the proposal appears to be feasible, workable, practical, affordable, *and*
4. objections to the proposal seem to be outweighed by the benefits, *and*
5. no better alternative course of action seems to be available.

The key condition is the presence or establishment of a need or desire. For instance, if a person does not want to donate money to the Alumni Scholarship Fund, presenting a variety of donation plans will be futile. Some interviewers mistakenly assume that an interviewee sees a need or has a desire, and thus, they end up introducing a proposal prematurely to an uninterested or hostile person. Following the nine steps illustrated in figure 10.1 will help you meet the five interrelated conditions for successful persuasion.

Analyzing the Interviewee

Learn everything you can about the interviewee prior to the interview, and do not overlook any potentially valuable source of information. What do you know from previous contacts or interviews with this party? What information is included in personal or organizational files? What can other members of your organization tell you about this interviewee? What information is included in church, professional, or community directories? How has the interviewee expressed interest in the topic, problem, or solution? Often little opportunity or insufficient information may be available to analyze the interviewee ahead of time. In such cases, use the first few minutes of the interview to discover important information by observing the interviewee's dress, manner, and attitudes and by carefully asking questions and listening to what the person says and does not say.

Figure 10.1 Stages in the persuasive interview

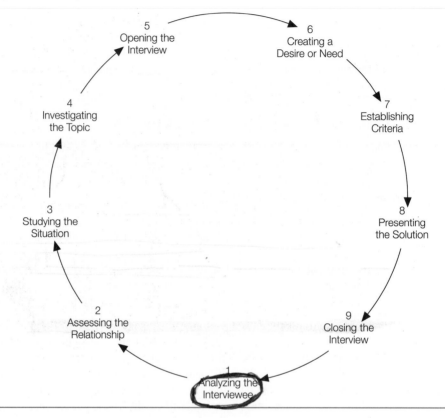

◑ *Physical and Mental Characteristics*

Consider potentially important physical characteristics such as age, sex, race, size, health, handicaps, and physical appearance. Studies have suggested, for example, that women may be more easily persuaded than men, perhaps because they are more sensitive or have fewer or different experiences.[9] Mental characteristics potentially important in an interviewee include intelligence, mental health, and quantity and quality of education.

◐ *Socioeconomic Background*

Important socioeconomic data may include the interviewee's group memberships because attitudes are strongly influenced by the groups people belong to or aspire to, and the more attached people are to groups the less they are persuaded by efforts that conflict with group norms.[10] Investigate the interviewee's occupation, avocations and hobbies, superior/subordinate relationships, marital status, dependents, work experiences, war or military experiences, and geographical background. "Frames of reference"—ways of viewing people, places, things, events, and issues—are created and altered by experiences, associations, and surroundings.

Do not overlook any potentially valuable source of information, including interviews, surveys, previous contacts, and reports.

Psychological Makeup

The interviewee's psychological makeup includes temperament (optimistic or pessimistic, suspicious or trusting) and whether it may change rapidly or unexpectedly. To what extent does the interviewee rationalize—attempt to find socially acceptable reasons—for feelings, beliefs, or actions?

Motives and Values

A motive prompts an interviewee to think, feel, or act in a particular manner. Sometimes a simple physical drive such as hunger, thirst, or sexual satisfaction may serve as a motive. But frequently people are motivated by one or more of the values they hold. Values are "a type of belief . . . about how one ought or ought not to behave, or about some end state of existence worth or not worth attaining."[11] The following are some American values often appealed to in persuasive interviews:[12]

1. Comfort and convenience (striving for a comfortable, pleasant life)
2. Health, safety, and security (for self, family, friends, others)
3. Pride, prestige, and social recognition (for personal achievements)
4. Affection and popularity (among family, friends, workers, others)
5. Happiness (an exciting, stimulating, and pleasurable life)
6. Ambition (to be successful through hard work)

7. Cleanliness (of self, home, environment)
8. Companionship (friends and relationships, a sense of belonging)
9. Competition (striving to be number one)
10. Conformity and imitation (being the same as others externally)
11. Accumulation and ownership (material goods, records, achievements)
12. Power and authority (while resisting others' authority)
13. Freedom from authority and restraint (independence, free choice)
14. Sexual satisfaction (mature love and affection)
15. Sense of accomplishment (a lasting contribution)
16. Peace and tranquility (in home, neighborhood, nation)
17. Education and knowledge (to be well-trained and knowledgeable)
18. Equality and value of the individual (equal opportunity for all)
19. Change and progress (to improve, advance, reach new goals)
20. Efficiency and practicality (to produce practical, useful benefits)
21. Generosity and compassion (to help others less fortunate)
22. Patriotism and loyalty (to home, employer, community, nation)

The interviewer's task is to determine which values are relevant to the interviewee and then to decide when and how to appeal to those values. For example, a life insurance sales representative might employ numbers 1, 2, 3, and 10, while a United Way campaign worker might use 3, 9, and 21.

Beliefs

Try to discover the interviewee's political, economic, social, and religious beliefs that relate to your topic. For instance, if equality is an important value, an interviewee is likely to support rights for women, African Americans, or Hispanics. If freedom from authority is an important value, the person is likely to advocate a free economy and elimination of governmental controls. People view themselves as paragons of consistency in beliefs, but actually they are consistently inconsistent. For example, interviewees may decry excessive taxes and government spending but demand superhighways to every point on the map; preach law and order but cheat on their income taxes; worry about permissiveness in American society but deny schools the right to punish their children. Discover the persuadee's beliefs and look for apparent conflicts and contradictions that might affect the interview.

Attitude Toward the Interviewer

If an interviewee dislikes or distrusts you or your organization, there is little chance of success unless you can alter your image during the interview. To create or to maintain a favorable image, your appearance, reputation, attainments, personality, and character should reveal to the interviewee a confident, poised person who is restrained and even-tempered, who exhibits physical energy, mental alertness, and knowledge, who is sincere in convictions, and who is fair, honest, sympathetic, and decisive in actions.[13] Studies reveal that interviewees pay more attention to highly credible interviewers and trust ones who are similar to themselves and seem to share important beliefs, attitudes, and values.

At the same time, however, interviewees expect authoritative interviewers to be a little wiser, braver, more knowledgeable, more experienced, and more insightful than they are themselves.[14]

Credibility is initially affected by what the interviewee knows or believes about the interviewer's reputation, attainments, personality, beliefs, and intent beforehand. When the parties are unacquainted prior to an interview, stereotypes (fixed conventional images such as the dumb blonde, the absent-minded professor, or the unethical politician) may play a significant role in creating an image and determining the outcome. Interviewers may enhance or lower credibility during interviews depending on their lines of argument, persuasive tactics, language, evidence, nonverbal communication, dress, physical appearance, and mannerisms. A few years ago, a young female Fuller Brush salesperson dressed in a tee shirt, blue jeans, and tennis shoes found it difficult to gain entry into homes or make sales. Residents felt she did not "look like" a Fuller Brush representative. Many people believe you are what you look like.

Attitude Toward the Proposal

Try to determine the interviewee's probable attitude toward your proposal along an imaginary linear scale, such as the following:

For				Undecided				Against
1	2	3	4	5	6	7	8	9

From what you know about the interviewee, where along the scale is the party's attitude likely to rest? If on positions 1 or 2, little persuasive effort will be required. If on positions 8 or 9, persuasion may be impossible beyond a small shift in feeling or thinking. If the attitude is on positions 4, 5, or 6, you should be able to alter behavior with a good persuasive effort unless the interviewee is highly committed to being undecided or has ego involvement that clashes with your proposal.

An interviewee may oppose a proposal for many reasons; you must discover which ones might operate during the interview. You or your ideas may threaten established (and perhaps cherished) habits, routines, rules, or traditions or seem incongruent with the interviewee's beliefs, attitudes, or values. The person may prefer to do something else or have a counterproposal. Or perhaps the party is uninformed, misinformed, or against all change.

Assessing the Relationship

Once you have become "acquainted" with the interviewee, you are ready to assess the relationship that is likely to exist. This is important because the relationship differs with each interview and interviewee and often determines the success of the persuasive effort.

Persuasive interview relationships range from cooperative to hostile. The following profiles of each extreme illustrate how the dimensions of inclusion, affection, and control vary from interview to interview:

Situation 1: The interviewee is thinking about purchasing a sophisticated word processor for the main office. The interviewer, a highly respected employee in the organization, has a great deal of experience with computers and has decided that it is time to purchase a word processor. She has in mind both a specific model computer and a software package. Because she is a respected member of the organization and a recognized expert, she is likely to control the interview. The parties like one another, want to take part in the interview, and are interested in the subject, so trust and cooperation should be high and conflict low. Only monetary aspects of the proposal may cause problems.

Situation 2: The interviewers, a husband and wife, are angry about the cost of a recent addition to their home. They want to persuade the contractor to redo some of the work and to reduce their bill. The contractor sees no need to do either and has high ego involvement because the interviewers are questioning his work, his charges, and his integrity. Both parties share control because the interviewers can refuse to pay the bill and the interviewee can refuse to redo the work or reduce the charges. Neither party wants to take part but both must. The relationship has deteriorated over time, so both parties are angry and have reached the point of enmity. Trust and cooperation will be low and conflict high.

③ Studying the Situation

Consider carefully the physical and situational atmosphere in which the interview will take place, including size of the room, furniture arrangement, seating, noise level, heat, and lighting. Try to obtain privacy and control interruptions, especially telephone calls. Make an appointment if possible because it is very difficult to guess how much time a persuasive interview will take. As interviewer, will you be the host (the interview is in your office or residence); a guest (the interview is in the interviewee's place of business or residence); or on neutral ground (a conference room, restaurant, hotel, club)? Will you be in a superior or subordinate setting—sitting behind or facing a desk? If selling life insurance, for example, you might prefer to meet in the interviewee's home, surrounded by the family. If selling business insurance, you might prefer to meet in the interviewee's place of business.

Timing and correct setting are important in persuasive interviews. For instance, a husband or wife may take the other spouse to dinner before proposing a move from Florida to Alaska. Be aware of events that have preceded your interview such as earlier interviews, experiences with other members of a group, and competition with others. Who would choose to be the fourth employee of the day to ask for a raise—or to request one from an employer who had just discovered a major financial loss for the previous quarter? Select the timing and setting that complement your persuasive effort, or at least try to neutralize the setting. For example, encyclopedia sales representatives have found sales brisk wherever a major labor strike is underway. Presumably, striking workers want a better life for their children and the set of encyclopedias, as an educational product, seems to offer a step in that direction. Try to discover forces beyond the interviewee's control that might weaken your persuasive effort, such as company policy, the interviewee's superior, other obligations or contracts, or financial limitations.

Investigating the Topic

Solid, up-to-date information not only helps sell your proposal, but also enhances your credibility by showing that you are knowledgeable and authoritative. The greater the risk involved in your proposal, the greater the likelihood that an interviewee will expect and demand proof that what you say is worth believing and acting upon. Investigate all aspects of the topic, including events that may have contributed to a problem, reasons for and against a change, evidence for all sides of an issue, and possible solutions.

Do not overlook any potentially valuable source of information: interviews, personal experiences, letters, pamphlets, questionnaires, surveys, unpublished studies, reports, newspapers, periodicals, professional journals, and government documents. Search for a variety of information on the topic and update your materials continually. Collect examples, both real and hypothetical, that illustrate your concern or proposal. Gather statistics on relevant areas such as inflation, growth rates, expenses, benefits, coverages, profits. It may help to know the sizes of organizations, populations, memberships, families, facilities, and cities. Gather statements of authorities on the topic as well as testimonials by persons who have joined, attended, purchased, signed, or believed. Compare your proposals with actual situations, showing what has happened to other people or organizations who have faced similar decisions. Evidence tends to have little impact if interviewees are familiar with it prior to the interview, so always seek new and unusual information. Remember that the interviewee may demand support, challenge generalizations, or ask for a source at any moment during the interview.

Opening the Interview

With your homework completed, you are ready to structure the interview to fit the interviewee and situation. A carefully planned structure is important, but you must remain flexible, ready for the unexpected, and cautious about assumptions concerning the interviewee's makeup and reactions.

Design the opening to gain attention and interest and to motivate the interviewee to take part actively. Adapt the opening to each interviewee, resisting the temptation to rely on a "standard" formula. Some writers estimate, for example, that "roughly 75 percent" of all sales representatives "fail in the attention step."[15] Review the opening techniques discussed in Chapter 3 and select the ones most suitable for each interview.

Begin with a warm greeting and do not make it sound like a question. "Good evening, Mr. Adams?" suggests you are unsure of the name and not well prepared. Introduce yourself (name, position, and perhaps background), your organization (name, location, nature, and perhaps history), and the purpose of the interview. If appropriate, you may make *sincere* personal inquiries or small talk about the weather, sports, and so on. Do not prolong the rapport stage, and be sure to involve the interviewee in the conversation. Interviewees may take an inactive role after the first few minutes if you seem to prefer doing all the talking.

When the opening ends, both parties should be aware of the degrees of interest and warmth that will pervade the interview. They should also know the agenda, how they will share control, and the interest levels of both parties. An inappropriate opening may mislead one or both parties or create a defensive rather than cooperative climate.

Creating a Need or Desire

Selecting Main Points

Select three or four points that illustrate a solid case for a need. These points should also help maintain interest and attention, enhance comprehension, and assure retention. Do not rely on a single reason or point. The interviewee may see little urgency in a problem that seems so simple or find it easy to attack "only" one reason. On the other hand, eight or nine points will either make the interview too long or very superficial from trying to move too quickly. An interviewee overloaded with information may become confused or bored.

As a general rule, begin with your strongest point because (1) you do not want it to get lost in the middle of the interview, (2) you may be able to move to the criteria/solution phases sooner than expected, and (3) the interviewee may terminate the interview before you can present all of your points.[16] *Develop one point at a time.* Explain the point thoroughly. Provide sufficient evidence that is factually based, authoritative, recent, and well documented. Use a blend of logic and emotion, with appeals to important motives and values. Encourage interaction, stressing how this point *affects and concerns this interviewee.* And finally, do not go to the next point until you have obtained at least tentative agreement from the interviewee. With point one presented and agreed upon, move to point two, then three, and so on. Do not rush through a point or jump to the next one if the interviewee states objections or asks insightful questions. Move on only when the interviewee is ready.

Developing Reasons into Acceptable Patterns

It is not enough to know which reasons or points to develop in an interview and in what order to present them. You must also know how to develop them into valid, acceptable patterns. The most effective interview is a carefully crafted blend of the logical and the psychological. Once again you have choices to make.[17]

Reasoning from an accepted belief, assumption, or proposition may involve three steps. For instance, an interviewer might argue: (1) Tetanus shots are necessary to prevent lockjaw; (2) you have not had a tetanus shot since you were in the Air Force; (3) therefore, you may get lockjaw from that cut. The strength of this pattern rests on the strength and acceptance of the belief, assumption, or proposition on which it is based. If the interviewee refuses to believe that a tetanus shot prevents lockjaw or that the old shot is no longer effective, the reasoning will fail. In most interviews, the interviewer seldom states explicitly all three parts of this pattern but allows the interviewee to supply one or more parts. For instance, a physician may simply say, "You've not had a tetanus shot since you were in the Air Force, so you need a booster to be safe," or "You need a tetanus shot." The patient will supply the reasons or the conclusion. The belief, assumption, or proposition is critical in this pattern because if the interviewee does not accept the *premise,* the interviewee will not accept the conclusion.

Reasoning from condition is based on the assertion that if something does or does not happen, something else will or will not happen. A person might reason, "Look, if I can afford $50,000 in life insurance, you can afford such coverage. I can, and so can you." The stated or implied condition is highly important to the strength of conditional reasoning. If, for instance, your financial status is significantly above the interviewee's, the interviewee is likely to reject the point. You must be able to show that your financial status is below or equal to the interviewee's. Weigh conditions carefully. For example, the conditional statement, "If we build the house east of the creek, we will have a dry basement," may be ignoring the water table or an underground spring east of the creek.

Reasoning from two choices is based on the assertion that there are only two possible proposals. The interviewer removes one proposal by showing it does not meet major criteria and concludes the obvious. For example, "Look John, either our company will conform to EEO guidelines in interviews or we will face embarrassing and costly lawsuits. We have no choice but to conform to EEO laws." The interviewer's task is, first, to convince the interviewee that only two possibilities exist and, second, to remove one of the possibilities so the preferred point or solution remains.

Reasoning from example is a generalization about a whole class of people, places, or things based on a sampling from that class. Recall the treatment of sampling techniques in Chapter 6. For instance, a physician might try to convince a reluctant parent to have a child vaccinated for mumps by stating, "A study of 15,000 children vaccinated for mumps showed that only 1 percent of vaccinated children got the mumps. It's evident that the vaccination works." The interviewer is reasoning that the results of this sample can be generalized to all other children who are vaccinated.

Reasoning from cause-effect is related to reasoning from example because interviewers often use a sample as proof of a causal relationship. For instance, a person might argue, "A study of 50 fatal accidents involving teenage drivers revealed that 35 had been drinking. It's clear that drinking causes most fatal accidents involving teenagers." Valid cause-effect reasoning relies on sampling and the range of possible causes.

Reasoning from facts is offering the conclusion that seems to explain best the evidence that is available—the best accounting for a body of facts. For instance, a campaign manager might reason, "Campaign workers are sending in good reports; our candidate is getting good turnouts for speeches; there is general discontent about unemployment; and the polls show us five points ahead. So I'm sure our candidate will win." The amount and type of evidence makes a conclusion more or less convincing to an interviewee.

Reasoning from analogy occurs when an interviewer points out that two things have a number of characteristics in common and then draws a conclusion about one of the two things. For example, a minister trying to convince a parishioner that the United States is in grave danger might reason, "Ancient Rome and the United States share many disturbing characteristics. Both controlled birthrate, had serious political corruption, were overly affluent, were materialistic, and suffered disintegrating morality. This country is likely to fall, too, if it does not change soon." Analogical reasoning is based on the assumption that if two things have a great deal in common, they share other important traits.

Adapting to the Interviewee

You must tailor each part of the persuasive interview to the identifiable beliefs, attitudes, and values of the interviewee. As Kenneth Burke writes, you persuade people only insofar as you can talk their language with "speech, gesture, tonality, order, image, attitude, *identifying*" your ways with theirs.[18] The first step is to determine the probable disposition of the interviewee, and the second is to select strategies appropriate for that disposition.

If an interviewee is likely to be *indecisive, uninterested,* or *uncertain,* you may have to educate the person to see reality for the first time. Present your strongest argument first to get the interviewee's attention and show the seriousness of the problem. Use probing questions to draw out feelings and perceptions, then use these revelations to show the urgency of the problem and the advantages of acting immediately. Avoid real or perceived pressure, but use moderate fear appeals to awaken the interviewee; "avoidance of loss" (of property, family, freedom, jobs) motivates people. Exhibit some of the emotion you want the interviewee to feel. Show how the person can solve the problem or reduce the danger.[19]

If the interviewee appears *hostile,* first be sure your impression is accurate. Do not mistake legitimate objections or a gruff demeanor for hostility. If the person is truly hostile, try to determine why early in the interview. A *common ground* approach, in which you stress beliefs, attitudes, and values that you share with the interviewee, may avoid or reduce hostility.[20] In a *yes-but approach,* begin with areas of agreement and gradually lead into points where you disagree, in an attempt to soften opposition. In the *yes-yes approach,* you hope that a series of agreements will lead to further favorable replies through habit. In an *implicative approach,* you want the interviewee to see the implication of your message because explicitly stating it may yield a "knee-jerk" negative reaction. Interviewees who perceive implications may end up feeling that the points or proposals were their own ideas. When dealing with hostile interviewees, listen, be polite, and try to avoid defensiveness or anger. Be willing to accept minor points of disagreement and to admit that your proposal is not perfect. Employ "shock-absorber" phrases that reduce the sting of critical questions: "That's a very good question, but . . ." "I'm glad you brought that up . . ." "A lot of people feel that way, however, . . ." Hostility often results from lack of information, misinformation, or rumors, so respond with facts, expert testimony, and examples that clarify, prove, and resolve issues.[21]

A *closed-minded* or *authoritarian* interviewee tends to rely on trusted authorities and may be more concerned about *who* supports your proposal than with the proposal itself. Facts alone will not do the job; you must demonstrate that the interviewee's authorities support your proposal. Closed-minded authoritarians have strong central beliefs and values, so you must identify yourself and your proposal with these values. Approach the persuasive interview in the normal, established way without bypassing hierarchical channels or altering prescribed methods. Authoritarians react negatively to interviewers who "don't belong here" or appear out of line, and they may demand censure or punishment.[22] Do not assume that a person is closed-minded or authoritarian because someone else says so or because of a few traits associated with these personalities. Don't be an amateur psychologist!

If the interviewee has a *low opinion* of you or your organization, try to determine why. You might begin the interview by expressing some views held by the interviewee— a yes-but or yes-yes approach. Maintain positive nonverbal cues such as a firm hand-shake, good eye contact, a warm, friendly voice, and appropriate appearance and dress. If the interviewee feels you are inexperienced, allude tactfully to your qualifications, experiences, and training, giving authoritative evidence. If the interviewee thinks you are too young, employ the above methods while avoiding undue informality and a cocky, egotistical attitude. If the interviewee sees you as argumentative, avoid confrontations, attacks on the person's position, and categorical demands. If the interviewee thinks you are a know-it-all, be careful when referring to your qualifications, experiences, and achievements. When presenting a need and solution, use a two-sided approach to appear objective and fair. Avoid appearances, actions, and approaches that stereotype you as a "typical" professor, lawyer, police officer, sales representative, or whatever. If the interviewee dislikes your organization, you might (1) distance yourself from it, (2) withhold the name of the organization until you have created good rapport with the interviewee, (3) explain how the organization has changed from what it used to be, or (4) try to improve the image of the organization.

If the interviewee will face *counter-persuasion,* forewarn and prepare the person for those efforts. Provide the interviewee with supportive arguments and evidence, and give small doses of the opposition's case (the so-called inoculation theory of persuasion) to show the strengths and weaknesses of both sides. When you discuss the opposition, have the facts straight and avoid emotional comments or heavy-handed criticism. Develop a positive, factual, non-emotional approach that addresses the competition when necessary but dwells primarily on the strengths of your position and proposal.[23]

The *highly intelligent* or *highly educated* interviewee tends to be less persuasible because of knowledge level, critical ability, and faculty for seeing the implications behind evidence. When working with such an individual, support all ideas thoroughly and develop a two-sided approach that compares your proposal with others. Minimize emotional appeals, particularly if the interviewee is neutral or disagrees with your position. Encourage the interviewee to ask questions, raise objections, and be an active participant. If the interviewee is of *low intelligence* or *education,* develop a simple, one-sided approach to minimize confusion and maximize comprehension. Use examples and comparisons rather than statistics and expert testimony, and appeal to such emotions as anger, fear, and pity. Do not determine intelligence or education merely on the basis of diplomas, degrees, grades, or appearance. A person may not be unintelligent, merely inexperienced or uninformed.[24]

Asking Questions

Although you will rarely come to a persuasive interview with a schedule of questions, questions can serve a variety of functions during persuasive interviews. Some sales professionals in fact believe you should never *tell* when you can *ask.* But you must select appropriate questions and have a fairly accurate idea of how the interviewee will respond.

Information gathering questions ascertain an interviewee's background, needs, desires, attitudes, and knowledge level. Be sure to listen and probe to get accuracy and details.

"What do you know about . . . ?"

"What experiences have you had with . . . ?"

"How do you feel about . . . ?"

Verification questions such as reflective probes, mirrors, and clearinghouse probes may serve two functions. (1) They check the accuracy of your assumptions, impressions, and information obtained before and during the interview. (2) They verify that an interviewee understands what you are saying and grasps the significance of your evidence and points.

"Am I correct in assuming . . . ?"

"As I understand it, you have . . . ?"

"Does that answer your concern about . . . ?"

Encouraging interaction questions urge the interviewee to take an active role and can serve as a "warm-up" so that answering/talking/questioning become natural. Interviewees may feel freer to ask questions and provide feedback once they have become an active part of the process. Use questions to discover how a quiet or noncommittal interviewee is reacting. A poker-faced person may give no feedback except in response to direct questions.

"Weren't you with Smith Enterprises when . . . ?"

"Haven't I noticed your name in the paper a good bit lately in connection with the library bond issue?"

"Well, what do you think?"

"Now do you see why I think we should delay consideration of this policy?"

Attention and interest questions are designed to keep the interviewee tuned in and alert to what you are saying. They are interesting, challenging, and thought-provoking.

"What would happen if . . . ?"

"Suppose you or your wife lost your job tomorrow . . . ?"

"Think about a situation in which. . . ."

Agreement questions try to obtain small agreements that will lead to big agreements. Be careful, however, of asking for agreement or commitment before you have developed or supported your point. The "yes-response" question can control the interview and lead to agreement if asked at the right time.

"This certainly makes sense, doesn't it?"

"I think you'll agree that this is the best solution to . . . ?"

"Isn't it amazing that we didn't come up with this sooner?"

Objection questions may draw out unstated questions or address stated objections tactfully, getting them "on the table" at the proper time. These questions can also discover what an interviewee knows about an issue and reveal the importance or reasons behind an objection.

"I understand that cost is your major concern?"

"Why do you ask?"

"Is that a major concern of yours?"

"Why do you feel that way?"

Questions can be valuable tools in persuasive interviews if you ask them *tactfully* and *tactically*. Select the correct question and phrasing for the specific moment. Beware of asking questions prematurely or using leading or loaded questions that interviewees might perceive as high-pressure tactics. And do not attempt to substitute questions for substance. You must know your topic thoroughly and present a tailored set of reasons why your proposal is acceptable.

Establishing Criteria

When you have presented the need, summarize your points and then try to get agreements from the interviewee before establishing criteria, the next phase of the interview. If the interviewee is obviously ready to move to the next stage before you have presented all your points, move on. Do not talk interminably until the interviewee becomes unconvinced or ends the interview because of boredom or frustration. The interview is not a speech, so you need not present everything you have prepared if it proves unnecessary.

Establish a set of criteria with the interviewee for evaluating all solutions to the problem. This step "presupposes that, consciously or unconsciously, any persuadee evaluates a persuasive proposal in terms of the degree to which that proposal appears to meet various kinds of criteria."[25] In selecting a college, for example, a person may consider size, areas of study, nearness to hometown, cost, housing, reputation, and athletic programs. In selecting a position, applicants consider type of work, salary, hours, job security, advancement potential, geographical location, and fellow workers.

Establishing a set of criteria *with the interviewee* involves the interviewee in the process and shows that you are attempting to tailor your proposal to his or her needs, desires, and capabilities. The criteria phase provides a smooth transition from the need to the solution and reduces the impression that you are overly anxious to sell your point. Agreed upon criteria enable you to build the interview on a foundation of agreements. When you move to the solution phase, criteria provide a clear and structured means of presenting and evaluating all proposals, including competing ones. They may also help you eliminate or handle objections that arise. Eventually, criteria provide a means of closing the interview by summarizing how your proposal has met the requirements agreed upon earlier. With criteria established, you are ready to present your proposal.

Presenting the Solution

Details and Evaluation

If more than one proposal is to be considered, deal with one at a time. Explain it in detail and use a variety of visual aids whenever possible: booklets and brochures, drawings and diagrams, graphs, letters, pictures, slides, computer printouts, sketch pads, swatches of

Explain your solution in detail and use visual aids whenever possible.

materials, objects, and models. Some sources claim that interviewees remember only about 10 percent of what they hear, 50 percent of what they do, and 90 percent of what they both see and do.[26] Evaluate the proposal according to one criterion at a time. Try to anticipate objections or respond as soon as the interviewee raises them. As you proceed through the solution phase, show how your proposal meets the criteria better than any other, and get agreement on its appropriateness, quality, and feasibility.

Always approach the solution phase of the interview in a positive, constructive, and enthusiastic manner—believe in what you are doing, and show it. Emphasize the strengths and benefits of your proposal rather than the weaknesses of the competition. Avoid "negative selling." Make no claims about advantages or disadvantages that you cannot prove. Help interviewees make decisions that are best for them at this time. Encourage the interviewee to ask questions and be actively involved. Use repetition— what one writer calls the "heart of selling"—to enhance understanding, aid memory, gain and maintain attention, and make the interviewee aware of what is important.[27] Educate interviewees by informing them about options, requirements, time constraints, and so on. Be prepared to deal with misinformation and misconceptions.

Handling Objections

Probably nothing is more threatening to an interviewer than the thought of an interviewee raising unexpected or difficult objections. But you should encourage the interviewee to do so because most objections voice the need for more information and reveal the interviewee's concerns, fears, misunderstandings, and misinformation. Some people enjoy objecting because they see persuasive interviews as games in which interviewers and interviewees joust until a proposal is rejected, modified, or accepted. Do not assume agreement because an interviewee does not raise overt questions or objections. Watch for nonverbal clues such as restlessness, fidgeting, poor eye contact, confused expressions, or signs of boredom.

Out of an infinite variety of possible objections, the most common are procrastination, money, tradition, an uncertain future, and need.[28]

Procrastination

We'll think about it later.

Why don't we get together again sometime?

Well, we have a lot of time left before we have to make that decision.

Let's give it more thought.

Money

We can't afford it right now.

Gee, $150.00 is a lot of money for a gun club.

I'm concerned about the security of my investment.

Tradition

We've always invested in government bonds.

This is the way it's always been done here.

All of my family has attended Baylor, starting with my grandfather.

We tried that once, several years ago.

Uncertain Future

I don't know what the future is going to bring.

With the economy the way it is, I'm not sure this is the time to act.

We're planning to retire to Florida in a few years.

I'm just not sure I want to commit myself that far ahead.

Need

I haven't had any problem getting more insurance when I needed it.

I already belong to the national association, so I don't see any reason to join the regional association.

I agree that the people near campus have a zoning problem, but that doesn't seem to affect us much out here.

We've done okay with the old system.

The first step in handling objections is to *anticipate* them and plan how you will respond. Planning removes the surprise and reduces the danger of being put on the spot with no answer in mind. The second step is to *listen* completely and objectively. Do not assume you understand the other person's point until you have heard it all. The third step is to *clarify* the objection, making sure you understand its importance before you respond. Did the interviewee raise the objection merely out of curiosity or because it is critical to agreement? And the fourth step is to *respond* appropriately, diplomatically, tactfully, and professionally. Do not become defensive!

Five common strategies for handling objections are minimize, capitalize, convert, deny, and confirm.[29] These strategies can be combined for effectiveness. You can *minimize* an objection by restating it to make it sound less important or by comparing it to other weightier matters. Providing evidence may also help reduce the importance of the objection, as in the following example:

Interviewee: Well, we feel our current investments are the best hedge against inflation.

Interviewer: That was very true a few years ago but with inflation now consistently below 5 percent a year, there are plans that will give you higher income and more flexibility.

You can *capitalize* on an objection by using it to clarify your own points, review your proposal's advantages, offer more evidence, or isolate the motive behind the objection.

Interviewee: I've heard so many stories about computers going "down" and information being lost that I'm reluctant to rely too heavily on them.

Interviewer: Yes, everyone seems to have favorite stories about computers, but think of the advantages. The complete file of every customer will be available to each sales representative, even when the representative is out of town. Orders can be placed immediately into the system without telephone calls, travel time, or recopying—where many mistakes are made. Revisions in orders can be made just as quickly.

You can *convert* an objection into agreement by explaining that it is not a liability, but an asset.

Interviewee: But I'm still in my twenties.

Interviewer: Actually now is the best time to consider life insurance because you can get greater coverage at a fraction of the cost you will pay when you reach forty.

You can *deny* an objection directly or indirectly by offering new or more accurate information, by introducing new features of your proposal, or by showing how circumstances have changed.

Interviewee: Well, I've heard that HMO health plans don't cover specialists you might have to go to.

Interviewer: That's true only if an HMO physician does not refer you to the specialist, but most specialists accept only referrals, so the HMO does cover specialists who are not part of the system.

Finally, you can *confirm* an objection by agreeing with the interviewee or by responding and then asking if you have relieved the concern.

Interviewee: But $17,000 a year tuition is an awful lot of money.

Interviewer: Yes, it is, but the very best law firms in the country recruit on our campus each year.

These, then, are five strategies for handling an objection. You can minimize it (reduce it), capitalize (take advantage of it), convert (reverse it), deny (answer it), or confirm (admit it).

Closing the Interview

Approach the closing of the interview confidently, but do not pressure the interviewee or appear too anxious to obtain a final agreement. Most people hesitate, fearing they will make wrong decisions. But be persistent, and remember that the average sale takes place after the fifth request or contact.[30] Hesitation to ask for the sale is the major cause of failure cited by most sales professionals.[31]

The closing usually consists of three stages: (1) trial closing, (2) filling out the contract or agreement, and (3) leave-taking.

Trial Closing

Begin the closing as soon as it seems appropriate. You do not want to continue talking if the interviewee is sold on your proposal. You may talk yourself out of an agreement by giving an interviewee more opportunities to ask questions, raise objections, and generate reasons not to be persuaded after all.

Be perceptive as you approach the end of the solution phase of the interview. Watch and listen for verbal and nonverbal cues that the interviewee is moving toward a decision. Verbal cues include questions and statements such as the following:

How soon could we complete such a program?

How could I finance a plan like this?

A government agency controls the investment of these funds?

It certainly would be nice to settle this issue soon.

That's interesting.

It makes a lot of sense.

Nonverbal cues may include enthusiastic vocal expressions, nods, and smiles. Interviewees may exchange glances as if to verify interest or begin handling brochures, models, and pictures.

Ask yes-response questions such as the following to verify that the interviewee is ready to close:

This seems to be an ideal time to computerize our operations, doesn't it?

You can see why so many college freshmen are joining ROTC units, can't you?

The cost seems very reasonable, doesn't it?

After you ask the trial closing question, be quiet! Remove any semblance of pressure and give the interviewee time to think. Your silence communicates confidence in the interviewee and allows an opportunity to ask questions or raise objections not brought out before. If you get a no to your trial closing question, try to discover why. Perhaps you need to review the criteria, compare advantages and disadvantages of acting now, or provide more information. Above all, get the cause for resistance out in the open. If you get a yes, ask a question that will lead into the contract or agreement stage:

Would you like to settle this here or come to the plant tomorrow where you can meet our staff and see our facilities?

I'm sure you'll be relieved when you have decided which college to attend next fall, won't you?

Contract or Agreement

If you have completed a successful trial closing, you are ready for the contract or agreement stage. This is a dangerous time in the persuasive interview because the interviewee knows the closing is coming and may be frightened or unsure about making a serious commitment. Be natural, pleasant, and maintain good communication with the interviewee during this stage.

You can use a variety of *closing techniques* during the contract or agreement stage.[32] In the *assumptive close,* you address part of the agreement with the phrase "I assume that . . ." For instance, you might say, "I assume from our previous discussion that you want an IBM-compatible system?" In the *summary close,* you may summarize the need, criteria, or agreements made earlier as a basis for decisions. In the *elimination of a single objection close,* you respond to the single objection that stands in the way: "Well, I can understand your reluctance to leave a position you're comfortable with, but think of the opportunities you'll have to influence a whole industry." In the *either/or close,* you try to limit the interviewee's choices to a manageable number, usually two, and then show that the alternative you advocate has the most advantages and the fewest disadvantages. In the *I'll think it over close,* you acknowledge the interviewee's desire to think about a decision, but try to assess interest or find out why the person is hesitating: "That's a good idea, and I know you wouldn't be taking time to think it over if you weren't really interested!" or "Just to clarify my thinking, which phase of the program do you want to think over?" In the *sense of urgency close,* you stress why the interviewee should act now: "This record low interest rate will end on the 31st." "We have only a few openings left for next fall's freshman class in electrical engineering." "We must fill this position before the fiscal year begins." In the *price close,* you stress the savings possible or the bottom line of the offer: "This furnace is 98 percent efficient and will save you from 30 to 50 percent on a year's heating bill." "The very best offer I can make is a $53,000 annual salary and 10 percent in commissions." "The best price I can make on that model is $1,995.00."

Leave-Taking

Once you have completed the contract, determined that no agreement can be reached, or discovered that another interview will be necessary, conclude pleasantly and positively. Do not make the leave-taking phase abrupt or curt, or you may undo the rapport and trust you worked so hard to establish. The verbal and nonverbal leave-taking techniques discussed in Chapter 3 may be adapted or combined to suit each interview. Above all, be sincere and honest in the final closing phase, and make no promises you cannot keep due to personal limitations, organizational policies, laws, or time constraints.

Sample Outlines

Let us summarize the structuring of a persuasive interview first through a blank outline and then through two developed outlines.

I.   Opening the interview
   A.   Select the most appropriate techniques from Chapter 3.
   B.   Establish rapport according to relationship and situation.
   C.   Provide appropriate orientation.

II. Creating a need or desire
   A.   Provide an appropriate statement of purpose, need, or problem.
   B.   Present a point-by-point development of reasons, causes, or aspects of the need or problem.
      1.   Provide a variety of evidence and appeals to motives, beliefs, and values.
      2.   Involve the interviewee in the discussion of each point.
      3.   Point out how *the interviewee* is involved.
      4.   Summarize the point and get at least a tentative agreement before moving to the next point.
   C.   Summarize the need or problem and get overt agreement from the interviewee.

III. Establishing criteria
   A.   Present the criteria you have in mind, explaining briefly the rationale and importance of each criterion.
   B.   Involve the interviewee in the discussion of criteria.
   C.   Encourage the interviewee to add criteria.
   D.   Summarize and get agreement on all criteria.

IV. Presenting the solution
   A.   Present one solution at a time.
      1.   Explain the solution in detail.
      2.   Evaluate the solution using agreed upon criteria.
   B.   Respond to anticipated and vocalized objections.
   C.   Get agreement on the appropriateness, quality, and feasibility of the preferred solution.

V.   Closing the interview
   A.   Begin a trial closing as soon as it seems appropriate to do so.
   B.   When the trial closing is successful, move to a contract or agreement with the interviewee.
   C.   Use appropriate leave-taking techniques from Chapter 3.

A student used the following sample outline to convince a student playing the role of a state legislator to support a *no-fault* divorce law at the next session of the general assembly. This outline develops all parts of the prescribed structure.

I. Opening
    A. Introduce self and position with Family Service Agency.
    B. Mention pending legislation on divorce laws.
    C. Allude to the high percentage of marriages ending in divorce.
    D. Refer to own recent divorce and its problems.

II. Need
    A. Show the problems created by divorce laws that require the establishment of guilt.
    B. Show how divorce laws are not constructive in nature.
    C. Show how children's needs are not properly considered.

III. Criteria
    A. Divorce laws must maintain our society's structural solidarity.
    B. Divorce laws should be constructive and positive for all involved.
    C. Divorce laws should be based on modern standards and theories.

IV. Solution
    A. The preferred solution:
        1. Eliminate the issue of guilt by establishing a nonguilt issue such as irreconcilable differences or irretrievable breakdown.
        2. Require counseling for possible reconciliation before divorce hearing and voluntary counseling therapy to help in adjustment if divorce takes place.
        3. Have independent representation of children to eliminate either side from using them in the divorce.
    B. Evaluation of the solution:
        1. Counseling and elimination of guilt would aid in maintaining society's structural solidarity.
        2. Elimination of guilt, counseling, and independent representation of children are constructive, positive approaches aimed at helping husband, wife, and children.

V. Closing
    A. Brief summary of need and solution.
    B. Encourage persuadee to express these views to other members of the general assembly.

Not all parts of an outline need be developed for every interview. For instance, if the persuadee agrees with the need or problem before the interview, you may summarize the need in the opening and move directly to criteria. A student used the following outline in a class interview to sell skis to a woman who wanted to purchase skis for the season rather than rent them as in the past.

I. Opening
    A. Greeting to an old customer.
    B. Determine the customer's seriousness in purchasing rather than renting skis.

II. Criteria
    A. Performance.
    B. Price.
    C. Durability.
    D. Resale value.

III. Solution
    A. Blue Star Superlight Skis
        1. Excellent recreational ski, stable, steady, and easy turning.
        2. A low price for a quality ski.
        3. Strong fiberglass with double-layered base to increase life of the ski.
        4. Great demand for quality secondhand skis.
    B. Comparison to other brands if interviewee asks.

IV. Closing
    A. Offer a free tryout with purchase.
    B. Urge to buy while a wide selection is still available.

In other persuasive situations, the interviewee may like the solution but see no need to take action. For instance, a person may like the speed and graphics of a new computer system but see no need because the old computer system is still in good working order and does *most* of the functions needed. You might devote nearly all of the interview to establishing need or desire. The point is, you must know the interviewee and the situation well and design the interview accordingly; be flexible and realistic.

The Interviewee in the Persuasive Interview

When you are an interviewee in a persuasive interview, you cannot afford to be passive because the result will usually be important to you, your family, or your associates. A good offense is the best defense in persuasive interviews, so be an active and critical participant. However, you also have ethical responsibilities in each interview. Too often interviewees are interested more in quick fixes, good deals, good news, and something-for-nothing rather than detailed interviews that analyze needs thoroughly, establish criteria, and evaluate a number of possible solutions. The results range from poor decisions to outright fraud. As the old saying goes, "If an offer seems too good to be true, it probably is."

Keep three guidelines in mind. First, don't be gullible. You are responsible for a reasoned skepticism about assertions, claims, and promises. Second, be an active participant in the interview. Provide thorough feedback to persuaders so they clearly understand your needs, limitations, and understanding of what is taking place and being agreed to. And third, do not make instant or unreasoned judgments for or against people, ideas, or proposals. Reject only after analyzing and evaluating a person, idea, or proposal carefully. To meet these guidelines, you must be familiar with the persuasive interviewing process outlined in this chapter, and you must be aware of common persuasive tactics and how to judge the soundness of content and evidence used to support claims about needs and solutions.

Persuasive Tactics

Interviewers use a variety of persuasive tactics to enhance their credibility, create a feeling of trust, and sell their points or solutions.

Identification is used to show how similar the interviewer's beliefs, attitudes, and values are to your own.

> I live in this neighborhood and have made the same investment you have made, so I would not be supporting a rezoning petition that would lower the values of our homes.

Are these alleged similarities real or merely claimed for a persuasive edge?

Association is used to establish a connection between the interviewer's proposal and an object, person, organization, cause, or idea that you revere.

> This zoning petition has the support of the Barberry Heights Homeowners Association and the City Planning Commission.

Is the connection real or merely claimed, and does it signify a major endorsement or simply no opposition from the "supporting" group? Is the interviewer sincere—or opportunistic like the politician who wears a Star of David only when campaigning in a Jewish neighborhood?

Disassociation is used to remove any connection between the interviewer's proposal and an object, person, organization, cause, or idea that you dislike.

> This rezoning petition was not developed and is not supported by the Ace Development Corporation that has been trying to build apartment complexes in this single-family neighborhood.

What evidence do you have of this disassociation? What is the possibility that the interviewer represents a group similar to the one you oppose? Is the denial sincere or merely a ploy to get your guard down?

Bandwagon is used to urge you to follow the crowd—to act now because "everybody's doing it" or "before it's too late!"

> Nearly half the homeowners have signed this rezoning petition already, and we should reach 100 percent by the end of the week.

How do you know everybody is doing it? Listen for qualifiers such as "nearly," "probably," "almost," and "majority." Ask for specific numbers and learn exactly who has signed, agreed, or joined. Be particularly skeptical of phrases such as "every knowledgeable person," "all clear-thinking owners," or "experienced investors." Do not be pressured or flattered into jumping on the bandwagon too quickly.

Testimony, the word of another person or group, is used to support a need or proposal.

> Wilma Rogers, president of the Homeowners Association, says this rezoning should "enhance property values and prevent commercial development in this neighborhood."

How credible and authoritative is the quoted person? When did the person make the statement?

Bifurcation is an attempt to polarize a situation into only two possibilities, proposals, or sides. The interviewer then removes one choice and concludes the obvious.

> It's either rezoning or commercial development. We have no choice but to rezone now to protect the integrity of our neighborhood.

Are only two choices possible? If so, do you agree that the choice being discarded is the least appealing? Beware of interviewers who try to oversimplify complex problems and solutions.

Cause-effect is an attempt to explain how a problem or issue developed.

> We didn't have this problem until the Board of Zoning Appeals began to make exceptions to the zoning ordinance to attract industry and builders. This petition will put an end to these variances.

Is this *the* cause, a *major* cause, or merely a *possible* cause? What evidence can the interviewer provide to connect the alleged cause with the effect? Is coincidence being confused with cause-effect?

Comparisons and analogies point out similarities between the known and the unknown in order to draw a conclusion about one or the other.

> Our problem is just like the one faced by the Knox Hill area a few years ago. That area was rezoned and commercial development was stopped cold.

How similar are the two things, events, people, places, or actions? How different are they? Which points of similarity are given and which are left out?

Tests of Evidence

Look very closely at the evidence interviewers use to support needs, criteria, and solutions and to answer your questions. Keep four tests of evidence in mind, with appropriate subquestions for each. First, *how reliable is the source of evidence?* Is the authority reputable and unbiased? Was the source in a position to observe the facts? Did reliable media report the evidence? Second, *is the evidence communicated accurately?* Are alterations or deletions apparent in reports, quotations, or explanations? Is material reported out of context? Is evidence documented sufficiently so you can tell its origin? Are statistics "rounded out" for effectiveness? Are opinions stated as facts? Is material being interpreted fairly and accurately? Third, *is the evidence sufficient in quantity and quality?* Are enough witnesses, authorities, or examples cited? How adequate is the sample of evidence? Do authoritative facts and statistics outweigh analogies and hypothetical examples? Was the evidence selected fairly? And fourth, *is the evidence recent?* Are newer statistics or authoritative statements available? Is some material too dated to be relevant? Has a quoted source altered his or her view since making the original statement?

Use probing questions, including reflective and mirror techniques, to be certain you understand what is being said, what you are agreeing with, and what commitments you are making. The following excerpt from a classroom interview using the "Rezoning

Petition for an Apartment Complex" case at the end of this chapter illustrates how seemingly convincing evidence may be challenged by an alert and critical interviewee. Notice how the interviewee's questions reveal weaknesses in the interviewer's case.

Interviewer: We have a real shortage of multiple-family housing in this community.

Interviewee: How can we have a shortage of multiple-family housing when the *Daily Tribune* has long lists of vacancies every evening?

Interviewer: Well, there's always a turnover rate in rental housing and it gives the impression of a renter's market. Did you see the article in the recent issue of the *National Homebuilder's Journal* by the Secretary of HUD? She said, "The greatest demand in the next ten to fifteen years will be for condominiums in which a person owns his or her own apartment."

Interviewee: Yes, I saw the article, but it appeared more than a year ago and reported a study conducted nearly three years ago. And wasn't she talking about geographical areas with large populations of fifty- to sixty-five year olds? We have a very small senior citizen population in this county.

Interviewer: But there is a growing demand for multiple-family housing, especially condominiums. We get inquiries nearly every day.

Interviewee: I haven't detected such a demand in this area, especially for condominiums. That development east of town has been sitting unfinished for nearly two years.

Interviewer: Yeah, well, that's not a good area for condominiums.

Interviewee: How many serious contacts have you received in the past six months?

Interviewer: I can't give you exact figures, but it's probably 15 or more.

Interviewee: Well, I'd have to see some impressive figures before I'd be willing to sign a petition to rezone 75 acres that could be a nice city park.

Be an active participant during each persuasive interview. Use carefully phrased questions to discover an interviewer's real purpose, qualifications, and preparation and to unravel complicated or vague points and proposals. Do not be rushed into making a decision; you have nothing to gain and much to lose through haste. Insist on clear points and adequate evidence that establish the problem, mutually acceptable criteria by which to evaluate all proposals, and thoroughly explained solutions. Do not tolerate "smears," innuendos, or half-truths aimed at an interviewer's competitors. And remember your ultimate defenses: termination of the interview or an emphatic "No!"

Summary

Good persuasive interviews are not debates or confrontations involving categorical demands and statements; they are efforts to establish a common ground during which both parties recognize the necessity of compromise and the virtue of realistic goals. Good persuasive interviews are not canned efforts designed to fit all situations; they are carefully planned and adapted to each interviewee, yet they remain flexible enough to meet unforeseen disruptions and reactions. Good persuasive interviews are not speeches to an audience of one; they are conversations involving the interviewee as an active participant and requiring the interviewer to listen as well as to speak effectively. Good persuasive interviews are not aimed exclusively at either emotion or reason; they appeal to both the head and the heart. Good persuasive interviews are not efforts in which anything goes as long as the interviewee does not catch on; they are honest endeavors conducted along basic ethical guidelines.

A Persuasive Interview for Review and Analysis _____

This interview is between Marty Weinberg, an adjunct professor at Bailey State University and city editor of the *Tribune-Star,* and Dr. Sarah Fleming, the chair of the Journalism Department at Bailey State. During the past five years, Marty Weinberg has taught a variety of journalism courses for Dr. Fleming, including basic reporting, newspaper reporting, and advocacy journalism. He believes the department's journalism writing laboratory must be updated to provide journalism students with the education they need to be competitive for positions in the 1990s and the future. The interview is taking place in Dr. Fleming's office at 8:45 in the morning.

How thoroughly has the interviewer done his homework? Assess the relationship between interviewer and interviewee and how this affects the interview. How satisfactory are the major parts of the interview: opening, need, criteria, solution, and closing? How well does the interviewer adapt to the interviewee (beliefs, attitudes, and values) and to the situation? How does nonverbal communication affect this interview? When do exchange of persuader and persuadee roles occur, and how do these exchanges affect the interview? How effectively does the interviewee play her role as a critical participant? What tactics does the interviewer use? How satisfactory is the evidence to support claims?

1. **Interviewer:** Good morning Dr. Fleming. (cheerful and smiling) Got a few minutes to discuss a problem with me?
2. **Interviewee:** Sure Marty; (pleasant tone of voice, looks at her watch) have a seat. I don't have to leave for a department chair's meeting for about ten minutes.
3. **Interviewer:** (serious tone of voice, takes a seat in front of the interviewee's desk) As you know Dr. Fleming, I've been teaching courses for you on a part-time basis for about five years now, and I've thoroughly enjoyed working with the journalism students at Bailey State. In fact, several of the students have had internships with me at the Tribune-Star. I believe these internships have gotten many of them good reporting positions.
4. **Interviewee:** (looking the interviewer directly in the eyes, serious but pleasant tone of voice) Yes, I know, and we've been very fortunate to have you, particularly since we have been unable to get additional faculty positions. And the students benefit from your professional background and connections.
5. **Interviewer:** Well, thanks. (smiling, glances around the office) I've sometimes wondered about how you and the regular faculty felt about me and my teaching. I'm sure you're aware that I'm one of the major users of the writing lab.
6. **Interviewee:** Yes, I am. (pleasant but forceful tone of voice) You said you wanted to talk about a problem? (glances at her watch, and pulls a file from her briefcase)
7. **Interviewer:** (hurriedly, smiling) Indeed. We simply have to get new computer equipment for the writing lab; what we have is a collection of antiques! Tech-Write stopped making these models years ago.

8. **Interviewee:** (pause) What we have is far better than the ancient typewriters we had five years ago when I became department chair. (a tone of irritation, and slow rate of speaking) We had very little money then, only enough to buy used word processors from another journalism school, and we have no capital funds now because of the state budget crisis! (defensive manner)

9. **Interviewer:** (quickly) Please Dr. Fleming, I didn't mean to criticize your leadership or what you have accomplished, but I do want to explain to you my frustration, and my students' frustration, with the lab. Will you hear me out?

10. **Interviewee:** Of course, (sits back, frowns, looks Marty directly in the eyes) but realize the financial limitations I'm operating under.

11. **Interviewer:** (grave tone of voice and manner) Well, first of all, the equipment is breaking down so frequently now that I rarely have more than twelve or thirteen word processors working for a class of eighteen to twenty students. Students must double-up, and often a student cannot get access to a machine during an entire class period.

12. **Interviewee:** (appears shocked) I had no idea they were breaking down that often; no one has mentioned this to me. Why haven't students or faculty come to see me?

13. **Interviewer:** We're all aware of how scarce funds are right now, and have been trying to make do. Unfortunately, it's getting more and more difficult to find parts for these old processors, and Joe (our part-time technician shared with the television department) is having to cannibalize some machines to keep the best ones working.

14. **Interviewee:** (deliberate manner) We're hoping to inherit the Tech-Write computers from the student newspaper when they go to PC's next year. These could replace the worst of the lot and provide parts for others.

15. **Interviewer:** I'm afraid that would only prolong major problems. These old machines don't allow students to work with the latest journalism software or to interface with other writers and editors on campus, at the student newspaper, and the *Tribune-Star*. This is essential learning for the twenty-first century. It's what all other journalism programs are turning to.

16. **Interviewee:** *All* other programs? (sounds skeptical) I may agree with you, but I don't see how we can afford a new writing lab. Even if money became available, the dean and executive vice president would demand a solid, data-based case for both need and proposal.

17. **Interviewer:** Well, (smiling) if I can sell you, I think I can sell the dean and vice president. Our old lab is preventing some of our students from landing good reporting positions. Do you have time to hear my proposal?

18. **Interviewee:** Only a couple of minutes. (sounds irritated) I do have a chair's meeting in less than five minutes.

19. **Interviewer:** Okay, here it is quickly. I propose we purchase twenty Model 235s from Elec-Write. They're the latest, the cheapest, and the best on the market. And they are IBM compatible and can handle any current software. Believe me, I've checked them all out. (hurried manner and fast speaking rate)

20. **Interviewee:** I don't doubt that you've done your homework, but we haven't even decided upon specific requirements for our situation here at Bailey. And how do I know they're the latest, cheapest, and best? If you think I'm demanding, wait until you try the dean.

21. **Interviewer:** Well, I know we don't have time now to go into all the details; that's why I didn't bring a lot of stuff with me.

22. **Interviewee:** You've made me think; I'll admit that. But this is not something that can be proposed or brought about without a lot of research, some careful thought about criteria or requirements for our program, and some notion of how we might pay for the equipment. By the way, what's your best estimate of total cost?

23. **Interviewer:** Twenty machines, all the necessary wiring, software, printers, and an instructor's module would run about $45,000.

24. **Interviewee:** $45,000! (sounds shocked) I had a terrible time convincing the administration to come up with $5,000 for the current lab. And that was when funding for higher education was relatively robust. What would it be without the instructor's module?

25. **Interviewer:** The instructor's module is absolutely critical to teaching journalism classes! We can't eliminate anything and remain competitive with other journalism programs.

26. **Interviewee:** Come now. (sounds skeptical and frustrated) I know of many programs who have labs as old as ours is.

27. **Interviewer:** Well, the module allows the instructor to communicate directly with each student station and to project a particular student's story up on the board for discussion and revision. It's a fabulous teaching tool.

28. **Interviewee:** I've seen a few in operation at major journalism schools. But the bottom line remains, where are we going to get the money?

29. **Interviewer:** I thought we might make an appeal to our alumni, maybe even a phone-a-thon, and tell them what we need and why. Other schools with fewer alums have been successful at fund raising.

30. **Interviewee:** Marty, (sounds exasperated) aren't you aware that the university is in the midst of a major development campaign and have frozen all school and departmental fund raising? The administration does not want anything to interfere with the Twenty-First Century Fund campaign.

31. **Interviewer:** I wasn't aware of the freeze and, yes, I know about the Twenty-First Century Fund. I've been tapped already.

32. **Interviewee:** Corporations are always telling us in higher education that we don't involve them enough in the training of their employees. How about the World Press Foundation owned by your parent company? It gives large sums of money to research and development projects, churches, and private schools. Forty-five thousand dollars would be small potatoes for the Foundation.

33. **Interviewer:** I had not considered the Foundation because it has a policy of not giving to state supported schools and programs.

34. **Interviewee:** It seems to me that when a university like Bailey gets only about 35 percent of its funding from the state, foundations such as the World Press Foundation ought to be willing to help. After all, we're not an engineering or science department that needs help but a journalism program. We produce a good many reporters and editors for World Press papers like the *Tribune-Star.*

35. **Interviewer:** (quietly, looks at floor) I guess it's worth a try; anything's worth a try to improve our writing lab.

36. **Interviewee:** (standing up) I'm late for the department chair's meeting.

37. **Interviewer:** I apologize for holding you up, but I do believe in this cause. Could we get together soon to discuss some specifics of a new lab?

38. **Interviewee:** Monday at ten would be a good time. But come with some guidelines for lab equipment and needs, and bring specifics on comparative costs for each item. I don't want to involve the faculty or the dean's office until *we* know exactly what we think is needed and why. Then we can see how the faculty reacts.

39. **Interviewer:** Sounds good to me. See you on Monday.

Persuasion Role-Playing Cases

Rezoning Petition for an Apartment Complex

The interviewer has been active in Citizens for Development and Progress, a group pushing for housing and industrial developments in and near Rockland, a city of 85,000. There are seventy-five acres in northern Rockland that the interviewer and others want to see developed into an apartment complex, and the interviewer is trying to get property owners to sign a petition in favor of rezoning the land. The interviewee, a very influential member of the community, is opposed to using this land for commercial development and would like to see it turned into a city park. The interview is taking place in the interviewee's home at 8:00 P.M.

The interviewee, a high school science teacher in Rockland, has above average intelligence and belongs to local and national ecology groups, including the Sierra Club. The interviewee enjoys all forms of sports, is married, has two children, tends to be optimistic and open-minded, and is beginning to question the notion of "progress." The interviewee believes that urban sprawl must be stopped and sees the interviewer as overly progress-minded—a petition carrier for any cause that might "develop" the area and a supporter of another move by the Citizens for Development and Progress.

Installation of a National Credit System

The interviewer is a partner in Westlake Farm and Garden, a store started ten years ago by the interviewer and interviewee. Net profits have grown to nearly $75,000 a year which is divided equally between the partners. Westlake Farm and Garden has always extended credit on a very informal basis. Volume of credit business (about 50 percent of all sales) has grown to a point where a full-time accountant will be necessary. Nearly $10,000 in credit purchases is not being paid back on a regular basis. The interviewer has decided to convince the interviewee to install VISA bank card as the only credit extended. The interview is taking place in the office area at 7:30 A.M.

The interviewee has above average intelligence, completed two years of college in horticulture, belongs to the Westlake Optimist Club and the Small Business's Club, and is a Boy Scout leader. The interviewee is optimistic, fairly open-minded and likes to help and get along with people. The interviewee sees the interviewer as more business-minded than people-minded and thinks the interviewer's M.S. in Agricultural Economics sometimes gets in the way in a small-town, personal business like Westlake Farm and Garden.

Proposal for Additional Funds for the Next Fiscal Year

The interviewer is manager of the research and development division of Smith Tools, a manufacturer of home and commercial power tools. Three years ago, during an economic recession, budgets of all departments were cut severely. Only the production division came out fairly well. Budgets and staff are now being considered for the next fiscal year, and the proposed budget for research and development is $2,777,000, a 2 percent increase. The interviewer has made an appointment with the vice-president in charge of budget to ask for at least a 15.5 percent increase. The interview is taking place in the vice-president's office at 3:30 P.M.

The interviewee, a highly intelligent and successful executive, makes $113,000 a year and is one of three vice-presidents answerable only to the president and board of directors. Three division heads (personnel, public relations, and sales) met with the interviewee earlier in the day with requests for substantial increases in budget and staff. The interviewee is serious, somewhat moody, suspicious, and closed-minded. The vice-president's goal is to forge ahead economically but maintain an austere budget until the company is clearly out of danger. The interviewer is perceived to be a bright young climber and an empire builder, although a bit pushy. Ego involvement is fairly high because the interviewee and staff have created the proposed budget.

Adoption of a New Line of Clothing

The interviewer is twenty-four years old and is the assistant manager of the College Shop, a clothing store for men and women near a state university campus. The interviewer's goal is to convince the manager to drop one of three brands of clothing and adopt another. The interview is taking place in the manager's office after the shop closes at 8:00 P.M.

The interviewee has been with the College Shop for several years, and never forgets who is manager. Ego involvement is high because the interviewee selected the three brands nearly twenty years ago. The interviewee is generally open-minded but likes things to stay the same and tends to be very slow to change. The interviewer is perceived to be intelligent, but young and inexperienced.

A New Home in the Country

The interviewer is a real estate sales representative for Oaks Realty who knows that the interviewees (husband and wife) have been looking at a variety of homes—new and used, in town and in the country—as well as at plans for constructing a new home. Oaks Realty has contracted to sell a ten-year-old ranch home located on five acres of rolling land about eight miles from town. The interview is taking place in the interviewees' apartment at 7:00 P.M.

The interviewees are both teachers at the local high school, with a combined income of $54,000. They have no children but plan to have one or two within the next five years. They are currently living in Riverbend Apartments and like the location's closeness to the high school. After hunting in a very systematic fashion, they became discouraged and stopped looking because of the high cost of homes, high interest rates, and increased travel expenses that would result from a move. They see the interviewer as pleasant but a "typical" real estate sales representative eager to make a sale. They know that sales commissions are the interviewer's only income and that sales have been slow for several months.

An Increase in Salary

The interviewer was out of work for nearly a year-and-a-half after his public relations position at a local manufacturing firm was eliminated. Then, nearly a year ago, the interviewee, founder and president of a new public relations and advertising firm, M & J Associates, hired the interviewer at an entry level salary far below what the interviewer had been making. M & J Associates has flourished beyond all expectations, and the interviewer, who has been primarily responsible for the firm's winning several advertising awards, wants a sizable increase in salary but does not want to appear ungrateful.

The interviewee has been very pleased with the success of M & J and is grateful for the interviewer's contributions. However, the interviewee is concerned about maintaining a solid financial base, has a number of loans to pay off, and knows that the loss of a few big accounts, an ever-present danger in advertising and public relations, could jeopardize the future of the firm. The interviewee feels the interviewer "came on board" with the understanding that salaries would remain low for a few years; otherwise, the firm would have hired younger employees.

Student Activities

1. Visit several department stores or car dealers and observe the persuasive approaches employed. How much information about you did the salesperson get before making a presentation or suggestion? How did your personal characteristics such as age, sex, race, dress, physical appearance, and apparent wealth seem to affect these interviews?

2. Invite an encyclopedia or insurance sales representative into your home for a sales interview. Observe the structure of the interview, the strategies and tactics employed, and the values appealed to. How close is persuasion in practice to persuasion in theory? Warning: You might end up with a set of encyclopedias or an insurance policy.

3. Interview a college coach who actively recruits high school students for his or her program. Probe specifically into how the coach adapts to each recruit's desires, needs, beliefs, attitudes, and values. What kinds of information does the coach provide? When and how does the coach try to "close" the persuasive effort? How does the coach handle objections?

4. Select a current controversial issue and a potential interviewee who feels differently about the issue than you. Make a thorough analysis of the interviewee, including physical and mental characteristics, socioeconomic background, psychological makeup, and attitudes. What difficulties did you encounter in finding relevant materials? How did you determine what information was relevant? How would this analysis affect your persuasive strategies?

5. Select a person you either admire or dislike—a casual acquaintance, fellow student or worker, relative, or national figure. Make a list of descriptive adjectives (such as honest/dishonest, competent/incompetent) that you think adequately describe this person. Which of these traits are important facets of credibility? How was this image formed in your mind? What could the liked or disliked person do to alter this image in your mind?

Notes

1. Roderick P. Hart, "Teaching Persuasion," in *Teaching Communication: Theory, Research, and Methods,* John A Daly, Gustav W. Friedrich, and Anita L. Vangelisti, eds. (Hillsdale, NJ: Lawrence Erlbaum, 1990), 104–105.

2. "A Nation of Liars?" *U.S. News & World Report,* February 23, 1987, 54–61; "What Ever Happened to Ethics?" *Time,* May 25, 1987, 14–29; *Wall Street Journal,* September 18, 1987, 1 and 5.

3. *Wall Street Journal,* September 18, 1987, 1 and 5.

4. Gary C. Woodward and Robert E. Denton, Jr. *Persuasion & Influence in American Life* (Prospect Heights, IL: Waveland Press, 1992), 388–401; Richard L. Johannesen, "Perspectives on Ethics in Persuasion," in Charles U. Larson, *Persuasion: Reception and Responsibility* (Belmont, CA: Wadsworth, 1992), 28–53.

5. Richard L. Johannesen, *Ethics and Persuasion: Selected Readings* (New York: Random House, 1967).

6. Karl R. Wallace, "An Ethical Basis of Communication," *Speech Teacher* 4 (1955), 6–9. Wayne C. Minnick, *The Art of Persuasion* (Boston: Houghton-Mifflin, 1968), 285.

7. Kenneth E. Andersen, *Persuasion: Theory and Practice* (Boston: Allyn & Bacon, 1971), 327.

8. These conditions are based on materials developed by W. Charles Redding and the Purdue University staff. They are treated in Robert S. Goyer, W. Charles Redding, and John T. Rickey, *Interviewing Principles and Techniques: A Project Text* (Dubuque, IA.: Wm. C. Brown Publishers, 1968), 49–54.

9. Marvin Karlins and Herbert I. Abelson, *Persuasion: How Opinions and Attitudes Are Changed* (New York: Springer, 1970), 89–91; E. Maccoby and C. Jacklin, *The Psychology of Sex Differences* (Palo Alto, CA.: Stanford University Press, 1974); and Charles Montgomery and Michael Burgoon, "The Effects of Androgyny and Message Expectations on Resistance to Persuasive Communication," *Communication Monographs* 47 (1980), 56–67.

10. Mary Ann Smith, *Persuasion and Human Action* (Belmont, CA.: Wadsworth, 1982), 165–70; Victoria O'Donnell and June Kable, *Persuasion: An Interactive-Dependency Approach* (New York: Random House, 1982), 27–31.

11. Edward D. Steele and W. Charles Redding, "The American Value System: Premises for Persuasion," *Western Speech* 26 (1962), 83–91; Milton Rokeach, *Beliefs, Attitudes, and Values* (San Francisco: Jossey-Bass, 1968), 124.

12. See Steele and Redding, 83–91; Milton Rokeach and Seymour Parker, "Values as Social Indicators of Poverty and Race in America," *Annals of the American Academy of Political and Social Sciences* 388 (1970), 101–2.

13. Robert N. Bostrom, *Persuasion* (Englewood Cliffs, NJ: Prentice-Hall, 1983), 71–74; Charles U. Larson, *Persuasion* (Belmont, CA.: Wadsworth, 1986), 238–41.

14. Herbert W. Simons, *Persuasion: Understanding, Practice, and Analysis* (New York: Random House, 1986), 129–33; Ellen Berschied, "Opinion Change and Communicator-Communicatee Similarity and Dissimilarity," *Journal of Personality and Social Psychology* 4 (1966), 67–80.

15. James F. Robeson, H. Lee Mathews, and Carl G. Stevens, *Selling* (Homewood, IL.: Richard D. Irwin, 1978), 109.

16. Ralph L. Rosnow and Edward J. Robinson, *Experiments in Persuasion* (New York: Academic Books, 1967), 99–104.

17. Woodward and Denton, 118–141; Larson, 176–205.

18. Kenneth Burke, *A Rhetoric of Motives* (Berkeley: University of California Press, 1969), 55.

19. Simons (1976), 12–14; Gerald L. Manning and Barry L. Reece, *Selling Today: A Personal Approach* (Dubuque, IA.: Wm. C. Brown Publishers, 1984), 312–13.

20. Karlins and Abelson, 120.

21. Gary A. Miller and C. Winston Borgen, *Professional Selling: Inside and Out* (New York: Van Nostrand Reinhold, 1979), 151, 198, 202, 263; Robeson, Mathews, and Stevens, 207–8.

22. Karlins and Abelson, 99–101; Bostrom, 181–82.

23. Manning and Reece, 149–51; Smith, 284–304.

24. Karlins and Abelson, 22–26.

25. Goyer, Redding, and Rickey, 50–51.

26. Manning and Reece, 12.

27. Tom Hopkins, *How to Master the Art of Selling* (Scottsdale, AZ.: Champion Press, 1982).

28. Charles J. Stewart, *Pre-Need Sales Manual* (Indian Rocks Beach, FL.: M. K. Jones & Associates, 1986), 6–13 to 6–15.

29. Stewart, 6–15 to 6–20.

30. Sal T. Massimino, *The Complete Book of Closing Sales* (New York: AMACOM, 1978), 103.

31. Lee Iacocca, *Iacocca: An Autobiography* (Toronto: Bantam Books, 1984), 34; Manning and Reece, 368.

32. See, for example, Manning and Reese, 372–76.

Suggested Readings

Karlins, Marvin, and Abelson, Herbert I. *Persuasion: How Opinions and Attitudes Are Changed*. New York: Springer, 1970.

Larson, Charles U. *Persuasion*. Belmont, CA.: Wadsworth, 1992.

Manning, Gerald I., and Reece, Barry I. *Selling Today: A Personal Approach*. Dubuque, IA.: Wm. C. Brown Publishers, 1989.

Massimino, Sal T. *The Complete Book of Closing Sales*. New York: AMACOM, 1981.

Miller, Gary A., and Orgen, C. Winston. *Professional Selling: Inside and Out*. New York: Van Nostrand Reinhold, 1979.

O'Donnell, Victoria, and Kable, June. *Persuasion: An Interactive-Dependency Approach*. New York: Random House, 1982.

Robeson, James F.; Mathews, H. Lee; and Stevens, Carl G. *Selling*. Homewood, IL.: Richard D. Irwin, 1978.

Simons, Herbert W. *Persuasion: Understanding, Practice, and Analysis*. New York: Random House, 1986.

Smith, Mary Ann. *Persuasion and Human Action*. Belmont, CA.: Wadsworth, 1982.

Woodward, Gary C. and Denton, Robert E. *Persuasion and Influence in American Life*. Prospect Heights, IL.: Waveland Press, 1992.

11

The Health Care Interview

Health care interview situations vary widely from a routine physical checkup, treatment for the flu, filling of a cavity, setting a broken arm, and minor or major surgery, to long term care for a curable disease such as breast cancer or an incurable disease such as AIDS or Alzheimer's. The interview may be scheduled days or weeks in advance or occur without warning because of an accident, act of violence, or physical emergency such as a heart attack or stroke. Health care interviews are often tense and emotional, whether involving the embarrassment of the gynecological examination, the happiness of childbirth, the trauma of cancer detection, or the sadness of death. Nearly all health care interviews are influenced by anxiety over the unknown, traditions, societal expectations, the medical bureaucracy, and relationships that may last for minutes (brief consultations with specialists) or years (examinations and treatments by the family dentist or general practitioner).

Many health professionals have assumed that their colleagues would "acquire interpersonal skills through role-modeling or by trial and error without exposure to a formal teaching program."[1] But research during the past twenty years has led to some startling discoveries. In Great Britain, a study of communication between medical personnel and couples facing the death of a partner concluded that "poor communication causes more suffering than any other problem except unrelieved pain."[2] Another study reported that "students in clinical training actually decreased in their interviewing skills when not exposed to instruction."[3] When training does take place, some medical professors argue that "too much emphasis has been given to the content of the interview and not enough to the process of the interview."

The apparent shortcomings of the health care provider have led most researchers to focus on the professional as *the cause* of all communication problems in the health care situation.[4] As we have stressed throughout this book, however, the interview is a two-way process with both parties involved in and responsible for behavioral interchanges. Thompson emphasizes that "patients play an equally important role in both effective and ineffective communication."[5] She has discovered, for instance, that both provider and consumer fail to ask questions at critical times during interviews.[6]

Although the medical interviewer may have a single dominant role to play in an interview, such as gathering information during an intake interview or a counseling session following surgery, the interviewer is most likely to "switch hats" frequently, depending upon the need of the moment. Within a single ten to fifteen minute interaction with a patient, a physician, nurse, or dentist might act as information seeker, information giver, counselor, and persuader—all of the major roles we have discussed so far in this book.

Because the interviewer plays so many roles in the typical health care interview, no series of stages we outlined in previous chapters is possible for health care interactions. This chapter begins with an extensive review and analysis of the health care relationship because it is critical for patient satisfaction and compliance.[7] Then the chapter focuses on three tasks interviewers encounter most often in health care interviews: information getting, information giving, and counseling.

The Health Care Relationship

Although the relationship between interviewer and interviewee is important in all interview settings, its importance is greatly magnified in the health care interview. A person's apprehension before a job interview or a performance appraisal pales in comparison to a pending pelvic examination or revelation of tests for cancer or AIDS.[8] And the status of the interview parties in the health care interview cannot be matched in any counseling, persuasive, or journalistic setting. A medical professional who is highly trained, seemingly in control of both self and situation, seldom emotionally involved, and fully clothed in a suit or uniform, talks with a patient who may be uninformed, have little or no control over self or situation, and may be partially nude, highly medicated, in severe pain, or chronically anxious about life and death matters.

The relationship between health care professional and patient is vitally important to the medical interview because, as Kreps concludes, it "facilitates exchange of relevant health information, coordination of efforts, and provision of emotional support between interdependent health care consumers and providers."[9] The history of health care has influenced communication between provider and consumer and thus the relationship between them.[10] During the nineteenth century when physicians could do little scientifically to combat germs and bring persons back to health, they established relationships by being always available and through caring and listening skills. During the twentieth century as science and technology enabled physicians to attack germs that cause diseases, caring and listening seemed less important and, for a time, scientific language, manner, and procedures brought new respect to providers. During the past twenty-five years, however, consumers have been satisfied with medical care but increasingly dissatisfied with the communication that accompanies it.[11]

Ineffective communication and relationship-building has led to dissatisfaction with health care services and alienation between providers and patients.[12] Patients complain of lack of friendliness and warmth, lack of communication with themselves and their families, excessive technical language and jargon, and inadequate explanations. Health care professionals complain of unrealistic expectations, control struggles, and lack of patient compliance with instructions.[13] It is important to become aware of the perceptions, roles, and forces that mold the health care relationship to understand and improve communication in the health care setting.

The Health Care Professional's Perspective

Health care professionals learn from training, role models, peer pressure, and the actions and comments of their superiors that they are to be "in control" at all times.[14] Many are understandably reluctant to share this control with patients and their families or even with other professionals, particularly physicians, nurses, emergency medical technicians, or staff members who are lower in the medical hierarchy. To maintain control under difficult and emotional circumstances, health care professionals often adopt a "professional distance" or an impersonal attitude toward patients and other associates. Health care professionals tend to be busy, "task-oriented" individuals who are reluctant to waste time on inconsequential chats with patients. They want to diagnose and treat the disease as quickly and efficiently as possible so they can treat the next patient.[15] Researchers have found that physicians tend to view most medical visits as *relatively routine* and, in routine situations, interviewers assume "their behavior is appropriate and their interpretations are accurate."[16]

Patients are often stereotyped. The perception of the patient as a child-like dependent is often revealed by the use of condescending attitudes and baby talk with adult patients. And, although the physician or nurse may call the patient by a first name or nickname, the patient nearly always refers to the professional as "the EMT," "the nurse," or by *Doctor, Miss,* or *Mr.* Thus, the patient is partially to blame for the parent-child relationship. Health care providers often have very positive attitudes toward certain kinds of patients such as the middle-aged and very negative attitudes toward others such as adolescents.[17] The "good" patient is cooperative, quiet, obedient, grateful, unaggressive, considerate, and dispassionate. "Good" patients tend to get better treatment than "bad" patients. Patients seen as lower class tend to get more pessimistic diagnoses and prognoses. Overweight patients are deemed *less* likable, seductive, well-educated, in need of help, or likely to benefit from help and *more* emotional, defensive, sincere, warm, and likely to have continuing problems.[18] One writer concludes, "It is not so much the patient's needs but the doctor's individuality that determines the form of the doctor-patient relationship."[19]

The Patient's Perspective

Unlike providers who see most medical visits as routine, patients view visits "with apprehension and uncertainty, especially if they normally enjoy good health," and when people are uncertain and anxious, they closely monitor their own and providers' behavior and communication.[20] When people seek medical care, they are openly admitting that their health problems are beyond their control and that they must turn to others for help.[21] People in this position are disappointed with themselves and feel guilty, weak, or inadequate. If the problem affects their looks or results in the removal of an organ or limb, patients may not feel like whole persons and may experience changes in personality, ego, self-image, and identity. Hospitalized patients often feel exceedingly vulnerable because they lose the security and familiarity of homes, jobs, routines, and normal relationships. They find themselves in threatening environments, deprived of their dignity, autonomy, authority, and freedom. Unlike the health care professional who focuses on diagnosis and treatment, the patient focuses on being ill and the *care* received. Care is most often equated with relationship-building: listening, empathy, warmth, ease of communication, and ability to explain things in understandable ways rather than scientific efficiency.[22]

Facing the unknown or an uncertain future frightens patients and their families and affects their perspectives. As Barnlund writes, "To be uninformed is to be communicatively impotent, and this dependent state is not one mature people tolerate gracefully."[23]

The development of positive relationships between health care professionals and patients is essential for effective communication and health care.

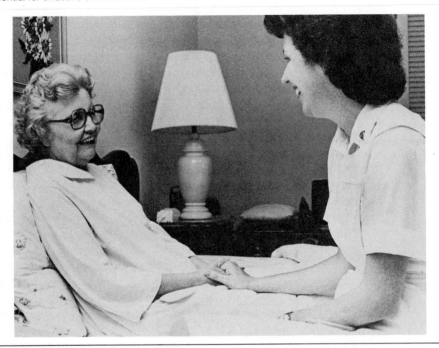

Patients are surrounded by authority figures in lab coats, nurse's uniforms, and three-piece suits who appear to have unlimited power to foster or to deny life. It seems dangerous to displease medical authorities in any way, and since patients detect that time must not be wasted, they generally try to be patient, brave, and above all, cooperative. People react to these altered and threatening circumstances in a variety of ways. Some become conservative, rigid, and suspicious. They see small incidents as affronts or signs of rejection. Others react angrily and lash out at nurses, technicians, staff members, and visitors. Still others withdraw into themselves, becoming self-centered or overly dependent; some may even want to remain ill to get attention, escape from the world, or achieve personal ends. Poor interpersonal communication is a major factor in patient dissatisfaction, patient noncompliance, and incidence of malpractice litigation. Dissatisfied patients often change physicians on this basis alone, sometimes even turning to medical quacks in search of reassurance, kindness, consideration, and communication.[24]

Positive relationships between health care professionals and patients are essential for effective communication and good health care. Mutual trust, cooperation, maximum self-disclosure, meaningful feedback, and a sharing of content are needed. However, too many situations are characterized by one-sided control and an impersonal setting, with neither party wanting to be involved in the interview. Such an atmosphere produces relationships in which conflict and fear prevail. Patients tend to agree with medical authorities during interviews and then ignore prescriptions, regimens, and advice afterward. The professional-patient relationship can be positive, but only if both parties work at it.

Ways to Enhance Interview Relationships

Health care professionals and patients must realize that both interview parties, while unique in some ways, also share many perceptions, values, needs, attitudes, and experiences.[25] Professionals and patients are real persons, not "medical magicians" or "disease carriers," and both need to maintain dignity, privacy, self-respect, and comfort. Each party must strive to understand and identify with the other. Professionals must realize how their messages can frighten and confuse patients, and patients must realize how important it is for them to explain their symptoms clearly and fully to receive appropriate treatment.[26] Some nursing and medical programs encourage students to spend a day lying in a hospital bed or using a wheelchair or crutches to experience being a "helpless" patient. Additionally, some medical schools are using mock patients "to test both the competence and compassion of medical students."[27] While other medical schools are replacing plastic models with real patients, sometimes medical students themselves, to train students how to conduct physical examinations.[28]

On the other hand, future patients could benefit from visits to hospitals or stints as volunteers to see what it is like in the professional's shoes. Medical personnel can reduce professional distance by not hiding behind uniforms or hospital gowns and emotional distance by encouraging two-way discussions of feelings. However, neither party should push the relationship too quickly—before the other is ready to talk about personal matters. Zakus and others suggest five ways for professionals to enhance relationships with patients: (1) try to be relaxed, confident, and comfortable; (2) show interest in the patient as an individual; (3) maintain objectivity; (4) be sincere and honest; and (5) maintain appropriate control over the structure of the interview without shutting the patient off.[29]

Because the quality of communication directly affects the relationships and outcome of health care interviews, the remainder of this chapter focuses on principles and practices that enable health care professionals to get information, give information, and counsel effectively.

Getting Information in the Health Care Interview _____

Barriers to Getting Information

Health care professionals spend a great deal of time trying to get vital information about patients—no easy task. Often physical or emotional factors make it difficult for interviewees to remember or articulate information accurately and completely. For example, frightened and anxious patients often unintentionally leave out significant parts of their medical histories or intentionally minimize symptoms. Mothers spontaneously recall only about half of their children's major illnesses. When patients feel ashamed or embarrassed, they may camouflage the real problem and make allegorical statements such as, "You know how women (men) are at this stage in their lives." Depth of self-disclosure is likely to be shallow if the patient does not trust the emergency medical technician or physician or is not assured of strict confidentiality. Interviewees may give short answers in hopes of ending an uncomfortable interview as soon as possible. And some patients give answers they think interviewers want to hear to please revered or feared medical authorities.[30]

The traditional history-taking interview, with its long inventory of closed questions, has produced more problems than it has solved. The manner is typically impersonal, and the questions often have little or nothing to do with a patient's current problem. As one patient remarked after such an experience, "He spent so long on things not wrong with me—two pages of lists—that it made me feel the interview had nothing to do with my illness at all."[31]

It is not surprising that patients in great pain or discomfort become angry or numbed, what one researcher calls "negative weakening," when responding to a series of seemingly irrelevant questions. One study revealed the following wearing down of a patient:[32]

Doctor: Is there any incidence of high blood pressure?
Patient: No. (strongly)
Doctor: Tuberculosis?
Patient: No. (average stress)
Doctor: Epilepsy?
Patient: No. (weakly)
Doctor: Neurological or psychological problems?
Patient: (shakes head)
Doctor: Allergies?
Patient: (no response)

A series of rapid-fire closed questions (sometimes referred to as the Spanish Inquisition approach) clearly set the tone for the health care relationship: the interviewer is in charge and wants short answers (usually yes or no), and is uninterested in explanations. But simple yes or no answers may not reveal comical but potentially tragic misunderstandings of simple medical terms. Too many health care professionals assume that everyone is familiar with medical jargon. The following real examples illustrate not only patient misunderstanding of jargon but the dangers of bipolar questions.[33] What if the patients had simply answered yes or no? The interviewers would not have detected any problems with this portion of their interviews.

1. **Interviewer:** Have you ever had a history of cardiac arrest?
   Interviewee: We never had no trouble with the police.
2. **Interviewer:** How about varicose veins?
   Interviewee: Well, I have veins, but I don't know if they're close or not.
3. **Interviewer:** Multiple births?
   Interviewee: (after a long pause) I had a retarded child once.

Apart from medical jargon, too many health interviewers ask ambiguous questions such as "Do you have regular bowel movements?" and "Do you feel tired?" What is a "regular" movement, and how tired must you be to be ill?

Medicine has yet to reach the point scientifically or mechanically where simple checklists are sufficient to determine diagnoses, prognoses, or treatments. Neither have patients, despite television dramas, become familiar or comfortable with medical jargon and abbreviations. Too many health care providers fear that if they "push the right button" they will end up with a thirty minute-conversation when they are already four patients behind.[34]

Ways to Improve Getting Information

Many techniques can improve getting information in health care interviews. First, provide an atmosphere in which the interviewee feels free to express opinions, feelings, and attitudes—even ones with which you might disagree. Because health care providers and patients rely so heavily on interviews to get information, the process is simply taken for granted, and both parties fail to realize that cooperation is necessary for a sharing of information.[35] A sense of collaboration leads to more information as well as greater patient satisfaction and compliance with instructions.[36] Select, if at all possible, a comfortable, quiet, private location free of interruptions, where questions and answers will remain confidential.

Second, open the interview with a pleasant greeting. Introduce yourself (name and position) if unacquainted with the patient or family, and explain what is needed and why. A simple orientation may reduce anxiety, satisfy curiosity, and allay suspicions. Do not prolong rapport building unless trust is very low; most patients would rather get on with it than make small talk about the drive to the hospital. If you are late for an appointment, apologize for the inconvenience and explain the reason for it. Simple politeness—treating people the way you like to be treated—can defuse an angry or impatient interviewee, and show that you are sensitive to the person's perceptions and needs. Too often medical personnel and institutions treat individuals like numbers or objects on an assembly line, then cannot understand why they encounter hostility or lack of cooperation.

Use individualized rather than routine approaches and try to adapt to each patient.[37] Be aware of communication apprehension common in medical interviews, particularly ones dealing with sensitive or embarrassing topics. You can reduce communication apprehension by carefully explaining examination procedures, being attentive and relaxed, treating patients as equals, and talking with them in their street clothes rather than backless hospital gowns.[38]

Third, employ a funnel sequence that begins with open-ended questions and gradually narrows to specific symptoms, diagnoses, or treatments. Open-ended questions communicate interest in what the interviewee has to say and show that you trust the interviewee to give valuable information. Such questions may evoke a wide range of information, are relatively free of interviewer bias, and (as noted in Chapter 4) allow the interviewee to volunteer information you might not think to ask for. Open questions tend to invite rather than demand answers and give patients a greater sense of control over what is being discussed.[39] Early questions should not be too open-ended, however. A patient may have difficulty responding to "How are you today?" or "Tell me about yourself." Use more focused questions such as "What kind of difficulties are you having with your back?" "What sort of night did you have?" and "Tell me about the kind of work you do."

Use inverted funnel sequences with caution because closed questions early in the interview may set a superior-to-subordinate tone. Such questions communicate that you want closed, specific answers. Thus that is what most patients will provide—and nothing more. By the time you reach the open questions in the sequence, interviewees may be unable to adjust to new expectations and continue giving brief answers.

And fourth, as interviewees respond to your questions, listen actively and carefully.[40] Listen also for hidden as well as obvious answers and requests and for evidence of confusion, hesitation, apprehension, or uncertainty.

Most people will respond if you appear interested, attentive, and relaxed. Research indicates that patients want most a chance to tell their stories, but they are often interrupted within eighteen seconds by interviewers who ignore what they are saying and try to transform stories into medical terms and logic.[41] Patients often try in vain to get physicians to pay attention to their personal sense of illness rather than the technical cause and treatment. Avoid unnecessary interruptions, especially if the interviewee becomes overwhelmed with emotion. Some writers suggest that the success of medical interviews may be due to the number of words the physician, nurse, or emergency medical technician does *not* say. Malcolm Coulthard and Margaret Ashby note that physicians tend to control interviews, and that the patient's main, and sometimes only, opportunity to give the facts he or she wishes is at the beginning when answering the opening question.[42] A recent study discovered that physicians tend to control interviews through questioning and topic change, and by introducing, developing, and dissolving topics.[43]

Be patient, and use nudging probes to encourage interviewees to continue answering. Avoid irritating interjections such as "right," "fine," "okay," and "good." Do not get into guessing games. Ask, "When does your knee hurt?" not "Does it hurt early in the morning? When you walk? How about climbing the stairs?" The patient may go along with whatever your series of questions seems to suggest. Be careful of multiple or double-barrelled questions such as the following:[44]

1. **Interviewer:** And in your family, were there any heart problems—any heart disease? Do you talk to your parents a lot?
   Interviewee: Yes.
2. **Interviewer:** Did you ever have rheumatic fever? Did you ever have scarlet fever? Break out in a rash?
   Interviewee: No.

What do the yes and no responses mean in these excerpts from a real interview? Is the patient saying yes or no to all three questions, to two of them, or to only the last one in the series? If you have any doubt about what a patient has said, employ reflective probes and mirror questions to be sure you understand thoroughly and accurately. Use these probing questions carefully, however. Some patients will go along with your reflectives or mirrors even if their answers are error-filled, feeling that you as a medical authority know what they should have said. Listen for important cues in answers—what patients are suggesting or inferring both verbally and nonverbally. A study of medical students at Oxford University revealed how important it is to learn the art of cue detection:

All the patients provided many useful cues about the nature of their problems. Hence, it was disconcerting that 74 percent of the students failed to pick up more than a fraction of these. Only 4 percent of the students were able consistently to detect and use the cues given them. Patients were often forced to repeat key phrases such as "I was feeling very low" as many as ten times to get the students to acknowledge their mood disturbance.[45]

Learn to listen and observe and, above all, do not be in a hurry to ask your next primary question. Avoid leading questions such as "You are staying on your diet, aren't you?" Few patients will say no when the interviewer clearly wants a yes or will give a different answer if the question reveals the *correct* or expected answer. Do not ruin a good open-ended question with a follow-up before the interviewee has a chance to respond. The health professionals below succumbed to the "open-to-closed-switch:"[46]

1. **Interviewer:** Well, how do you feel? Did you have a fever?
   Interviewee: No.
2. **Interviewer:** How long have you had that? All your life?
   Interviewee: Yes.

Ask the open question and stop talking until the patient has responded. At times you may have to make it clear to parents, spouses, relatives, or friends that you want the *patient* to answer. This is particularly prevalent when interviewing children in the presence of a mother or father.[47] Stifle "helpful others" tactfully and sensitively.

Sometimes, like a good journalist, you must ask a closed question (who, what, when, where, how, or why) to make diagnoses and recommend courses of action. It takes skill to ask the correct type of question at the proper time as well as to know when to remain silent and let the interviewee talk. Remember that active interviewees not only volunteer more information and opinions but understand more clearly what is taking place and experience a better medical outcome than inactive interviewees.[48]

Giving Information in the Health Care Interview

Giving information and having it remembered accurately and acted upon satisfactorily is a difficult process, particularly in the health care setting. One study revealed that within ten to eighty minutes, less than 25 percent of patients remembered everything they had been told, and the patients who remembered most had received only two items of information. Another study of twenty-five patients discovered that within a short time, ten showed significant distortions of information and four showed minimal distortions. Several studies reveal that from 30 to 50 percent of prescribed drugs are either not taken or are taken improperly.[49] Even though patients are guilty of forgetting and distorting facts, still they criticize lack of sufficient information more than any other aspect of hospital care.[50] Health care professionals give important information constantly so they should learn what causes loss and distortion and how to transmit information more effectively.

Causes for Loss and Distortion of Information

Inaccurate or inadequate communication of health care information is usually caused by attitudes of medical personnel, problems of patients, or ineffective transmission methods. Health care professionals place much greater emphasis on eliciting information than on giving information and explanations.[51] Although the strongest predictor of patient satisfaction is how much information is given on the condition and treatment, two-thirds of physicians in one study underestimated patient desire and overestimated how much information they had given. In a typical twenty-minute interview, less than two minutes is devoted to information giving.[52] And health care providers tend to give information selectively. For instance, they tend to give more information and elaborate explanations to educated, older, and female patients than to others.[53]

A patient's illness, fears, and anxiety often directly affect his or her ability to hear, comprehend, and remember. Some people protect themselves from unpleasant experiences by refusing to listen or understand. Many patients interpret information and instructions according to their personality type. For example, if a physician says, "You have six months to a year to live," a pessimist may tell friends, "I have less than six months to live," while an optimist may declare cheerfully, "The doctor says I might live for years." The physical and psychological condition of a patient may lead to extreme distortions in simple interactions. The patient in the following exchange was a sixty-three year old chronic paranoid schizophrenic:[54]

Nurse: Oh, Elsie, you're having some difficulty, aren't you? Let me give you a hand . . .

Patient: (Elsie gazes downward rather blankly. She stares first at her own right hand and then at her left hand, and then looks at the nurse's hand.)

Nurse: (The nurse looks down to see what Elsie is staring at; there is a pause, then . . .) No, Elsie, I don't mean I can really give you a hand! Of course, I can't! (pause) I would just like to help you.

Patients, like Elsie, often take words quite literally, and metaphors (that by their nature require the receiver to complete the implied comparison) may confuse persons who are frightened and anxious. Patients may not understand or comprehend information because they are untrained and inexperienced in medical situations. Few settings are as replete with communication-stifling gadgets, smells, noises, and goings-on. Patients are bombarded with unfamiliar abbreviations (IV, EKG, ICU, D & C, Pre-Op), and strange jargon (adhesions, contusions, nodules, cysts, benign and malignant tumors, steroids, chemotherapy, and metastases). The aura of authority may inhibit patients from asking for clarification of information even though they must rely on the professional to evaluate and understand technical information.[55] For instance, a woman who did not understand what nodule meant did not ask questions "because they all seem so busy, I really did not want to be a nuisance . . . and anyway she [nurse] behaved as though she expected me to know and I did not want to upset her."[56] The strange setting combined with hope for a favorable prognosis may lead patients to oversimplify complex situations or to interpret information as not really aimed at *them.*

Physicians, nurses, and medical technicians may contribute to information loss and distortion in a number of ways. On one hand, they may underestimate what patients know and give them little additional information. But on the other hand, they may assume

A patient's fear and anxiety are barriers to effective communication.

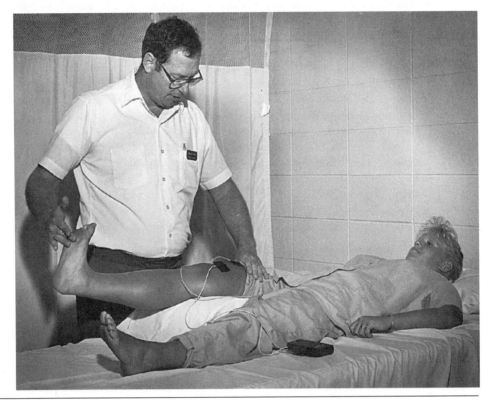

patients understand all they just told them and take few steps to verify that *assumption*. The physician in the following example was trying to give a thorough briefing to a patient about what tests had revealed:[57]

> Well, Mrs. Jones, I expect you'd like to know exactly what is wrong with you. (pause) Well, we here at this hospital believe in telling you and all our patients the truth about their illnesses and their treatments. I promise you that we will tell you everything you want to know. Well, now, in your case, we have carried out all the investigations and tests, and sadly, we have found that you have a rather nasty tumor on your ovary . . . I am sure you know what a tumor is . . . Well, now, we have had some very good results from giving our patients a course of treatments which involves a series of injections of platinum. . . .

This patient later exclaimed to family and friends, "Thank goodness I haven't got cancer. I only have a tumor." Five days later she learned that she had cancer from another patient, not from her physician.

Many health professionals are reluctant to give coherent information because (1) they don't want to get involved, (2) they fear patients' reactions, (3) they feel they are not allowed to give information, or (4) they are afraid of giving incorrect information.

Nurses, for example, often have insufficient data about the patient's condition; or they may be uncertain about what the physician wants the patient to know or what the patient already knows.

Information is also lost and distorted because of ineffective transmission methods. Sometimes patients are overloaded with data, details, jargon, and explanations far beyond their abilities to comprehend. Ley discovered in a study that 82 percent of patients could recall two items, but the percentage dropped to 36 percent for three or four items, 12 percent for five or six items, and 3 percent for seven or more items.[58] Ley also discovered that physicians tend to give diagnostic information before instructions. Not surprisingly, patients remember diagnostic information twice as often as instructions because the diagnosis seems more important to them and they are still thinking about it during the instructions. Some interviewers, by habit or intent, deal in confusing and meaningless ambiguities: "Now, Mr. Brown, you will find that for some weeks you will tire easily, but you must get plenty of exercise."[59] How long is "some weeks;" what does "easily" mean; and how much is "plenty"? Simple repetitions of jargon, slang, or unknown procedures do not help. The patients learned nothing from these repetitions:[60]

1. **Interviewer:** I'm afraid you'll be nil by mouth for a little while.
   Interviewee: I'll be what?
   Interviewer: Nil by mouth.
   Interviewee: Oh.
2. **Interviewer:** We need to get you ready for an EKG.
   Interviewee: A what?
   Interviewer: An EKG! (vocal stress)
   Interviewee: Oh.

Often medical personnel rely on a single medium such as a written note or a brief oral exchange with a patient. Neil Davis and Michael Cohen relate numerous problems caused by such efforts.[61] For example, a physician treating a patient for a painful right ear wrote a prescription with "R" and "ear," leaving out the period. The person administering medication read the directions as "rear," and the patient received the medication in his rectum. A nurse coming on duty on a ward asked one patient if he was Mr. Thomas, and he said, "Wright." Mr. Wright received Mr. Thomas's medication.

Transmitting Information More Effectively

There are many ways to improve information given in health care interviews.[62] First, establish a relationship of trust and confidence with each patient by being informative, helpful, understanding, and communicative—listening, touching, looking at the patient, and sounding confident, friendly, and sensitive. The information you give must seem authentic, a judgment patients often base upon effective presentation.

Second, do not overload the patient with information or professional language. Discover what the patient knows and proceed from that point, eliminating unnecessary or irrelevant facts. Relate new information to information the interviewee already understands. Reduce explanations and information to the simplest terms. You might present information in two or more brief interviews instead of a single long one. As a rule, provide only enough information to satisfy the patient and the situation.

Third, use a variety of media to present information: pamphlets, leaflets, pictures, slides, models, and audio and video recordings. Employ both the spoken and written word. Receptionists or patient representatives, in addition to physicians, nurses, and technicians, can serve as sources. Use visual aids. Dentists often use models of teeth to explain dental problems; emergency medical technicians use mannequins to teach CPR; and knee surgeons use facsimiles of the knee joint to explain injuries and treatment. Provide written records of conversations, prescriptions, and instructions. When giving information orally, emphasize important words, dates, and figures to aid patients' memories. Use your voice (pitch, loudness, speed, tone, pauses) to substitute for the underlining, highlighting, and italicizing you might use if providing information through printed materials. Be sure that important words and phrases stand out from less important ones. Give information to a group, such as several patients who share the same problem or a patient accompanied by family members. This tactic provides several memories to rely upon.

Fourth, practice good communication skills. For instance, define technical terms and procedures or translate them into words and experiences the patient understands. Organize items of information systematically so they are easy to recall. Listen and watch for nonverbal signs that the interviewee is confused, unsure, or overwhelmed. Common cues are gasps, moans, puzzled expressions, and raised eyebrows. Do not rush through information. Repeat items strategically two or more times during an interview. Try presenting important instructions first so they do not get lost in reactions to the diagnosis.

Fifth, involve patients in the information giving process. Encourage them to ask questions as you go along, not at the end of your presentation, and listen for implications and misinterpretations. Ask the interviewee to repeat or recall what you have said so that you can listen for losses and distortions. See if the person can apply what you have said or tell you why certain procedures must be followed.

And sixth, be aware that all staff in the organizational hierarchy should be thoroughly informed about patient status. Take the time to review available data and know exactly what you can and cannot tell each patient. Do not *assume* you are informed because if you are uninformed, the patient will not only be uninformed but misinformed and perhaps treated erroneously.

Counseling in the Health Care Interview

Most health care professionals are trained to be task-oriented. Not surprisingly, they perceive their tasks to be the care and treatment of physical ailments they were trained for in medical, dental, nursing, or technical school. They tend to rely more on verbal expertise to gain compliance rather than empathy to gain understanding of a non-physical problem.[63] But with ever greater emphasis on treating the whole patient, the health care professional needs to become a counselor to help a patient understand and deal with a problem. Unfortunately, many barriers inhibit effective counseling in the health care setting.

Barriers to Effective Counseling

Patients and their families often make counseling difficult by becoming silent, withdrawing, or complaining about a physical problem rather than admitting a psychological one.[64] When nothing is found wrong physically, the patient is often dismissed with a diagnosis being stress, a case of nerves, or an overactive imagination. The emotional or physical problem remains intact until its seriousness demands attention and proper treatment, if it is not too late. A patient may take days to get up the nerve to ask a nurse or physician about death, physical impairment, or cancer, and even then is likely only to hint at the concern rather than ask directly.

Typical health care professionals spend little time actually talking to patients because they have many tasks to perform and see talking as "social activity" rather than "nursing" or "doctoring."[65] The interviewer initiates most interactions and usually makes them short. Care and treatment are considered more important than getting acquainted with the patient. Predictably, interviewers often fail to detect subtle cues that a patient wants to talk about a serious topic. Because they find silence awkward, many interviewers talk instead of listening and observing. They employ a variety of "blocking" tactics to avoid having to counsel or get involved. Some make jokes or deny the seriousness of a problem, while others pursue the least threatening line of conversation. Common tactics are to ignore the patient's comment, become engrossed in a physical task, change the subject, pretend a lack of information, hide behind hospital rules, or simply run away. The nurse in the following exchange illustrates common blocking tactics:[66]

Nurse: There we are, dear. OK? (gives a tablet to the patient)
Patient: Thank you. Do you know, I can't feel anything with my fingers at all nowadays.
Nurse: Can't you? (minimal encouragement)
Patient: No, I go to pick up a knife and take my hand away and it's not there anymore.
Nurse: Oh, I broke my pen! (walks away)

As a health care interviewer, you must understand yourself—your reactions to counseling situations and outside factors that may influence them. For example, when a patient started talking about his father's death, a resident physician switched to the less emotional topic of the patient's mother. The resident later explained that he had changed the subject because he thought the patient might cry. Upon further questioning, however, it was discovered that the resident's own father had died eight months earlier; he was protecting himself rather than the patient.[67]

Guidelines for Effective Counseling

Review carefully the principles and guidelines presented in Chapter 9 on counseling interviewing. These are easily adapted to the health care situation. Approach each interview with the realization that five relational factors are critical: empathy, trust, honesty, validation (when a person feels others accept and respect what he or she has to say), and caring.[68]

Set aside time to talk to each patient and establish a close relationship.[69] Even if only a few moments, this time is likely to be a major event in the relationship and good therapy for both parties. You will become someone the patient can confide in and better able to detect subtle requests for help. Therefore, you should strive for comradery in the interview by showing respect for the patient's agenda and encouraging mutual sensitivity.[70] Ballard-Reisch has created a model of participative decision making for physician-patient interactions (see figure 11.1).[71] Her model involves the patient as a partner, not a bystander in the interview process. Input and feedback from both parties is critical in

Figure 11.1   Model of participative decision making for physician-patient interactions

Diagnostic Phase

    Stage 1: Information Gathering
    Stage 2: Information Interpretation

Exploration of Treatment Alternatives Phase

    Stage 3: Exploration of Alternatives
    Stage 4: Criteria Establishment for Treatment
    Stage 5: Weighing of Alternatives against Criteria

Treatment Decision, Implementation, and Evaluation Phase

    Stage 6: Alternative Selection
    Stage 7: Decision Implementation
    Stage 8: Evaluation of Implemented Treatment

each phase and stage of the participative decision making model. This model is based on the common sense theory that health care counseling is not likely to be effective unless information about a problem is gathered and evaluated, possible treatments are identified and weighed, and treatment decisions are implemented successfully.

You must use directive, nondirective, and combinations of these approaches to enhance communication and self-disclosure. Sharf and Poirier have used a theoretical framework developed by psychiatrists Szasz and Hollender to teach medical students how to select appropriate interviewing approaches.[72] An active (directive) approach is recommended when a patient is passive and unable to participate. An advisory (nondirective) approach is recommended when a patient is compliant because of acute illness and thus not at full capacity. And a mutual participation (combination directive-nondirective) approach is recommended when gathering data, solving problems, and managing an illness of a patient who can participate fully.

You can encourage patients to talk in a number of ways. For instance, if you share your own experiences and feelings, the patient is more likely to confide in you, thus enhancing self-disclosure. Employ nonverbal communication (smiles, nods, touches, and eye contact) to show that you care about the patient. Listen with comprehension and empathy (not sympathy) so you can see the situation as the patient does. Avoid making judgments as you try to clarify and interpret a patient's problem. Use open-ended, reflective probe, and mirror questions to encourage the patient to talk and clarify his or her meaning. Do not ask too many questions or seem overly curious. Use a range of responses and reactions (from highly nondirective to highly directive) and avoid giving advice unless the patient lacks information, is misinformed, or will not react to less directive means.

Employ positive and reinforcing techniques for past performance such as following prescribed regimens, taking prescribed medicines, and showing up on time for treatments.[73] Avoid fear appeals and threats because more often than not they lead to patient denial or avoidance of regimens, medicines, and checkups.[74]

Approach a solution to the problem when the patient is ready; do not push for a solution too soon. Present clear courses of action, not bland reassurances. Fully one-third of all patients fail to comply with medical advice, and the figure jumps to 50 percent "when treatment instructions are 'preventive,' when patients are without symptoms, and when the treatment regimen lasts for a long period of time."[75] You must present specific instructions and demonstrate that they are easy to follow. You should also convince the interviewee that the remedy will work and that dire consequences may result if instructions are not followed (stroke brought on by high blood pressure, liver damage caused by drinking too much alcohol, gum disease due to not flossing, and so on).[76] Remember, however, that you need not, and indeed cannot, solve the problem for the patient.

Summary

The health care interview is a difficult and complex process. Situations vary from routine to life-threatening, and the relationship between health care professional and patient is affected by tradition, professional and societal expectations, and the perceptions of both parties. Both medical personnel and their patients often feel threatened and may take defensive measures ranging from reticence to hostility to escape. The health professional may act as information giver, information seeker, and counselor all within a brief interview. Each role is fraught with difficulties, but the difficulties can be recognized and overcome. Above all, the physician, nurse, medical technician, and staff member must realize that good communication does not come naturally or merely with experience but requires thorough training and practice.

A Health Care Interview for Review and Analysis

This interview is between a surgeon and a forty-seven-year-old patient who has undergone microsurgery on a vertebra two days before. The surgeon is making his usual rounds and is checking the patient's progress.

Assess the relationship between patient and surgeon by using the dimensions of inclusion, affection, and control. How effectively does the surgeon get information? How effectively does the surgeon give information? How effectively does the surgeon counsel the patient? How appropriate is the blend of directive and nondirective reactions and responses? How effectively does the surgeon detect cues from the patient? How effectively does the surgeon use questions? How does the patient aid and hinder the interview process?

1. **Surgeon:** Good afternoon, Bill. How have you been doing?
2. **Patient:** Hi, Dr. McSween. Well, (serious tone of voice) I haven't gotten much sleep because every time I drop off, a nurse or someone will come in for a temperature or blood pressure check, or jab me with a needle, or wake me up for a sleeping pill. And that vampire with her blood samples . . .
3. **Surgeon:** (laughing) Yeah, we train them down in the dungeon.
4. **Patient:** (not smiling) *You* ought to try it some time.
5. **Surgeon:** (more serious tone of voice) Well . . . the first few days after surgery are rather busy for patients. We try to keep track of how well your system is reacting and handling the situation.
6. **Patient:** You succeeded . . . I was uncomfortable most of last night.
7. **Surgeon:** Uh-huh. We need to talk about some rehabilitation procedures for the next several weeks, until the scar tissue gets in place.
8. **Patient:** I don't think it was quite so uncomfortable the first night.
9. **Surgeon:** What do you mean by uncomfortable? Do you mean you've experienced some pain in the area of the incision?
10. **Patient:** Yeah, that too. It's a sharp pain in the back when I try to change positions and . . .
11. **Surgeon:** Movement is going to be painful for awhile. Where exactly did you feel the pain?
12. **Patient:** Right about here, near the operation, and then sort of down into the hip.
13. **Surgeon:** I see. Well, that's normal for this type of surgery, and you're likely to experience some pain for a few days. I'll make sure you're given some pain killers. Did you get out of bed today?
14. **Patient:** Well, it was a struggle, but I made it to the john on my own, in spite of that damned IV I had to drag along.
15. **Surgeon:** Very good. You ought to be able to go home in a few days or so.
16. **Patient:** Good . . . when do you think I'll be able to get back to work, Dr. McSween?
17. **Surgeon:** Hey, it's too early to talk about that; let's worry about getting this back in good shape first. There are some exercises you'll need to do to strengthen the muscles . . .
18. **Patient:** (anxious tone of voice) Well, do you have any idea when I might be able to get back to work for a few hours a day at least?
19. **Surgeon:** That depends on how quickly the incision heals and the scar tissue forms to replace the part of the disk we removed. (looking at Bill's chart) I would like you to remain at home for a month before you go back to work, and then work only for a few hours at a time.
20. **Patient:** (loud, shocked voice) A month!
21. **Surgeon:** (speaking softly) Yes, I'm sure it'll take that long for you to get moving again. (continues to look at the chart)
22. **Patient:** A month!
23. **Surgeon:** I'll want you to do some exercises and be up around the house as much as you can.
24. **Patient:** A month's a long time to be away from a job like mine.
25. **Surgeon:** Um-hmm?
26. **Patient:** They can't afford to wait for me to wander back months from now.
27. **Surgeon:** Oh, it won't be months, and I'm sure your employer will understand.
28. **Patient:** (low voice) You don't understand the advertising business.
29. **Surgeon:** (looks Bill directly in the eyes) Try me.

30. **Patient:** Advertising is a tough, highly competitive business, and you can lose good accounts easily—much easier than you get them. The agency can't put accounts on hold because of my back . . . I've just got to get back in a couple of weeks.

31. **Surgeon:** (firmly) No way, Bill! We'll try to get you up for a short walk tomorrow after we get the IV out, and I think you'll discover that you're not going to be ready to work for awhile. Let's take a look at that incision.

32. **Patient:** How can I see an incision on my back?

33. **Surgeon:** Good point. (laughing) Let *me* take a look at the incision.

34. **Patient:** (anxious tone) Well?

35. **Surgeon:** Not bad.

36. **Patient:** Not bad?

37. **Surgeon:** It's okay, don't worry.

38. **Patient:** That's easy for you to say; you're not lying in this bed.

39. **Surgeon:** Let's talk about some exercises. I want you to do a lot of walking when you get back on your feet, and until then, I want you to do some back pressing and flexing.

40. **Patient:** Like what?

41. **Surgeon:** I want you to lie on the floor and press the small of your back flat against the floor.

42. **Patient:** No problem; I do a lot of sit-ups.

43. **Surgeon:** No, no, I don't want you to put that kind of pressure on your back. Just lie flat and press the small of your back against the floor. Back flexing is acting like a cat when the cat gets up from a nap and arches its back. Now, take it easy!

44. **Patient:** I hear you, Dr. McSween, but I may surprise you with how soon I'm back on my feet.

45. **Surgeon:** Uh, huh. I'll drop by again this evening on my rounds. Just lie there and relax. Pretend it's a bit of a vacation.

Health Care Role-Playing Cases

An Emergency Room Patient

The patient was brought into the hospital by EMTs at 2:30 in the afternoon after suffering severe chest pains at his law office. He wants to go home and is insisting that the pains were caused by indigestion. The nurse is twenty-two and must get a medical history from the patient. She knows he is impatient and may become hostile if the interview seems irrelevant and prolonged. The EKG indicates that a mild heart attack did take place. The nurse's age and lack of experience may pose a problem in trying to control the interview.

A Terminally Ill Patient

The patient is nineteen and a sophomore at a nearby university where she stars on the volleyball team. She was admitted for exploratory surgery after suffering blurred vision and severe headaches. She hopes to get back to school within a few days and eventually to attend law school. The interviewer is the patient's surgeon who has asked to speak with the patient and her family about the results of the surgery and tests on tissues taken from behind the right eye. The surgeon must explain that untreatable cancer has been found in brain tissues, and that the patient is unlikely to live more than six to nine months.

A Young Child and His Family

The patient is eight years old and has experienced nausea and diarrhea on and off for several days. At first his parents did not think much of the problem and did not begin the usual treatment until two days ago. Prescriptions seemed too expensive, so they did not give them very faithfully. Now they are afraid their lack of concern may have caused or prolonged a serious problem. They feel guilty for having been negligent. The interviewer is an emergency room nurse who must try to get information about the condition and treatment from the child. The child's parents, however, are now anxious to be helpful and will attempt to answer most of the nurse's questions. The nurse must be very tactful, and above all, must avoid leaving any impression that the parents are to blame for their child's problems.

A Hostile and Disturbed Patient

The patient is a long-term patient at Fairview Convalescent Home. He rarely has visitors or receives telephone calls, and has become increasingly reticent. When staff members try to talk with him or cheer him up, he becomes hostile and withdraws even more. He views minor incidents as personal affronts and insults. The interviewer is a counselor at a local mental health facility who is often asked to counsel patients at Fairview. In this first discussion, the interviewer hopes to start establishing a trustful and cooperative relationship and to discover why the patient avoids visits and conversations.

A Rehabilitation Program

The patient was struck by a car while riding his motorcycle, and in addition to scrapes and bruises, has a broken right arm and ankle. He plays soccer for his high school team and is very concerned about when he will be able to play again. He is also very depressed. The interviewer is the orthopedic surgeon who set the patient's arm and ankle in plaster casts. He wants to review the X-rays with the patient and his family and explain the fractures, care of the casts, when the casts will be removed, and a future rehabilitation program. The interviewer is concerned that the patient will try to be too active and retard the healing process. He has recently had several problems with teenagers damaging their casts.

Student Activities

1. Analyze the sample health care interview. What are its strengths and weaknesses? How well is the surgeon following the suggestions made in this chapter and related chapters? How much information does the physician obtain about the patient's concerns and attitudes? How might the patient have helped the information giving, information getting, and counseling processes?

2. Visit a health care facility in your community. Observe how physicians, nurses, emergency medical technicians, and staff conduct medical interviews. Talk with some of the staff about their communication training and interview techniques. How does the health care interview seem to differ from the typical probing interview?

3. Pick one of the health care role-playing cases and develop an approach for it. How would you select or arrange the setting? How would you begin the interview? What types of questions would you ask? How much would you disclose about yourself and your experiences? What kind of solution, if any, would you propose? How would you close the interview?

4. Arrange to observe a medical counseling interview. Try not to be an obvious third party. Observe the opening, questions and responses, nonverbal behavior of both parties, self-disclosures, effect of interruptions, suggestions, directive and nondirective techniques, and the closing. Write a detailed criticism of the interview with suggestions for improvement.

Notes

1. Alan S. Robbins, et al., "Teaching Interpersonal Skills in a Medical Residency Training Program," *Journal of Medical Education* 53 (1978), 998; Loyd S. Pettegrew, "Some Boundaries and Assumptions in Health Communication," in *Explorations in Provider and Patient Interaction,* Loyd S. Pettegrew, ed. (Louisville: Humana, 1982), 3–5.

2. Averial Stedeford, "Couples Facing Death II—Unsatisfactory Communication," *British Medical Journal* 24 (1981), 1098–1101.

3. R. A. Barbee and S. A. Feldman, "Three Year Longitudinal Study of the Medical Interview and Its Relationship to Student Performance in Clinical Medicine," *Journal of Medical Education* 45 (1970), 770–76; Nicholas G. Ward and Leonard Stein, "Reducing Emotional Distance: A New Method to Teach Interviewing Skills," *Journal of Medical Education* 50 (1975), 605; Sonia L. Nazario, "Medical Science Seeks a Cure for Doctors Suffering from Boorish Bedside Manner," *Wall Street Journal,* March 17, 1992, B1.

4. Teresa L. Thompson, "The Invisible Helping Hand: The Role of Communication in the Health and Social Service Professions," *Communication Quarterly* 32 (1984), 150.

5. Thompson, 152.

6. Thompson, 154.

7. Gary L. Kreps, "Applied Health Communication Research," in *Applied Communication Theory and Research,* Dan O'Hair and Gary L. Kreps, eds. (Hillsdale, NJ: Lawrence Erlbaum Associates, 1990), 273–274.

8. Sandra L. Ragan and Lynda Dixon Glenn, "Communication and Gynecologic Health Care," in *Applied Communication Theory and Research,* Dan O'Hair and Gary L. Kreps, eds. (Hillsdale, NJ: Lawrence Erlbaum Associates, 1990), 313–330.

9. Gary L. Kreps, "Relational Communication in Health Care," *Southern Speech Communication Journal* 53 (1988), 344–59; James M. Honeycutt and Jacqueline Lowe Worobey, "Impressions about Communication Styles and Competence in Nursing Relationships," *Communication Education* 36 (1987), 217–227.

10. Stewart Auyash, "Medicine and Health," *Communication Quarterly* 32 (1984), 92–93.

11. Thompson, 107.

12. Kreps, 344; Nazario, B1.

13. Thompson, 148–163.

14. This discussion is based on Ruth Purtilo, *The Allied Health Professional and the Patient: Techniques of Effective Interaction* (Philadelphia: Sanders, 1973); Lewis Bernstein and Rosalyn S. Bernstein, *Interviewing: A Guide for Health Professionals* (Norwalk, CT: Appleton-Century-Crofts, 1985); and Patricia MacMillan, "The Bridge Builders' Guide—1," *Nursing Times* (22 January 1981), 151–52.

15. Barbara F. Sharf and Suzanne Poirier, "Exploring (Un)Common Ground: Communication and Literature in a Health Care Setting," *Communication Education* 37 (1988), 229.

16. Richard L. Street Jr. and John M. Wiemann, "Differences in How Physicians and Patients Perceive Physicians' Relational Communication," *Southern Speech Communication Journal* 53 (1988), 425.

17. Street and Wiemann, 424.

18. Linda M. Breytspraak, et al., "Sensitizing Medical Students to Impression Formation Processes in the Patients Interview," *Journal of Medical Education* 52 (1977), 47–54; F. S. Hewitt, "Cool It Man (Feelings in the Making)," *Nursing Times* (16 September 1981), 33–36.

19. Michael Balint, *The Doctor, His Patient, and the Illness* (New York: International Universities Press, 1975).

20. Street and Wiemann, 425.

21. This discussion is based on Purtilo; Bernstein and Bernstein; Patricia MacMillan, "What's in a Word?" *Nursing Times* (26 February 1981), 354–55; and Patricia MacMillan, "Getting Through Without Words," *Nursing Times* (16 March 1981), 554–55.

22. Sharf and Poirier, 229; Vince S. Di Salvo, Janet K. Larsen, and Dencil K. Backus, "The Health Care Communicator: An Identification of Skills and Problems," *Communication Education* 35 (1986), 233–34.

23. Dean C. Barnlund, "The Mystification of Meaning: Doctor-Patient Encounters," *Journal of Medical Education* 51 (1976), 716–25.

24. J. Gregory Corrall and Judy Moore, "Teaching Medical Interviewing: A Critique of Educational Research and Practice," *Journal of Medical Education* 54 (1979), 398–500; Bernstein and Bernstein, 1–19; Nazario, B1; Honeycutt and Woroby, 217.

25. This discussion is based on Bernstein and Bernstein; Patricia MacMillan, "Role-Playing for Nurses," *Nursing Times* (28 May 1981), 960–61; H. Brunning, "Social Skills and Personal Effectiveness Training for Student Nurses," *Nursing Times* (21 May 1981), 919–20; and Ward and Stein.

26. Gary L. Kreps and Barbara C. Thornton, *Health Communication: Theory and Practice* (New York: Longman, 1984), 4.

27. Nazario, B1.

28. Ragan and Glenn, 316.

29. Sylvia E. Zakus, et al., "Teaching Interviewing for Pediatrics," *Journal of Medical Education* 51 (1976), 325–31.

30. O. Eugene Baum, "The Difficult Patient," *Pennsylvania Medicine* 70 (1967), 82–83; Kathryn Woods and J. Regis McNamara, "Confidentiality: Its Effect on Interviewee Behavior," *Professional Psychology* 11 (1980), 714–21; Ward and Stein, 605–13.

31. Allen J. Enelow and Scott N. Swisher, *Interviewing and the Patient* (New York: Oxford University Press, 1986), 47–5; A. D. Wright, et al., "Patterns of Acquisition of Interview Skills by Medical Students," *The Lancet* (1 November 1980), 964–66.

32. Roger W. Shuy, "The Medical Interview: Problems in Communication," *Primary Care* 3 (1976), 376–77.

33. Shuy, 376–377.

34. Ron Winslow, "Sometimes, Talk Is the Best Medicine," *The Wall Street Journal* (5 October 1989), B1.

35. Daniel Goleman, "Physicians May Bungle Part of Treatment: Medical Interview," *New York Times* (22 January 1988), 12.

36. Kreps, 350–51.

37. Barbara M. Korsch, "Current Issues in Communication Research," *Health Communication* 1 (1989), 5–9; Sharf and Poirier, 224–229.

38. Virginia Eman Wheeless, "Female Patient and Physician Communication and Discussion of Gynecological Health Care Issues," *Southern Speech Communication Journal* 52 (1987), 198–211.

39. Korsch, 7.

40. Honeycutt and Worobey, 225; Vince S. Di Salvo, Janet K. Larsen, and Dencil K. Backus, "The Health Care Communicator: An Identification of Skills and Problems," *Communication Education* 35 (1986), 231–242.

41. Winslow, B1; Goleman, 12.

42. Malcolm Coulthard and Margaret Ashby, "Talking with the Doctor, 1," *Journal of Communication* 25 (1975), 140; K. Hopkinson, et al., "Psychiatric Interviewing Techniques III. Naturalistic Study: Eliciting Feelings," *British Journal of Psychiatry* 138 (1981), 406–15.

43. Marlene von Friedericks-Fitzwater, Edward D. Callahan, Neil Flynn, and John Williams, "Relational Control in Physician-Patient Encounters," *Health Communication* 3 (1991), 17–36.

44. Shuy, 376.

45. G. P. Maguire and D. R. Rutter, "History-Taking for Medical Students," *The Lancet* (11 September 1976), 556–58.

46. Shuy, 376.

47. H. B. Valman, "Talking to Children," *British Medical Journal* (15 August 1981), 482–83.

48. Analee E. Beisecker, "Patient Power in Doctor-Patient Communication: What Do We Know?" *Health Communication* 2 (1990), 105–122.

49. P. Ley, "What the Patient Doesn't Remember," *Medical Opinion Review* 1 (1966), 69–73; Joshua Golden and George D. Johnson, "Problems of Distortion in Doctor-Patient Communication," *Psychiatry in Medicine* 1 (1970), 127–49.

50. Ann Cartwright, *Human Relations and Hospital Care: Reports on the Institute of Community Studies, No. 9* (London: Routledge and Kegan Paul, 1964).

51. Sharf and Poirier, 225.

52. Winslow, B1; Goleman, 12.

53. Street and Wiemann, 423.

54. "Talking Points No. 12," *Nursing Times* 5 (16 April 1981), 676.

55. Street and Wiemann, 420–21; Beisecker, 117.

56. MacMillan, "What's in a Word?" 354.

57. MacMillan, "What's in a Word?" 355.

58. Ley, 69–73.

59. F. S. Hewitt, "Just Words: Talking Our Way Through It," *Nursing Times* (26 February 1981), 5–8.

60. "Talking Points No. 9," *Nursing Times* (26 March 1981), 556.

61. Michael Cohen and Neil Davis, *Medication Errors: Causes and Prevention* (Philadelphia: Stickley, 1981).

62. These suggestions are included in Purtilo, 85; Bernstein and Bernstein, 41–45; Ley, 69–73; F. S. Hewitt, "Getting Across Information," *Nursing Times* (16 July 1981), 25–28; Myron R. Chartier, "Clarity of Expression in Interpersonal Communication," *The Journal of Nursing Administration* (July 1981), 42–46.

63. Michael Burgoon, Roxanne Parratt, Judee K. Burgoon, Thomas Birk, Michael Pfau, and Ray Coker, "Primary Care Physicians' Selection of Verbal Compliance-Gaining Strategies," *Health Communication* 2 (1990), 13–27.

64. Bernstein and Bernstein, 137–38; "Breaking the Silence," *Nursing Times* (30 October 1985), 32–33; F. S. Hewitt, "The Interview," *Nursing Times* (25 November 1981), 41–44; "Talking Points 13," *Nursing Times* (30 April 1981), 765; "Talking Points 16," *Nursing Times* (21 May 1981), 922.

65. Pamela Smith, "Teaching and Learning to Communicate," *Nursing Times* (7 September 1983), 51–53; Ann Tait, et al., "Improving Communication Skills," *Nursing Times* (22/29 December 1982), 2181–84; Catherine Steers, "Talking to the Elderly and Its Relevance to Care," *Nursing Times* (8 January 1986), 51–54.

66. Jill M. Clark, "Communication in Nursing," *Nursing Times* (1 January 1981), 16.

67. Ward and Stein, 612.

68. Kreps and Thornton, 104–5.

69. These guidelines are based on materials in Don Minshull, "Counseling in Psychiatric Nursing—1," *Nursing Times* (7 July 1982), 1147–48; Don Minshull, "Counseling in Psychiatric Nursing—2," *Nursing Times* (14 July 1982), 1201–2; Bernstein and Bernstein, 139–48; F. S. Hewitt, "Cool It, Man (Feelings in Talking)," *Nursing Times* (16 September 1981), 33–36; Tait, et al., 2181–84; Hewitt, (25 November 1981), 41–44.

70. Korsch, 7.

71. Deborah S. Ballard-Reisch, "A Model of Participative Decision Making for Physician-Patient Interaction," *Health Communication* 2 (1990), 91–104.

72. Sharf and Poirier, 227–229.

73. Burgoon, et al, 25–26.

74. Korsch, 8.

75. Shelley D. Lane, "Communication and Patient Compliance," in *Explorations in Provider and Patient Interaction,* 59–69.

76. Herbert W. Simons, *Persuasion: Understanding, Practice, and Analysis* (New York: Random House, 1986), 33–35.

Suggested Readings

Bernstein, Lewis, and Bernstein, Rosalyn S. *Interviewing: A Guide for Health Professionals*. Norwalk, CT: Appleton-Century and Lange, 1985.

DiMatteo, M. R., and Friedman, H. S. *Social Psychology and Medicine*. Cambridge, MA: Oelgeschlager, Gunn, and Hain, 1982.

Enelow, Allen J., and Swisher, Scott N. *Interviewing and Patient Care*. New York: Oxford University Press, 1985.

Gerrard, Brian A.; Boniface, Wendy J.; and Love, Barbara H. *Interpersonal Skills for Health Professionals*. Reston, VA: Reston Publishing, 1980.

Hersen, Michel, and Turner, Samuel M. (eds.) *Diagnostic Interviewing*. New York: Plenum Press, 1985.

Jones, J. Alfred, and Phillips, Gerald M. *Communicating with Your Doctor*. Carbondale, IL: Southern Illinois University Press, 1988.

Klinzing, Dennis, and Klinzing, Debe. *Communication for Allied Health Professionals*. Dubuque, IA: Wm. C. Brown Publishers, 1985.

Kreps, Gary, and Thornton, Barbara C. *Health Communication: Theory and Practice*. Prospect Heights, IL: Waveland Press, 1992.

Pettegrew, Loyd S. (ed). *Explorations in Provider and Patient Interaction*. Louisville: Humana, 1983.

Stewart, Moira, and Roter, Debra. *Communicating with Medical Patients*. Newbury Park, CA: Sage Publications, 1989.

Stoeckle, John D. *Encounters Between Patients and Doctors*. Cambridge, MA: MIT Press, 1987.

Thompson, Teresa L. *Communication for Health Professionals: A Relational Perspective*. Lanham, MD: University Press of America, 1988.

Photo Credits

Chapter 1
Page 2, p. 7: © James L. Shaffer
Chapter 2
Page 26: © James L. Shaffer; p. 35: ©
Michael Siluk
Chapter 3
Page 43: © James L. Shaffer; p. 58: ©
Donna Jernigan
Chapter 4
Page 63, p. 71: © James L. Shaffer
Chapter 5
Page 95, p. 99: © James L. Shaffer
Chapter 6
Page 127: © James L. Shaffer; p. 131: ©
Alan Oddie/Photo Edit

Chapter 7
Page 149: © James L. Shaffer; p. 171: ©
Charles Harbutt/Archive Pictures
Chapter 8
Page 195, p. 208: © James L. Shaffer
Chapter 9
Page 225: © James L. Shaffer; p. 229: ©
Robert G. Gaylord/EKM Nepenthe
Chapter 10
Page 245, p. 256: © James L. Shaffer
Chapter 11
Page 278: © Donna Jernigan; p. 285: ©
James L. Shaffer

Photo Credits

Index